DOING REAL RESEARCH

D0025950

PRAISE FOR DOING REAL RESEARCH: A PRACTICAL GUIDE TO SOCIAL RESEARCH

'I am very impressed by the format of the book and the learning features. The practical step-by-step approach is better than any of the texts we currently use, and the book contains a valuable chapter on risk evaluation in the field, so often absent in research textbooks.' **Barry Turner, Senior Lecturer in Research Methodology, University of Lincoln**

'This textbook enables the student-researcher to learn very practical skills to prepare for the research journey. Providing a clear "how to" guide from research design, ethics, data collection and analysis through to presenting research data, much of what you need to know is here. Accessible and informative, this textbook will inspire students to get into the field and become researchers.' **Teela Sanders, Professor of Sociology, University of Leeds**

'This book provides such an extensive overview of how to plan, execute and write-up a research project that it will be invaluable for postgraduate students across the humanities. It is rich in detail, comprehensive in coverage and the addition of many real-life examples makes this book extremely accessible for students, teachers and researchers alike.' **Dr Rory Pilossof, University of the Free State, South Africa**

'A well-written, easy to read and very practical handbook to guide taught Masters students through all the key stages of their dissertation work.' **Ian Charity, University of Northumbria**

'A well-written book that highlights the different kinds of challenges and risks experienced by researchers and provides practical solutions. It includes valuable tools, strategies and tactics for doing research and overcoming the taken-for-granted difficulties that may potentially affect the viability of any research project.' **Dr Sizwe Phakathi, Senior Research Associate at the University of Johannesburg and Head of Safety and Sustainable Development at the Chamber of Mines of South Africa**

'This is an easy to follow, practical guide to entering the field of social research. Students will love this introduction, which covers key themes of research without getting bogged down in academic jargon.' **Brady Wagoner, Professor of Psychology, Aarlborg University**

ERIC ALLEN
JENSEN

CHARLES
LAURIE

DOING
REAL
RESEARCH

A PRACTICAL GUIDE
TO SOCIAL RESEARCH

Los Angeles | London | New Delhi
Singapore | Washington DC | Melbourne

Los Angeles | London | New Delhi
Singapore | Washington DC | Melbourne

SAGE Publications Ltd
1 Oliver's Yard
55 City Road
London EC1Y 1SP

SAGE Publications Inc.
2455 Teller Road
Thousand Oaks, California 91320

SAGE Publications India Pvt Ltd
B 1/I 1 Mohan Cooperative Industrial Area
Mathura Road
New Delhi 110 044

SAGE Publications Asia-Pacific Pte Ltd
3 Church Street
#10-04 Samsung Hub
Singapore 049483

Editor: Jai Seaman
Development editor: Sarah Turpie
Editorial assistant: Alysha Owen
Production editor: Ian Antcliff
Copyeditor: Richard Leigh
Proofreader: Neil Dowden
Indexer: Martin Hargreaves
Marketing manager: Sally Ransom
Cover design: Shaun Mercier
Typeset by: C&M Digitals (P) Ltd, Chennai, India
Printed and bound by Bell and Bain Ltd, Glasgow

© Eric Allen Jensen & Charles Laurie 2016

First published 2016

Apart from any fair dealing for the purposes of research or private study, or criticism or review, as permitted under the Copyright, Designs and Patents Act, 1988, this publication may be reproduced, stored or transmitted in any form, or by any means, only with the prior permission in writing of the publishers, or in the case of reprographic reproduction, in accordance with the terms of licences issued by the Copyright Licensing Agency. Enquiries concerning reproduction outside those terms should be sent to the publishers.

Library of Congress Control Number: 2015955044

British Library Cataloguing in Publication data

A catalogue record for this book is available from the British Library

ISBN 978-1-4462-7387-6
ISBN 978-1-4462-7388-3 (pbk)

At SAGE we take sustainability seriously. Most of our products are printed in the UK using FSC papers and boards. When we print overseas we ensure sustainable papers are used as measured by the PREPS grading system. We undertake an annual audit to monitor our sustainability.

CONTENTS

PREFACE: HOW TO USE THIS BOOK

The book is constructed in a roughly chronological order, so that a first-time researcher could follow the narrative spine of the book from the earliest stages of research design to a completed research report. Used in this way, the book is designed to flag up any concerns relating to future steps in the research process, which are likely to require early planning (e.g., research ethics approval is flagged up in the research design chapter as a future concern that may require advance preparation). This model for using the book would be most likely to apply to undergraduate or postgraduate students conducting their own empirical projects for the first time. However, individual chapters are also designed to be largely 'detachable' if you would like to use the book as a reference that you consult when you find yourself needing to undertake a task covered by one of the chapter headings. This way of using the book is most likely to apply to advanced under-graduate or postgraduate students working relatively independently (e.g., on a dissertation).

The book uses a consistent set of features:

- **Table of contents.** Each chapter begins with a brief table of contents providing a clear and accessible overview of the chapter.
- **Real world examples.** Throughout the book, we provide you with real examples of how people have dealt with common research challenges. Some examples come from published studies, while others come from behind-the-scenes stories from our friends, students and other researchers we've met. We've also constructed a few of the examples ourselves. These examples provide you with a concrete way of understanding these challenges, allowing you to learn from the experiences of others (including us). We include a range of examples, from large-scale international studies by established researchers to local, small-scale research conducted by university students.
- **Key tips.** This recurring feature provides short, sharp pieces of advice that will save you time and resources.
- **Further reading.** At the end of each chapter, a list of further reading will direct you to other sources of relevant advice and information, including Sage journal content.
- **Glossary.** Each chapter finishes with concise definitions of key concepts introduced in that chapter. This provides you with a quick reference option if you want to refresh your memory about a concept.
- **Companion website resources**. We provide you with free tangible resources you can use – editable documents containing examples of survey forms, informed consent letters, etc. – to get you started. You will also find videos from the two of us introducing each

chapter, and links to further videos and web resources we think you'll find useful. The website provides free downloads of good examples of published research using different approaches to give you some best practice models to draw on for inspiration.

These features are intended to make your journey through this book as straightforward and helpful as possible.

A ROADMAP FOR THIS BOOK: CHAPTER CONTENT

This section provides high-level summaries of each chapter to help orient you to the topics we cover in the book. To get you started, Chapter 1 takes you through the process of research design. It shows you how to develop a realistic plan to chart a good pathway through the uncertainties you face in any research project. Above all, this plan is guided by your research question(s). As such, we show you how to develop good, focused research questions and select the most appropriate and feasible methods to answer them.

The next step in developing your project is to engage with existing research knowledge and theory. Chapter 2 describes how to review published information to establish a strong foundation for your research. The task in a literature review can seem overwhelming: you are being asked to summarize and evaluate the current state of knowledge about your topic. Yet this task can be broken down into manageable steps. Chapter 2 explains each of these steps, including how to find sources, quickly assess their credibility, reference them and use them in your research report.

An important step when undertaking social research is to pre-emptively identify ethical challenges that can arise. This is a key issue when stepping away from ideal theoretical scenarios to confront the ambiguities, sensitivities and practical constraints that define real world situations. Chapter 3 begins by making the case for a duty-based framework for research ethics, which emphasizes your responsibility to safeguard your participants rather than rely on legalistic approaches. For instance, standard written consent forms are advocated by most existing methods book, yet they pose potential risks to both researcher and participant in some contexts. Moreover, this chapter addresses the role of official institutional ethics procedures, including advice on preparing applications for ethical approval and articulating ethical plans and procedures in a way that will reassure ethical committees, research supervisors and participants. In sum, Chapter 3 identifies the key ethical issues involved in real world research, and proposes practical solutions that achieve research objectives while maintaining high ethical standards.

Chapter 4 goes into further detail by identifying possible physical, economic and psychological risks to your well-being during the process of conducting research. Physical dangers to the researcher include those associated with travel in unfamiliar places, risks from aggressive participants, activists and security services that might be hostile to research. Emotional risks can affect both researchers and participants, such as from you unearthing disturbing stories and information about events in people's lives. This chapter helps you counter risks to your research and well-being from emotionally threatening situations, minimize risks to your personal safety, identify in advance threats you may encounter and how to safeguard your research equipment. Chapter 4 also addresses how technology such as encryption software can be used to mitigate risks.

Chapter 5 examines how we can develop reliable knowledge about a larger population through research with a smaller group of people. Qualitative and quantitative research paradigms answer this question very differently. In qualitative research, the goal is to develop an understanding of the range of possible perspectives within a population and the processes by which people come to their views and feelings about a topic. In quantitative research, the goal is typically to be able to make accurate quantitative generalizations about the prevalence of particular characteristics, attitudes and behaviours in a larger population. The practical implications of these different approaches to developing knowledge are spelled out in this chapter, along with practical advice about sample size and approach. The chapter provides tried and tested techniques and strategies for achieving the most representative sample possible within the constraints of a given research context. We also offer advice on sampling strategies you can use with hard-to-reach, transitory and low-profile populations. In sum, Chapter 5 addresses the issues of 'sampling' and 'generalizability' for qualitative and quantitative research.

Chapter 6 takes you through the challenge of finding participants and involving them in your research. Some participants may be difficult to locate because they want to remain unknown, such as computer hackers, or because the population is transitory, such as visitors to a festival, or because they might face negative consequences for participation, such as from an employer. Whatever the barriers might be, locating and approaching participants can be a major challenge. Start by understanding the needs of your potential research participants, as well as the language and framing that will be most appropriate to use when inviting their participation. Chapter 6 also describes how to develop and maintain good research relationships with your participants.

Chapter 7 provides detailed guidance on how to do survey research with limited resources. Surveys offer a standardized method of collecting both quantitative and qualitative data from individuals. The design and conduct of survey research must be very carefully developed to ensure the quality and accuracy of your results. Indeed, good survey research relies on the principle of beginning with the end in mind. What is the scope of the research claim you want to be able to make from the survey results? How much time do you have available to do the analysis? The answers to such practical questions feed into the process of designing survey research that effectively balances accurate measurement of individuals' thinking against your available resources and data analysis capabilities. The chapter addresses major dilemmas in survey research, including the use of self-report questions, how to phrase your questions and test whether your survey is effective.

Chapter 8 explains how to gather qualitative data, focusing on interviews and focus groups. Qualitative research offers unique opportunities for gaining insights into the social lives, experiences and viewpoints of participants. However, there are also a number of common pitfalls that can undermine the quality of qualitative research. Getting the most out of qualitative methods requires a step-by-step approach. Effective research questions must be translated into detailed plans for structuring qualitative data collection. Yet, such planning must be balanced against the need to maintain flexibility in qualitative research. Good qualitative research allows for 'emergent' research design in which new information emerging from the data collection process can trigger changes in the focus, approach and content of subsequent data collection. Chapter 8 offers detailed guidance on developing good semi-structured interview and focus group questions and how to structure such research interactions. The chapter also identifies the types of locations to use for data collection, as well as how to record and transcribe your data.

Chapter 9 addresses the challenges and opportunities involved in using existing data. Using data collected by other people can be an efficient and effective way to conduct social research. There are major practical advantages of this 'secondary analysis' approach. For example, you can avoid long hours of data collection and data entry, instead putting that time into developing your analysis. There are also advantages for enhancing the quality of your research, as this approach can give you a much larger sample size than you would be able to gather yourself. Using existing data collected for other purposes can provide insights that would not be possible to achieve in any other way. Yet such data also raise the same questions of quality and accuracy that apply to data you collect yourself, making it your responsibility to critically evaluate the methods used by the primary researcher(s). Moreover, you may need to adjust your research question to fit the available data. These challenges can lead to difficult decision-making that weighs research quality against available data sources. Chapter 9 provides step-by-step guidance on how you can identify and evaluate possible sources of data for your project. The chapter provides practical solutions to problematic qualitative and quantitative data sets, including collapsing categories to form new and more useful variables.

Chapter 10 gives you tips and strategies for managing your data at every stage in the research process. We outline specific strategies for documenting and maintaining the data you collect in a systematic way to avoid errors. For example, the chapter presents guidance on the 'coding' involved in entering quantitative data into a spreadsheet for analysis. In addition, Chapter 10 shows you how to store your data in a reliable, accessible and secure manner.

Chapter 11 explains the core principles of qualitative analysis, with particular focus on practical strategies and techniques to get you from raw data and notes to a completed thematic analysis. Qualitative data can be ambiguous and difficult to analyse. However, Chapter 11 takes the guesswork out of qualitative analysis by providing clear step-by-step guidance on how to systematically analyse data. Being systematic is essential to ensure results are a valid representation of participants' views and experiences. This approach also limits the risk of 'cherry-picking' convenient quotations that fit your pre-existing assumptions.

There are numerous approaches to qualitative data analysis including grounded theory, discourse analysis and interpretative phenomenological analysis. The focus in Chapter 11 is on the practical steps involved in identifying patterns in your data. We equip you with an approach that is broadly applicable across disciplines. Our advice in this chapter will help to demystify the qualitative analysis process, including showing you how to use qualitative data analysis software. Specific quality assurance techniques are outlined in detail, providing practical steps you can follow to ensure your analysis is as robust as possible.

Chapter 12 walks you through the process of analysing quantitative data, while also providing instructions for using SPSS statistics software. This chapter begins by introducing you to content analysis, which you can use to systematically quantify qualitative data. We then show you how to make the best use of numerical data. We also address practical tasks such as setting up tables and charts to present your research results and choosing what kinds of statistical tests you need to use. Chapter 12 explains in plain language how to use descriptive statistics for typical purposes such as describing your sample and identifying basic numerical patterns. The chapter also provides focused, plain-language and mathematics-free instructions on the selection, use and assumptions of chi-square tests, independent and dependent samples t-tests, and correlation analysis, as well as their non-parametric equivalents.

Chapter 13 shows you how to write up your research for academic and non-academic audiences. First, you will need to ensure you have all the content you need from the various parts of your project. You need to organize this content into the typical research report sections such as 'Methods' and 'Results', which we explain step by step. The chapter saves you time by showing you how to prepare a word processor template to include automated features and referencing. We also explain how to develop your writing in way that is focused and analytical, while following best practices in writing clearly and coherently in line with your audience's expectations.

HOW TO USE YOUR BOOK

Chapter Outlines List what is covered in each chapter at a glance and allow you to navigate between topics with ease

--- THIS CHAPTER COVERS THE FOLLOWING TOPICS ---

- Developing a sound research question.
- Finding appropriate and feasible ways of measuring key concepts in your research question.
- Matching your overall research goals to specific research methods.
- Anticipating and avoiding obstacles in your data collection, analysis and write-up.
- Deciding between qualitative, quantitative and 'mixed' methods research approaches.
- Choosing whether to use a cross-sectional or longitudinal research design.
- Selecting a research strategy, if appropriate.
- Planning and organizing your time to successfully complete your project.

Chapter Objectives Detail what you will learn in each chapter

--- REAL WORLD EXAMPLE ---

Access participants through a gatekeeper

Olivia was hoping to conduct a verbal survey of children at a local primary school about their dietary habits. She knew that it would be unethical to contact the children directly, so she contacted the head teacher of the school and explained the objectives of the research. Olivia was able to convince the head teacher that her research would be contributing to the valuable social objective of combating childhood obesity.

The head teacher then agreed to contact the parents of children in one class to ask for their written consent for participation in the study. After this was granted, Olivia was careful to fully explain her study to the schoolchildren and to obtain their consent before conducting the survey.

Real World Examples Provide insight into how people have dealt with common research challenges, from published studies to behind-the-scenes stories from the authors' friends, students and other researchers

--- KEY TIPS ---

Let your research question be your guide

It is easy to drift off course as your research project unfolds. Some diversions from your original research question will be necessary if, for instance, your planned participants refuse to be interviewed. However, you may also be drawn towards new, non-essential questions or interests that distract you. Following such distractions can cause you to stretch beyond the original scope of your project, thus making it harder to achieve your research goals on time and within budget. Commit a lot of time and effort to crafting your research question and then regularly refer back to it to ensure you remain on course in the face of enticing distractions.

Key Tips Provide practical advice on how to avoid common pitfalls and also save you time when executing your research

2.6 CONCLUSION

This chapter identifies how to establish what's already known about your topic to show the need for your research project and where it fits within the landscape of existing knowledge. Your literature review shows your path through the vast field of existing research in which your specific study sits. This chapter begins by explaining what a literature review is, and what it is not. Insightful and probing analysis of the literature in your field will help you more easily define 'gaps' in the field that your research can fill. Your literature review provides the rationale for your entire project.

By identifying and mapping where your specific project fits in the larger research literature relating to your topic, your study's contribution becomes clear. Also, you can rely on existing knowledge as a starting point for developing your claims and insights.

Conclusions Recaps what the chapter covers and is perfect for revision

--- SUGGESTIONS FOR FURTHER READING ---

- Fink, A. (2014). *Conducting research literature reviews: From the internet to paper* (4th ed.). Thousand Oaks, CA: Sage. This book is pitched to a broader audience than students by also focusing on users in marketing, policy-making and planning. It includes content on preparing grant proposals, methods to evaluate and use databases, and strategies to record and store information in a 'virtual file cabinet'.
- Machi, L. A., & McEvoy, B. T. (2012). *The literature review: Six steps to success* (2nd ed.). Thousand Oaks, CA: Corwin. This work advocates a six-step model to writing a literature review, and includes detailed activities and tasks to understand and achieve each step.
- Onwuegbuzie, A., & Freis, R. K. (2015). *Seven steps to a comprehensive literature review: A multimodal and cultural approach.* London: Sage. The authors advocate a thematic approach to literature reviews. It is especially useful in its coverage of multimodal texts – two or more communication modes (e.g., images and written language together) – and discussion about the role of culture in how we interpret knowledge.
- Ridley, D. (2012). *The literature review: A step-by-step guide for students.* London: Sage. Ridley's work outlines a series of practical strategies for conducting systematic searches. It is

Suggestions for Further Reading Every chapter end directs you to other sources of relevant advice and information, including SAGE journal content

--- GLOSSARY ---

Abstract – A short summary of an article which appears at the beginning and concisely presents the arguments and findings put forward by a publication.

Boolean search – A type of web search carried out using the words AND, OR and NOT to find more relevant search results.

Journal database – Electronic journal databases are a key method of sourcing literature for your review. Most are easily accessible and searchable, and your library will often have access to hundreds of different journals. Some journal databases even offer the option of downloading a citation directly into your citation software.

Literature review – A literature review goes beyond merely describing other people's research. It's an opportunity to analyse and critically evaluate existing literature so that you can apply it to your topic clearly and coherently, as well as identify gaps that your research can address.

Glossary Each chapter finishes with concise definitions of key concepts introduced in that chapter, and highlighted blue in the text

Companion website materials relevant to each chapter to help support your study

HOW TO USE THE COMPANION WEBSITE

Doing Real Research is supported by a wealth of online resources for students to aid study, which are available at https://study.sagepub.com/jensenandlaurie

For students

- **Editable documents**, including survey forms and informed consent letters to help get you started with your research.
- **Weblinks** direct you to relevant resources to expand your knowledge and are an ideal starting place for assignments.
- **Selected journal articles** give you free access to scholarly journal articles chosen for each chapter to expand your knowledge and reinforce your learning of key topics.

For lecturers

- **PowerPoint slides** featuring figures and tables from the book, which can be downloaded and used in presentations.
- **Author videos** featuring discussions of key concepts help integrate supportive content into your teaching and foster a rich learning environment for your students.

ACKNOWLEDGEMENTS

As fellow students at Cambridge, we ourselves were confronted with the practical research issues that form the basis of this book. It is our hope that by sharing our experience in *Doing Real Research,* we have provided a valuable resource to address the many challenges that exist throughout the research process.

Embarking on a project such as this is doomed to failure in the absence of support from so many people. We are indebted to Jai Seaman, Sarah Turpie and the rest of the SAGE team, who provided invaluable support, feedback and guidance throughout the process. A host of superb undergraduate and postgraduate students (acknowledged in a separate list) provided insightful contributions and thoughtful edits. Our colleagues and friends in Oxford, Warwick and all over the world added suggestions, critiques and ever-helpful challenges to our ideas. Our partners, Robyn and Samantha, have been the source of enormous support and encouragement.

For all the people who have helped us write and develop this book, we are truly grateful.

Charles and Eric

SEPARATE ACKNOWLEDGEMENT NOTE

We would like to thank the following students and friends for their contributions to this book:

- Benjamin K. Smith (University of California – Santa Barbara)
- Sizwe Phakathi (University of Oxford, University of Witwatersrand)
- Sarah Bromley (Wrap UK)
- Thomas Lister (University of Cambridge)
- Vicky Exley (Qualia Analytics Ltd.)
- Lauren Humphrey (National Marine Aquarium)
- Jonah Rimer (University of Oxford)
- Monae Verbeke (University of Warwick)
- Allison Plunkett (University of Oxford)
- Mireille Mazard (Max Planck Institute)
- Kelly Mcguire (Ipsos MORI)
- Vlad Glaveanu (University of Aalborg)

- Aaron Jensen (University of Strathclyde)
- Brady Wagoner (University of Aalborg)
- Deborah Biggerstaff (University of Warwick)
- Andrew Moss (Chester Zoo)
- Rachel McLenaghan (University of Warwick)
- Giulia Ceccon (University of Warwick)
- Joshua Simons (University of Cambridge)
- Mairi Jeffery (University of Warwick)
- The students in the 2014-15 Practice of Quantitative Research and Practice of Social Research classes at the University of Warwick

PUBLISHER'S ACKNOWLEDGEMENTS

The publishers would like to extend their warmest thanks to the following individuals for their invaluable feedback on the draft material for this textbook.

Rosaline S. Barbour, The Open University

Birgit Burböck, FH JOANNEUN Institute of International Management

Nicholas Cimini, Edinburgh Napier University

Grant Coates, University of Roehampton

Colin Howard, Worcester University

Duncan Jackson, Birkbeck, University of London

Gabriel Katz, University of Exeter

Teela Sanders, University of Leeds

ABOUT THE AUTHORS

 **Dr Eric Jensen** is from the United States, but now resides in England. He is an Associate Professor in the Department of Sociology at the University of Warwick, UK. He has previously taught at US and UK universities and colleges, including Portland State University, Clark College, University of Cambridge and Anglia Ruskin University. Eric has taught research methods courses at the undergraduate, master's and doctoral levels about research design and practice, qualitative, quantitative and mixed methods research across disciplines including psychology, sociology, business, communication, health, media and film studies, and social anthropology. He has supervised the successful completion of over 60 dissertations at the undergraduate, master's and doctoral levels. He regularly delivers research and evaluation training for practitioners working in non-profit and commercial sectors such as wildlife conservation, visitor attractions, museums and higher education.

Eric's research experience includes several grant-funded projects supported by funders such as the European Commission, the Arts & Humanities Research Council (UK) and the National Science Foundation (USA). Eric has published over 45 journal articles, book chapters and books, appearing in journals such as *Culture & Psychology*, *Public Understanding of Science*, *Media, Culture & Society*, *Journalism & Mass Communication Quarterly* and *Nature* (http://warwick.academia.edu/EricJensen/Papers). Eric's bachelor's and first master's degree are in communication, awarded by Portland State University, USA. He moved to the UK to do his Master of Philosophy and PhD in sociology at the University of Cambridge, UK.

Dr Charles Laurie was born and raised in Zimbabwe and later moved to the United States where he earned his bachelor's and a master's degree. His ambitious doctorate at the University of Oxford on political violence in Zimbabwe required mixed methods data collection in an environment that was hazardous, inhospitable and notoriously data-poor. He located and interviewed people in 24 countries, from victims of political violence, to senior government officials, and as a result, is extremely experienced at facing, and coping with, the practical challenges of doing real research. His research was funded in part by the Harry Frank Guggenheim Foundation.

Charles holds Master of Philosophy (University of Cambridge) and Doctor of Philosophy (University of Oxford) degrees in sociology and is currently Director and Head of Country Risks at Verisk Maplecroft.

INTRODUCTION TO THE RESEARCH JOURNEY

This book is your field guide to real world social science research. In it we aim to steer you along your social research journey from the earliest stages of planning to the final point of submitting your manuscript with pride and confidence. Along this journey, we will focus on the practical challenges faced by most early-stage researchers, and we include just enough theory to help you understand our reasoning. At every stage we focus on real world solutions and practical advice to help you identify, understand and successfully solve the broad range of challenges every researcher faces.

Thrift (2005, p. 338) offers one way of identifying a social scientist:

> I have what I think is a pretty good test of whether a person is a social scientist or not: do they eavesdrop on a fairly regular basis on other people's conversations on trains and planes, on buses, in the street, and so on?

Indeed, social research is primarily a matter of listening and watching social phenomena, while developing and applying conceptual tools to understand and explain what you find. Generally, research seeks to answer questions about what is happening (i.e., describing events, attitudes, distributions of characteristics in a population, etc.), why it is happening (i.e., describing the causal or contributing factors that explain why you are findings particular patterns of attitudes, characteristics in a population, etc.) and/or how it is happening (i.e., describing the processes by which causal or contributing factors lead to particular patterns or outcomes).

Motivations for conducting social research include the following:

- **To understand or 'to know'.** Aristotle wrote: 'All men by nature desire to know.' Social research can be used to create robust knowledge about social and cultural aspects of society. Motivations may include shedding light on your personal experiences, exploring a pattern you've observed in more depth and seeking answers to a 'puzzle' about why and how an event or issue occurred.
- **To decide between competing truth claims.** When different groups in society or within an institution make contradictory claims about what is happening in a given context, social research can produce evidence to resolve this disagreement. Moreover,

robust knowledge can be relied on by individuals, organizations and government to inform decision-making, practice and policy.

- **To build better explanations through theory.** You can use original research to shed light on the limitations and applications of an existing theory. It can also inform the development of your own theoretical concepts, models or explanations.

Research methods provide the foundation for knowledge claims. Details such as how sampling, data collection, measurement and data analysis were done in your research project can justify your claim to knowledge about your research topic.

This book takes you step by step through this process of developing knowledge through qualitative, quantitative or mixed methods social research. We take you from planning to data collection to analysis and how to write up your report. We focus on the most essential guidance you need during this process, pointing you towards further readings if you wish to know more.

WHY YOU SHOULD READ THIS BOOK

Many methods texts tell you what to do under ideal circumstances, but what about when conditions for social research are less than ideal (which is almost always!)? In such conditions, how can you achieve your research aims while maintaining validity, reliability and ethical research practice? The ideal and the practical are constantly in tension when conducting real world social research. As a researcher, you must negotiate this tension creatively to arrive at high-quality research results on time and on budget. Our approach in this book is above all realistic. It's designed to offer you frank, practical and empowering advice. We tend to strike an informal tone throughout the book in line with our role as supportive guides on your research journey.

This book articulates a real world approach through step-by-step discussion of the practical tasks and key principles involved in the research process. The book covers a range of decisions you will face when you venture into uncharted research territory. We help you navigate such difficulties as gaining and maintaining access to hard-to-reach, hidden or transitory populations, collecting data in chaotic or uncertain environments, using digital technology to gather and safeguard data, and maintaining ethical research practice. As authors, we apply our broad range of methodological experience and expertise from a wide range of challenging research contexts in both developed and developing countries. We provide detailed guidance about how to avoid common problems, how to conduct and account for suboptimal sampling and data collection and how to manage your relationship with participants. This book helps you take on the unexpected, the unusual, the uncertain and the hard-to-reach elements of social life around the world. The same advice is also useful for university students facing everyday obstacles such as how to find appropriate research participants. We use specific examples from a wide range of multidisciplinary researchers' experiences in developed and developing countries to show how our recommended strategies and techniques can be used. These examples come from a range of disciplines, including psychology, education, anthropology, health and social care, business, criminology, communication, sociology, behavioural economics, sociolinguistics and political science. These examples show you how general research principles play out in challenging, real world scenarios.

A key limitation in the existing crowded field of research methods books is that they offer broad theoretical guidance that can leave you without specific solutions to real world situations you almost always encounter. Moreover, when case studies are included in the current field of methods textbooks, they tend to stop short of elaborating detailed templates or advice for the reader. The result is that students are often uncertain about how to navigate the numerous situations where methodological compromises are unavoidable. This book offers a unique approach in that it provides direct and specific practical guidance on such issues. We walk you through the decision-making required at each stage of the research process, offering solutions informed by the latest methodological literature and the experience of the authors and a broad range of other social scientists. In every chapter, we provide further reading suggestions and useful links to give you the tools to get more detail on theoretical and methodological concepts and research that underpin our guidance.

This book starts from the premise that the ideal practices so often discussed in methods textbooks are frequently not possible in the field. It is not intended to be an abstract or theoretical methods text, as this is a space well occupied by existing research methods literature. Instead, it provides robust and tested guidance on how to navigate challenging real world research situations. It is this kind of guidance on practical considerations and problem-solving that is frequently absent from existing methods literature. Therefore, many students all over the world face such challenges without clear and specific advice. It is this need that the current book is looking to satisfy.

In addition to drawing on existing methodological literature published in peer-reviewed journals and books, the practical guidance in this book is informed by research undertaken by us in a range of contexts in developing and developed nations. For instance, the book draws on Charles's research in Zimbabwe on processes and practices of political violence. He interviewed 111 perpetrators and victims of state-sponsored violence such as murder and torture. He also surveyed 34 per cent of the nation's commercial farmers, and through careful document analysis identified 21,491 instances of violence nationwide. He has experience undertaking interviews with senior government officials hostile to investigations of political violence, perpetrators of criminal acts, as well as male and female victims of violence. As such, he brings to this book tested real world experience in topics such as: how to approach potential participants in chaotic and uncertain social conditions, how to undertake fieldwork in a context where participation in social research poses risks for both researcher and participant, how to use technology to handle sensitive data and how to locate hidden and inaccessible participants.

We also draw on Eric's research and consultancy projects in many diverse contexts, including studies of public attitudes about conventional and alternative healthcare, socially excluded young mothers' cultural experiences, who goes to art galleries and why, the effects of visiting a science, literature or jazz festival, young children's knowledge and attitudes about history, cultural heritage, animals, bioethics, science and conservation, science communication professionals' motivations and effectiveness, media coverage of political and scientific issues and religious discourse about scientific issues. He also has experience consulting on research projects in developing countries, including evaluating a conservation programme in Madagascar and a training programme for tour guides in Mauritius. He has helped design a survey in Bangladesh to assess the level of bushmeat consumption, a national survey about the role of science in society in Chile and a global survey of knowledge and attitudes towards biodiversity for the UN Decade of Biodiversity initiative. Many of these research examples involved limited resources and the use of technology such as tablets and online survey methods to achieve the research goals in the most efficient way possible. In each of these examples, the 'rulebook' for social research offered precious little direct practical guidance on how to handle challenges in data collection and sampling. However, the vast methodological literature offers general insights that we can help you apply to real world situations you encounter during your research journey.

LAYING THE FOUNDATIONS

It's crucial to have a well-designed research plan. Whether you have a polished design already in mind or just a basic sketch of what you'd like to investigate, we help you get started on the right track by understanding what you've got and what's missing. We encourage you to be opportunistic when choosing a research topic: use your existing experience, contacts and skills to give yourself a head start. We also advise you to be flexible about your research question in the early phases by adjusting it as you encounter obstacles, exciting new data sources or new research avenues that stimulate your interest. However, narrowing your focus – and sticking to it – is the key to ensuring that you can successfully address your research question(s) within the confines of available time and budgets.

Once you've started developing your research design, you need to find and use existing research and theory relevant to your topic. This process of reviewing the most relevant books and articles will help you understand the landscape you're venturing into with your research. Critically evaluate this existing research and probe for weaknesses and 'gaps' that your study can address. This process refines your focus, helps you avoid reinventing the wheel and establishes why your study is needed. In addition, you can build on other researchers' work, which allows you to venture further into unexplored research territory. We include step-by-step guidance so you can be confident that your review of the literature demonstrates a firm grasp of existing research and ideas on your subject.

Throughout your project, you must ensure that you are at all times being an ethical researcher. How you design your research, undertake your data collection, analyse your data and disseminate your results can affect people's lives. As such, ethical principles apply across the full range of topics we discuss in the book. Think about how you would feel if someone used data about you in a manner that you found intrusive or perhaps even damaging or upsetting. Make sure you do everything you can to ensure that you don't abuse a participant's trust or take away their right to decide whether they want you to use their data (and for what purpose). We explain your responsibilities as an ethical researcher by providing a framework for ethics that lets you understand best practices, especially when working with vulnerable people.

INTO THE FIELD

Having laid good foundations for your research by building on existing evidence and ideas and responsible ethical practices, you're ready to begin your data collection. Data collection can bring with it risks to your emotional and physical well-being, property and data. For example, being in an unfamiliar environment immediately increases risk because you may not know where you're going, you may not be aware of suspicious behaviour around you and you may appear out of place and therefore draw unwanted attention. Similarly, you may be carrying expensive and bulky equipment such as recording devices, laptops and smartphones for your research. You may also at times deliberately seek out individuals in high-risk professions, such as organized crime. We show you how to identify and mitigate these risks while you also protect your participants.

As you prepare to head into the field you must decide whose participation to invite for your project. For example, are you surveying people (and if so, what's your sample?)? Are you looking to do focus groups (and if so, with what kind of participants?)? These decisions directly affect the kind of knowledge you can develop through your research. This book walks you through your sampling options and their implications. We also explain how to save time and costs at both the data collection and analysis stage, for example by using digital data collection tools.

DATA COLLECTION METHODS

Once you have understood your sample and decided where to collect data, how do you gain participation? We explain that gaining participation is primarily about anticipating the needs and expectations of your potential participants. Establish your credibility by easily answering questions about the scope of your project, its potential implications, your funding sources and what you will do with your data. You should also be able to easily explain any potential positive and negative implications for the participants. Incentives can play a positive role in gaining participation, but you should be careful because they need to be appropriate for your research population. For instance, you are unlikely to gain a busy businessperson's participation by offering a free cup of coffee. Also, incentives can introduce bias, so they should also be appropriate to the research topic and the level of contribution you're requesting from your participants.

At this point in your research journey, you may reach a crossroads: how will you collect your data? First, we walk you through how and why to use surveys. If you decide that a survey is appropriate for your research, this book will help you ensure it's well designed and effective in achieving good results. A survey that follows established principles of good practice in question selection and design can set the stage for efficient and effective data analysis. Use pilot research to help you ensure that your survey design is clear, yielding the type and depth of data you need. It's far better to encounter obstacles and think through solutions before you get into the field! For researchers facing tight budgets, we also explain how to reduce the costs associated with conducting a survey such as simplifying your questions, reducing the sample size and using online, electronic survey tools. Also, think ahead to what kind of analysis you'd like to be able to do because your options are affected by the way you structure your survey questions.

Qualitative interviews and focus groups can be an invaluable means of answering the 'how' and 'why' in your research question. These methods are far more resource intensive than surveys in terms of time and cost per participant; think about how long it would take to administer a survey to ten respondents versus setting up and conducting interviews of an hour each for ten participants. Following our guidance will help you to ensure you don't waste resources by gathering more qualitative data than you need. We offer tested strategies to help you develop your interview and focus group questions, respond appropriately when participants talk too much or too little and deal with other challenges such as participants who evade questions. In addition, we highlight the importance of electronically recording your qualitative data to get the necessary detail for your analysis.

It's worth considering using existing data ('secondary data') because it is an efficient way to conduct social research. It enables you to access data on a scale that would otherwise be beyond your reach, such as census data or other government-funded population surveys. Using such secondary data can save time you can reinvest in your analysis and write-up to give you a stronger overall project. Unless you are extremely lucky, you will need to make adjustments to your research topic and question(s) to bring it into alignment with the existing data you wish to use. While existing data offer great opportunities, you will still need to carefully evaluate the methods used by the primary researchers. Look for weaknesses in the original research design and data collection because these will then be carried over into your research if you use the data.

MANAGING AND ANALYSING DATA

From the beginning of your project, you need to manage information about your research. Documenting your decision-making will help you down the road when you may not remember your thought processes as clearly. Decisions that seem obvious during data collection may become foggy later on as your perspective shifts with time. We also show you how to organize and arrange your data so you can find the information you need quickly and avoid the risk of accidentally deleting your files. The data management system we propose simplifies the process of compiling and quality checking your data, giving you greater assurance and clarity as you proceed with your research.

Once you've set up your framework for managing your data, your data analysis can begin. Qualitative analysis requires rigorous methods and sensitivity to the context in which data are generated. We show you how to take your raw data and transform them into 'codes' (i.e., categories). These codes can then be compared with each other and across different samples to identify the variety of viewpoints in your data. By linking the codes and your emerging ideas around them to theoretical concepts, you then begin linking your research to existing ideas in your research area. As your analysis deepens, particularly in the writing phase, you will begin developing insightful explanations about your data. This process of qualitative data management and analysis is made much easier and more robust with the help of qualitative data analysis software, which we walk you through step by step.

The value of quantitative data analysis is widely recognized in business, government, charities and social research. We provide step-by-step instructions for conducting some of the most commonly used statistical tests. In SPSS, you can use these statistics to concisely present your results, analyse relationships between variables and compare different categories to see, for example, whether one group of people enjoy an experience more than another. We highlight the assumptions inherent in parametric statistical tests, along with instructions for alternatives you can use if assumptions are violated.

PRESENTING YOUR RESEARCH

After all the hard work designing your research project, gathering your data and analysing them, you will be ready to complete your research report. This writing-up process is exciting because you are organizing and clarifying your ideas and findings into a coherent report that presents your contribution to knowledge on your topic. Of course, it is also challenging to see it through to completion.

Who will be reading your work? Considering your audience is a first key step in writing up. We offer guidance on different expectations of various types of audiences. Good writing for any audience requires multiples waves of writing and editing to shape and refine your report. Trying to get all your ideas down in one major writing session just doesn't work with research reports. Instead, let your ideas evolve gradually during the writing process while following the good writing principles we outline. Use the writing process itself as a chance to develop your thoughts. The more drafts you do, the better your writing becomes.

We guide you through how to structure a standard research report. We also show you how to keep focused on your work and what to do if you run out of steam. Start writing early in your project and keep making contributions to the write-up, even if it is just to sketch ideas out on the screen. This will give your writing more opportunities to evolve because you can track and develop ideas that emerge along your research journey.

When we began our university research journey, we found we struggled to decide exactly how to conduct our research. Methods books we looked to for help were often vague or overly focused on commentary to the exclusion of practical guidance. We found that we would finish reading a book, for example on how to do qualitative research, only to find we still didn't know where to begin or end this process. Our motivation in writing this book is to take the mystery out of the research process, while sparing you unnecessary stress, wasted time and resources. Throughout this book, we provide you with our honest advice about what is realistic for you to achieve within the constraints that researchers routinely face. Think of this book as a map that you take with you on your research journey, helping you decide which pathways to take. While the path may get muddy at points, we'll help you find a way through. If you stay focused, you'll make it to your destination with results you can be proud of. Now let's get started!

REFERENCE

Thrift, N. (2005). Panicsville: Paul Virilio and the esthetic of disaster. *Cultural Politics*, *1*, 337-348.

PART I

LAYING THE FOUNDATIONS

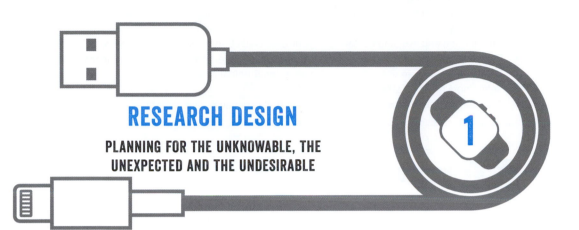

RESEARCH DESIGN

PLANNING FOR THE UNKNOWABLE, THE UNEXPECTED AND THE UNDESIRABLE

━━ **THIS CHAPTER COVERS THE FOLLOWING TOPICS** ━━

- Developing a sound research question.
- Finding appropriate and feasible ways of measuring key concepts in your research question.
- Matching your overall research goals to specific research methods.
- Anticipating and avoiding obstacles in your data collection, analysis and write-up.
- Deciding between qualitative, quantitative and 'mixed' methods research approaches.
- Choosing whether to use a cross-sectional or longitudinal research design.
- Selecting a research strategy, if appropriate.
- Planning and organizing your time to successfully complete your project.

1●1 INTRODUCTION

As you begin your research, you face many decisions. To achieve your research objectives, you need a roadmap to keep you on a feasible and appropriate path – this is your **research design**. Your research design is the plan you develop to identify the methods and procedures you'll use throughout your research project. This design will help you anticipate and navigate risks and uncertainties in a systematic and rigorous manner. A good research design gives you the best chance of successfully achieving your research objective: a completed report that effectively addresses your research question(s). In this chapter, we first identify the early decisions you need to make in order to develop a good **research question** to guide your research decisions. We then help you pinpoint precisely what you will measure and what research approach would be most suitable for your project.

1●2 GET STARTED ON RESEARCH DESIGN

1●2●1 BEGIN PLANNING BY LOOKING AT THE ROAD AHEAD

Crafting an appropriate research design involves matching the research goals motivating your study with methods for meeting those goals. For example, you might decide that the goal of understanding a social problem such as homelessness is best addressed through an ethnographic study, that is, observing and interviewing homeless people in their own environment. As your research design develops, you need to choose what kind of data to collect, from whom, in what setting and with which methods. This process rarely involves drawing a straight line from general idea to detailed plan. You are likely to adjust your research design to accommodate new information, face obstacles to your initial ideas and rethink some of your assumptions. Figure 1.1 illustrates the planning and decision-making process involved in research design.

As you develop your research design, remember that there is rarely one 'right' way to conduct a study. There will be a range of options, each involving trade-offs of some kind. Always document and justify the decisions you make along the way.

In Chapter 10 we show you how to track your decision-making by documenting the issues you face, options you consider and ultimately what choices you make and why.

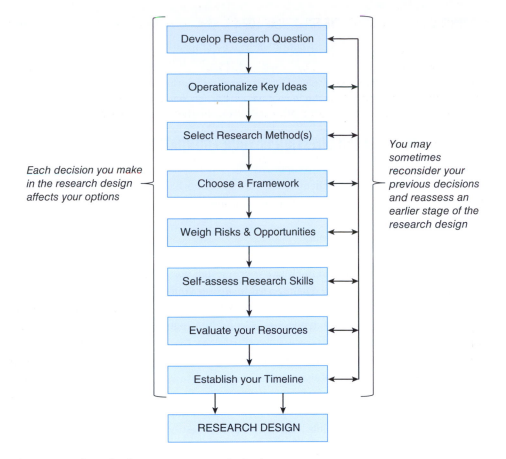

Each decision you make in the research design affects your options

You may sometimes reconsider your previous decisions and reassess an earlier stage of the research design

Figure 1.1   Developing your research design

Keeping a 'research diary' establishes an audit trail for your thought process as it develops along your research journey. A decision may seem obvious at the time, but it's easy to forget your reasoning later.

KEY TIPS

Crafting a research design is an ongoing process

You are unlikely to create a robust and defensible research design on your first attempt. More realistically, aim to start with a solid – but not necessarily perfect – research question. Then, as you move through the research design phases and encounter barriers or opportunities, you can double back and adjust your research question or other aspects of your research design. For most researchers this process is ongoing and carries on into the initial data collection phase. So your research design is only truly complete when you've finished the research. Consider this ongoing process of adjusting your research question or design, exploiting opportunities and circumventing

(Continued)

(Continued)

problems not as 'correcting mistakes' but rather as a natural part of the research design process. It is important to remain open to new ideas and innovations throughout this process, while also keeping your project focused.

1•2•2   YOUR RESEARCH QUESTION IS YOUR FOUNDATION

Your research question governs all components of your research project. It defines what data you collect and how you analyse them. It also needs to be both feasible and worthy of academic attention. Consider the following points when crafting your research question:

- What are you looking to find out?
- What are your key explanatory ('independent') and outcome ('dependent') variables?
- What information do you need to answer your research question?
- Will it be feasible to gather the data required to answer your research question in the time you have available? If 'no', you probably need to narrow or change your research topic.
- Does the answer to your research question offer useful insights that contribute to your field of study?
- Would your research results add to established knowledge by shedding light on a new or under-researched dimension of the topic?
- Would your research results help develop theory or shed new light on an existing theory?
- Is your question too broad, possibly leading you into an impossibly open-ended study? Remember, it is nearly impossible to have a research question that is too focused!

Developing a tightly focused, answerable research question is the crucial first step in the research design process and will be the foundation of your project. A poorly formulated question may result in a research project that is hopelessly broad and potentially unachievable within your budgetary and time constraints. By contrast, a carefully crafted question will enable you to focus your efforts, thereby putting you on a good track. Once you have your research question honed, you will build the rest of your project around it. Even as you develop your project around your initial research question, it is normal to use new ideas and information to refine your research question and focus further.

FIND AN APPROPRIATE RESEARCH TOPIC

Developing a good research question requires selecting a workable research topic. If you're already clear on your interests and the direction you wish to take your research, that's great. Some of the best research is driven by a strong personal interest. This interest can help you persist through challenges that you may face during the research process. Your topic should be important and vivid: 'Anything can be cocooned by studies and theories, but something beautiful emerges only if there lies, in its center, something alive' (Gray & Wegner, 2013, p. 550). However, it's important to ensure that your topic is of general interest in your academic field. Does it address an important theoretical concept, for example, or could it open up new avenues or areas for research? Interesting topics are often those that pursue unexpected angles or that may achieve surprising outcomes. A good test to evaluate your idea is to imagine the best and most surprising outcome possible, and think about whether this would be interesting (Gray & Wegner, 2013, p. 550). Toiling away on a subject that motivates you but is of limited interest to your field can undermine the value of your efforts and make securing funding, research participation and a positive outcome from your project difficult.

The following are key strategies to help you determine whether the research topic you're considering has relevance and value in your field:

- Thoroughly **explore the topic in existing academic literature**. Who is studying it and in what academic disciplines? This can indicate whether there is an academic audience for your topic in your discipline. Many journal articles include in their final section a discussion of 'directions for future research', which highlight unanswered research topics within the scope of that study. Finding any such discussion on your topic can help point you towards fruitful avenues of exploration.
- Evaluate whether **you are in a particularly good position to conduct research on the topic**. For example, if you have special access or a background that will make the topic easier to explore, this weighs in favour of selecting the topic.
- **Discuss your potential ideas with your supervisor, colleagues and other academics**. This process is particularly useful because you can gain insights and guidance from seasoned researchers who can recognize hidden pitfalls in your proposed research topic.
- Are there any **upcoming events** (e.g., elections, investigations, or likely discoveries) **that may affect the relevance and research interest** in your topic? Time-limited events can create a unique opportunity for conducting valuable research.
- Is there something about the topic **that appears to generate particular interest for your academic discipline's core concerns**? For example, in sociology a topic relating to societal inequality or to gender or ethnic discrimination is likely to find an interested audience.

However, you also need to remember through this process that if there are many researchers working on your specific topic already, this may cause problems. You may have difficulty finding a niche to research and your topic may be seen as being less original. Consider the advice: 'As soon as you find yourself surrounded by others, consider seeking out the dangerous freedom of the unexamined' (Gray & Wegner, 2013, p. 551).

REAL WORLD EXAMPLE

Finding a good topic in the Olympic Games

Allison wanted to do a research project on how the Olympic Games were planned. This was an attractive topic because the Olympics generate considerable public and media interest. Also, she was offered privileged access to key event organizers and decision-makers. But it was when Allison found an interesting theoretical angle that she knew she had a viable research topic. She

(Continued)

(Continued)

decided to focus on how institutional memory is transferred from one decision-making body to another. She could address this topic by focusing on the Olympics organizing committee's processes for communicating its institutional knowledge to the subsequent organizing committee. For example, Allison studied how officials from the 2010 Vancouver games transferred knowledge to the organizers of the 2014 games in Sochi. The theoretical angle focusing on the transmission of institutional memory helped her refine her research question so that it would interest both academic and non-academic audiences. As is often the case, the key idea to use institutional memory as her theoretical focus only emerged once her project was already under way, thus requiring her to circle back and refine her research question.

CRAFT YOUR RESEARCH QUESTION

Your research question defines the key issues you are investigating in your project. The points in Table 1.1 will help you craft a good research question.

Table 1.1   Principles to guide research question development

Target the research gap	**Aim your research question at a gap in the existing research literature** that you can demonstrate to your readers.
Keep it narrow and specific	**Your research question must be 'answerable'.** A narrow and specific research question means you are creating a manageable and feasible research task for yourself. A focused research question with clear boundaries can save time and resources by limiting wasted efforts.
Be analytical	The question should **demonstrate more than mere description** in order to contribute to general knowledge about your topic.
Be clear and brief	Maintain maximum clarity by ensuring **your research question is clear, focused and easy to understand**. Your question should simply and briefly communicate the key information about what variables you will be exploring.

 **REAL WORLD EXAMPLE**

Keep your research question narrow

Don't fall into the trap of thinking that choosing a broad research topic is necessary to demonstrate ambition or to do justice to the research topic. For example, Sizwe wanted to do in-depth **qualitative research** on different worker subcultures in South Africa's gold mines for his doctorate and initially proposed studying five different mines. When he mapped out how much data he would end up with if he did this, it became clear that such extensive data collection would generate far more data than he would have time to analyse. While he could have opted for a less in-depth form of data collection such as quantitative survey research, he didn't feel this would allow him to get the level of detail he needed to answer his research question.

Therefore, Sizwe decided to focus his efforts on just one mine. This focus still provided more than enough data for Sizwe's research and allowed him to delve deeply, rather than spreading his effort thinly. You are likely to find a similar pattern: a narrow focus can still yield plenty of data for your project.

You must be able to demonstrate that you can plausibly answer the research question with the data you are planning to collect. For example, consider the research question: 'Why do young people use Facebook?' If you only collect survey data from students in your class, you wouldn't really be addressing this large question. Instead, you would need a more focused research question. A sample of students in one university department could address a more specific question, such as: 'What are the self-reported motivations for using Facebook amongst first-year psychology students at a UK university?' Ask yourself the questions in Figure 1.2 as you devise your research question to ensure you have included the necessary elements.

USE SUB-QUESTIONS TO CLARIFY YOUR RESEARCH FOCUS

A clear and focused definition of your research question also enables your readers to quickly understand what you are setting out to achieve. However, a single research question may not fully encompass the different dimensions you wish to explore. The particular aspects of your

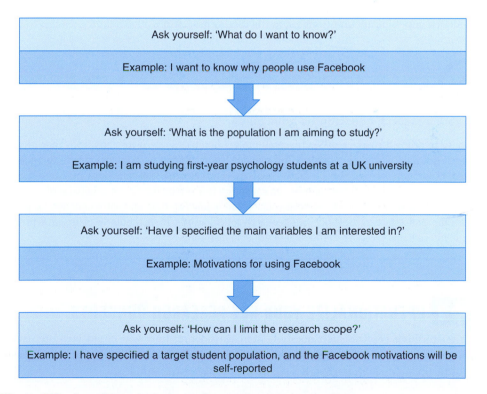

Figure 1.2   Questions to help craft your research question

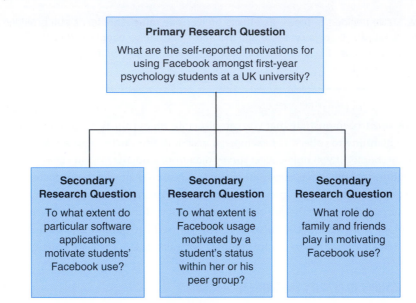

Figure 1.3   Developing sub-questions

topic that you will address can be spelled out in more detail by using sub-questions. Once identified, these sub-questions provide direction and structure for your research. Figure 1.3 provides examples of sub-questions using the Facebook example.

🔑 **KEY TIPS** ═══

Let your research question be your guide

It is easy to drift off course as your research project unfolds. Some diversions from your original research question will be necessary if, for instance, your planned participants refuse to be interviewed. However, you may also be drawn towards new, non-essential questions or interests that distract you. Following such distractions can cause you to stretch beyond the original scope of your project, thus making it harder to achieve your research goals on time and within budget. Commit a lot of time and effort to crafting your research question and then regularly refer back to it to ensure you remain on course in the face of enticing distractions.

1 ◖ 3 OPERATIONALIZE YOUR KEY RESEARCH CONCEPTS

After establishing your research question, start considering how you could measure its key concepts. Some concepts are easy to measure. For example, you can measure your participants' gender by asking them to tick a box next to 'male', 'female' or 'other'.

You may need to be creative in devising appropriate and feasible ways of testing other concepts. For example, when Eric needed to measure learning outcomes for children aged 7–15 visiting London Zoo, he decided to have them make drawings of 'a wildlife habitat and all the plants and animals that live there' before and after their zoo visits. This process is called **operationalization**.

Operationalization involves establishing a means of measuring an event or phenomenon that isn't easily or directly measurable. For example, if you are seeking to determine which brands of clothing are popular among web users you can measure this by operationalizing key words entered into websites they visit. If you find that a particular search term is popular, this will give you a good indication of what clothing brands are favoured by online consumers. Effective operationalization helps you develop your plans by establishing precisely what procedures and materials are required for your project.

REAL WORLD EXAMPLE

Measuring student satisfaction with university housing

Paulina wanted to evaluate how satisfied fellow undergraduate students were with their university accommodation. In order to capture – to operationalize – the range of student perceptions, Paulina decided to use a Likert-type scale to operationalize student satisfaction. She listed different aspects of university accommodation such as common areas, kitchen facilities and laundry, and provided five possible options: 1, very unsatisfied; 2, unsatisfied; 3, neutral; 4, satisfied; 5, very satisfied. This allowed Paulina to translate students' satisfaction with their accommodation into a scale that could be analysed statistically.

1•3•1 CHOOSE BETWEEN QUANTITATIVE, QUALITATIVE AND MIXED METHODS APPROACHES

Your research question will orient you towards a particular research approach: quantitative, qualitative or a combination of the two called '**mixed methods**'. It isn't always obvious which approach you should choose. This subsection will help you make this decision.

TRADITIONAL QUALITATIVE RESEARCH APPROACH

Qualitative methods involve data that are not numerical. Qualitative research is generally inductive, which means that it starts with data collection, then progresses to create theory or generate explanations. Qualitative research often aims to establish a new understanding of a previously under-researched topic, develop a preliminary theory or model and/or discover processes in human interactions.

Qualitative methods can have a number of strengths and weaknesses you should be aware of (see Table 1.2).

Table 1.2   Strengths and weaknesses of qualitative research

Strengths	Emergent research design	What you learn during data collection can influence your research design. This allows you the flexibility to make adjustments as your research unfolds.
	Exploration and theory development	Qualitative methods are useful as the first step in understanding ideas, perspectives and phenomena, especially when there is little existing research on the topic. Can be great for developing theoretical explanations that account for key processes and context.
	In-depth understanding	Qualitative research can enable deeper understanding of individuals' contexts, perspectives and experiences because you typically take more time with each participant. This can make qualitative methods uniquely effective at finding good explanations for quantitative findings.
Weaknesses	Lack of breadth	Emphasizing depth takes time away from gathering data from a larger number of people or organizations. Be alert to the risk of missing key perspectives because you didn't have time or resources to collect data from everyone who could have made a useful contribution.
	Time-consuming	Qualitative research can generate an enormous amount data (e.g., 10 minutes of recorded interviewing could take an hour to transcribe and be 15+ pages long). This can increase the cost and time required to prepare your data for analysis.
	Limited ability to generalize about population characteristics	Because you may be missing key perspectives if you have a small, possibly unrepresentative sample, it's hard to know whether your participants' characteristics apply more broadly.

TRADITIONAL QUANTITATIVE RESEARCH APPROACH

Quantitative methods are based on numerical data and are typically used to answer numerical questions: How many? What proportion? What is the statistical relationship between two variables?

Quantitative research can have numerous strengths, which help to explain its widespread use in public policy, business and academic research. However, it brings important potential limitations that you should be aware of when selecting the most suitable approach for your research (see Table 1.3).

MIXED METHODS RESEARCH APPROACH

A *mixed methods* approach to research design 'accepts that quantitative, qualitative, and mixed research are all superior under different circumstances and it is the researcher's task to make the decision about which research approach ... should be used in a specific study' (Johnson & Onwuegbuzie, 2004, pp. 22–23). Of course, more methods do not necessarily improve a

Table 1.3   Strengths and weaknesses of quantitative research

Strengths	Easy to generalize results	Quantitative approaches can be very appealing because they provide clear answers using methods designed with generalization as a goal. You can use statistical analysis to identify patterns that apply at the level of entire populations. Moreover, quantitative research can be used to predict the probability of a behaviour or other outcome occurring, given certain conditions.
	Large scale	Quantitative studies can make collecting data from large numbers of people more feasible. This can give you greater confidence that your results are not biased because of who you spoke with.
	Statistical analysis	Quantitative approaches can employ complex analysis that can identify subtle statistical patterns in the data. The use of statistics enables quantitative social scientists to benefit from scholarship in mathematics and statistics to develop more sophisticated analyses.
	Visualizations	Quantitative data easily translates into charts and graphs to illustrate your argument. Some audiences find such charts more persuasive than quotations on PowerPoint presentations and in reports.
Weaknesses	Loss of depth and context	While quantitative research can offer insights that are accurate at the population level, individual-level patterns can be obscured (Wagoner & Jensen, 2014). Moreover, important contextual factors may be neglected because the researcher is not immersed in the field or engaged in open discussion with participants.
	Limitations in accuracy	Quantitative research can suffer from lower levels of accuracy than qualitative methods for reasons such as limited depth of measurement or respondents not fully understanding or engaging with survey questions.
	Disconnected from the real world	Operationalizing concepts and turning them into survey questions can create measures that are too far removed from the real-world phenomenon you are trying to study.

research project. If you choose to use multiple methods, you must have a clear rationale for why this is the best approach for your project.

Mixed methods expert David Morgan (2013) identifies at least three reasons for combining research methods:

1   **Convergent findings about research topic**. Qualitative and quantitative methods can be used to address the same research question. If the different research methods yield similar results, you can have greater certainty in your findings. This motivation is also known as triangulation or cross-validation.

For instance, a research project evaluating racial bias in police 'stop and search' practices could include a quantitative analysis of how many times individuals of different races are stopped and searched. This could be supplemented by qualitative research in which police are interviewed about who they selected for search and why. If both forms of data pointed to racial bias, then the researcher could report this finding with greater confidence. If only one method had been used, the researcher would have to report findings with less certainty.

For example, it may be that the qualitative results in the above example show that police officers genuinely feel they are stopping people for search for legitimate reasons. However, structural factors such as the deployment of police to certain parts of the city or prioritization of certain crimes could be creating quantitative patterns demonstrating racial disparities.

2   **Additional coverage of topic.** This motivation for combining methods involves assigning each of the selected research methods to address different research goals. This leads to a division of labour in which each method's strengths are matched to separate goals or aspects of the research question within the overall project.

For example, a research project analysing media coverage of a new medical treatment might include quantitative analysis of how often a particular theme is mentioned in news coverage. This could then be supplemented with a qualitative focus group study to explore how doctors and patients are responding to that news coverage. This combination would make for a well-rounded study that addresses both the content and reception of the news coverage.

3   **Connected contributions to addressing research question.** This motivation links research methods together so one method enhances the effectiveness of another without necessarily overlapping in their coverage. Morgan therefore calls this 'complementary assistance'. The aim of linking the two methods is to use findings from one method to inform your use of another.

For example, when Caroline was conducting research on migrant workers in Arizona she used qualitative interviews of farm workers and government stakeholders to help shape the insights and questions for her subsequent survey of farmers.

It is also possible to mix two qualitative or two quantitative methods in a study. For example, some research questions might be most effectively addressed by combining qualitative interviewing and focus groups.

While combining research methods can be a powerful tool in helping you reach your research objectives, this approach also raises practical challenges. Deciding to combine research methods means you will need to be capable of planning for, gathering, analysing and writing up different kinds of data. This is not necessarily a problem, but you will need to allow time to develop any necessary skills you are currently lacking.

To some extent combining methods can mean 'doubling the work'. In addition to learning multiple approaches, each with their own implicit rules and expectations, you will almost certainly need additional time to undertake the other methods. This can increase your research timeline and thus lead to cost overruns. However, some researchers will scale back each method to compensate for the additional work and the possible negative impacts.

The decision to combine qualitative and quantitative methods should be driven by the value for effectively addressing your research question. Think about how Morgan's three reasons for combining methods might apply in your project. For example, will combining methods help you 'plug a gap' that might otherwise exist in your data? While combining methods is not universally appropriate, it is always worth reflecting on its potential value in your project.

1•3•2 CHOOSE BETWEEN A CROSS-SECTIONAL AND A LONGITUDINAL APPROACH

A **cross-sectional** study takes place at a single point in time. For example, public opinion polls take snapshots of public views about issues or events on a specific day, week or other defined point in time. Cross-sectional studies are an appealing option because they can be done at any time for relatively low cost (because only one round of data collection needs to be organized). The downside is that this snapshot may not represent longer-term patterns. For example, support for different political parties may shift over time due to changes in the economy or to major political events such as a corruption scandal.

The **longitudinal** research approach is designed to address the limitations of cross-sectional studies. Longitudinal research tracks changes in variables such as attitudes over time by collecting data from the same individuals on multiple occasions. However, longitudinal studies require a much greater time and resource commitment to keep track of individual respondents and gather data from them on multiple occasions. This greater level of cost may mean that you need a smaller sample size if you choose a longitudinal approach, which increases your vulnerability to participants dropping out because they move away, lose interest, or change contact details and become unreachable.

1•3•3 CHOOSE A RESEARCH STRATEGY

Once you have a sense of the research you want to do and the approach you want to use, the next question is whether there is a particular research strategy that applies to your project. Research strategies provide a general orientation for your project by relying on an established structure for your research design. There are many established research strategies. We focus on two here to get you started: action research and evaluation research.

ACTION RESEARCH

Action research is a strategy based on the dual aims of increasing knowledge or understanding, and acting in a practical way based on the newly produced knowledge to affect positive organizational or social change. Greenwood and Levin (2007, p. 2) think of action research as at once a 'research strategy' and a way to 'reform practice' in a given context: 'We view [action research] as a way of working in the field, of utilizing multiple research techniques aimed at enhancing change and generating data for scientific knowledge production.' The relative emphasis within the continuum between these two aims of practical 'action' and social 'research' varies from project to project. Action research is therefore cyclical, continuous and tightly interwoven within the entire research process.

Action research enables the researcher to intervene with the aim of improving a specific system, service, product or outcome, while creating new research knowledge. For example, if you were looking to improve the process of rehousing homeless people by local councils and charities, you could begin by designing an intervention based on the best available theory and research. You could then implement that intervention, evaluate its effectiveness and use that evaluation to inform a new and improved intervention. Interviewing homeless people using the new process could reveal insights to shape further alterations, continuing the action research project into a new cycle. The following example demonstrates how this cycle can work:

1   You develop a prototype website based on the best available theory and research to enable a local community to plan events together.
2   To learn more about how effective this website is in practice, you could conduct evaluation research with website users. This research would develop knowledge about how the website is used, and why. For example, this research could reveal how local communities bridge offline and online communications as they mobilize to improve their neighbourhoods. This knowledge would reveal processes and patterns that could be applicable well beyond this specific case.
3   At the review stage, the project team takes stock of what has been achieved and learned so far, and what should be done next.
4   The knowledge gained from this research then contributes to the plan for future action in the next round of website development, which will be evaluated again and so on (see Figure 1.4). In practice, there will be resource and time limitations that set the end point for this cycle. Most action research projects only go through one or two cycles.

This example demonstrates how the action research cycle can ultimately yield both a refined practical outcome and new social scientific knowledge. The decision about when to stop this cycle is usually a practical one based on available time and resources, or when a satisfactory 'action' result has been achieved.

Action research can take different forms. For example, 'participatory action research' involves much greater participant involvement in decision-making throughout the research and action process. This type of action research is defined as follows:

> (a) a collective commitment to investigate an issue or problem, (b) a desire to engage in self- and collective reflection to gain clarity about the issue under investigation, (c) a joint decision to engage in individual and/or collective action that leads to a useful solution that benefits the people involved, and (d) the building of alliances between researchers and participants in the planning, implementation, and dissemination of the research process. (McIntyre, 2008, p. 1)

In other action research projects, the researcher will make all of the major decisions using research data and theory to provide guidance.

Figure 1.4   Action research cycle

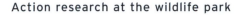

Action research at the wildlife park

Durrell Wildlife Park on the island of Jersey was looking to better understand visitors' experiences. To assist, Eric conducted a series of focus groups with different types of public visitors. He analysed what they said about the wildlife park, what they would like from the experience and how the wildlife park could most effectively reach them with messages about wildlife conservation. This was the first 'research' element in the action research cycle.

Eric presented these findings to staff at the Durrell Wildlife Park, working with them to create a change plan that the wildlife park then implemented. This was the 'action', that is, the practical intervention informed by the research. To assess how public visitors would respond to the 'action', Eric conducted another phase of research with another series of focus groups, including some participants from the initial research and some new participants. He analysed participants' views on the changes that had been made, again presenting these results to the wildlife park. The wildlife park used this information to inform new further 'action' to improve the experience and engagement with wildlife conservation messages in the park.

This two-year project finished with Eric's final round of research: a mixed methods survey conducted with the general population of visitors to the wildlife park to evaluate their response to the transformed visitor experience. Crucially, the research elements in this project were used to provide generalized knowledge about wildlife park visitors, public engagement with wildlife conservation and environmental communication. Therefore, the research contributed both to 'action' outcomes (improving the wildlife park) and 'research' outcomes (knowledge that could be applied to other settings and contexts).

EVALUATION RESEARCH

Evaluation research focuses on real-life events in social, policy, learning or business contexts. It aims to provide useful knowledge about how and why particular interventions or processes are working or failing in order to inform future decision-making. Scriven (1991, p. 139) explains that evaluation research is the 'process of determining the merit, worth, or value of something, or the product of that process'.

Evaluation research is defined by its focus on assessing whether objectives or intended outcomes have been achieved by a particular intervention or initiative. For example, an evaluation might assess the effectiveness of an intervention designed to improve childhood obesity rates by restricting junk food advertisements in children's TV programmes. Chelimsky (1997, p. 9) points out the enormous breadth of topics that could be addressed with an evaluation research strategy:

> to measure and account for the results of public policies and programs; to determine the efficiency of programs, projects, and their component processes; to gain explanatory insights into social and other public problems and into past and present efforts to address them; to understand how organizations learn; to strengthen institutions and improve managerial performance; to increase agency responsiveness to the public; to reform governments through the free flow of evaluative information; and to

expand results or efficiency measurement from that of local or national interventions to that of global interventions such as reducing poverty and hunger or reversing patterns of environmental degradation.

The effectiveness of such initiatives can be measured using a range of data collection methods, such as surveys, focus groups or qualitative interviews, but the strategic focus on effectiveness would apply in all cases.

Like action research, an evaluation research strategy can take many different forms. Indeed, many evaluation models have been articulated; for example, 'utilization-focused evaluation' (Patton, 1997) focuses on what will be most useful to the end user of the evaluation. The specifics of the different evaluation models are beyond the scope of this book. If you decide to use an evaluation research strategy, we recommend that you consult one of the evaluation methods books in the 'further reading' section at the end of this chapter.

 REAL WORLD EXAMPLE

Evaluation of a programme to reduce alcohol consumption

Lena wanted to evaluate whether a health organization's binge drinking reduction programme was achieving its goals. The programme's objectives were to reduce the volume of alcohol consumed by 18-20-year-old college students over a six-month period, reduce the frequency of binge drinking episodes, and raise awareness of the health risks associated with excessive alcohol consumption.

Lena used a mixed methods approach to shed light on the programme. She operationalized the term 'binge drinking' by using a standard measure: the consumption of five or more drinks in a row for men and four or more drinks in a row for women. The organization funding the programme had no specific demographic focus other than 18-20-year-old college students, so Lena selected a probability sample of 354 students (49.2 per cent male) at a university in Pennsylvania where the programme was operating. She arranged for a pre-survey of this sample of students in their first week of university and a post-survey in the last week of their first term using a Likert scale to understand how much alcohol students were consuming and how often. She then interviewed students during the first and last weeks of their term to understand whether awareness of health risks associated with excessive drinking had changed.

With this approach Lena was able to test whether the organization's aims were being achieved. The organization was then able to use her data to inform them about what kinds of approaches were proving successful and which needed to be changed in order to bring about the desired change in student behaviour.

1•3•4 EVALUATE YOUR PROJECT'S LIMITATIONS AND OPPORTUNITIES

Good research planning requires you to realistically assess the strengths and weaknesses of your research options as well as your capabilities as a researcher. Particular challenges may arise as you develop your research design; data may be hard to find, difficult to access or challenging to analyse. For example, if you are studying socially undesirable behaviour, such as prostitution, can you access respondents and are they willing to participate? There may also be complex legal implications for such a project. On the other hand, you may have major research opportunities, such as locating previously unknown documentation, receiving privileged access to an institution or finding a good 'inside' source that offers ground-breaking insights into your topic.

Look ahead to identify potential difficulties with your data collection and analysis plans. What aspects of your data sources or collection plans are unpredictable or uncertain (e.g., in terms of quality or availability)? Table 1.4 outlines areas of your research design that will benefit from advanced planning and detailed evaluation of your research capabilities.

Table 1.4   Anticipate your research needs

Approval and access

- Do you need approval from a government or major institution to access certain archives, participants (e.g., members of a group or institution) or other data sources? The uncertainty here could apply to both the initial granting of access and its possible withdrawal during your project.
- Are you relying on one person or organization to provide all your data?
- Are you assuming that a key gatekeeper will be appointed to a certain post, get permissions from their superiors, or remain cooperative in assisting you?

Ways to address these issues

- **Start seeking approval and access early** in your research process. Don't be waylaid by non-responses or administrative procedures. Be polite but persistent in ascertaining whether approval will or will not be granted.
- Wherever possible, **avoid hinging your research on one person or data source**.
- Try to **gain interest and approval from multiple stakeholders** who can approve your access to key archives, participants or other data sources.
- Seek out **backup or alternative sources of key data.** Even if your alternative sources are not ideal, other sources are worth having in case your first choice becomes unavailable. For example, you may want to interview US senators but find that they don't easily commit to interviews. Think about other legislators who – while not your ideal choice – can provide sufficient data for your research.

Budget

- Does your funding or sponsorship come with constraints about who, where, or what you can research, and with which ethical procedures?
- Are your resources sufficient for the scope of research you are envisioning?

Ways to address these issues

- **Before you seek and receive funding, clearly understand terms and restrictions** from any funding providers. Account for these in your research design.
- **Establish and frequently update a budget**. This budget should be sufficiently detailed to provide a clear sense of your project costs. It should account for the various expenditures and support needs involved in your project such as compensating participants for travel costs, help with data entry or translation and any equipment you may need.
- **Take action to ensure your available budget will cover your anticipated costs**. Start seeking additional funding early on for any shortfall. Don't wait until you have nearly run out of funds or your entire project may be jeopardized. Alternatively, you can cut the scope of your project to fit your budget.

(Continued)

Table 1.4   (Continued)

Timeline

- Are key aspects of your research relying on the successful completion of preceding tasks? For example, do you need to complete part of your research before a key gatekeeper changes jobs?
- If you are an international student or planning foreign travel, do you have visa or passport requirements that might take several months to resolve?
- Are you assuming that events beyond your control will occur, such as a particular election result? What is your contingency plan if this doesn't occur?

Ways to address these issues

- **Establish a detailed timeline** (see Section 1.4) which includes all your major project milestones and objectives.
- **Update your timeline** to reflect completed milestones, changing dates and shifting research requirements.

Research skills

- Are you considering a project that requires higher levels of skill than you currently possess? For example, if your proposed research requires a statistical test you are unfamiliar with, you will need to plan time for the relevant statistics training or tutorial support.

Ways to address these issues

- **Be realistic and frank about what new skills you may need to develop**. Speak to your supervisor, colleagues and others who have undertaken similar research. Seek advice on what additional expertise you may require and at what stages in your research you will need these skills.
- **Plan additional training early but when it is most useful in your research**. If you are doing a particular statistical test in two years' time, it probably makes sense to do the training closer to when you will be applying your new skills.
- **Factor any additional training into your timeline and include any associated costs in your budget planning**.

🔑 KEY TIPS

Rely on your existing research skills to shape your research focus when short of time

We argue in this chapter that you should not start with a research method, but rather you should arrive at the method after considering how best to address your research question. However, you may find yourself in a situation where you have only developed skills in one or two data collection or analysis methods (or more rarely, that a client commissioning research pre-specifies research methods).

If you don't have the time to develop additional skills, you will realistically need to rely on the method(s) you can competently use. What aspect of your topic can you address effectively using your current skills? In other words, what skills do you currently possess and how best can your research question be addressed using these skills?

To do this, refer to the chapters on data collection and analysis, which discuss each method's relative strengths and weaknesses. Choose a research question within your general area of interest that uses the strengths of the method(s) you're committed to using. For example, if your method is qualitative interviewing, your research question should probably seek to understand individuals' perspectives on a topic.

Once you've scrutinized your plans for possible challenges, you can prepare for them and maximize opportunities. Ensure you prepare before undertaking data collection; don't just hope you will find solutions as you go. The steps required for your project will depend on the specific issues you're facing, but solutions will include:

- **Have a backup plan for sourcing alternative data**. Rank your ideal data sources on a hierarchy. How reliable is each source and what challenges (e.g., timeline constraints or the granting of permission) do you need to consider? Establish second and third backup options in case your ideal source is unavailable. For example, if your ideal source is the Vice President of Technology for Google (who may deny you access), who else at Google could provide useful data? Could someone at another technology company provide the information you need? Could you use any publically available sources if all access channels are denied?

  While such contingency planning is important, do remember that using alternative data sources may also require you to adjust your research question or other aspects of your research project. The best alternative data sources require minimal such adjustments.

- **Have a realistic timeline when dealing with challenging data**. The more challenging the data (e.g., unreliable sources, poor-quality data), the more time needed to contend with the various challenges that could arise.

REAL WORLD EXAMPLE

Have a backup plan for an alternative data source

Javier was researching the influence of employees' ethnicity in the performance appraisal process in a government department. He wrote letters in advance and was surprised at the good cooperation and access to confidential departmental information he was given. Initially he was elated at the unique and privileged data this access provided. Because Javier's access appeared to be so certain and the data so interesting, he didn't 'waste time' finding backup sources.

Four months into his seven-month project, a departmental lawyer heard about Javier's project. Citing confidentiality concerns, the lawyer immediately blocked Javier from conducting further research. Because he did not have approval in writing to use the data, the lawyer was also able to block his use of the information he had already collected. Without alternative data sources, Javier had no means of continuing his project, which he was over halfway through. Javier sought an extension to his deadline and didn't complete the project in time with his classmates.

Having a backup data source, even if it would be an inferior option, is preferable to having no data and needing to start again from scratch. Javier could also have been more diligent in seeking broad, written consent from departmental leaders indicating their willingness to provide access. Your data collection plan is more vulnerable if it relies on one person (who could suddenly leave the organization) than if multiple stakeholders have given approval in writing.

1●4 MANAGE YOUR TIME IN THE RESEARCH DESIGN PROCESS

Now that we've walked you through the core components of developing your research design, let's think more deeply about the unifying element for your research: your timeline.

Establishing a detailed and realistic timeline is essential to meeting deadlines without making drastic last-minute changes to your research project. Your timeline also helps you determine the feasibility of your research plan. It's easier and more efficient to remove part of your planned research early in your project than to complete work that later becomes unusable. For example, if you only had time to analyse five of the 10 qualitative interviews you conducted, you would have wasted both your and your participants' time. Inexperienced researchers tend to underestimate – sometimes severely – the time necessary to complete a project, so be detailed and conservative with your time estimates. Moreover, it can be particularly helpful to get feedback on your planned timeline from an experienced researcher.

 **REAL WORLD EXAMPLE**

Narrow your research scope early on

When Eric wrote his PhD proposal he wanted to research science journalists and their reporting on the scientific controversy surrounding therapeutic cloning in the United States, the United Kingdom and New Zealand. However, after drawing up a research timeline Eric realized that it wouldn't be feasible to conduct in-depth research in all three countries. Therefore, he decided to remove New Zealand because it required the greatest travel costs in order to carry out face-to-face data collection. In addition, he already had some understanding of the US and UK policy and media context for his topic, so he also saved the time required to develop this knowledge about New Zealand. This was also an easy way to reduce the scope and therefore the size of his research project, which had downstream benefits in terms of reducing the amount of data he had to analyse. He also decided to conduct about half of his qualitative interviews over the phone to further save costs (focusing his face-to-face interviews on the geographical areas he could most easily reach). The phone interviews were successful, but he wanted to conduct some of the interviews on-site at news organizations in the US and UK to see for himself the context in which science journalists operate. If he didn't have the funding to do this, he could have also used online options such as Skype, Google Hangout or FaceTime to conduct video interviews.

1•4•1 AVOID TIME-WASTING RESEARCH PRACTICES

While the quality and depth of your research is of course important, make sure you don't get bogged down in time-wasting practices that could throw off your timeline:

- **Keep writing.** Don't do more and more reading instead of getting on with your writing. You could spend years reading all the literature on your topic!
- **Avoid making so many preparations that you don't make substantial progress in your data collection and analysis.** For example, you might spend weeks locating a handful of hard-to-find interview respondents rather than getting on with interviewing your existing sample.
- **Don't collect more data than you have time to analyse.**
- **Avoid collecting data you don't really need**, such as interviews with respondents who, although interesting, may only hold limited value for your research.

It's easy to lose control of your time management. Procrastination often causes this, for example when you can't face a full day of such tedious tasks as transcribing interviews. We therefore recommend that you try to overlap tasks within your timeline; you could begin transcribing while still collecting data collection. Completing the less exciting research tasks in smaller chunks increases the likelihood that you will get on with it! Thinking early on about what each task requires will enable you to create a more effective and achievable timeline.

1•4•2 CREATE A TIMELINE FOR YOUR RESEARCH PROJECT

Begin by creating a timeline, a chronological list of the tasks required to complete your research on time. Here are the steps to follow when you create your research timeline:

1 Determine the **start and end date for your research**.
2 Decide on the **time unit you'll use to set targets**. For most projects of three months or longer, weekly units are sufficient. However, if you're working on a short project, consider setting daily goals. Biweekly or monthly intervals can work for projects of a year or longer. Remember that you want your timeline to be specific enough to let you effectively track your progress.
3 Decide on the **major phases of your research** and assign timeframes, normally overlapping, for these steps:

   - Proposal writing
   - Research design and planning
   - Literature review
   - Pilot testing
   - Data collection
   - Analysis
   - Write-up.

4 Define and **include your major milestones for each phase of your research**. For example, you may have preliminary deadlines to provide your supervisor with survey or interview questions, or to deliver a draft report. Also include milestones such as any required examinations and presentations.
5 **Populate your timeline with more detailed goals for each major milestone.** What specific tasks are involved in each major research task? Which tasks need to be completed early or prepared in advance because they depend on other people? For example, you'll need to arrange interviews or focus groups well in advance.
6 **Identify forks in the research road**. You could set up checkpoints in your timeline to review and see if a backup 'plan B' is needed.
7 After distributing your tasks over your timeline, fully **evaluate whether your time allocations are realistic**, and adjust as necessary. Build some slack into your timeline. Your project is a venture into the research unknown for you, so assume that parts of it will overrun your expected timeframe. An unrealistically tight schedule can make you feel like you're constantly behind.
8 Don't forget to **plan holidays and any other inactive periods into your timeline.** Again, be realistic and include planned relaxation breaks from your research, especially when you are working on tedious or emotionally draining content.

Being flexible and planning some slack into your timeline

Making apparently efficient plans that use all available time can end up causing you stress due to a lack of flexibility. Duncan was undertaking a research project on how European trade unions are reacting to globalization of the labour market. In an effort to maximize a short research trip to the Netherlands, Duncan arranged interviews and archive visits for the entire time of his trip. However, Duncan's departure was delayed by a day due to food poisoning and there was little he could do to reschedule his planned activities into an even shorter timeframe.

Even with the most carefully planned timelines, things can go wrong and fieldwork can generate all sorts of surprises. Your schedule needs to be flexible enough to deal with unexpected delays.

There are many tools that you can use to prepare your timeline. One option is to use Microsoft Word or Excel (see Table 1.5 for an example). Such layouts are quick and easy to create and don't require you to locate and learn how to use new software. However, this method does not easily allow for the more complex functionality offered by purpose-built timeline software, such as the easy creation, understanding and updating of concurrent timelines. Timelines created in Word or Excel can also get unwieldy if they are long or detailed; imagine following Table 1.5 if it was extended over five years, for example.

You have innovative options for creating timelines and tracking your progress on a calendar using software that is flexible and easily updated. You should create a basic timeline that shows key milestones over the duration of the research project to ensure you've allowed sufficient time for your research tasks.

We recommend using a calendar-based tool that allows you to make the timeline as detailed as needed. Creating automatic reminders in your personal calendar also helps you remain focused on your established milestones. Consider the following software tools:

- **Preceden** allows you to create complex, easily updatable and interactive timelines. Timelines can be in colour and are printable. It is an excellent tool for basic timeline needs. You can currently try this software for free with limited features; there is a fee for the full access version.

Table 1.5 Sample timeline extract

Week	Major goal	Minor goal	Activity	Status
29 May–5 June	Transcribe interviews	Transcribe interview with Robert Smith	Transcribe interview	Complete
		Transcribe interview with Bill Jones	Transcribe interview	Complete
		Transcribe interview with Chris Stephens	Transcribe interview	Ongoing
6 June–12 June	Begin qualitative coding	Code interview with Robert Smith	First coding pass	Not started

- **Google calendar** gives you access to a free online calendar system that connects to your email account. This enables texts and emails to be sent automatically as reminders.
- **OS X Calendar** is Apple-specific software that tracks events, makes calendar entries and sets basic timeframes for events. It offers a range of reminder options and features. You can create a calendar theme specifically for your research to make it clear, at a glance, when important research-related activities are coming up. This application comes free with OS X.

While the above tools offer the capability to develop and update your timeline, the timeline will only be as good as you make it. Frequently update your timeline as your project develops, and keep to your milestones.

Having both a short-term and long-term view of your research is crucial. Know what you intend to accomplish in the coming days and weeks. This is where calendar software can be particularly useful. But maintaining a wider overview of your research over, for example, monthly or even yearly intervals is crucial to seeing what you have already accomplished and what is yet to be completed. You can annotate your timeline with notes about the decisions you made at key points during your project.

Experienced researchers don't view updating their timelines as an unpleasant 'chore' or something to be done only a few times at the beginning of a project. Instead, consider your timelines as your yardstick for assessing and maintaining your progress, highlighting where adjustments are needed to move forward. In other words, closely attending to your timeline is one of the easiest and most effective ways of keeping your research on track.

KEY TIPS

Establishing accurate timelines is a major challenge for researchers

It is easy to be overly ambitious with your deadlines. This problem often stems from your enthusiasm for your project and from the fact that the complexity of some tasks may not be apparent until you start working on them. The general rule for research planning is that everything will take much longer than you think!

Pay particular attention to planning the phases of your project that may be emotionally draining, tedious, repetitive or tiring. For example, transcribing interviews, coding and data entry can be very tiring at the best of times and can be particularly gruelling for poor-quality audio recordings. Your attention may lapse, technical challenges may arise and, for a myriad other reasons, these tasks can therefore take longer than anticipated to complete. The overriding principle is to be realistic with your expected timeframes for key tasks, erring on the side of caution, yet remaining focused and diligent in striving to complete your objectives on time.

1.5 CONCLUSION

This chapter has provided ways for you to develop and maintain a robust research design, narrowing your focus through a series of decisions to arrive at a feasible project plan. Throughout the research process, your research question leads the way. Remember that the purpose of your research design is to 'ensure that the evidence obtained enables [you] to answer the initial [research] question as unambiguously as possible' (de Vaus, 2001, p. 9). We have identified ways for you to develop a sound research question that will lead you towards feasible and useful research.

You may find you need to reduce the scope of your project along the way. In this case, look for places where you can make a clean cut (a whole section, one out of three comparison cases, etc.) so that you don't create more work by having to edit the section you cut down in size. At the time, cutting down your scope may be hard to accept, but you will be much happier in the long term if you make this decision early on before investing a lot of time and resources in a direction you don't have time to fully develop. By developing and refining your clear and achievable research question, you will keep your research on track as you encounter many interesting paths along your research journey. Your mantra once your project is well under way should be 'stay focused!'.

We have illustrated each step as you develop your research plan with examples from the real world so you can see how others have resolved research design challenges. These examples demonstrate how careful and realistic planning and strategies can keep your project on track. It is important that you avoid the temptation of overlooking research limitations during this planning process. Be honest about them and generate solutions early on; problems are much harder to resolve later in your research project.

Finally, we have offered guidance on how you can develop a comprehensive yet flexible research timeline. We advocate being ruthlessly realistic with your project plans and scope so they reflect what can feasibly be delivered in the available time. Use a software-based approach to create and update your timeline. This approach allows you to focus on the work required to reach specific research objectives each day and week, while enabling you to 'zoom out' and see a monthly or even yearly view of your past and future research journey. Regularly orienting yourself within your timeline is crucial for keeping on course to achieve your research objectives on time and within budget.

SUGGESTIONS FOR FURTHER READING

- de Vaus, D. (2001). *Research design in social sciences*. London: Sage. This book provides a straightforward and helpful introduction to research design, which goes into more detail than is feasible in this chapter. It is one of the best research methods texts available, and is particularly good at helping you work through research design dilemmas.
- Johnson, R. B., & Onwuegbuzie, A. J. (2004). Mixed methods research: A research paradigm whose time has come. *Educational Researcher, 33*(7), 14-26. This article gives a useful overview of 'paradigm' debates in the methodological literature. The authors detail the fundamentals of mixed methods research, and you may find their 'eight-step process' particularly useful.
- Kelle, U. (2006). Combining qualitative and quantitative methods in research practice: Purposes and advantages. *Qualitative Research in Psychology, 3*, 293-311. This article takes a pragmatic approach to research design by asking fundamental questions such as: What kinds of research questions are qualitative and quantitative methods best able to answer? What are the main strengths and weaknesses of quantitative and qualitative research with respect to particular domains?

- **Morgan, D. L. (2013).** *Integrating qualitative and quantitative methods: A pragmatic approach.* **London: Sage.** This is the best book on mixed methods research design currently available. It spells out in clear and accessible language why you would want to conduct research using a combination of qualitative and quantitative methods. The book also provides practical guidance about how to justify and structure such research.

Action Research Strategy

- **Mertler, C. A. (2014).** *Action research: Improving schools and empowering educators* **(4th ed.). Thousand Oaks, CA: Sage.** This book gives a good introduction to action research and then takes you through the key stages to completion. You may find the sections on planning for action research and developing a research plan especially useful.
- **Stringer, E. T. (2014).** *Action research (4th ed.).* **Thousand Oaks, CA: Sage.** One of the most authoritative and approachable books on action research available. The book guides you through the action research process, illustrating key elements with case studies so you can easily see how to implement the guidance in real situations.

Evaluation Research Strategy

- **Dane, F. C. (2011).** *Evaluating research: Methodology for people who need to read research.* **Thousand Oaks, CA: Sage.** This is a systematic and comprehensive book on evaluation that is especially suitable for beginning students and those on master's programmes. The book relies on selected published research articles that provide detailed and illustrative examples.
- **Shaw, I. F., Greene, J. C., & Mark, M. M. (2006).** *The SAGE handbook of evaluation.* **London: Sage.** This book offers a broad account of evaluation methods, and different approaches to using this research strategy. It features chapters from different authors offering detailed accounts of their favoured strategic approaches to evaluation.

Visit the companion website at **https://study.sagepub.com/jensenandlaurie** to gain access to a wide range of online resources to support your learning, including editable research documents, weblinks, free access SAGE journal articles and book chapters, and flashcards.

▬ GLOSSARY ▬▬▬▬▬▬▬▬▬▬▬▬▬▬▬▬▬▬▬▬▬

Action research – A process of research involving an iterative cycle of theory-driven action that is evaluated, with research results feeding into further changes in practice that can then be evaluated. This approach can be conducted by researchers or by practitioners to inform and evaluate improvements in their own settings, for example to benefit outcomes for patients, clients and customers.

Cross-sectional research – The analysis of individuals' perspectives at *a specific point in time*; for example, a survey of voter satisfaction with the performance of their national leaders.

Evaluation research – A type of social research focusing on the effects of interventions and programmes within social, policy, learning and business contexts. The focus on testing the intended objectives of the intervention distinguishes this type of social research from other approaches.

Longitudinal research – The analysis of individuals' perspectives over a period of time. For example, a longitudinal study might follow how a set of children exposed to different childhood traumas develop into adulthood.

Mixed methods research – Also referred to as 'combed research methods', this term describes the use of more than one research method in a single research project. This often involves using quantitative and qualitative methods in a coordinated manner to gain from the strengths, while mitigating the weaknesses, of each method.

Operationalization – The process of defining how you will measure something (usually an abstract concept).

Qualitative research – A category of social research that refers to methods of data collection and analysis that use words, images, observations and other non-numerical data. Major qualitative research methods include focus groups, in-depth interviews and ethnography.

Quantitative research – A category of social research that refers to methods of data collection and analysis that use numerical data.

Research design – The plan detailing how you will answer your research question(s). Good research design decision-making requires understanding both your range of options and how to evaluate the strengths and weaknesses of each option.

Research question – The central question that your research seeks to answer. This question provides the guiding focus for your project.

■■ REFERENCES ■■■■■■■■■■■■■■■■■■■■■■■■■■■■■

Chelimsky, E. (1997). The coming transformations in evaluation. In E. Chelimsky & W. R. Shadish (Eds.), *Evaluation for the 21st century: A handbook* (pp. 1–27). Thousand Oaks, CA: Sage.

de Vaus, D. (2001). *Research design in social sciences*. London: Sage.

Gray, K., & Wegner, D. M. (2013). Six guidelines for interesting research. *Perspectives on Psychological Science, 8*(5), 549–553.

Greenwood, D. J., & Levin, M. (2007). Part 1: What is action research? In D. J. Greenwood & M. Levin (Eds.), *Introduction to action research* (2nd ed., pp. 2–3). Thousand Oaks, CA: Sage.

Johnson, R. B., & Onwuegbuzie, A. J. (2004). Mixed methods research: A research paradigm whose time has come. *Educational Researcher, 33*(7), 14–26.

McIntyre, A. (2008). *Participatory action research*. Thousand Oaks, CA: Sage.

Morgan, D. L. (2013). *Integrating qualitative and quantitative methods: A pragmatic approach*. London: Sage.

Patton, M. Q. (1997). *Utilization-focused evaluation* (3rd ed.). Thousand Oaks, CA: Sage.

Scriven, M. (1991). *Evaluation thesaurus* (4th ed.). Newbury Park, CA: Sage.

Wagoner, B., & Jensen, E. (2015). Microgenetic evaluation: Studying learning in motion. In G. Marsico, R. Ruggieri & S. Salvatore (Eds.), *The yearbook of idiographic science* (Vol. 6, *Reflexivity and change in psychology*). Charlotte, NC: Information Age Publishers.

HOW TO DO A LITERATURE REVIEW

USING EXISTING EVIDENCE AND IDEAS TO BUILD A FOUNDATION

2

▬▬ **THIS CHAPTER COVERS THE FOLLOWING TOPICS** ▬▬▬▬▬▬▬▬▬▬▬▬

- Recognize the boundaries of your research area, and define your specific research focus.
- Systemically search for good sources.
- Evaluate your sources.
- Organize your sources by logically grouping them.
- Define a gap in what is already known and published on your topic for you to address in your research.
- Ensure your literature review is well organized and persuasive.

2◗1 INTRODUCTION

At a general level, research is a social process. Ideas, research methods and knowledge all develop over time, with researchers critiquing and building on each other's work. This collaborative way of creating knowledge involves explicitly referencing, summarizing, evaluating and applying ideas from previously published research and theory to establish the foundation for your own project. Therefore, you must develop a good understanding of what is already known about your topic in relevant, credible publications. Then you'll need to effectively communicate this understanding in your research report. Your understanding of this prior research affects your research design, selection of research methods and interpretation of findings. Your account of existing knowledge on your topic normally appears as a major section in your research report, commonly referred to as your **literature review**.

Your research should test an existing idea or introduce and evaluate new ideas. Establishing where your planned research sits within the context of other research can help you identify your project's major contribution(s), such as:

- filling in an under-researched area, a 'gap' in the literature;
- testing an existing idea;
- building on an existing idea.

For example, if you imagine researching the role of women in the garment industry, you might find that, while there is extensive research on this topic, there is a surprising lack of coverage of the role of black women. You could then shape your study to focus on this underdeveloped area within the larger topic. On the other hand, if you found that your planned research had already been done recently by someone else, then you might want to refocus your study so that your work is viewed as making an original contribution.

2◗2 ORIENT YOUR RESEARCH THROUGH YOUR REVIEW OF THE LITERATURE

In order to understand what is already known about your topic and therefore where you can make a valuable contribution, you'll need to conduct a literature review. A literature review is a systematic account of what is known about a specific topic using research, policy and theory that have been published by credible sources of information. A literature review can be a research output in its own right. More commonly, a literature review is written as one part of a research project.

A literature review should go beyond merely describing other people's research. It should analyse and critically evaluate both the methods and results of such research, applying it to your topic in a clear and coherent manner.

A good literature review will achieve the following:

- Establish a **base of existing knowledge** that you can build on.
- **Categorize relevant literature** so you can group sources coherently.
- **Stay tightly organized and focused around** your research question.
- **Critically evaluate the methods and claims of your sources**, as well as summarizing key findings relevant to your topic.
- **Identify general trends in strengths, weaknesses or gaps** in relevant literature.
- Highlight when aspects of your topic have received **particular attention, disagreement or controversy**.
- If possible, **offer insights** into how research trends, controversies and areas of particular focus have emerged.

You can use these aspects of your literature review to lay the foundations for framing your research as clearly needed to address unresolved issues in the existing research on your topic.

Often people begin the literature review before having a firm **research question** (just having a general topic idea). Indeed, starting to read relevant literature can help you craft and refine your research question. However, before you can write up and finalize the literature review section in your research report, you'll need your specific research question so that you can ensure your literature review creates a strong rationale for your research.

2●3 FOCUS YOUR LITERATURE REVIEW WHILE ACCOUNTING FOR THE BIG PICTURE

In your literature review, you'll first need to place your topic within a relatively broad research and policy context to establish why your topic is interesting and to orient your readers (Creswell, 2014, p. 28). For example, if you're studying how intravenous drug users amongst homosexual men in Barcelona engage with police there, you might start off your literature review section by showing how this behaviour connects to government and law enforcement policies, healthcare issues or changing social norms about drug use in Spain, or Europe more generally. You could think of this process as being like a picture puzzle: if you are trying to place your single piece of the puzzle, you need to see how it will fit next to the surrounding pieces and the overall picture.

As you begin your literature review, you can save time by defining your focus as narrowly as possible. For example, the topic about homosexual male intravenous drug users in Barcelona would be hopelessly large and vague if the topic was 'drug use in Spain' or 'illegal activities in Europe'. The more tightly focused your topic, the more efficient and effective your research can be. So, if you don't yet have a specific research question, at least try to sharpen your focus by talking to your colleagues, speaking to your supervisor or doing initial reading about your general topic area.

KEY TIPS

What if I have too many or too few relevant sources?

When preparing a literature review, you may find yourself overwhelmed by too much existing research or cast adrift with only a few islands of existing research relevant to your topic. 'Too many' or 'too few' can be decided based on how much time you have and how much space you have to write in your literature review (e.g., in a small 3000-word research report, you may only have space for 5-10 sources at the most in your literature review). To cope with too many existing research studies for you to handle, the quickest solution is to more narrowly define your scope. You could do this geographically by focusing on a smaller area (e.g., focusing on the situation in Scotland, rather than the UK as a whole) or narrowing by discipline (e.g., reviewing the psychological literature on this topic). To address the challenge of too few sources, you'll need to widen your search to include nearby topics. Research from these different but related topics will then need to be applied in a tentative and provisional way to your specific topic.

For both challenges (over- and undersupply of existing research on your topic), it can be helpful to take each aspect of your general area of study and map it out from its least focused to a more focused part. For instance, if one part of the study included the city of Lagos, you might map the following: Africa > West Africa > Nigeria > Lagos > Ikoyi (a suburb of Lagos); this way you could easily slide up and down the scale of focus depending on your research needs and the availability of sources for your literature review. You can also identify different categories within your general topic, which will allow you to focus on a particular category. For example, if you're interested in studying education in Nigeria, you might identify education levels as the key categories: primary education, secondary education, tertiary education, international education, education for special needs students, etc. If you had too many sources to deal with at this level (e.g., if you selected secondary education as a focus), then you could narrow further by looking at a specific year or type of schooling (e.g., private, or specialist schools for dropouts) in order to reduce the number of sources you have to contend with.

2•3•1 KEEP MAKING ADJUSTMENTS AS YOU DEVELOP YOUR LITERATURE REVIEW

As Figure 2.1 shows, preparing a literature review involves circling back to make adjustments, refine your focus and shore up your evidence multiple times as you move towards a completed research project. You will be looking for sources, reading and synthesizing the information and writing up your literature review mostly at the beginning and end of your project, but be sure to continue this process of reading literature as you go to reinforce and check your emerging ideas. Double back, adjust your search, explore new avenues while shutting off others and then gradually move towards the goal of understanding what is already known or claimed about your specific research topic. On the other hand, don't let yourself get caught in a hamster wheel of aimlessly exploring one topic after another with no focus. Maintain a laser-like focus on your research question, and keep writing throughout the literature review process.

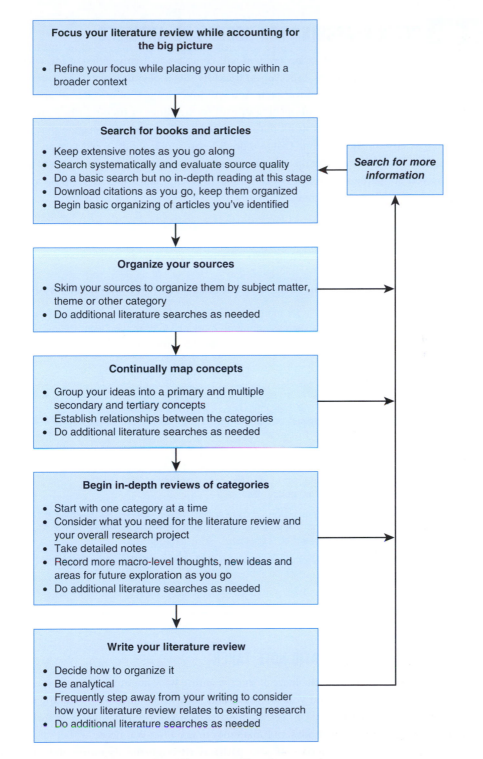

Focus your literature review while accounting for the big picture

- Refine your focus while placing your topic within a broader context

Search for books and articles

- Keep extensive notes as you go along
- Search systematically and evaluate source quality
- Do a basic search but no in-depth reading at this stage
- Download citations as you go, keep them organized
- Begin basic organizing of articles you've identified

Search for more information

Organize your sources

- Skim your sources to organize them by subject matter, theme or other category
- Do additional literature searches as needed

Continually map concepts

- Group your ideas into a primary and multiple secondary and tertiary concepts
- Establish relationships between the categories
- Do additional literature searches as needed

Begin in-depth reviews of categories

- Start with one category at a time
- Consider what you need for the literature review and your overall research project
- Take detailed notes
- Record more macro-level thoughts, new ideas and areas for future exploration as you go
- Do additional literature searches as needed

Write your literature review

- Decide how to organize it
- Be analytical
- Frequently step away from your writing to consider how your literature review relates to existing research
- Do additional literature searches as needed

Figure 2.1   The process of writing your literature review

2 ● 4 BEGIN SEARCHING FOR BOOKS AND ARTICLES

As you embark on your literature review, you will come across many different ideas about a broad range of research concepts. Especially at the early stages of your research, you are exploring a topic and not following a linear path. You will investigate a lot of different approaches and ideas, some being fruitful and opening up still further lines of inquiry, while others will prove to be dead-end streets you won't pursue any further. For example, imagine that you are visiting a new city for the first time that you don't know much about. You'd take an exploratory approach where you wander up different promising streets and alleys, stopping to explore further as you go, perhaps doubling back at times to re-explore certain areas while avoiding others that don't inspire your interest.

 KEY TIPS

Use Boolean searches to improve your success rate finding relevant sources

Boolean searches enable you to be far more precise when entering search terms by using words such as AND, OR, NOT or symbols such as quotation marks to indicate you want to limit a search to an exact phrase. These search options can save you a lot of time, so we strongly recommend you get to know them.

Quotation marks " "	*Searches for words and phrases in the exact order.* This is useful when a phrase has a specific meaning. For instance, if you searched for **"US war on drugs"** you would find all instances where those precise words appear in that order.
Excluding terms -search word	*Excludes the word immediately after the symbol* **-**. For example, if you wanted to know about the policies of politician Jeb Bush but not his more famous brother George, you would enter: **"Jeb Bush" policy -George**
Allow more than one term OR	*At least one of the terms joined by OR will appear.* For example, if you search for **"social housing" OR welfare** then you would get results that have either "social housing" or "welfare".
Default Boolean operation AND	*All words joined by AND appear unless you have entered a different Boolean command in your search.*

2 ● 4 ● 1 BECOME A SYSTEMATIC NOTE-TAKER

As you make your way through the maze of sources during your literature review, it is essential that you take careful notes about your decisions and your initial ideas while reading articles. Tracking this process means you can get the most benefit out of your time by ensuring you don't have to reread articles or books multiple times to get what you need.

Take notes to establish a record of your pathway through the literature and the decisions you make along the way about where to focus. It may be tempting to track your decision-making by hand in a written journal, but you'll be making so many changes and recategorizations as you go that doing it in an electronic format, such as Word, will be much easier for you. The note-taking process evolves as you progress through your project. Begin by tracking the following:

- Research **topics you have explored**, and **what you decided about each one**.
- **Promising articles, books and authors** you've uncovered, separated into categories. Thinking back to the drug use in Barcelona example, literature categories might include 'Homosexuality in Spain', 'Drug use in Spain' and 'Drug policy in Barcelona'. You would also need subcategories for each of these clusters of relevant literature.
- A **list of search terms** you've used (see forthcoming sections).

As you go through the process of writing your literature review, keep your notes continuously updated.

2•4•2 DEVELOP A SEARCH PLAN

Before you begin actually searching for sources, you need a clear **search plan**. Come up with a list of search words and phrases that would likely lead to information on your research topic. Incorporate synonyms, slang terms, alternative spellings, foreign languages and different phrasings into this plan. This plan both ensures that you maintain good coverage in your search and that you can explain how you went about your search in your research report.

Table 2.1 is a brief example of part of this search planning using the male homosexual intravenous drug users in Barcelona topic. When you begin searching, you'll find that certain word combinations – that may not be obvious initially – will reveal a much richer set of sources than others. Preferred usage of certain terms amongst researchers, policy-makers or people within a particular culture can affect keyword selection, and be hard to predict in advance. You should therefore keep a continuously updated record of which search terms are turning out to be most effective, as shown in Table 2.1. See Ford (2012, p. 29) for further guidance about selecting appropriate search terms to avoid missing important information.

Table 2.1 Example of search plan

Ranking	City	Drugs	Homosexuality
Strongest results	1. Barcelona	1. Heroin	1. Homosexual
	2. Catalonia [autonomous community where Barcelona is located]	2. Smack, junk, China white, etc. [slang terms for heroin]	2. Gay
	3. Population centres Spain	3. Intravenous drug use (IDU)	3. Queer
	4. City Spain	4. Inject	4. LGBT
Weakest results	5. Urban Spain	5. Needle	5. Same-sex
	6. Street Spain	6. Needle exchange	6. Lesbian

Once your search plan is in place, electronic **journal databases** are likely to be the best choice for starting your literature search. There is a vast array of electronic sources that are easily accessible and searchable, often from anywhere in the world. These have the major convenience of being downloadable (in most cases), easily organized and stored, and viewable from multiple devices. Some software, such as Papers (www.papersapp.com), allows you to organize downloaded sources, annotate PDFs, manage citations and then easily search this modified content. Moreover, journal databases sometimes offer the option of downloading a citation directly into your citation software such as Endnote.

Many researchers favour electronic resources, but it's important to also draw on printed sources when necessary (some older books are only available in a printed format).

REAL WORLD EXAMPLE

Printed sources still relevant today

The major convenience offered by electronic sources in terms of storage, searching and portability makes them an easy choice for most researchers. However, printed materials can still be essential for some topics.

When Charles was researching political conflict in Zimbabwe, he found that much of the information he needed from southern Africa was not available electronically (a more common situation in the developing world). Most relevant government documents and major newspapers were available only in printed form. Locating these sources posed major challenges because Charles had to gather them in person when travelling in the region. Moreover, even archives in the region tended not to hold complete records and were often poorly organized.

He found one solution with the British Library (http://www.bl.uk) which offers copies of many global newspapers (some, but not all, are available online). This plugged some of the gaps but in many cases these newspapers were not current. Charles found another solution in the form of friends and research assistants who could gather copies of these records in Zimbabwe for him and send them by mail.

In practice, you'll need to improvise as you conduct your search, sweeping up the most interesting and promising articles, books and reports in whatever ways you can. Consider using informal approaches to gathering sources, such as asking a friend or acquaintance working on a similar topic for a copy of their Endnote library (or other bibliographic software) file, folders of downloaded articles, etc. (you can offer to share what you find in return). Once you've identified a few recurring names in the relevant literature on your topic, you can go straight to those researchers' institutional websites and any other research sharing accounts they may have (e.g., on websites such as academia.edu or Research Gate) to try to access a full set of relevant publications from those authors.

EVALUATE AND ACCESS YOUR POTENTIAL SOURCES

It's important to weigh the strengths and weaknesses of your various sources (Table 2.2). The gold standard for source credibility across all sciences, including social science, is **peer review**. When an article or book is peer-reviewed, this signifies that experts in the topic of the article or book have

Table 2.2 Comparison of sources

Type of sources	Strengths	Weaknesses
Books	• In-depth analysis and write-up • Extensive information on a topic • Reputable publishers tend to publish higher-quality information • References section in a relevant book can highlight other useful sources	• Tend to be less current because it usually takes longer to write a book • Often include information you don't need. Don't feel you need to read everything in a given book • Very time-consuming to read whole books. Focus on parts most relevant to your topic • Less likely to be in electronic format, thus difficult to search for key words • Can be expensive to purchase if not available in a library
Journal articles	• All have an abstract at the start summarizing the article for you • Tend to be more current • Sharper focus on a specific issues • Reputable publishers publish higher-quality work • Shorter, less time-consuming to review • References section in a relevant article can highlight other useful sources	• Tend to be less current than newspapers and magazines due to often slow review process (1–9 months) and long lag time between article acceptance and publication (3–24 months) • Subscriptions can be expensive and individual article purchase prices are untenably high
Completed theses/ dissertations	• Insight into recent research on a topic • References section in a relevant thesis can highlight other useful sources	• Not professionally peer-reviewed, so the source carries less weight when supporting your research • Time-consuming to read a thesis, especially a PhD dissertation • Can be difficult to locate (many may not be in electronic format) • Quality is inconsistent
Government documents, white papers and official reports	• Present official research, analyses and viewpoints • Provide credible sources for describing government policy details and goals • Often freely accessible and free to access if published online • Can be biased documents driven by implicit political agendas • Usually less time-consuming to review than books	• No traditional academic peer review • Quality can be inconsistent • May be difficult to locate if not published online
Magazines and newspapers	• Information is very current • Can offer insights into topics circulating in the public sphere • Can offer detailed insights into events in specific geographic locations • Less time-consuming to review and easier to read • Can be used to help orient your understanding of what is going on with issues relevant to your topic	• Claims may not be rigorously supported by evidence • Basis for knowledge claims can be vague or unspecified • Not peer-reviewed, so the source carries less weight when supporting your research • May not provide a list of sources • Generally shouldn't be used to support knowledge claims • Quality is highly variable across different newspapers and magazines, and sometimes within the same publication

critically assessed it and decided it was worthy of publication. While the peer-review process is far from perfect, and its quality can vary substantially, it is the widely accepted quality control mechanism in social research (O'Leary, 2014, p. 95). Here are some other points to keep in mind:

- Books from highly regarded publishers and peer-reviewed journal articles tend to provide the same high level of credibility.
- Research published in journal articles can be more current than that in books, due to the shorter timeframe to get an article written and published (although social science journals can have gaps of up to 2 years from submission to publication).
- Books and articles that are not peer-reviewed provide much less credibility; many researchers will avoid them unless absolutely necessary. You can cite non-peer-reviewed publications if you are using them to point out a representation or argument, but you generally should avoid using them as a source of evidence or scholarly ideas.

Journal articles will probably be your largest category of sources. Therefore, much of our guidance in this chapter focuses on how to review and manage journal articles for your literature review.

While you consider what sources to use, you will also need to think about how to access these sources. Printed materials such as books, newspapers, maps and historical documents are typically located in libraries, and can be found by using library catalogues and electronic resource search tools. Electronic resources, such as journal databases, are also accessible through library systems (including university libraries). See Table 2.3 for a comparison of different ways of accessing sources for your literature review.

Table 2.3   Comparison of options for identifying sources

Source	Strengths	Weaknesses
Journal databases – JSTOR, EBSCO, ProQuest, etc.	• Focused source of content on specific fields • Access to high-quality research that is often peer-reviewed. • Content is filtered to provide specific content, i.e., you don't receive advertisements, etc. • Systemically organized content	• Usually subscription based • Will not provide information outside of a specific set of providers
Search engines – Google, Safari, etc.	• Easily accessible • Enormous source of varied information • Output tends to be less organized • Free	• Quality can be highly variable • More difficult to do a highly focused search • Volume of search results can become unmanageable • May not access useful content that is offline or requiring a subscription
Specialist search engine – Google Scholar, etc.	• Easily accessible • Database is continuously growing • Free	• Sources are usually incomplete • Breadth of coverage is sporadic

===== KEY TIPS =====

Get to know your library's resources

You might think that most academic libraries are fairly similar, but they aren't. Libraries concentrate their investment in resources around the current and past interests of key stakeholders in the university. Beyond the obvious variation in printed book collections, a range of different journal databases is available: each library must decide how to spend its scarce funds on subscriptions to such databases. This means that once you understand what resources your library does have, your next question should be how they will help you access resources they don't currently have.

Most libraries have orientation sessions where the differences in libraries at, for example, a university, are explained. Most libraries also offer some training on how to use their electronic resources. Get to know the resources available to you as soon as possible in the literature review process (if not before).

Most university libraries also offer online content covering everything from tips and guides, to digital media such as photographs and maps. For example, Anglia Ruskin University library provides guidelines on using the APA style for your citations (libweb.anglia.ac.uk/referencing/apa.htm).

2•4•3 BEGIN SEARCHING FOR RELEVANT SOURCES

Now that you have focused and planned your search, know how to use your library's available resources and are prepared to critically evaluate potential sources, it's time to begin your search in earnest. At this stage you want to be thorough in terms of the breadth of your search but not to get bogged down in the details of individual sources. Save the in-depth reading for the next stage, once you've narrowed down your sources to those that are most relevant and credible. For now you just want to identify the range of possible sources. Start with electronically accessible journal articles because they give you a clear sense of the current literature in your field, the content is easily searchable and **abstracts** can be quickly reviewed. Save books and other printed content, and electronic sources that are more difficult to access, for later when you can do a more detailed search.

===== KEY TIPS =====

How recent should your sources be?

The lazy assumption that recently published research will be more cutting-edge and valuable is widespread in parts of the social sciences. It's impossible to know in advance whether the best sources for your literature review will be from the last few years or from a few decades ago. In some fields of research, there is clear progression in ideas and research, which means that if you're focusing on work that was published five years ago then you've missed the boat because it's been superseded by new research. However, many research fields have major, defining publications

(Continued)

(Continued)

(sometimes called 'keystone' articles or books) that have become 'must-cites'. You'll soon see which publications hold this status when you see most of your relevant sources citing them. You fail to read, understand and cite these key works at your peril. Thus, to tell the story up to the present day for your topic, you may need a mix of recent research, major works from within the last 20 years, and (more occasionally) even older classic literature in your field.

Using your search plan (Section 2.4.2), begin looking for relevant articles, reports and books. Ensure relevance by first reading the title. If that seems relevant, then read the abstract or summary. If you find an abstract or summary to be relevant, then download or record the details of the publication and gather its citation information (many journals have a button that allows you to download citation details pre-formatted for bibliographic software such as Endnote).

Even at this stage of only reading titles and abstracts, you should begin making notes about how the information you're finding is shaping your ideas about your topic. Does your research still seem feasible? Do you need to sharpen the focus? (Usually the answer is 'yes'!) Do you need to branch off in a different, more promising direction? What are the key tips and author names you're seeing, and should you be focused more on them? What ideas are you getting about forming a possible research question?

 **KEY TIPS**

Prepare your references as you go along

Gathering citation details as you go through the literature review process is far easier than having to go back later to find the article again. We strongly recommend using citation software, such as Endnote, to manage your citations. This software provides a consistent template for entering your citations. Once entered, you can easily insert citations as you write in whatever format you specify. This approach will save you lots of time when compared to manually entering citations, which is both tedious and prone to errors. For example, if you wrote a 100-page thesis using APA 5th edition style and wanted to change it to Chicago Manual 15th edition style, this would only take a few clicks with bibliographic software. To do it manually would require you to adjust every single citation one at a time – a gruelling and entirely avoidable task.

Having more citations recorded in the bibliographic software than you ultimately need is fine. Indeed, you may be able to use them in later research.

2●4●4 ORGANIZE YOUR DOWNLOADED AND RECORDED SOURCES INTO CATEGORIES

Once you've gathered your first set of sources, start organizing them into categories, with a folder on your computer for each category. Place downloaded publications into these folders along with a document containing copied and pasted details of publications you couldn't download. Err on the side of being overly specific with your categories early on, as you can always combine them later. It usually doesn't make sense to categorize by author since you'll be reviewing research conducted by a range of researchers on overlapping topics.

Once you've created a preliminary set of categories for your initial set of sources, take stock to see if you can combine categories, if you need to expand your search to get more sources for a category or if you should refocus away from any categories.

KEY TIPS

What do I do when I find the perfect source but can't get access to the full-text version of it?

If you find you can't download the article or access the book you want, then try to use your library's system for requesting such unavailable resources. If this proves too difficult or slow, you can consider emailing the article authors to request a full-text version of the article. If you do this, explain that you're very interested in reading the article, and that your institution does not have access. If you're doing this, it is often worth also asking if the author has any recent papers on a similar topic that have not yet been published (this can enable you to get your hands on sources that are very recent). Most researchers will be pleased you're interested in their work, and will happily send you the article you requested. This procedure can also be used to request a chapter from an edited book (this is less widely accepted than sharing articles, but it is sometimes your only feasible option). You generally shouldn't expect an author to provide you with a copy of their entire book: this is much more likely to be considered an impolite request.

2•4•5 BEGIN REVIEWING YOUR LITERATURE IN DETAIL

Start with one category and begin reviewing each article one at a time. To guide you through this process, ask yourself the following questions while reading. These are adapted from the Cornell University Library (2015):

1 **Evaluation of core content**

- Has the author clearly defined the topic under investigation? How significant is it?
- What is the author's **theoretical framework** (if there is one)?
- Does the information come across as opinion or propaganda?
- Are assumptions reasonable?
- Does the author take a radically different approach from others examining a similar topic? Could it have been better if approached from a different perspective?
- Can you spot any errors, gaps or omissions?

2 **Assessment of evidence**

- Are there methodological shortcomings? If so, how fundamental to the author's claims are they? What are the implications for the author's claims? Is the chosen research method leading the author to make certain claims?

- Are claims supported with sufficient and credible evidence? Is the author overreaching with the publication's claims?
- Does the article rest on primary or secondary research (or just the author's arguments or application of theory)?

3 **Coverage of the topic**

- Does the source confirm or support other sources you've read, update other material, or provide new insights?
- Does the publication appear to be of good quality?

You shouldn't merely report a researcher's conclusions. You should critically evaluate your sources' evidence and claims.

Beyond the credibility of the source you're thinking of using, for research articles and books you also need to evaluate for yourself whether the methods used in the study provide sufficient evidence for its knowledge claims. Don't assume that established researchers are producing good research. Maintain a critical stance when reading for your literature review. As Becker (2007, p. 47) points out, 'real authorities on any subject know that there is never one right answer, just a lot of provisional answers competing for attention and acceptance'. Think about whether the evidence presented in a publication justifies its claims, thereby meriting your attention and acceptance. Look for important issues that have been overlooked or analysed inappropriately.

To document your assessment of sources, take two different sets of detailed notes. In the first set capture information relating to the list of questions above. Be detailed, critical and analytical in your write-up. Summarize the methods, findings and a few quotes that effectively describe the research results or conclusions. In your second set of notes, start identifying connections (similarities or divergences) with other literature. Are you seeing patterns emerging, the same major issues, etc.? Are certain themes becoming clearer? Are authors coming to similar conclusions (why or why not?)? As you prepare both sets of notes, clearly document the reference details for the publications you are reviewing.

2●5 WRITE YOUR LITERATURE REVIEW

Now that you have gathered most of the sources you need and done your in-depth reviews, it's time to start writing your literature review in earnest. Writing in small batches as you gather and read your key sources can be helpful.

2●5●1 FIND A CLEAR ORGANIZATIONAL STRUCTURE AND STICK WITH IT

Clearly organize your literature review. The widely used thematic organizational structure presents sources within each category relevant to your topic. Your literature review should include an introduction to the research topic that emphasizes its importance, as well as signposting what research has been conducted and how the section will be structured (i.e., what comes next after the introduction, then after that, etc.). You'll need a body section next, that is, the main part where you present your summaries, evaluation and application of the literature to your topic. If you're organizing your literature review thematically, you can start

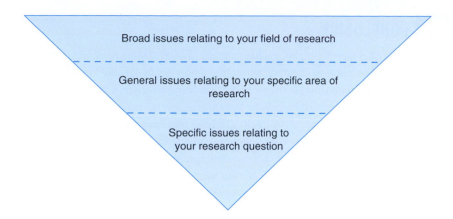

Figure 2.2 Contents of the 'body' of your literature review

with the most macro-level categories relating to your topic before gradually narrowing to your specific research. You should conclude your literature review section by summarizing the gaps your research will be addressing.

2•5•2 BE ANALYTICAL

The content of your body section must be analytical and directed towards telling a clear story about existing knowledge and debates on your topic. Summarize publications as just one step towards presenting any major patterns in the literature and relationships between studies. Use quotations only when the author says something in a particularly pithy way, or when you are going to be disagreeing with the author's claims (so that you ensure you are fairly representing the author's views).

Keep your own 'voice' as you write. You may feel pressure to mimic the style or terminology of your sources. But keeping your own authentic voice helps to ensure the review presents your analysis, not just a summary of other people's work.

2•5•3 IDENTIFY KEY GAPS IN THE LITERATURE

Identify gaps in the literature by asking yourself the following questions:

- Are there areas of worthwhile study relating to your topic that have not yet been covered by other researchers?
- Are relevant studies neglecting a particular type of evidence, for example are they all qualitative or all quantitative?
- Is there a relevant theoretical concept that has not yet been applied to the topic?

Sometimes gaps exist because other researchers haven't thought to take a particular research approach, or the data needed to address a research question could be difficult or costly to obtain. Finding a research gap that you can address is a good way to demonstrate the value of your research.

2 ● 6 CONCLUSION

This chapter identifies how to establish what's already known about your topic to show the need for your research project and where it fits within the landscape of existing knowledge. Your literature review shows your path through the vast field of existing research in which your specific study sits. This chapter begins by explaining what a literature review is, and what it is not. Insightful and probing analysis of the literature in your field will help you more easily define 'gaps' in the field that your research can fill. Your literature review provides the rationale for your entire project.

By identifying and mapping where your specific project fits in the larger research literature relating to your topic, your study's contribution becomes clear. Also, you can rely on existing knowledge as a starting point for developing your claims and insights.

This chapter offers advice about searching for literature review sources, including the following points:

1   **Focus your search** and **develop a search plan**. If you start too broad you will end up with a hopelessly large number of sources.
2   **Start with journal articles**. Come back to other sources when you've refined your focus.
3   Use the **search words and phrases from your search plan**, making adjustments and adding new terms as you go. When you find a relevant publication **read the abstract**, saving the in-depth review for later.
4   If the article still seems relevant after reading the abstract, then **download it** if you can, and **capture the citation**; don't put this off until later. Start your search with as tight a focus as you can, gradually widening it to broaden your coverage.
5   **Take detailed notes as you go**, tracking search terms, key authors, etc.
6   Use your reading to **understand your topic and help shape your future research project**.
7   Download and **enter references into your citation software as you go** and then only use the ones you actually need for your write-up. Start this process at the beginning of your research.

As you conduct your search, take detailed notes. What key tips are proving more fruitful? What research areas seem like they'll be worth investigating further? What authors and issues are recurring in the literature? Track your thoughts and document your journey. What seems obvious at the time can be forgotten later.

Your sources need to be relevant and of high quality. A good study from, for example, five years ago will be far more important than weaker work published recently. However, you may still be expected to review the most recent research to show you're up to date.

A secondary, implicit goal when writing your literature review is the need to demonstrate awareness of the academic field you're writing in. So you may need to include a paragraph or two that situates your research within the bigger picture in this field, even if it is not strictly necessary to establish what is known about your topic.

We advocate categorizing your sources to organize the research you gather during the literature review process. Make your literature review organized by telling a story step by step about what is known (and unknown) on your topic. Most reviews are organized thematically (by category). Whatever organizational method you choose, keep your review analytical, with an eye to defining the gap in the literature that your study will address.

SUGGESTIONS FOR FURTHER READING

- **Fink, A. (2014).** *Conducting research literature reviews: From the internet to paper (4th ed.). Thousand Oaks, CA: Sage.* This book is pitched to a broader audience than students by also focusing on users in marketing, policy-making and planning. It includes content on preparing grant proposals, methods to evaluate and use databases, and strategies to record and store information in a 'virtual file cabinet'.
- **Machi, L. A., & McEvoy, B. T. (2012).** *The literature review: Six steps to success (2nd ed.). Thousand Oaks, CA: Corwin.* This work advocates a six-step model to writing a literature review, and includes detailed activities and tasks to understand and achieve each step.
- **Onwuegbuzie, A., & Frels, R. K. (2015).** *Seven steps to a comprehensive literature review: A multimodal and cultural approach. London: Sage.* The authors advocate a thematic approach to literature reviews. It is especially useful in its coverage of multimodal texts – two or more communication modes (e.g., images and written language together) – and discussion about the role of culture in how we interpret knowledge.
- **Ridley, D. (2012).** *The literature review: A step-by-step guide for students. London: Sage.* Ridley's work outlines a series of practical strategies for conducting systematic searches. It is particularly strong for students looking for strategies to evaluate online sources and literature, and guidance on how to cope with copyright and permissions issues.

Visit the companion website at **https://study.sagepub.com/jensenandlaurie** to gain access to a wide range of online resources to support your learning, including editable research documents, weblinks, free access SAGE journal articles and book chapters, and flashcards.

GLOSSARY

Abstract – A short summary of an article which appears at the beginning and concisely presents the arguments and findings put forward by a publication.

Boolean search – A type of web search carried out using the words AND, OR and NOT to find more relevant search results.

Journal database – Electronic journal databases are a key method of sourcing literature for your review. Most are easily accessible and searchable, and your library will often have access to hundreds of different journals. Some journal databases even offer the option of downloading a citation directly into your citation software.

Literature review – A literature review goes beyond merely describing other people's research. It's an opportunity to analyse and critically evaluate existing literature so that you can apply it to your topic clearly and coherently, as well as identify gaps that your research can address.

Peer review – Peer review is the accepted method of scrutiny of academic work by other academics, in order to hold research publications within the discipline to a high standard. Work that has been peer-reviewed can be seen as more reliable than work which has not been critically assessed by peer review.

Research question – Your research question is the specific question your research will be asking. Often your research question is informed by assessing other research in the field and identifying gaps in research which you can contribute to, and so your research question is usually presented at the end of your literature review.

Search plan - A search plan is a plan of key search words and phrases, including synonyms, slang terms, alternative spellings and foreign languages that you can put together before beginning your search for literature for your review, to ensure that you cover all relevant literature.

Theoretical framework - The theoretical framework of a piece of research is the philosophical basis and assumptions within which the research takes place. For example, you may be approaching your research from a 'realist' or 'positivist' standpoint. It is sometimes necessary in your literature review to critique the theoretical framework that other researchers have used.

━━ REFERENCES ━━━━━━━━━━━━━━━━━━━━━━━━━━━━

Becker, H. S. (2007). *Writing for social scientists: How to start and finish your thesis, book, or article* (2nd ed.). Chicago: University of Chicago Press.

Cornell University Library (2015). Critically analyzing information sources: Critical appraisal and analysis. Retrieved 8 March 2015 from http://guides.library.cornell.edu/criticallyanalyzing

Creswell, J. (2014). *Research design: Qualitative, quantitative, and mixed methods approaches* (4th ed.). London: Sage.

Ford, N. (2012). *The essential guide to using the web for research*. London: Sage.

O'Leary, Z. (2014). *The essential guide to doing your research project*. London: Sage.

HOW TO BE AN ETHICAL RESEARCHER

3 ● 1 INTRODUCTION

Ethics refers to values or principles that are integral to your research objectives and define your responsibilities to your participants, your institution and yourself. While ethical principles are underpinned by complex philosophies, you can focus on applying them to your research practice. This chapter outlines the specific procedures that you can follow to ensure you are being an ethical researcher.

It is important to distinguish between ethics and **legal requirements**. When you seek ethical approval from an institution, such as a university, they are likely to focus more on legal requirements and liability. Satisfying your institution that legal requirements are covered will be a practical necessity in many cases in order to be allowed to conduct the research. However, your paramount concern as a researcher needs to be ethics. Being ethical helps you maintain a positive long-term relationship with your research participants. You need to ensure that you are protecting them in whatever ways you can. Don't take advantage of them or put them at risk of **harm**, even if you're legally allowed to do so.

Harm can come to participants because of your research. They can feel victimized if their information is used improperly. Moreover, they can feel a loss of control and breach of trust if, for example, you don't adequately protect their **privacy**. Any person or institution associated with your research can be brought into disrepute by reckless or manipulative behaviour, so taking steps to be ethical is essential.

3 ● 2 RESEARCH ETHICS MATTERS

In practice, **research ethics** helps to achieve the following:

- **Maintain your integrity.** Ethics promotes **integrity** in research by establishing that you should be consistently truthful, seek to gain knowledge and avoid error. Ethics establishes a set of expectations for your conduct that prohibits falsifying information, deception or other acts that might bring disrepute on you, the quality of your research or your institution.
- **Protect the welfare of others.** A fundamental principle of research ethics is to do no harm to others. You must ensure your research does not put at risk the welfare or reputation of those directly or indirectly involved in your research.
- **Build support for you and your research.** Good ethical conduct means that those who participate in or who view your research will have a more positive view of both you and your research. This support means that you are more likely to be able to recruit participants for your future research and gain help from colleagues.
- **Give you direction when facing challenging situations.** Ethical principles help you find your way through challenging situations.

3•2•1 FOLLOW BASIC ETHICAL PRINCIPLES

There are three main areas of consideration for research ethics. These are paraphrased in part from the Code of Ethics of the American Sociological Association (2015):

1   **Develop your research competence.** You should always strive for the highest levels of **competence** in your research practices so that you can make the most of your participants' contributions. You should seek to improve your education, hone your skills and reflect on strategies to improve your performance. Meanwhile, know the limitations of your ability, skills and training. Don't take on research tasks that you are not yet ready to handle. If you need help with your research, consult people in your department and others working in similar areas who can guide you.
2   **Maintain your personal integrity.** When engaging in all aspects of your research – but particularly any stage that involves participants – always maintain a high standard of personal integrity. Don't mislead, deceive or show a lack of respect to anyone engaged in your research.
3   **Be respectful.** Ensure that you always remain respectful of differences in gender, race, sexual orientation, physical ability and national origin. Recognize that people are different from you. This does not mean you always have to agree with other people, but you should remain respectful at all times.

In addition to these considerations, there are three ethical principles that all researchers must abide by: **informed consent**, **confidentiality** and **anonymity**. Informed consent will be discussed in more depth later, but in short, it is the responsibility of the researcher to explain clearly the purpose of the research, who is undertaking it, who is financing it, how it will be used and who will have access to the data (British Sociological Association, 2002, p. 3). Part of this process involves explaining how much confidentiality will be afforded to the participants; researchers are permitted only to share information with parties to which the participant has consented, and the participant may also refuse to allow recording of their personal information (British Sociological Association, 2002, p. 3). Finally, researchers must respect their participants' right to anonymity. Ideally, data should be anonymized as soon as it is stored to minimize the risk of a breach of privacy (British Sociological Association, 2002, pp. 4–5). The British Sociological Association's 'Statement of Ethical Practice' is a must-read before conducting any research.

============ **KEY TIPS** ============

You can't automatically use data for a different purpose than originally specified

Researchers might wonder whether informed consent gives them the right to use the information they have gathered from participants for a purpose that was not originally declared to the participant. For example, can you provide survey data from your project to another researcher investigating a similar topic?

(Continued)

(Continued)

A key consideration in ethics is to make it clear to participants how you will use the data collected from them. The person giving you permission to use their information has a right to know how it is going to be used and then decide whether this is an acceptable purpose or not.

Think of it differently. Have you ever given your contact details to a company which has sold them to an advertiser that then bombards you with spam emails and nuisance phone calls trying to sell you things? If so, you probably get an idea of why it is important to represent the intended use of the data fairly. Now imagine that you had given a researcher personal information and the researcher was using it for a different purpose than the one you authorized.

In general, you can only use the information gained from participants for the specific purpose that you declare to them and that they authorize. This applies even under the following conditions:

- Another research purpose is similar to the purpose you specified to the participant.
- You are '99 per cent sure the participant would not mind'.

If you decide that you would like to use the research data for other purposes, you should try to get the direct permission from the participant who provided the information in order to be on solid ethical ground.

3•2•2 YOUR OWN PRIVACY

One of your first ethical decisions is how you present yourself to your participants. If you avoid telling them certain details about yourself, are you deceiving them? To what extent are you entitled to privacy?

As with most aspects of ethics, you will need to make a judgement call based on a range of considerations. You are entitled to privacy. However, you also need to provide information to participants that might have *a significant influence* on their decision to participate in the research. For example, if you are researching smoking habits, people might feel very differently about participating depending on whether a tobacco company or the World Health Organization is funding your research.

You will find that your participants ask you many different questions about your identity. Most of these questions stem from friendliness or curiosity. However, sometimes participants genuinely want to know about your identity and agenda in order to decide whether to participate in the research. For example, if you were investigating illegal migrant workers in a rural farming area, participants might ask if you are from the area (i.e., if you are a 'local' and 'understand' the community) or if anyone in your family works in law enforcement. It is worth thinking ahead about how you will answer such likely questions about yourself.

You must not lie to participants. At the same time, you do not have to reveal the complete truth in all instances, such as if the information you don't mention could not reasonably be expected to affect the participants' decision-making about contributing to your research. For example, while having a family member in law enforcement would need to be declared to the participant if you were asked, you do not need to relay your entire family history. It would also be acceptable to not proactively raise this issue – assuming, of course, that the family member's law enforcement role was totally unrelated to your research.

3•2•3 INSIDER RESEARCH AND ITS ETHICAL DILEMMAS

Related to the boundary between researcher and researcher participant is the idea of insider research. **Insider research** is where a researcher conducts their study with a community to which they already belong. For instance, a student researcher may conduct interviews with their peers as part of a project seeking to understand what students get out of their university experience. Insider research is different than **outsider research**, where the researcher gathers their data in an unfamiliar environment.

As with most methods, insider research has several advantages and disadvantages. Imagine that you are conducting the study mentioned above – you are a student researcher, hoping to gain insights about what people enjoy and dislike about university. Possible obstacles and benefits to this research method are shown in the Table 3.1.

While being an ethical researcher is *always* important, it is especially so when conducting insider research – just because you know the participants and the research setting well, informed consent cannot be assumed. It is therefore crucial to fully explain the project and define your role as researcher as distinct from your role as insider to all participants before commencing your research (Humphrey, 2012).

You also need to be careful when relying on personal stories and accounts from participants, as 'some of the stories expose significant failings in agencies and personal anguish in families.

Table 3.1 Evaluation of insider research

Advantages	Disadvantages
• Greater cultural understanding of the group, including an ability to 'speak the language' and a knowledge of taboo subjects (Bonner & Tolhurst, 2002; Coghlan, 2003; Rouney, 2005; Tedlock, 2000; Unluer, 2012). This gives you an advantage over novice researchers who would have to spend time learning information that you would already know (Smyth & Holian, 2008; Unluer, 2012).	• It may be possible that your researcher role and your insider role conflict, and balancing the two may become difficult (DeLyser, 2001; Gerrish, 1997; Unluer, 2012). For example, if you have a professional disagreement with someone in your insider role, this may affect their willingness to interact with you in the research setting.
• As you are already part of the group, your presence may have less of an impact on the flow of social interaction because participants are used to you being there (Bonner & Tolhurst, 2002; Unluer, 2012).	• Familiarity could lead to a loss of objectivity. For example, some routine behaviours that you are so used to might be overlooked (DeLyser, 2001; Hewitt-Taylor, 2002; Unluer, 2012). Similarly, your close familiarity means that you might make assumptions about the meanings of events, rather than attempting to gain your participants' interpretations. Alternatively, participants may assume that you already know what they mean, so it is always worth remembering to clarify everything with your participants (Unluer, 2012).
• As the participants already know you, they may be more willing to share personal insights and information (Bonner & Tolhurst, 2002; Unluer, 2012).	• There is a need for stringent ethical compliance when conducting insider research. Your insider role may afford you access to sensitive information that you may not have been privy to had you been 'just' a researcher (Smyth & Holian, 2008; Unluer, 2012).

Would all the actors have consented to these stories being circulated, albeit in anonymized form and for a defensible reason?' (Humphrey, 2012, p. 6). For example, in certain professions, people are regulated as to what information they can and can't provide you with. This is particularly true for bodies controlled by central government departments. So, if you were conducting research with NHS workers, service users or their families, for example, you would need to ensure that your work complied with the Department of Health's Research Governance Framework for Health and Social Care. Such regulations are put in place for the following reasons:

1   **To protect participants who are potentially or particularly vulnerable**. This is because they may not be able to give informed consent.
2   **To protect participants whose professional lives might compromise their ability to give consent freely**. If you are working with someone who has a particularly busy or stressful job, then participation in your research may add to this and negatively affect their work performance.
3   **To ensure safeguards on data access and data use.** Professionals who themselves are told things in confidence by, for example, patients, are bound by their own rules of confidentiality. You therefore need to ensure that you are complying with these rules, as well as your own (Research Ethics Guidebook, 2015a, 2015b).

The Research Ethics Guidebook is a very useful resource and contains a lot of information about the relevant regulatory bodies for certain professions.

It may be possible for your researcher role and your insider role to come into conflict. For instance, you may learn something during your research that affects your professional opinion of a colleague. At all times, you must respect participants' right to confidentiality – anything that they tell you *as a researcher* has to remain with you as researcher, not with you as an insider (Humphrey, 2012, p. 7). You always need to consider your primary role and any information obtained as a researcher has to be documented as such and can only be used for research purposes. Likewise, if information is gathered in a professional context, it cannot be used for research without the colleague's informed consent (Coghlan & Brannick, 2005; Humphrey, 2012).

3•2•4 YOUR ETHICAL DUTIES APPLY TO ONLINE RESEARCH

Conventional ethical practices cannot easily be applied to Facebook, LinkedIn, Twitter and other social media sites. It is worth considering the sometimes unusual and unique issues posed by internet-based research. You will need to seek out contact details for participants, which may require extensive searching for a phone number or email address listed somewhere on the internet. You may also need to do background research on people to find relevant personal information.

This can feel like 'snooping'. But as long as you are not gathering deeply personal information or using secretive methods (e.g., gaining access to their Facebook page using the login information of one of their friends), then you're acting in accordance with widely accepted ethical guidelines. Keep in mind that people can present themselves online in ways that are misleading. For example, posing for a photo in front of empty beer bottles may be a private joke among friends, not evidence that they drink heavily.

Where you need to be most careful is if you start trying to get information that someone is keeping, or trying to keep, private. The fact that you can access such information does not mean you should. Violating someone's online privacy is ethically just as wrong as doing it in person. Personal information online should be treated with the same level of consideration, courtesy, privacy and ethics as anywhere else. Moreover, you should be honest about where you found online information if your participant asks you. This will help you maintain a positive relationship with your participant, which is one of the most important aspects of data collection.

The Association of Internet Researchers (AoIR) offers valuable guidance on this relatively new field of social research. The AoIR is a group of international academics from a range of disciplines who specialize in internet studies. The Executive Committee, who are the primary decision-makers of the Association, establish working parties, such as the current Ethics Working Group, who have produced guidelines for ethical internet-based research.

The Ethics Working Committee emphasizes that these are 'guidelines' rather than pro-scriptive rules, as every research project involving online data will be unique and have its own ethical considerations. Indeed, the Committee's guidelines state that, 'while regulations or disciplinary traditions are intended to encourage ethical practice, they can also inadvert-ently function to restrict the researcher by making universal declarations and a priori determinations about what constitutes harm and what will cause harm' (Markham & Buchanan, 2012, pp. 7–8). The Committee stresses the importance of considering harm, vulnerability, respect for persons and beneficence at every stage of the project, while acknowledging the difficulty of ethics in online research, as 'multiple judgements are pos-sible, and ambiguity and uncertainty are part of the process' (Markham & Buchanan, 2012, p. 5). The rules concerning online research ethics are quite vague at this stage; however, the EU's data protection laws are currently being reviewed and are due to be finalized during 2015, which may bring greater clarity. It is also important to recognize that personal infor-mation is also governed by national laws. In the UK, this is the Data Protection Act 1998, which states that your information can only be used fairly, lawfully and accurately, for a limited and stated purpose, and must be kept securely and for no longer than necessary (Gov. uk, 2014). For the full list of proscriptions, see the suggestions for further reading at the end of the chapter.

If you are sifting through a large data set, such as a collection of tweets, then it may be easy to lose track of the fact that each tweet represents the thoughts of an individual participant, and in turn it can be easy to think that ethical considerations do not apply. If you are conduct-ing online research, it is best to check a website's or social media platform's terms of service, to ensure that you are acting in accordance with their legal framework.

3•2•5 GAINING APPROVAL FROM YOUR INSTITUTION'S ETHICS COMMITTEE

As your research project begins to take shape, you will need to begin thinking about gaining approval from your institution's **ethics committee**, using guidance from a supervisor or instructor. This step should come before you begin any research with participants. The granting of ethics approval is your 'permission' to begin interacting with participants. It is often also linked to the provision of funding. For example, from January 2006, the European Social Research Council's 'Research Ethics Framework' stated that all research requesting funding for projects involving human participation had to undergo ethical review in order to receive funding.

For more information, see the ESRC's (2012) framework for research ethics. The procedures necessary for you to achieve ethics approval vary by department and institution, but there are some typical features. Ethics committees want to know that you are aware of basic ethics concepts (outlined in this section) and how they affect your research plans and procedures (outlined in the following section).

Think of your engagement with the ethics committee as an opportunity for reflection. It shouldn't be a 'rubber stamp' or 'box ticking' exercise. Make the most of the process, using it as a chance to think about your responsibilities and ways you can engage with participants constructively.

 **REAL WORLD EXAMPLE**

What to do if you breach ethical good practice

Ricardo was researching flows of money from migrants living in the EU to West Africa in order to understand how much was being sent and why. After assuring participants that their anonymity and privacy would be protected, he completed 22 in-depth semi-structured interviews with migrants.

Ricardo made an error early on in his research by not immediately anonymizing his respondents and replacing their actual names with numerical identifiers or pseudonyms. A problem then arose when Ricardo sent a journal article out for review that contained the actual names of his respondents. This was a clear breach of ethical good practice.

In such cases you need to discuss any breaches of good practice with your supervisor, your department's ethics committee or an equivalent authority figure. You will need guidance on how to proceed in your particular situation. While the correct action depends on the nature of the ethical problem, you will most likely need to contact the affected participant(s) to apologize and explain what has happened.

After consulting his supervisor and the ethics committee, Ricardo immediately contacted the journal and asked them to withdraw his article from review. The editor of the journal asked the reviewers to delete their copies of the article. Ricardo then sent a message to the respondents explaining the situation, reassuring them that the breach was limited and detailing the specific steps taken to correct the problem. He also apologized for what had happened. Ricardo then added pseudonyms to all his drafts chapters and articles in order to prevent the breach from happening again. He also committed to not send future drafts of the article to the same journal to limit the likelihood that the same reviewers would read the original and amended versions of the article.

3 ● 3 BUILD YOUR RESEARCH ON INFORMED CONSENT

You must consider informed consent whenever you are gathering data from human participants. Ensuring you have informed consent from your participants is the bedrock principle of social research ethics. Informed consent develops through a process where you, as a researcher, *inform* potential participants about your research in order to gain their voluntary *consent* to join that research. So, informed consent is 'a procedure for ensuring that research participants understand what is being done to them, the limits to their participation and awareness of any potential risks they incur' (Social Research Association, 2003, p. 28).

The key reason behind informed consent is that social research often intrudes into the lives of participants. People have a right to privacy, control over their lives and ownership of the ideas they express. To breach any of these norms in order to gather and use data from participants requires explicit consent. You therefore need to clearly explain to them what your research is about, how it will be used and what consequences they might face if they participate.

━━━━━━━━ **REAL WORLD EXAMPLE** ━━━━━━━━

Are 'mild' ethical breaches acceptable to achieve 'major' social gains?

Havier was researching the illegal trade of pharmaceutical products by healthcare workers. He wanted to better understand how these workers used their privileged access to supply the local drug trade and their own recreational use.

Havier tried to access participants in the healthcare industry to record interviews, but no one gave permission due to privacy concerns and fears of prosecution. He then decided to secretly record five interviews to show his supervisor that there were valuable insights to be gained from this line of research.

Havier justified his decision to himself because he believed that the illegal trade in pharmaceuticals by healthcare providers was such a problem that it threatened the local community. He thought that the 'greater' public good of better understanding the illegal trade of pharmaceutics justified his 'minor' ethical breach. Moreover, since his participants were behaving unethically – and illegally – they did not deserve the normal level of ethical protection.

Havier's justifications were flawed. You must be ethical at all times. You cannot lower this standard because of a perceived greater good. There have been countless studies, including medical experiments, that have cited a great social benefit to justify lower standards of ethics. These have been roundly criticized and many have resulted in severe damage to the careers of the researchers involved, not mention the participants who were subjected to unethical treatment and the reputation of social research more generally.

You also cannot lower your ethical standards because you perceive that a participant is untrustworthy, of poor character or criminal. The same ethical considerations still apply regardless of your subjective judgement of a person's character. Think about how you would feel if someone justified treating you unethically by citing benefits to other people or perceived flaws in your character.

Also emphasize that your participant can choose to withdraw from the research at any point, asking for their data not to be used.

3•3•1 WHEN DO YOU NEED INFORMED CONSENT?

The need for informed consent applies to all the information participants reveal to you. However, your responsibility to 'do no harm' extends to non-participants, whose words or behaviours are revealed during your research. For example, if you were investigating work practices in an office in New York by interviewing employees, you may be told personal information about other non-participating employees. While you don't need to get the non-participants' permission to use such data, you do need to fully anonymize your findings so that you are not inadvertently revealing information about a non-participant to others in the office who later read your research report.

It may not be practical or desirable to follow informed consent procedures in some cases. Information obtained unobtrusively in public spaces (including media) where people do not have a reasonable expectation of privacy does not typically require informed consent. However, you cannot assume that activity in public spaces does not require informed consent. For example, a couple having a private conversation in a public park should be entitled to privacy.

A journalist's published articles are obviously meant to be public (and therefore informed consent is not required to use them as data), but this same individual writing a personal letter to the editor of the newspaper is entitled to privacy (i.e., consent would be required). For more information on the difference between journalistic and social science research, see the suggestions for further reading at the end of this chapter. Likewise, public documents and statements by government and corporate officials are generally freely available for research purposes without any need for consent procedures. Similarly, studying crowds, such as people attending a sporting event, would be practically impossible if you had to obtain informed consent from each individual. It is best to think of privacy as encompassing personal details about an individual, whether this is in public or not. An individual has a reasonable right to privacy about such information and it is off-limits without their consent.

The use of online data such as YouTube comments or chatroom conversations published by non-professionals is a more controversial issue than other forms of data in the public domain. While some argue that you should seek permission from the authors in all these cases, we think that it is helpful to divide online content into two main categories with regard to seeking consent:

1   **Information that is intended to be public.** Everything that has a broad potential audience and that does not require any kind of password access so could be easily read by strangers at any time. This category should not generally require informed consent procedures. YouTube video comments would generally fall into this category.
2   **Information that is intended to be private.** Information that is more personal and is visible only to those within the author's network, such as content on non-public online forums or on Facebook. This category generally requires seeking the consent of the author. For Facebook posts that the user has decided to make fully public, anonymizing the post may be the best option for making your research ethically compliant by doing no harm, rather than contacting the user to request permission to analyse their content for your research.

Finally, the validity of your research can be compromised by needing to follow informed consent procedures. Sometimes people behave differently if they know a researcher is watching them. In particular, studying socially undesirable behaviour, such as illegal drug use and racism, can be affected by participants adjusting their self-presentation when they know they are speaking to researchers. Considering how to handle ethical procedures in these exceptional cases is very challenging. You should consult your supervisor or ethics committee to get further guidance. For a good discussion of occasions when informed consent may not be desirable, see Spicker (2007).

REAL WORLD EXAMPLE

The ethics of analysing Twitter content without informed consent

Although data from Twitter are effectively public, this does not necessarily mean that you can use tweeted information without permission. If the author of a tweet is not intending it to be public (you can generally tell this by the content of the tweet) then it may be your ethical duty to seek informed consent. Research on Twitter (e.g., Marwick, 2011) users suggests that even though their tweets are open to all, their imagined audience is much smaller (mostly people they know). Therefore, there is often an expectation of privacy despite the globally accessible nature of the content. Moreover, Twitter's Terms of Service state that users retain ownership of their tweets, which may reinforce users' belief that their tweets cannot be used without consent.

While it would be convenient to use content from Twitter without contacting the author, using tweets that are intended to be private could be an ethical breach. You have a responsibility to think carefully about privacy, ownership of information and associated ethical obligations, even when data are easily accessible.

3•3•2 HOW DO YOU ACHIEVE INFORMED CONSENT?

There are two different methods of confirming consent to participate in research, but these do not always have equal validity and you need to consider what the appropriate level of informed consent is for your project. *Written* consent is the gold standard and will give you and your institution the most protection from a legal standpoint. Therefore, your institution may insist on using this method of gaining consent, even when it is less appropriate to the situation.

Oral consent is only acceptable in some circumstances and is generally considered a weaker form of consent. However, in some situations, gaining consent verbally is superior to using a written form, such as when a signature can be incriminating in cases where you are trying to maintain a participant's anonymity. You need to carefully weigh the relative strength of the form of informed consent against the privacy needs of your respondents. Be sure to make your specific research context clear to the ethics committee at your institution when seeking ethics approval in order for committee members to make an informed decision about what scenarios and constraints you are likely to face in your fieldwork.

KEY TIPS

When seeking informed consent be prepared for likely questions

During the process of obtaining informed content, be prepared for a broad range of questions. Make sure you have the basics covered: what your research is about? Who is funding you? Will the participants' contributions be anonymized?

Privacy is a key issue. Who will have access to your data? How will the data be used? If you are working on a wider project as part of a research team, you need to make it clear that others

(Continued)

(Continued)

apart from yourself will be able to access the data. You also need to be prepared to explain the implications of participating in your study. Will they be at risk? Depending on your research topic, participation could entail very different consequences. You need to ensure that potential participants consider these consequences prior to giving consent.

You might be asked about other research participants. If this should happen, you need to consider their privacy. For instance, if the population you are researching is small, some of your participants may know each other and could even be friends. You should respectfully decline to provide any information about other participants, including whether they are part of the study. If asked, the best strategy is to gently deflect the question to another topic and perhaps offer an explanation that you have promised a certain level of privacy to all participants.

Finally, if you are asked questions about your research that you don't have answers for, just say so. (For example, what will the findings of your study be? You don't know until you've done it!) If it is a question you should be able to answer, then write it down, investigate later and get an answer to the participant without delay.

When seeking informed consent, make it clear that participation is voluntary and that people have a right to refuse to participate and can withdraw from participation at any point for any reason. Moreover, they do not have to tell you what that reason is. However, you should also note that it is not possible to withdraw the data they have contributed once the results have been published. Even when you use written informed consent, it is important to talk the participant through the key points to ensure they understand what they are signing.

Your participants have a right to privacy and this should be respected in the way you handle their data. You should specify early in the informed consent process whether data will be anonymized (identity not visible to the researcher or in the report) or held confidentially (identity is known to the researcher, but hidden in the report). You may need to explain what steps you will take to ensure that the data they provide will be held safely and securely. When obtaining informed consent, you may need to make it clear that there are limits to the confidentiality you can offer. For instance, if you see someone engaged in violent behaviour or learn that someone else's life is in danger, you have an obligation to report it to appropriate authorities.

 **KEY TIPS**

Make an information sheet for prospective participants

When you first engage prospective participants, you may be providing them with a lot of information. Some of it may be complex and all of it will probably be new to the participant. A useful way of helping the prospective participant retain and understand your research information is to prepare a detailed but user-friendly information sheet. This will also give participants the impression that you are professional, organized and thoughtful – and that you are serious about your research and their time.

Make sure your information sheet is very **user-friendly**! If the sheet looks like it will be onerous to read, it may give a negative impression of your research.

- Use a **professional and accessible layout** and font (i.e., avoid clutter or looking too artsy).
- Your layout should also be **informative and approachable** (e.g., avoid small print or cramming the text into paragraphs). Use plenty of white space on the page.
- Ensure your **language is friendly and jargon-free** (i.e., avoid complicated words, technical terms and vocabulary that is overly academic).
- Cover the most **basic questions**:

  o Who are you?
  o What is your research about?
  o What institution do you belong to?
  o What are you seeking from the participant?
  o How long will it take?
  o What compensation or other benefits are being provided to participants?
  o Is participation required?
  o How will the research be used?

- Make a special effort to assure confidentiality.
- Keep the document as **short as possible**. Most information sheets are just one single-spaced page.
- Don't forget to include your **contact details**, listing different ways that participants can reach you (i.e., email, telephone [if appropriate] and post).
- Include the **contact details of your supervisor** or university ethics committee to reassure prospective participants that there is someone else they can contact if they have concerns or questions about your research.

When seeking informed consent, also consider the issue of recorded interviews. Permission to electronically record a research interaction must be explicitly granted. For example, you might say:

> I would like to record this interview to ensure I have accurate notes and can focus on listening to what you are saying rather than quickly writing things down. Once I transcribe the audio recording, I will delete it permanently to ensure your confidentiality. Can I record?

If permission is not clearly granted then you cannot record the interview. Secretly recording an interview – even if you don't plan using any transcribed content in your research – is also a breach of your ethical obligations.

━━━━━━━━ **KEY TIPS** ━━━━━━━━

How to handle different types of participants

The eager participant

Some participants are not all that concerned about informed consent. What do you do when prospective participants are dismissive of informed consent because they are so eager to

(Continued)

(Continued)

participate? One method of highlighting the importance of informed consent is to explain that you are **required by your university to review the document**. Also, assure the participant that **you will only need a couple minutes to go through the document**. These reasonable strategies almost always prove effective.

The informed consent sceptic

What do you do when prospective participants are sceptical of the informed consent process? Perhaps they are concerned that the documents you have provided might not fully reflect your true research intentions. Perhaps they are unsure about how much legal protection such a document can provide them.

Your first step is to always **ensure that you maintain a pleasant, professional, patient and open disposition**. Looking hurried or unwilling to take the time to reassure the participant doesn't convey trustworthiness. **Reassure the participants that they are totally in control** of the process and can stop at any time in the research for any reason. **Offer to explain each part of the form**. When you do so, maintain your pleasant and patient disposition. It's helpful to provide examples to illustrate each part, providing details about the measures you are taking to ensure their privacy and secure data storage.

If you are patient and friendly, it is possible to reassure prospective participants. If you sense continued hesitation, you can leave the informed consent document with them so that they can review it on their own. Tell them you can contact them at a later date to see if they want to participate. In many of these instances, when people have had time to read and reflect, they will agree to participate. If not, be sure to thank them for their time and consideration, leaving the interaction on a positive note.

---

3 ● 4 ETHICS AND VULNERABLE PEOPLE

There are additional ethical implications to consider if you intend to conduct research with vulnerable individuals, such as children, people with learning disabilities or the elderly. You should carefully consider whether you are prepared and qualified to tackle the additional ethical responsibilities associated with such research because the potential for causing harm to your participants is much greater. Some **vulnerable people** may be more prone to finding your research intrusive and stressful. Consider that you may need additional training before embarking on a research project with a vulnerable population.

Your foremost concern when researching individuals from vulnerable populations is whether they are capable of giving informed consent. They must be able to understand what participating in your research would mean, as well as the nature of the risks associated with it. Not everyone is able to give such consent. For example, elderly people with dementia or people with severe mental disabilities may not fully understand the implications of participating in your research. If there are guardians responsible for the well-being of your prospective participants, you should also seek their informed consent. Also keep in mind that even if you gain informed consent with vulnerable people, you may need to take additional steps to enable their participation in ways they will find comfortable.

Table 3.2 Sample informed **consent letter**

Title of Research Project: Female Managers in the British Auto Industry

Principal Investigator: [The name of your supervisor and his/her contact details] Professor Kate X
Student Researcher: [Your name, along with your contact details] Susan Y

Purpose of this Study
This study is seeking to understand barriers facing female managers in the British auto industry in the period after Tony Blair's New Labour Government. The research seeks to explore how male-only informal networks are created and how they affect the promotion of female managers in the British auto industry. This study also seeks to understand how male-only informal networks are created.

The findings of this study will be used in academic books and articles focusing on the role of gender in the workplace.

Confidentiality
All the information you provide in this study will be kept strictly confidential. Your name will not appear on the questionnaire and the answers you provide will only be linked to the research by anonymized number. Only the principal investigator and student researcher will know your real identity and it will not be disclosed or made public. In addition, your identifying information will be kept in a secure location in a locked cabinet, in a locked office on the university campus and a password-protected computer.

Voluntary Nature of this Research
Your participation is voluntary. You are not required to participate in this research. You can withdraw at any time and for any reason, or for no stated reason at all.

Compensation
While this research offers no monetary compensation, your contribution will be used to advance knowledge of the role of gender in the British auto industry. We are able to offer you reimbursement for reasonable travel expenses (with receipts). If you will be claiming travel-related expenses, please contact the student researcher for more details before making your travel commitments.

Agreement to Participate
If you agree to take part in this study, please sign your name below.

....

I have read the information provided in this document. I voluntarily agree to participate in this study.

_____

_____

Name (printed)   Date

_____

Signature

Professor Kate X _____   Susan Y _____
Principal researcher's name (printed)   Student researcher's name (printed)

_____

_____

Principal researcher's signature   Student researcher's signature

You should not work with children and teenagers without the written consent of their parent, guardian or school (if it has the delegated authority to grant consent), unless you gain very specific guidance and authorization from your supervisor on these kinds of participants. There is a wide literature asserting that children should speak for themselves, without the consent of their parent, guardian or school. Minors are now increasingly thought of as autonomous agents, capable of providing their own informed consent, rather than needing protection from researchers and the consent of their parents (Williams, 2006). See also Rogers and Ludhra (2011) for a discussion on research as a means of providing a social voice and empowerment for young people. However, if you proceed without parental consent, you may be in violation of child protection laws or norms. It is also important to gain the direct consent of the child. While this is not usually a legal requirement, respecting the autonomy of the child by offering a simple explanation of who you are and why you are asking questions is part of your duty as an ethical researcher.

Research with children requires special considerations. For more information on the guidelines for ethical educational research, for example, see the suggestions for further reading at the end of this chapter. You may also have certain legal requirements towards the protection of minors. For example, in the UK, under the Children Act 1989, you would be obliged to waive confidentiality if you discovered a minor to be in danger and would have to report your findings to the relevant authority. Your duty of care to children must be fully explained at the start of the process in order to gain fully informed consent (Williams, 2006).

Participants of all ages may also be emotionally vulnerable. You could face a difficult decision about whether to engage someone in research that will likely be personally upsetting (e.g., recounting a painful personal experience). You should first consider that you may not be appropriately trained or emotionally capable of handling such research. As discussed elsewhere in the book, accounts of sexual abuse, torture and even illness and medical treatment can be too much to handle. If your participant is fully aware that recounting such information may be painful and even emotionally damaging to them and they consent to this, then it is ethically permissible to proceed. You should not push a participant to provide such information. But ultimately it is their choice whether to share this information or not.

REAL WORLD EXAMPLE

Human Trafficking and Commercial Sex Workers

Henry was researching the commercial sex industry in Amsterdam in order to understand connections between organized crime and human trafficking. He did not have much experience of researching vulnerable people and was unsure about whether his study would bring harm to participants who may be emotionally vulnerable due to their status as sex workers or the circumstances that led them to become sex workers.

Henry located two researchers at nearby universities who were experienced in researching sex workers. While they didn't know the specific context in Amsterdam, they provided him with strategies he could use with potential participants, including ways to frame questions and explore sensitive topics. Henry found the insights from these experienced researchers especially useful because their strategies helped him confidently approach his emotionally challenging research topic.

You should find official information about the national and local legal requirements for researching vulnerable populations before beginning your research project. For example, in the UK, the Department of Health (2005), the Scottish Educational Research Association (2005) and the British Educational Research Association (2011) all publish guidelines on researching vulnerable people. Sometimes formal background checks or supervision are required, which can involve a lengthy wait and a fee. In the UK, for instance, you will need to undergo a detailed police background check called a Disclosure and Barring Service check (previously known as a Criminal Records Bureau check) before you are permitted to conduct relatively long-term or intensive research with vulnerable adults or children.

3 ● 5 CONCLUSION

This chapter provides a framework for you to understand why ethics is important in your research. Research ethics is about establishing good practices when seeking participants, engaging with them, and using the data they provide. You have a responsibility to behave ethically through all phases of your research, particularly when dealing with personal or sensitive information. Moreover, your ethical responsibilities are most essential when you are working with vulnerable people.

Informed consent is the foundation of social research ethics. The key behind informed consent is recognizing and respecting the participant's privacy. So a good general rule is that any information that might reasonably be considered private requires the participant's informed consent before you seek it or use it.

Although informed consent is essential for most social research, it may be unnecessary or even counter-productive in some circumstances. These circumstances are exceptions though, and you should always think about whether consent is needed. When you conduct your research, you must make judgement calls about how you will handle ethical issues. Some ethical issues are 'grey' areas, that is, there is no simple right or wrong answer. In this chapter, we have provided principles and examples to help you find your way through such uncertain situations.

━━━ SUGGESTIONS FOR FURTHER READING ━━━

- About Education, *Ethical considerations in sociological research: Five principles of the American Sociological Association's Code of Ethics.* Available online at: http://sociology. about.com/od/Research/a/Ethics.htm. This website provides a succinct overview of some of the main ethical principles of competence, integrity, responsibility and respect.
- British Educational Research Association. (2011). *Ethical guidelines for educational research.* Available online at: http://content.yudu.com/Library/A2xnp5/Bera/resources/index. htm?referrerUrl=http://free.yudu.com/item/details/2023387/Bera. A very useful resource with guidelines on how to conduct research in an educational setting ethically. Pages 5–8 highlight the researcher's responsibilities towards their participants.
- British Sociological Association. (2002). *Statement of ethical practice for the British Sociological Association.* Available online at: http://www.britsoc.co.uk/media/27107/ StatementofEthicalPractice.pdf?1435594584410/. This is the British Sociological Association's official statement on research ethics, and as such is essential reading!

- **Dahlberg, L. and McCaig, C. (2010). Practical research and evaluation: A start-to-finish guide for practitioners. London: Sage.** Chapter 4 of this book provides useful commentary on informed consent and the code of professional standards. For guidance on ethical approval applications, see page 53.
- **ESRC (2012).** *ESRC framework for research ethics.* Available online at: http://www.esrc. ac.uk/_images/framework-for-research-ethics-09-12_tcm8-4586.pdf. This document outlines the European Social Research Council's official position on research ethics. While the document in its entirety should be read before conducting research, pp. 2–3 outlines the ESRC's six main ethical research principles.
- **Gov.uk (2014)** *Data protection.* Available online at: https://www.gov.uk/data-protection/ the-data-protection-act. This web page explains data protection laws in the UK, your rights as an individual and how your data can be used, and how to legally use other people's data.
- *The research ethics guidebook: A resource for social scientists* **(2011).** Available online at: http://www.ethicsguidebook.ac.uk/. This is a very useful resource with a whole host of tips and advice. Of particular note is the 'Permission and Approval' section that provides information and external links to various legal and institutional requirements for how research should be conducted in a compliant manner.
- **Rogers, C. and Ludhra, G. (2011). Research ethics: Participation, social difference and informed consent. In S. Bradford and F. Cullen (Eds.),** *Research and research methods for youth practitioners.* **New York: Routledge.** Available online at: http://www.academia. edu/1106391/Research_ethics_participation_social_difference_and_informed_consent_in_ Bradford_and_Cullen_eds._Research_and_Research_Methods_for_Youth_Practitioners. This text aims to address the issue of research ethics from the perspective of the young researcher. Pages 48–50 are particularly useful on informed consent.
- **Sieber, J. E. and Tolich, M. B. (2013) Journalistic ethics ≠ social scientist ethics. In** *Planning ethically responsible research.* **London: Sage.** As journalistic ethics was mentioned in this chapter as being distinct from research ethics, this text has been provided to expand on the differences between the two.
- **Spicker, P. (2007) Research without consent.** *Social Research Update, 51,* **1–4.** Available online at: http://sru.soc.surrey.ac.uk/SRU51.pdf. This short article, conversely, discusses instances where consent may not be desirable.

Visit the companion website at **https://study.sagepub.com/jensenandlaurie** to gain access to a wide range of online resources to support your learning, including editable research documents, weblinks, free access SAGE journal articles and book chapters, and flashcards.

▬ GLOSSARY ▬

Anonymity – Respondents should be anonymized as soon as possible to protect their identity. As well as their name, this may also include places where they live and work as well as any other identifying information.

Competence – Research competence improves over time, with experience and self-reflection. Your research should always be conducted to the highest standards, and to ensure this you shouldn't attempt complex tasks that you don't yet feel ready to handle.

Confidentiality – Part of your ethical duty as a researcher is to ensure that your participants are aware of your confidentiality policy. In general, this means that anything they tell you cannot be used outside the specific research parameters that the participant understands and agrees to allow. However, this does not always apply; for example, if children are in danger you are legally obliged to protect them. You must tell your participants at the beginning of your study if you cannot maintain confidentiality.

Ethics committee – This is the body from which you have to gain approval for your research before you can begin. They ensure that your research plan is legally and ethically compliant and can help you to improve your plan where necessary.

Harm – Participating in your research may cause some participants psychological, emotional or, in extreme cases, physical harm. For instance, participants may feel abused if their right to privacy is not honoured. Your primary concern is to protect their well-being, so you always need to abide by ethical guidelines.

Informed consent – You need to secure informed consent from your participants before commencing any research with them. This involves making them fully aware of the purpose of the research, the parties involved, what is expected of them, who will see their data and how it will be stored. Consent is usually recorded with a signed declaration. You can only proceed in a manner that they agree with. For example, if they are happy to answer your questions, but don't wish to be recorded, then you have to respect their decision.

Insider research – This is when you conduct research within a community or setting with which you are personally or professionally familiar.

Integrity – Research integrity is very important; by abiding with ethical principles, you can ensure that the reputation of your work, your institution and yourself remain in good stead.

Legal requirements – These differ from research ethics (below). When seeking approval for your project, your institution will outline what you are and aren't legally allowed to do. For example, you may legally be allowed to interview an adult who is not vulnerable, but if in the interview you find that the participant is experiencing a high level of distress then continuing with the interview would conflict with your ethical duty to protect your participants.

Outsider research – This is when you conduct research in a setting or community with which you are not familiar.

Privacy – Both your participants and you as researcher are entitled to privacy. This means that you should not push respondents too hard if they appear unwilling to divulge personal information. It also means that you are not obliged to respond to their questions about your personal life, but should be prepared in case they do so.

Research ethics – These define how you should act towards your participants throughout the course of your project. Their well-being is always paramount, and you have a responsibility to cause no harm as a result of your research project.

Vulnerable people – You may need to do research with vulnerable people, who might find involvement in your research particularly stressful, or who may not be able to understand the process sufficiently to be able to give fully informed consent. Examples of vulnerable groups include children, the elderly, people with learning difficulties, and people who do not share your first language.

━ REFERENCES ━

American Sociological Association (2015). *American Sociological Association Code of Ethics.* Retrieved 8 August 2015, from http://www.asanet.org/about/ethics.cfm

Bonner, A., & Tolhurst, G. (2002). Insider-outsider perspectives of participant observation. *Nurse Researcher, 9*(4), 7–19.

British Educational Research Association (2011). *Ethical guidelines for educational research*. London: BERA. Retrieved 2 September 2015, from https://www.bera.ac.uk/wp-content/uploads/2014/02/BERA-Ethical-Guidelines-2011.pdf?noredirect=1

British Sociological Association (2002). *Statement of ethical practice for the British Sociological Association*, March. Retrieved 2 September 2015, from http://www.britsoc.co.uk/media/27107/StatementofEthicalPractice.pdf?1435594584410

Coghlan, D. (2003). Practitioner research for organizational knowledge: Mechanistic- and organistic-oriented approaches to insider action research. *Management Learning, 34*(4), 451–463.

Coghlan, D., & Brannick, T. (2005). *Doing action research in your own organization*. London: Sage.

DeLyser, D. (2001). 'Do you really live here?' Thoughts on insider research. *Geographical Review, 91*(1), 441–453.

Department of Health (2005). *Research governance framework for health and social care* (2nd edn). [London:] Department of Health. Retrieved 2 September 2015, from https://www.gov.uk/government/uploads/system/uploads/attachment_data/file/139565/dh_4122427.pdf

ESRC (2012). *ESRC framework for research ethics*. Available online at: http://www.esrc.ac.uk/_images/framework-for-research-ethics-09-12_tcm8-4586.pdf

Gerrish, K. (1997). Being a 'marginal native': Dilemmas of the participant observer. *Nurse Researcher, 5*(1), 25–34.

Gov.uk (2014). Data protection. Retrieved 20 July 2015, from https://www.gov.uk/data-protection/the-data-protection-act

Hewitt-Taylor, J. (2002). Insider knowledge: Issues in insider research. *Nursing Standard, 16*(46), 33–35.

Humphrey, C. (2012). Dilemmas in doing insider research in professional education. *Qualitative Social Work, 12*(5), 1–15.

Markham, A., & Buchanan, E. (2012). *Ethical decision-making and internet research: Recommendations from the AoIR ethics working committee*. Retrieved 2 September 2015, from http://aoir.org/reports/ethics2.pdf

Marwick (2011) http://nms.sagepub.com/content/13/1/114

Research Ethics Guidebook (2015a). *Assessing risk and harm*. Retrieved 18 July 2015, from http://ethicsguidebook.ac.uk/Assessing-risk-and-harm-21

Research Ethics Guidebook (2015b). *Risks to researchers*. Retrieved 1 August 2015, from http://ethicsguidebook.ac.uk/Risks-to-researchers-68

Rogers, C., & Ludhra, G. (2011). Research ethics: Participation, social difference and informed consent. In S. Bradford & F. Cullen (Eds.), *Research and research methods for youth practitioners*. New York: Routledge.

Rouney, P. (2005). *Researching from the inside – does it compromise validity?* Retrieved 2 September 2015, from http://arrow.dit.ie/ltcart/5/

Scottish Educational Research Association (2005). *Ethical guidelines for educational research*. [Edinburgh:] SERA. Retrieved 2 September 2015, from http://c.ymcdn.com/sites/www.weraonline.org/resource/resmgr/a_general/sera.pdf

Smyth, A., & Holian, R. (2008). Credibility issues in research from within organisations. In P. Sikes & A. Potts (Eds.), *Researching education from the inside* (pp. 33–47). New York: Routledge.

Social Research Association (2003). *Ethical guidelines*. Retrieved 2 September 2015, from http://the-sra.org.uk/wp-content/uploads/ethics03.pdf

Spicker, P. (2007). Research without consent. *Social Research Update, 51*, 1–4.

Tedlock, B. (2000). Ethnography and ethnographic representation. In N. K. Denzin & Y. S. Lincoln (Eds.), *Handbook of qualitative research* (2nd ed., pp. 455–486). Thousand Oaks, CA: Sage.

Unluer, S. (2012). Being an insider researcher while conducting case study research. *The Qualitative Report, 17*(58), 1–14.

Williams, B. (2006). Meaningful consent to participate in social research on the part of people under the age of eighteen. *Research Ethics Review, 2*(1), 19–24.

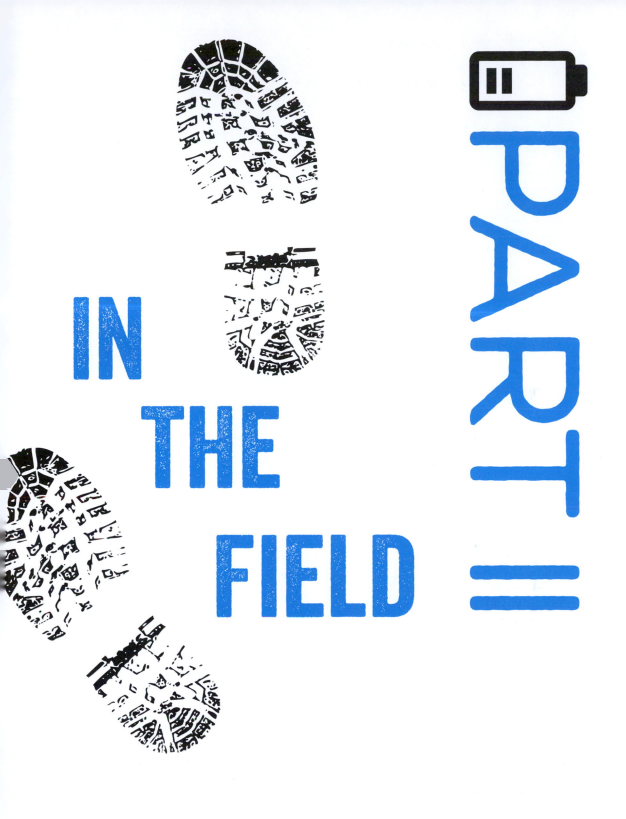

PART II

IN THE FIELD

HOW TO MANAGE RISK

PROTECTING YOURSELF AND YOUR EQUIPMENT

4

4●1 INTRODUCTION

Whether you are researching your local community or travelling abroad, you may find yourself negotiating new and unfamiliar situations. Undertaking **fieldwork** offers the prospect of real adventure and the opportunity to provide insight into ideas, people and places that are unknown to most of the world. However, in visiting these people and places, you may encounter threats to your safety and **emotional well-being**. The goal of this chapter is not to alarm or discourage you. Rather, it is intended to help you stay safe when conducting your research. Through raising your awareness of problems that can arise, you can anticipate and successfully mitigate **risks** to you and your research.

We begin by identifying identify potential psychological risks you may encounter. Then we turn to examining possible physical threats you could face. Throughout this chapter, we discuss real world solutions that can help you minimize or manage these risks.

4●2 RECOGNIZE AND MANAGE THREATS TO YOUR EMOTIONAL WELL-BEING

Because social research often aims to dig beneath the surface with participants, it is not unusual to encounter emotionally charged topics, especially during open-ended qualitative research. Even seemingly innocent topics, such as someone's childhood experiences at school, can unearth an emotional issue, such as a participant's unresolved psychological trauma about having been bullied. Effectively managing emotionally challenging situations is therefore an essential skill you need to develop as a social researcher.

4●2●1 MINIMIZE DISRUPTION FROM PARTICIPANTS' EMOTIONAL RESPONSES

When participants get upset, they can occasionally become defensive and verbally lash out at you as the researcher. Such outbursts, or the threat of them, can undermine your sense of safety and your ability to carry out your research if it focuses on a particularly sensitive topic. Concern about upsetting your participants can lead you to avoid certain lines of questioning, which could potentially undermine the quality of your research. More commonly, feeling anxious about how your participant may respond can prevent you from feeling comfortable and confident in the interview, limiting your ability to probe further on interesting topics that emerge during the data collection process.

To minimize the risk of encountering these negative outcomes, you can use a **pilot study** – a small preliminary project – to refine your ability to strike a good tone and practise the steps discussed below.

Employ neutral phrasing. When discussing sensitive topics with participants, keep your language as neutral and non-judgemental as possible.

- **Investigate what words, phrases and references may be viewed as upsetting or insulting by participants in your area of study.** Speak to gatekeepers or those with knowledge of the participants or the participants' social group. Think about it from the perspective of the participants. Create a list for yourself of these verbal 'no-go' terms or topics.
- **Be familiar with your participants' preferred phrasing to help you navigate controversial topics.** For example, if you were researching the commercial sex industry, some participants may be offended by whatever label you use to describe workers in their industry. The term 'sex workers' or 'escorts' may be preferred to other terms such as 'prostitutes'. You could ask your participants directly about their preferred terms early in the data collection process to minimize the risk of inadvertently offending them. At minimum, you should be attuned to the language your participants use. For example, if you found that a participant referred to herself as an 'escort' rather than a 'sex worker', you should attempt to use this phrasing for the rest of the interview.

Distance yourself from controversial questions. If you ask a question outright or your phrasing comes across as too direct, participants might typically assume that the question reflects your views or assumptions about them. For example, if you asked, 'Have you ever been tempted to take advantage of your position?', your participant may feel defensive. To avoid this, you can use phrases such as 'Some people might wonder whether you …' to begin your question, rather than 'Have you ever …'. By carefully phrasing the question as if it is coming from others and not from you personally, the participant may feel less 'put on the spot'. It also helps to avoid the impression that you, the researcher, have critical or biased views.

A further strategy is to ask direct questions by pointing the direction of the question to others. For example, you could ask 'Do you know of fellow co-workers who …' or 'Some people believe that workers in your office …', instead of 'In your workplace, do you …'. This strategy allows you to dissociate yourself from the question and provide the participant with 'cover', so that they can avoid directly admitting to have taken part in any embarrassing or socially undesirable activities.

━━━━━━━━━━ **REAL WORLD EXAMPLE** ━━━━━━━━━━

Use a distancing strategy for controversial questions

Toby encountered a negative response when he asked users of alternative therapies, such as acupuncture or homeopathy, about what evidence they relied on in deciding to use such therapies. His participants interpreted the questions about their (non-)use of scientific evidence in selecting alternative health treatments as the researcher viewing these treatments in a negative light. This led to defensive responses from the participants.

(Continued)

(Continued)

A **distancing strategy** could have helped to lessen the perceived threat in this line of questioning and encouraged the participants to be more open. Instead of saying 'Do you use scientifically verified evidence when choosing acupuncture instead of treatment from your doctor?', Toby might have said, 'Some people think they need to find scientifically verified evidence for acupuncture before choosing it as a means of therapy. What do you think?'

Finally, you can employ a distancing strategy by prefacing your question with a statement that lowers the risk of embarrassment or **stigma** for the participant. For example, if you were to ask students at a religious university about their romantic relationships by saying 'How many sexual partners have you had in the last 12 months?', it might be viewed as too forward or as assuming they have been promiscuous. An alternative would be to say something like: 'It is well known that many couples meet during their time at university. Have you had any romantic experiences in the last year?' Once participants responded to this question, follow-up questions could establish the number and nature of those romantic experiences.

Use 'buffer' questions to reset a research discussion when it becomes heated. If your participant starts to react badly during a line of questioning, you can follow the strategy of inserting a **buffer question** to neutralize negative emotions before they fully emerge. Buffer questions have the following characteristics:

- The question should take the form of an entirely non-threatening topic that the participant can answer in a confident manner.
- Topics you can ask about should ideally be focused on issues the participant would enjoy speaking about.

Buffer questions can 'reset' the conversation by distracting the participant from negative thoughts that appear to be emerging. It is worth being prepared with phrases that explain the interruption. For example, if a participant begins to look angry, upset or defensive, you could use an interrupting question such as 'Sorry, what you said a moment ago reminded me of something: I wanted to ask you why you chose to enter law enforcement to begin with'. Once the conversation has returned to a more neutral tone, you may able to re-engage the topic using a different approach. However, it is usually best to side-step the sensitive area that initially elicited a bad reaction.

Consider ending the interaction if the participant shows strong negative emotions. Strong, negative emotions could include hostility towards you or evident emotional upset while describing a particular experience from their past or present. This can be a challenging situation for any researcher, but you have a few options:

Option 1. Give the participant time to regain composure.

- Provide gentle indications of empathy, such as nodding your head slowly and showing your recognition of the participant's emotion with a correspondingly empathetic facial expression of your own.
- Remind participants in this situation that they have complete control over the interview. Reiterate that they have been very helpful and provide them with the option of proceeding or stopping.

- After taking these steps you may be able to continue with the interview, albeit taking extra care not to appear at all aggressive or insistent in your manner.

Option 2. End the interview.

- *Discontinue the interview quickly* (without appearing hurried) as soon as it becomes apparent that the situation is deteriorating.
- If participants choose to end an interview, respect this decision. Politely thank them for their time before you leave. If there is an opening, you can ask if it is possible for you to reschedule the interview for a later time or date. But, it may be prudent to simply get back in contact the next day.

You have the primary responsibility for protecting your participants' well-being. If you suspect that you are causing a participant to feel distressed, you are obliged to end your interaction in the quickest and least harmful way possible. Your duty of care extends beyond the interview itself – if you have (unintentionally) upset participants as a result of your study, you should point the participant in the direction of appropriate emotional support.

4•2•2 MANAGE THE EFFECTS OF EMOTIONAL STRESS ON YOUR RESEARCH

Many researchers experience some kind of emotional toll from undertaking their study. You may have anxieties about the research. Will the study be successful? Will you get enough participants? Will the data provide insights to answer your research question? You may have anxieties about your own abilities. Can you complete a survey successfully? Have you left out a crucial question? What if you do not know how to analyse all the data you have collected? Other concerns may relate to the duration of your research. You may worry about not being able to complete your work before your deadline. You may feel anxious that you will be 'scooped' by another researcher publishing on your topic before your research is completed. Or you may worry that your funding will run out before you have completed your study.

Exposure to these kinds of emotional **stress** from your research – even from seemingly small, ongoing worries and anxieties – can affect your emotional and physical health. You may experience sleeplessness, bad dreams or more serious mental health problems, such as depression. Indeed, you may find yourself with physical health problems that you feel are unconnected, such as a heightened propensity for illness; this could be related to prolonged exposure to stressful research. It is also worth keeping in mind that over time exposure to emotionally stressful information and experiences can have a cumulative effect on you.

━━━━━━━ **KEY TIPS** ━━━━━━━

Keep a work-life balance

Keep in touch with friends, family and institutional sources of support. Do not isolate yourself in your research. Maintaining contact with friends, family and research supervisors may help you to put concerns you have with your research into perspective. They can also provide you with an important emotional support network during emotionally challenging periods.

(Continued)

(Continued)

Maintain interests and activities outside your research. Participating in other activities outside your research work – potentially including sports or hobbies – can help you put your research into perspective. This may be particularly important if you are conducting research in a foreign country away from your loved ones, so be prepared with solutions such as long-distance calling cards or Skype software to be able to maintain regular contact.

Know where you can seek emotional support. Most universities have a counselling service that you can turn to, and many organizations run free listening services (such as the Samaritans). If you suspect that you are developing depression, you should consider seeking advice.

You need to be attuned to possible emotional threats to your well-being in order to take steps early on if you start to experience symptoms. Generally speaking, the following may increase the likelihood that you will be facing emotional risks:

- **Addressing emotionally challenging research content.** Research on distressing subject matter, such as terminally ill hospital patients, is more likely to have a serious emotional impact.
- **Gathering data directly from those affected by tragedy.** Speaking face-to-face with people who have experienced deep sadness or suffering can stick with you much more than written accounts.
- **Visiting locations where distressing incidents occurred.** The project becomes more 'real' if you are exposed to the physical context in which distressing events took place.
- **Maintaining 'secret' data.** The responsibility to maintain the secrecy of sensitive data can impose a substantial emotional burden on you.
- **Conducting your research in a stressful research context.** If your research context is stressful, such as an intense, busy city or a foreign country where even ordering food is challenging, this can add to the overall strain on your emotions.

Stress can negatively affect your decision-making. You should be self-aware and alert to possible biases that emotional stress may induce:

- **Stressful emotions can distort, rather than clarify, your research perspective.** Your emotional response can be instructive, pointing you towards important insights. However, it can also override your objectivity, making you vulnerable to bias.
- **Repeated exposure to emotionally charged content could give you the impression that upsetting incidents are more widespread than they really are.** This may cause you to lose perspective and overestimate a phenomenon's importance or relevance to your research.
- **Raw emotional experiences can make you identify too closely with your participants.** While you certainly want to be able to empathize with your participants' perspectives, you must maintain emotional boundaries. Your primary purpose as a researcher is to develop new knowledge. Getting too emotionally involved in your participants' problems can get in the way of successfully completing your research.

There are several strategies you can use to mitigate the negative effects of stressful and emotional information. Figure 4.1 provides a summary of indicators of emotional risk in research.

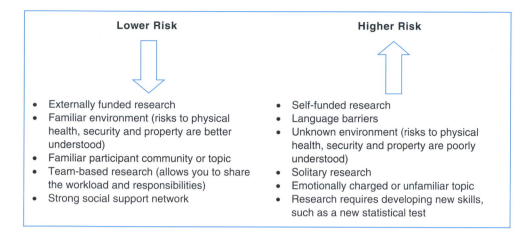

Lower Risk

- Externally funded research
- Familiar environment (risks to physical health, security and property are better understood)
- Familiar participant community or topic
- Team-based research (allows you to share the workload and responsibilities)
- Strong social support network

Higher Risk

- Self-funded research
- Language barriers
- Unknown environment (risks to physical health, security and property are poorly understood)
- Solitary research
- Emotionally charged or unfamiliar topic
- Research requires developing new skills, such as a new statistical test

Figure 4.1   Indicators of emotional risk in research

These guidelines are not universal. For example, some researchers may find the social interactions and expectations of team-based research more stressful than solitary research. Yet, being attuned to these emotional risk indicators can help you detect and evaluate potential emotional risks to your well-being at an early stage when you can more easily implement the steps described in this chapter to mitigate negative impacts.

Keep perspective. You can do this by placing new information you encounter into the context of what you already know. You can employ this strategy to reduce the negative effect of emotionally charged research experiences.

- **Find perspective through facts, such as examining statistics on the issue.** For example, if you just held a focus group with convicted burglars, the increased awareness of burglary could make you feel like you could be burgled. To re-establish your perspective, you might turn to official crime statistics. For example, in 2011–12 there were just 653 burglaries in England and Wales (CSEW, 2012). In addition, statistics would show that most burglaries occur in a small number of high-risk areas, highlighting that the risk of your being a victim is extremely small.
- **Talk to an expert in the field or to someone you trust.** Simply 'talking it out' can allow you to express your feelings, while helping you to alleviate some of the emotional pressure. Indeed, regularly 'checking in' with your supervisor or a friend is strongly recommended during fieldwork to help you keep emotional perspective.

Reframe your experience of negative emotions. Find a new, more positive way of perceiving potentially upsetting or stressful information. For example, change your internal focus from 'These interviews are upsetting and I am worrying about the effect that listening to these accounts will have on me' to 'While these interviews are emotionally challenging, this research holds the promise of gaining new insights that will ultimately improve people's lives'.

The following are some examples to help you redirect your emotions towards a focus on positive outcomes:

- My research is contributing to the greater good of academic knowledge.
- By hearing these accounts, the world will know more about what these individuals or groups have experienced.
- Emotionally challenging findings will provide a richer research output and have a greater impact on readers.

Create an intellectual distance to shift away from an emotional response. You can keep emotional distance from distressing content by seeing it as an intellectual challenge. For example, if you are researching the coping strategies of families who have experienced the death or serious illness of an infant, you might shift away from an understandably emotional perspective on your research to the intellectual challenge of coming up with improved strategies to help families in the future. The idea is to compartmentalize the research as an intellectual effort, and not as a part of your broader personal life.

REAL WORLD EXAMPLE

Keep your research and home lives separate

Jonah's research project included several in-depth interviews with internet sexual offenders. During this time, he encountered detailed histories of online sexual offences, listened to accounts of participants' decision-making and justifications, and heard about consequences for their families. This exposure caused him to experience emotional distress and personal conflict over the actions of offenders.

To avoid feeling overwhelmed by the upsetting content in his research, Jonah was strict about seeing his research as a 'job' – a specific, focused activity that took place between certain hours of the day. By being disciplined about not bringing his 'work life' back home, Jonah rebalanced his life with more 'normal', everyday thoughts that kept his research in perspective. He found that playing sports regularly, seeing friends and reading for pleasure helped him see the merits and value of his research without being overwhelmed by it.

Finally, you should consider at an early stage in your research if the risks to your psychological well-being when taking on an emotionally challenging topic are worth it to you. This is a personal decision, which must be based on your own experience, level of sensitivity and the particular range of emotional risks you may be facing. It is worth thinking deeply and honestly about how your research is likely to affect you emotionally. Some research may be too emotionally challenging for some people, making the emotional cost of the research too high. It is far better for you and your participants if you can come to a clear decision early in your research process.

The Research Ethics Guidebook (2015a, 2015b, 2015c) has additional focused guidance on how to identify harm, understanding risk to researchers and steps on how to undertake a risk assessment.

—————————— **REAL WORLD EXAMPLE** ——————————

Coping with societal inequality: Emotional experiences at a UK food aid charity

Adriana's research project included participant observation research at an Italy-based Somali food aid charity. This charity collected surplus food from outlets, cooked it and distributed the meals to Somali migrants in Sicily. Primarily Adriana ate meals with the users of the charity. She encountered a range of individuals from different backgrounds, who were all vulnerable emotionally, physically or financially. The participants provided detailed life stories, including struggles to obtain basic necessities such as food. The accounts she heard were often traumatic, unjust and exposed the personal toll of societal inequality. During her research, Adriana witnessed the segregation and stigmatization of individuals who have been labelled as unworthy by society, and the dehumanizing process of accepting charity. This experience was distressing for Adriana. She felt overwhelmed by the scale of the migrants' poverty, and she particularly struggled to return to her daily life without feeling guilty.

To help address her feelings of distress, guilt and hopelessness, she discussed her experiences with other researchers and her support network. Adriana was careful not to disclose personal information about participants in order to respect ethical guidelines, but found that talking about her experiences and listening to others helped put her research into perspective. Adriana also became active on a number of social networking sites in supporting charities and debates which sought to combat food poverty. This allowed Adriana to feel not only that the research was being carried out for academic reasons but also that she was helping in some way.

4●3 RECOGNIZE AND MANAGE RISKS TO YOUR PERSONAL SECURITY AND PROPERTY

4●3●1 LIMIT THREATS TO YOUR PHYSICAL HEALTH THROUGH GOOD PREPARATION

Threats to your physical health are unlikely to be among your main concerns when conducting research in a developed country. Nevertheless, you should take sensible precautions, even when researching in your home country. For example, if you are researching the use of pesticides in agriculture, make sure that you wear the correct safety equipment when carrying out field visits and follow the specified safety procedures.

Threats to your health are often elevated if you are carrying out research abroad. In some parts of the world, there may be no clinics for hundreds of kilometres; in other cases, medical facilities are severely overcrowded and underequipped. These limitations in medical care are particularly problematic if you have a pre-existing medical condition that requires advanced medicines. It is essential that you plan for such needs well in advance and do not presume that medical supplies and facilities are readily available.

Before travelling to a tropical location, seek professional medical advice on the main disease threats and how to avoid them. For example, official government websites such as for the Centers for Disease Control and Prevention (http://www.cdc.gov) can help you find out if you need to start taking preventative medication before your trip. Some anti-malaria medicines need to be taken at least one month before entering a malarial zone. If you can afford it, go for the more expensive Malarone anti-malarial medication to reduce the risk of distracting side effects undermining your ability to carry out your research effectively.

Investigate whether you need additional travel insurance, including medical coverage. Whether doing your research in developed or developing countries, purchase travel insurance to make certain that you are covered if there's a medical emergency. Depending on where you travel, ensuring you have provision for medical evacuation by aircraft may be particularly important. The cost of medical evacuation is unaffordable to most people unless they have insurance. This coverage provides for you to be airlifted to the nearest medical facility, even if it is in another country. Moreover, it allows you to fly to a location where specialist services can be provided.

Don't forget that in some cases medical insurance could also be useful when carrying out research in developed countries where disease risks are lower. For example, you may wish to purchase additional insurance if you are working with drug addicts or in other situations where your physical health might be compromised.

Keep your important health documents organized in a centralized location. You should store your medical insurance documents, any backup prescriptions you may have, and contact details for emergency medical services on your person or somewhere you can easily access in an emergency. Storing them in a waterproof bag or container is a sensible additional precaution.

4•3•2 PREPARE FOR THREATS FROM CRIMINALITY

Threats from criminality are present all over the world. If you are carrying out research in a developed nation, you may be vulnerable if you are researching issues such as drug use or prostitution, which may require you to spend time at night in areas with high crime rates. In some cases, such as urban gang research, you could even face risks of crime from the participants in your research.

The threat of crime can be heightened when you are travelling in a foreign country, or even in an unfamiliar part of your own country. If you are recognized as being from out of town, thieves may see you as an easy target. They may assume that you don't know your way around the area and are carrying valuables with you: your laptop, recording equipment, camera or mobile phone are obvious targets for thieves. Moreover, as a visitor in an unfamiliar context you may not be as alert and attentive as you should be.

You may also be uncertain of whom to trust. For example, when an apparently kind person offers to assist you, it can be difficult to know whether the offer is genuine. Pickpockets – working alone or in pairs – often use distraction as a tactic. You could be the victim of a more serious crime if a criminal lures you into an isolated area.

In addition, you may encounter unwanted sexual advances. In some parts of the world, Western women may be viewed as being more willing to tolerate sexually suggestive behaviour. Unwanted attention may range from eye contact to lewd comments and, in some cases, physical contact and serious assaults. It is usually best to ignore suggestive comments, rather than provoke a confrontation. Wearing a wedding ring can help both women and men avoid unwanted advances. See Duncombe and Jessop (2012) on dilemmas faced by some researchers when striking up rapport with participants. See also Gurney (1985) and Lumsden's (2014) research on challenges faced by female researchers in the field.

To be prepared for the range of possible threats you might face during your fieldwork, do a thorough search online for information on the risks in the cities and countries you are visiting in advance of your visit. Bear in mind that during certain times of year, some areas may be less safe due to sporting events, religious festivals or political demonstrations. Arriving at your research location at a time of heightened risk is often completely avoidable. For example, the US State Department's Bureau of Consular Affairs and the UK Foreign and Commonwealth Office have useful online information for identifying such risks.

The specific location for your data collection can also affect your level of risk (see Chapter 5 for further discussion). Local residents, or recent visitors (e.g., from your university or business), can be valuable sources of information about risks in a given area. You can also review relevant discussions online to see if people have been discussing any particular concerns relating to the area you will be visiting. In developing countries, staff from non-governmental organizations (NGOs) who work in the local area can be a good source of advice. Be persistent, but courteous, and ask people if they can provide contact details of other locals who may be able to help you. Learning from the locals is especially valuable because it gives you a realistic sense of what you are likely to face. The mitigation strategies they suggest are likely to be tried and tested.

REAL WORLD EXAMPLE

Find creative options for mitigating criminality risks

Jonathan determined there was a risk of being mugged when carrying out research after dark in the Bronx district of New York, so he devised a scheme in which he had a tailor sew a pocket on the inside of the leg of his jeans where he could store most of his money and documents. He then carried a separate wallet with a small amount of money. The idea was that if criminals demanded his cash, he could provide what was in his wallet and they would overlook the concealed pocket in his jeans. While this precaution would be unnecessary in most contexts, it demonstrates the kind of innovative thinking that can help mitigate threats you would otherwise have little control over. If you don't know a tailor, consider using a body wallet (e.g., one that goes around your waist, under your shirt), as these are much harder for a pickpocket to access.

4●3●3　BE PREPARED WHEN TRAVELLING IN UNFAMILIAR PLACES AND FOREIGN COUNTRIES

Travel in foreign countries and unfamiliar places can make basic considerations challenging.

Do your homework and learn about where you are going to before you leave. It is useful to start with the bigger considerations:

- How reliable is the transport system and does it service the areas you will be visiting?
- Are any of the transport hubs you are likely to use in more crime-ridden parts of town? If so, are there alternative hubs?

You can then start focusing on more detailed questions:

- What kind of transport do locals use or avoid and why?
- Are you bringing certain kinds of luggage (e.g., oversize suitcases or a bike) that may not be allowed on forms of public transport?
- Are there certain times of year when public transport should be avoided?
- How much do tickets cost, where do you buy them, on what days/times are they available, and what forms of payment can you use? Do you need to bring coins with you (e.g., for automatic ticket machines)?

In the UK, travel advice is provided by the Foreign Office and it would be useful to make this your first port of call. Additionally, many universities have their own travel policies governing the conduct of their students abroad, so keeping abreast of these is very important. After that, you can find the answers to most of your questions with some persistent web searching. Travel guides answer some questions, but many commercial publications fall short of providing 'real', up-to-date insights about what challenges you can expect to encounter. Friends or colleagues with first-hand experience can be a great resource. Another really useful means of getting detailed 'on the ground' information is from travel blogs, which often provide detailed accounts of travellers' experiences. A number of these sites cater specifically to student or budget travellers.

 **KEY TIPS**

Be prepared when you travel

Maps and documents. Bring hard copies of maps and documents when going out to your research site. Copies saved on smartphones and other electronic devices may be useful in some cases, but can become inaccessible if your device runs out of power or you can't connect to the internet.

Check your passport. Check whether you need a special visa for visiting a country well in advance (ideally as soon as you decide you are going to travel there). Always ensure that you have at least 6 months left on your passport when you return from your trip, as this is a (poorly advertised) requirement for entry in many countries. Make sure you have backup photocopies of your passport and other relevant travel documents, including visas, which you keep in a separate location from your original documents.

Make sure someone knows where you are and how to find you. When travelling somewhere dangerous or unfamiliar, tell someone responsible what route you are planning to take, when you are expected to arrive and what they should do if they do not hear from you.

If travelling by public transport, you need to work out where departure and drop-off points are, as well as operating times. You also need to know how to book tickets in the least expensive manner. The system may have quirks that are well understood by locals but are not obvious to a foreign visitor. For instance, in parts of Italy bus tickets are normally purchased from the local tobacco shops, which are often closed on Sundays (though ticket inspectors still operate!).

Driving in foreign countries is likely to present a variety of different risks. Even in countries with high levels of crime, road accidents often present the greatest safety risk. In some countries you may find that locals routinely drive at excessive speeds and operate old, poorly maintained vehicles. In addition, roads worldwide often have uneven surfaces and can be severely potholed, while there is a lack of traffic management systems.

To mitigate these driving risks, you should:

- Familiarize yourself in advance with any special driving conditions you are likely to face. You are likely to find numerous official sites detailing formal rules, along with informal advice from blogs and other websites.
- Avoid driving in urban areas wherever possible until you gain experience. Typically urban areas in developing countries are congested not only by vehicles, but also by pedestrians and various other obstacles and distractions.
- Avoid driving at night in developing countries. There may not be working street lights, cars may not have working lights and there may be hard-to-see obstacles on the road.

4•3•4 PROTECT YOUR PROPERTY

During your research, your property – including the laptops and recording devices you need for your project – can be at risk from loss, theft or damage. This risk is greater during fieldwork in unfamiliar settings where you cannot easily rely on routine conveniences such as access to safe equipment storage. Also, the more you use your equipment the more likely it is that at some point it may be damaged. We suggest considering the steps detailed in Table 4.1 to minimize the wide range of risks to your equipment and data deriving from theft, loss or damage.

Table 4.1 Steps to store and protect your data

Step	Details
Select robust equipment	• Choose equipment that is known to be durable to minimize risk of damage. • Consult expert equipment reviews, such as on www.expertreviews.co.uk. Customer reviews on websites such as www.amazon.com can also be helpful in identifying whether a given piece of equipment tends to break down.
Use specialized protective cases	• Water, dust and sand can damage electronic equipment. You need a sealed and padded protective case to fully protect your equipment.
Take precautions against power surges	• Power surges that can damage electrical goods are common in the developing world. Use a surge protector and unplug items when they are not in use or charging (especially during any power blackouts).
Keep spares of essential equipment	• Assume something will go wrong and buy a spare. • Basic voice recorders can be purchased cheaply. A second laptop or tablet may be worthwhile if you are in the field for an extended period in a location where buying a replacement would not be feasible.

(Continued)

Table 4.1   (Continued)

Step	Details
Avoid taking your equipment with you on non-research excursions	• Have a 'base' where you can store your equipment safely when it is not needed. • Keep backup devices in a separate location from your main equipment so you could at least recover your data and carry on with your research if your main equipment were lost.
Consistently back up your data	• Try to back up your data at least once a day if you are gathering important information. • External hard drives are useful, but storing data in a managed network ('the cloud') is preferable as it safeguards your data even if your other equipment is lost or stolen (see Table 4.2).

An important decision as you prepare for your research is which physical devices you will use to save your data. In Table 4.2 we help you weigh up the merits of using external hard drives or USB flash drives compared to web-based storage. There are also ethical implications relating to securing confidential participant data (see Chapter 3). If you can afford it, using both an external hard drive and cloud storage is usually the ideal.

Table 4.2   Strengths and weaknesses of external drives and cloud storage

	External storage (hard drive or USB)	Cloud storage
Strengths	• One-off cost • Ability to access data without an internet connection • Greater direct control over your data • Ability to encrypt the drive and data	• No risk of physical damage • Can set up automatic file sync to ensure continuous updates • Can access files from anywhere there is an internet connection • More secure – cloud storage companies will usually back up your data across multiple servers for added backup security
Weaknesses	• Target for theft • Easily lost, stolen or physically damaged (e.g., from dropping, although flash-based drives are less susceptible to impact damage) • Data corruption risk (can occur from physical damage or hardware malfunction) • Unable to access files without the device	• Subscription fees (although some will provide some free storage) • No physical control over data once on the cloud • File access can be slower, depending on server speed

You will also need to consider the other kinds of equipment that you take with you to your research site. Think about having redundant backups so that you never find yourself unable to collect data because of equipment failure.

KEY TIPS

Select the right equipment for the situation

Equipment choices depend on where you are conducting your fieldwork, your budget, the level of weather protection required and how replaceable the item is.

Batteries and electrical power. If you will be in an unfamiliar setting during field research, don't assume you will have easy access to electrical power to charge your devices.

- Fully charge your devices before going into the field.
- Bring backup batteries for your electronic devices.
- In practice, you might not be able to obtain reasonably priced backup batteries for larger electronic devices such as laptops, which rely on expensive lithium batteries. For these devices, consider purchasing a mobile wind-up emergency charger if you are going to be in a setting with limited power sources.

Basic and dependable mobile phone. Always carry a mobile phone in case unexpected issues arise during fieldwork. People get lost and meeting times can get mixed up, so be prepared to contact relevant parties at short notice (and make sure your participants can contact you if they are unable to make it for whatever reason). In a research setting where mobile data service is good, smartphones can be very useful. Indeed, your smartphone can act as a backup voice recorder in case your primary recorded fails. However, in developing countries or rural parts of developed countries, a smartphone may not be the best choice:

- Its 3G or 4G functions may not work reliably in some areas.
- Smartphones tend to be more expensive, increasing the financial risk if lost or damaged.
- The battery life is usually shorter on smartphones than on more basic devices.

If you are travelling in a foreign country to conduct your research, it is a good idea to acquire an additional cheap mobile phone that is 'unlocked' and not tied to any mobile phone carrier so that you can use foreign SIM cards and you have a backup phone.

4●4 CONCLUSION

In this chapter we have helped you identify and mitigate risks to your emotional well-being, health and property. We have advised thorough preparation before going into the field rather than relying on coming up with solutions once you get there. Knowing in advance what risks you are likely to face – by consulting reviews of equipment and travel destinations, and asking how experienced researchers, travellers and locals handle the risks – means you know how to identify, avoid and respond to problems if they occur.

We discussed how to identify and reduce the risks from participants' emotional responses. We also evaluated risks to your well-being that can arise if you have to deal with highly emotive research content, or if you are working in a stressful situation. We identified strategies that can help you maintain emotional balance while conducting your research. By following these steps you can identify and navigate emotional issues inherent in all research. From the basic stress and worry all researchers feel, to more challenging situations, the approaches discussed in this chapter will give you the best possible chance of arriving at positive outcomes for your research and your own mental and physical well-being.

━━ SUGGESTIONS FOR FURTHER READING ━━

- **Gov.uk (2015)** *Foreign travel advice.* Available at: http://www.gov.uk/foreign-travel-advice. The British Foreign and Commonwealth Office provides up-to-date information and advice on all foreign countries in the world at this address. You can search for the country you are due to travel to and access a wealth of advice, including maps, safety advice, terrorism status, local laws and customs, currency, and natural disasters. This is also where you can see if the FCO advises against travel to a country at a particular time.

- **Duncombe, J., & Jessop, J. (2012). 'Doing rapport' and the ethics of 'faking friendship'. In T. Miller, M. Birch, M. Mauthner & J. Jessop (Eds.),** *Ethics in qualitative research* **(2nd ed., pp. 108-122). London: Sage.** This article discusses an ethical issue often neglected by qualitative research literature. The authors discuss the dilemmas they faced when trying to interview vulnerable or reluctant participants. The dilemma concerns the professional need to gain information versus the human act of striking up 'rapport' and friendship. The dilemma occurs as the authors construct rapport as a tool to initiate information exchange, rather than genuine friendship – thus, an ethical dilemma arises as the participants are 'tricked with kindness' into revealing information.

- **Gurney, J. N. (1985). Not one of the guys: The female researcher in a male-dominated setting.** *Qualitative Sociology, 8*(1), 42-62. Although written 30 years ago, this article remains a relevant piece on gendered research interactions. Gurney discusses how status characteristics (gender, age, social class, etc.) affect women's ability to gain access to a community and maintain a relationship with those they wish to study. The article discusses the dilemmas faced by female researchers in male-dominated settings and argues that sound advice on this issue has historically been lacking, save from listening to the experiences of other female researchers in the field.

- **Lee, R. M. (1993).** *Doing research on sensitive topics.* **London: Sage.** Although this book is somewhat dated, it is worth reading Chapter 8 for content on how to manage research interactions with hostile and challenging participants.

- **Liamputtong, P. (2007).** *Researching the vulnerable: A guide to sensitive research methods.* **London: Sage.** Chapter 4 investigates the impact on the researcher from emotional experiences and ways to safeguard the vulnerable researcher.

- **Lumsden, K. (2014).** *Use of Ethnography as a Method in the Context of Adopting a Reflexive Approach: A Study of Boy Racer Culture.* **SAGE Research Methods Cases. London: Sage.** This is a useful real world example of a female researcher conducting fieldwork in a male-dominated setting. The researcher adopts a reflexive approach to ethnography and, as such, discusses in detail her experience of gendered interactions in a male-dominated community. Lumsden discusses unwanted sexual attention and sexist treatment in her project.

- **Fielding, N. (2004). Working in hostile environments. In C. Seale, G. Gobo, J. F. Gubrium & D. Silverman (Eds.),** *Qualitative research practice* **(pp. 248-260). London: Sage.** Fielding draws on his own research experiences with US communes and the National Front (a British far-right extremist group) to highlight some of the working practices and personal justifications of people who research in hostile environments. As well as being a personal account, Fielding offers a great deal of advice on how to protect your welfare as a researcher in such an environment.

- **Silverman, D. (2013).** *Doing qualitative research: A practical handbook* **(4th ed.). London: Sage.** Chapter 17 provides insights on impression management and relationships with participants that will be useful for a range of qualitative data collection scenarios.
- **Social Research Association (n.d.).** *A code of practice for the safety of social researchers.* Available online at: http://the-sra.org.uk/sra_resources/safety-code/. The SRA's code takes a particular focus on staying safe when you're working in private or unfamiliar settings and covers five main areas to avoid: physical threats or abuse; psychological trauma; compromising situations; causing harm to others; and increased exposure to every day risks, such as accidents and infections. While this sounds quite serious, the SRA's main aim is to minimize any anxieties you may have that could negatively affect your research.
- **Research Ethics Guidebook (2015).** *Assessing risk and harm.* Retrieved 18 July 2015, from http://ethicsguidebook.ac.uk/Assessing-risk-and-harm-21. This resource has a lot of good information on how to approach risk assessment prior to conducting any fieldwork. The links at the bottom of the page take you through to discussions on 'what is harm?', 'risks to researchers' and 'how to assess harm to researchers'.
- **US Department of State. (2015).** *U.S. passports and International travel: Learn about your destination* **[Online].** Available at: http://travel.state.gov/content/passports/english/country.html. This is the US Department of State's website advising on travel to all foreign countries. You can search for the country you are intending to travel to and the site will advise you on many things, including: visa requirements, vaccinations, local laws, health, and travel information. Any messages advising against travel, or warning of specific dangers are displayed at the top of each country's information page.

Visit the companion website at **https://study.sagepub.com/jensenandlaurie** to gain access to a wide range of online resources to support your learning, including editable research documents, weblinks, free access SAGE journal articles and book chapters, and flashcards.

■ GLOSSARY ■

Buffer questions – These can be used to reset the (calm) tone of the interview if the conversation becomes heated, as a result of the participant becoming defensive or offended. Buffer questions should be on non-threatening topics so that the participant can answer confidently, and they should be on issues that the participants enjoys speaking about.

Distancing strategy – This is a tactic to aid the asking of difficult or controversial questions. By phrasing the question in a way that ensures the respondent doesn't think that *you* are judging them, you can avoid some tricky situations. For example, saying 'it is thought that' rather than asking someone directly about something could avoid this situation.

Emotional well-being – This refers to your state of mind, which can be affected by emotionally challenging research situations. For instance, you may find your participants' personal accounts to be distressing, upsetting or disturbing – all of which might negatively affect your emotional state.

Fieldwork – This is conducting research 'in the real world'; you are in a certain community as opposed to conducting desk research.

Neutral phrasing – This is important, especially when discussing sensitive topics with your participants. This involves using non-judgemental language and ensuring that your questioning or comments do not offend your participants. An offended participant is unlikely to be willing to continue the conversation or give meaningful answers!

Pilot study – This is a small, preliminary project, designed to minimize the risk of encountering negative outcomes in your main research project. Pilot studies are a good way of practising before you commence your project in its entirety; they can be seen as a 'trial run'.

Preferred phrasing/terms – This is the language that your participants like to use about themselves. Before you start your research you should consult with gatekeepers or your participants themselves about which words they like to use. Asking such questions would be advisable when, for example, conducting research with transgender participants, who may well have a preference as to which personal pronouns ('he' or 'she') you use.

Risks to the researcher – These can be either avoidable or unforeseen events that can pose a problem, or cause harm to you throughout the course of your research. Such events can cause emotional harm, endanger your personal safety or damage your personal property.

Stigma – Some lifestyles, habits or communities are stigmatized or have a history of stigmatization by society. This is when something is seen as socially undesirable by 'the mainstream', and often such people or habits are avoided, looked down on, or cast out entirely. For example, being gay or lesbian has historically carried a social stigma.

Stress – On occasion, research can cause you stress if it is emotionally or psychologically challenging. This can also have a detrimental effect on your research, in three ways: it can distort your research perspective; it can lead you to believe that upsetting incidents are more widespread than they are; and it could make you identify too closely with your participants.

▬ REFERENCES ▬

CSEW (2012). Crime survey of England and Wales (CSEW). Retrieved 28 February 2013, from http://bit.ly/1Eyaq1h

Duncombe, J., & Jessop, J. (2012). 'Doing rapport' and the ethics of 'faking friendship'. In T. Miller, M. Birch, M. Mauthner & J. Jessop (Eds.), *Ethics in qualitative research* (2nd ed., pp. 108–122). London: Sage.

Gurney, J. N. (1985). Not one of the guys: The female researcher in a male-dominated setting. *Qualitative Sociology, 8*(1), 42–62.

Lumsden, K. (2014). *Use of Ethnography as a Method in the Context of Adopting a Reflexive Approach: A Study of Boy Racer Culture.* SAGE Research Methods Cases. London: Sage.

Research Ethics Guidebook (2015a). *Assessing risk and harm.* Retrieved 18 July 2015, from http://ethicsguidebook.ac.uk/Assessing-risk-and-harm-21

Research Ethics Guidebook (2015b). *Permission and approval.* Retrieved 1 August 2015, from http://www.ethicsguidebook.ac.uk/Permission-and-approval-Key-questions-79

Research Ethics Guidebook (2015c). *Risks to researchers.* Retrieved 1 August 2015, from http://ethicsguidebook.ac.uk/Risks-to-researchers-68

HOW TO FIND A REPRESENTATIVE SAMPLE

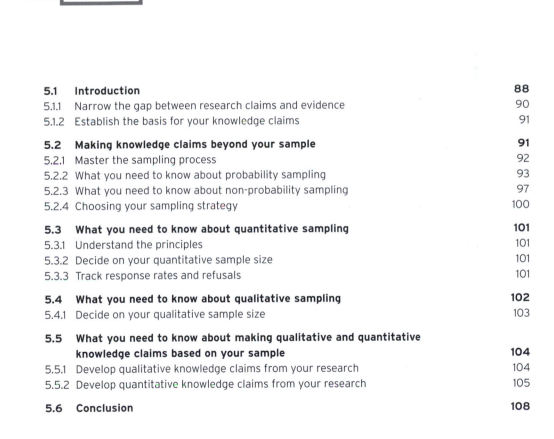

5 ● 1 INTRODUCTION

Social researchers face a central challenge: how can you develop reliable knowledge about a group without studying all its members? In this chapter, we discuss how you can make new knowledge claims through social research. We explain 'sampling' and 'generalizability' in this context. We outline tried and tested techniques and strategies used to select participants. Along the way, we give special attention to the practical steps you should take to develop robust knowledge claims.

As you learned in previous chapters, the **population** is the group of people that your research is designed to generate knowledge about. If the population you're investigating is small – such as all the students in a class – then it may be feasible to study all members of the population. Such a 100 per cent coverage of the population is known as a 'census'. Most populations, however, are too large to gather data from all members. You can instead select a subset of the population to study, which is called a **sample**.

Qualitative and quantitative research paradigms use samples to make knowledge claims about larger populations. In quantitative research, the goal is to make accurate **generalizations** about a population's characteristics. You may use sampling to address quantitative questions such as 'Do more people hold view X or view Y?' or 'Has the proportion of people holding view X changed over time?' Qualitative research uses sampling to address questions such as 'What is the range of views being expressed by a group of people?' or 'How do people come to hold certain views or feelings about a topic?'

This chapter spells out the practical implications of these distinct paradigms for sampling and making research claims. In sum, this chapter engages with a fundamental challenge of social research: on what basis can you claim to know something about people, organizations or society? To do this, we address the more specific question: if you only talk to a few people for your research, how can you say anything about the broader population?

 **REAL WORLD EXAMPLE**

Sampling children's attitudes towards smoking

Catherine was interested in attitudes about smoking among school pupils aged 11–13 in Birmingham, the UK's second largest city. It would be impractical to get every student in this age range to fill in a questionnaire about their attitudes to smoking, so Catherine decided she would use a sample. Catherine randomly selected 10 schools in Birmingham to sample. She then used the school registers to randomly select 30 students per school from appropriate year groups. This resulted in a sample of 300 teenagers, a more manageable population size for her project.

The fact that everyone in her target population had an equal probability of selection allowed Catherine to generalize the results of her survey to make claims about levels of pro- and anti-smoking attitudes among the thousands of pupils aged 11–13 in Birmingham schools.

When you draw conclusions about a population as a whole based on the results obtained from studying a sample, you are engaging in generalization. When thinking about how to make legitimate new knowledge claims based on your research, you should first consider some basic principles of generalization in social research:

- **Look for patterns**. Sometimes you may encounter a situation, participant perspective or behaviour that appears to be irrational or hard to understand. Your first step is to approach the topic systematically with the aim of identifying any patterns that might explain what is going on.

  In qualitative research, what is often most important are the processes underpinning a situation, viewpoint or action. For example, if your research focuses on alcohol abuse by single mothers, you may find that cyclical processes involving abusive relationships are underpinning the issue. In quantitative research, the connections between different variables within your sample will often be a primary focus. For example, alcohol consumption may be linked to number of hours worked per week, gender or other variables.

- **Look for deviant cases**. When doing any type of research, it is completely normal to encounter exceptions to the norm. How you work with deviant cases depends on whether you are conducting quantitative or qualitative research.

  Qualitative researchers tend to be more prepared to keep 'deviant cases' in the picture (see Chapter 11). In contrast, quantitative researchers are typically focused on generalizing about the 'typical' pattern or the most common outcomes. They usually exclude from their analysis any cases that vary significantly from the norm (see Chapter 12).

- **Beware of the ecological fallacy**. There is a natural human tendency to presume that trends at the group level apply at the level of the individual. For example, we may make the mistake of thinking that because men on average earn higher salaries than women, an individual man will always earn more than an individual woman. This logical fallacy can lure even experienced researchers into making inaccurate research claims.

- **Understand the types of new knowledge claims**. You can generally make two types of knowledge claims in social research. First, you can make new knowledge claims based on the evidence you have collected (i.e., your research claims). Second, you can make larger claims about the way your new evidence fits into the broader picture of existing research and knowledge (i.e., the implications of your research).

- **Your research claims need to be narrow and specific**. You can use relatively strong phrasing when discussing these claims (e.g., 'these data show …'), but their scope is limited by the data you have actually collected. The possible implications you identify can be much broader. This is because the implications of your research are based on the total picture of available evidence, not just the data you collected. However, implications are generally more speculative, and should usually be tentatively phrased (e.g., 'one possible implication of this finding is …').

- **Make the most of critical review**. You were introduced to the concept of peer review in Chapter 2. Many of the same principles apply as well to the development of your own research and sampling strategies. Seeking critical feedback from more experienced researchers will help you feel assured that your reasoning is as solid as possible. Such feedback can reveal hidden assumptions and gaps that might otherwise go unnoticed.

At this point, it's also worth acknowledging that gathering an appropriate sample is a particularly difficult real world challenge. Your sample will almost certainly fall short of the ideal in some way (as this is true of the largest and most well-funded research projects). This is fine, as long as you understand and acknowledge how this affects your analysis and limits the kinds of knowledge claims you can make based on your research.

5•1•1 NARROW THE GAP BETWEEN RESEARCH CLAIMS AND EVIDENCE

When starting your research project, you face a gap between what you'd like to know and what the available data can tell you. Given constraints such as your available time, resources and skills, you will rarely be able to access data that perfectly answer your research question. Even if everything in your research project goes perfectly, there will always be a degree of uncertainty when deciding what your research data mean. Therefore, having some level of humility and restraint when making research claims based on your data is always wise. You should never see good academic social researchers claiming to have 'proved' something or discovered a universal law of human behaviour.

Acknowledging the limits of your research does not make it less valuable. The social world is messy, complicated and constantly changing. Therefore, making relatively restrained knowledge claims based on the best available evidence is what social scientists do. Indeed, such knowledge claims can be highly accurate. For instance, in 2012, the political scientist Simon Jackman used a detailed study of public opinion polls to predict the result of the US presidential election. Even though people can change their minds at any time, these polls, based on **representative** sampling, proved to be very accurate. Using these data, Jackman correctly predicted the presidential election results in every US state.

Although you can never claim to have perfect knowledge about a social phenomenon, you can narrow the gap between your available evidence and your research claims in several ways:

1 **Reduce the scope** of your research so that you aren't trying to make sweeping knowledge claims that you won't be able to adequately support with your research evidence.
2 **Use representative sampling and acknowledge any limitations**. By following clearly defined sampling procedures, you will reduce the risk of having an unrepresentative sample that can lead you to make misleading knowledge claims.
3 **Use existing knowledge** (from your literature review; see Chapter 2) to narrow the range of possible interpretations of your data. It is important that you build on the good-quality research work that has already been done on your topic.

While these steps help to narrow the gap between your evidence and your knowledge claims, your main bridge across this gap will be **inference** – the logical process of drawing general conclusions from available evidence. You rely on inference throughout the research process, including when you get to the stage of making knowledge claims at the end of your project. The important point is that you must constantly work to recognize your biases and be as rigorous as possible when making sense of the evidence available to you.

5•1•2 ESTABLISH THE BASIS FOR YOUR KNOWLEDGE CLAIMS

When publishing or presenting your research results, you must always include a section describing your research methods. This section allows your readers to independently assess the validity of the claims you make, and to identify any flaws in your research design that might undermine your conclusions. The methods section, along with your literature review, serves as the justification for all knowledge claims made within your results section. In it, you should explain the following:

1 Why you opted for a particular sampling strategy and who you collected data from.
2 How you gathered your data.
3 How you identified and measured the variables you investigated.
4 How you analysed the data.

Readers can then use this information to understand your decision-making and judge the credibility of your knowledge claims.

5●2 MAKING KNOWLEDGE CLAIMS BEYOND YOUR SAMPLE

Social research is generally motivated by a desire to know something about a group of people: your population of interest. For example, in a recent study, Eric and his co-authors wanted to survey people visiting zoos and aquariums around the world to understand their views about biodiversity – a scientific concept encompassing all plant and animal life (Moss, Jensen, & Gusset, 2015). As discussed previously, however, it is rarely possible to collect data from everyone in the population you're studying. In order to develop knowledge that applies beyond your research participants, sampling is required. In Eric's zoo survey, the sample was drawn from about 6000 visitors attending 32 zoos and aquariums that were members of the World Association of Zoos and Aquariums (WAZA).

Sampling is based on the principle that you can use data collected from a smaller number of individuals to represent the larger group from which they were drawn. A 'representative sample', then, is one whose characteristics closely match those of the population from which it is drawn. In the zoo survey example, Eric's sample of about 6000 people at 32 zoos and aquariums were standing in for millions of visitors to thousands of zoos and aquariums around the world. Therefore, Eric and his co-authors had to address the question of whether their sample is likely to be representative.

Accurate generalization from a quantitative research perspective requires a precisely defined population, from which a representative sample can be drawn. Henn, Weinstein, and Foard (2013, p. 335) note that for a sample to be fully representative, it needs to be 'theoretically possible to select any member of the population for inclusion in the research ..., although practical limitations, such as access ... may make this impossible'. In the case of Eric's zoo survey, all zoos and aquariums that are not members of WAZA were excluded, raising immediate questions about representativeness. The practical limits on who you can sample have to be taken into account when you're defining the boundaries of your population. In this case, Eric did not have a big grant to support this research, which meant he had to rely on participation from zoos and aquariums that were willing to put their resources into administering the survey data collection. This further biased his sample of zoos and aquariums, as smaller institutions with fewer resources would be less likely to participate.

Many qualitative researchers also have an interest in making generalized knowledge claims that extend beyond their participants. However, qualitative research tends not to focus on having a statistically representative sample, but rather on having a diverse sample that shows a range of perspectives from within the population. A qualitative researcher may observe processes and patterns within a small group of individuals, and then build a working theoretical model based on these observations. This working model is then tested against additional observations, adding to and refining the model based on new information. Thus, qualitative research can be used to build theoretical models that explain behaviour in general. For example, Tracy and Tracy (1998) analysed problematic interactions during emergency phone calls for police assistance. These calls were problematic in the sense that they ended in either the emergency operator or the person who originally called for help putting the phone down in anger or frustration. In this qualitative study, patterns of miscommunication are identified within this particular, rather extreme, context. However, by discussing the implications of miscommunication patterns, they were able to show that they are indicative of general flaws affecting human communication, which lead to mutual misunderstanding.

While many qualitative researchers aim to generalize their research findings beyond the confines of their sample, some reject this approach. Somekh and Lewin (2011, p. 323) warn that the concept of generalization 'is regarded as highly problematic by many social science researchers who argue that knowledge is always context-dependent'. Indeed, some researchers argue that generalization beyond the context in which the research was conducted is not legitimate. These researchers question whether we can directly measure any phenomenon using either qualitative or quantitative methods, given that our research participants are thinking, self-aware beings who inevitably adapt their responses based on how and in what context they are approached. Researchers who follow this way of thinking emphasize 'thick description' (i.e., lots of descriptive detail both of the interesting and the seemingly mundane) of the setting, the context of the research and the participatory role of the researcher. Good qualitative research in this tradition aims to enlighten the reader with thorough explanations of the particular situation and participants.

5•2•1 MASTER THE SAMPLING PROCESS

The first step of the sampling process is identifying and defining the population you're interested in, such as students in your university, teachers at a nearby school who smoke regularly, men who work night-shifts at a local factory, etc. The next step is to decide the most appropriate sampling method based on the details of your target population. You can choose from a range of different techniques for acquiring your sample. These are grouped together as probability sampling techniques and non-probability sampling techniques. Every technique has its own benefits and limitations, which are discussed in detail below.

5•2•2 WHAT YOU NEED TO KNOW ABOUT PROBABILITY SAMPLING

Probability sampling techniques are designed to ensure that in principle any of the individuals in your target population may be selected to be part of your sample. Generally, this includes some form of random selection, which helps to ensure the sample is statistically representative. This kind of sampling is considered the strongest for quantitative research, and helps to avoid the major sources of sampling bias that can skew your sample. Qualitative researchers seldom use probability sampling. There are several different kinds of probability sampling, described below and summarized in Table 5.1.

WHEN TO USE SIMPLE RANDOM SAMPLING

Simple random sampling is conceptually the simplest form of probability sampling. It involves using a process where members of your population are selected completely at random for inclusion in the sample, ensuring that everyone has the same chance of being selected.

Imagine you want to investigate the attitudes of audience members towards a music concert they attended. There are 10,000 people in the audience, but you only have the resources to survey some of them. One way to obtain a representative sample would be to give each audience member a raffle ticket when they enter. At the end of the performance, you draw 50 raffle tickets from a hat, and the people with those tickets are the ones selected for your sample. Because the individuals were randomly selected, and because all members of the population had an equal probability of being selected, you could characterize this as a simple random sample.

This sampling technique requires little or no information about your population's characteristics and is easily the most robust form of sampling. This form of sampling can be performed with computer programs (like the website http://random.org) and can be very affordable for sampling some populations. However, the costs associated with simple random sampling can become prohibitive if you have a geographically dispersed population. If you were to randomly select households in America for an in-person survey, for example, the distribution of the sample would be so large as to make collecting the data almost impossible. This is one of the reasons why simple random sampling is often used in conjunction with other techniques.

It's worth acknowledging the practical limits of this approach. In order for a sample to be truly random, every member of your population must have an equal chance of selection, which means you must be able to access everyone in your population. In the example above, where you were sampling from audience members, this is relatively easy because the audience members are all in one place. It becomes considerably harder as the population size increases and the accessibility of your population decreases. Therefore, in practice you will at best be working with a 'nearly random' sample, which will have limitations you acknowledge when reporting your results.

WHEN TO USE STRATIFIED RANDOM SAMPLING

While it avoids sampling bias, simple random sampling also leaves the demographic distribution of your sample completely up to chance. For statistical reasons, you may need a minimum number of people in particular categories. One technique that can address this

Table 5.1 Types of probability sampling

	Pros	Cons
Simple random sampling *A process where members of a population are chosen using a random number generator to ensure all members of the population have an equal chance of being selected*	• Reduces the risk of sampling bias. • Since all members of the population have an equal chance of selection, it is easily the most robust form of sampling • Requires little or no advanced information about your population's characteristics. • Can be affordable for easily accessible populations (e.g., visitors to a museum or students at a particular university).	• Often difficult in practice to achieve a purely random sample. • Can be prohibitively expensive for dispersed populations, such as with nation-wide samples if you want to collect data face-to-face. • A purely random sample may not yield enough respondents in particular categories of interest for your statistical analysis (e.g., minority ethnic groups), as this method does not require a minimum number of people in certain categories.
Stratified random sampling *Divides the sampling frame into categories relevant to your analysis (e.g. ethnic categories). You then apply random sampling within those categories*	• More targeted than simple random sampling because you can require a minimum number of people in certain categories. This ensures you don't end up with a dataset that is too small in any one category for statistical analysis that uses that category. • Useful when comparing attitudes of particular groups is your primary motivation in the research (e.g., men and women). • Can be used to compare groups of different sizes because you can specify the number of respondents required in each category (e.g., you can require equal numbers of people from each ethnic category). • Can deliver what is widely regarded as a probability sample.	• May still be relatively expensive to undertake, for the same reasons as simple random sampling. • Requires more knowledge about the population than simple random sampling to determine the characteristics to select. • Choice of variables to use to stratify the sample may be complicated if the research has numerous important variables.
Cluster sampling *Random sampling of a geographical cluster, often divided along pre-existing lines (e.g., electoral district boundaries)*	• Enables face-to-face probability sampling when you don't already have contact details for your potential respondents. • If structured effectively, cluster sampling brings many of the same strengths as simple random sampling.	• Can be complicated to do. • Can be prohibitively expensive for populations spread over large geographical areas.
Multistage sampling *A combination of different sampling techniques*	• Enables you to address the constraints and analysis requirements of your particular project.	• Complex to define and implement. • Probably not a good choice for novice researchers.
Systematic sampling *Method that relies on 'selection rules', but not random selection.*	• Easy to implement, or to ask others to do when collecting data. • Can be more efficient and easier to implement in real-world situations than any form of random sampling. • Avoids risk of researcher inadvertently causing selection bias. • Widely considered good enough to treat data as if they were from a probability sample.	• Does not employ truly 'random' selection. • It is possible that selecting, for example, every 15th person systematically excludes certain people. For example, if used at a museum entrance, this system would almost guarantee that you would not get more than one person per family in your sample.

issue, stratified random sampling, involves dividing the population you are researching into exclusive subgroups, or strata. This can be along the lines of age, gender, country of origin, ethnicity or any other important characteristic. You can then gather part of your sample from each of these subgroups, usually by selecting an equal number of people from each category.

This sampling technique is useful if you are looking to compare the attitudes of particular subgroups (e.g., men to women), by ensuring those groups are represented in sufficient numbers within your sample. Under these circumstances, stratified random sampling is similar to, and in some cases superior to, simple random sampling, in that all members of the population retain a relatively equal probability of selection.

Stratified random sampling is also useful if you are trying to compare subgroups with drastically different sizes. In the 10,000-person concert audience example, you may be interested in knowing whether 16–24-year-olds (attending on discounted 'young person' tickets) enjoyed the concert as much as individuals aged 25 and over. If there are only, say, 130 people under the age of 25 in the audience, then a representative sample of 200 audience members may only yield 30 or 40 young adults. This is not a large enough group to make robust statistical comparisons with the rest of the audience population. By oversampling this demographic category (e.g., selecting 100 from this group and 100 from the rest of the audience) using stratified random sampling, you could ensure you have enough 16–24-year-olds to perform a statistical analysis with age category as the explanatory variable. This approach would yield a sample that is no longer truly random at the concert audience population level, as 16–24-year-olds have a higher probability of selection than all others do. However, the application of random sampling within each subgroup maintains the overall quality of the sample.

As you might have guessed, stratified random sampling requires significantly more information about your population and is much more complicated to perform than simple random sampling. If you want to produce a representative sample stratified by gender, then you first have to know the number of males and females in your population. The same is true of any other variable by which you may want to stratify your population for sampling.

WHEN TO USE CLUSTER SAMPLING

Cluster sampling is useful when your population is dispersed across a large geographical area and it would be expensive and time-consuming to travel to survey them. Taking a simple random sample of voters in a US Senate election in Texas, for example, would result in potential participants scattered over hundreds of miles. In order to reduce the costs associated with surveying far-flung participants, you can divide the population into geographical groups, or clusters. Often this is based on pre-existing boundaries, like counties, cities or electoral districts. Then, rather than selecting individuals – like in simple random sampling – you randomly select clusters. In basic cluster sampling, your sample consists of everyone in the cluster(s) you selected. If the clusters are proportionate in size (or weighted), then this method is similar to simple random sampling, in that all members of the population have a roughly equal probability of being selected. This technique can also be used to gather a representative sample when you have a large group of people in a space, such as protesters in a square or festival-goers. The physical space can be divided into imaginary grids of, for example, 1 square metre, which are randomly selected for sampling (i.e., this is where you go to collect data).

Using an online survey organization to conduct your quantitative sampling

If your study requires a sample that is representative of the population, geographically dispersed, or even just large, you may find it challenging to actually collect your sample in the time and with the resources you have available. Traditionally, it would have been incredibly expensive to rely on a professional organization to conduct your sampling for you. Depending on a number of factors – what kind of sampling you want, the interview medium (e.g., phone, mail, in-person), the time required from each participant, etc. – a survey company could charge anywhere from $5000 to $750,000 to conduct a quantitative survey study.

However, companies offering online sampling options have sparked a major shift in research sampling options over the last decade. These organizations usually have a large pool of respondents who are paid to be survey and experiment participants, with costs of roughly one-tenth of those of traditional samples. While there are trade-offs (especially for generalizability) these companies offer great, low-cost resources for studies requiring large sample sizes and/or samples from specific population categories. We've listed some of the major players in this domain below, (roughly) what you can expect to pay per respondent and some pros and cons for each service.

Organization/ Website	Median cost per participant (short survey; general population)	Pros and cons
Qualtrics http://www. qualtrics.com	$4.00–$5.00 per completion	Can be very narrowly targeted to a specific sub-population Largest flexibility in survey/experiment design Can be easily paired with other sampling options, including the creation of your own panel of respondents Often more expensive than other options Relies on other organizations to provide them with respondents

WHEN TO USE MULTISTAGE SAMPLING As you may have gathered by this point, these sampling techniques are not mutually exclusive. It is common, especially in large-scale surveys, to use a combination of techniques. For example, you could first randomly select clusters (to cut down on cost by limiting the geographic disbursement of your sample), then stratify the individuals in those clusters (to ensure your sample is representative), and then randomly select participants from the stratified groupings (to avoid sampling bias). This would be referred to as multistage stratified cluster sampling. In the example above, two stages are represented in the sampling structure (randomly selected clusters, and then random selection from strata).

WHEN TO USE SYSTEMATIC SAMPLING All the probability sampling techniques discussed so far have used some form of 'random' selection. Occasionally, however, you will find that it's just not practical or possible to use a truly random sampling method. In such instances, you can turn to systematic sampling, which uses 'selection rules' to mimic the objectivity of random selection. Often, the selection rule is as simple as picking every *x*th person to meet some criteria (like entering a room). While this approach is not as good as strict random sampling, it can come relatively close to producing a random sample. Moreover, it has the major virtue of avoiding the risk of the researcher introducing selection bias.

REAL WORLD EXAMPLE

Systematic sampling using the 'continual ask' method

When Javier conducted survey research with public visitors entering the Metropolitan Museum of Art in New York, he found that there were too many people flooding into this popular museum to be able to employ strict random sampling. He decided that the next best approach was to use systematic sampling, and establish a selection rule. He would select an imaginary line near where he was standing and approach the first person to cross it. Once this person either declined to participate or finished the questionnaire, he returned to his original position and focused again on the same imaginary line. This approach to systematic sampling within crowded, chaotic spaces is known as a 'continual ask' method. Its main virtue is in avoiding the introduction of research bias in selecting participants.

5•2•3 WHAT YOU NEED TO KNOW ABOUT NON-PROBABILITY SAMPLING

Non-probability sampling techniques (see Table 5.2) are defined by the fact that they don't meet the standard of equal probability of selection for all members of your target population. It's possible to obtain a representative sample using non-probability sampling, but there is no guarantee, nor is there any way to measure the statistical probability that the sample is representative. Non-probability sampling techniques are generally much cheaper and easier than probability sampling, but should be used with caution. The fact that you don't know if your sample is representative of the population means that you can't use the most powerful inferential statistics to generalize from your sample to the population as a whole (although there are alternative statistics you can use). Your knowledge claims may therefore need to be more tentative if you are describing the characteristics of the population using your sample data.

CONVENIENCE SAMPLING

Convenience sampling is a technique that selects the members of a population who are the easiest for the researcher to access. Psychology experiments in universities, for instance, will often recruit among students in psychology classes, as these are the easiest participants to gather. Convenience sampling can involve surveying your family or people you stop on the street, your Facebook friends, or anyone else who is easy to access. This sampling technique is very cheap, requires minimal effort, but has obvious drawbacks. It is usually unlikely that the people sampled through this method are representative of a wider population. If you stop people in the street to ask about their opinion on, say, proposed urban redevelopment, you may simply gather a representative sample of people in your neighbourhood with time to kill. That said, because convenience sampling is so inexpensive, it can be an effective way to test survey questions, or conduct other preliminary pilot-testing activities.

Table 5.2 Types of non-probability sampling

	Pros	Cons
Convenience sampling *Where you select the members of a population that are easiest to access (e.g., friends, classmates)*	• Often the lowest-cost option. • Easy to do: as it says in the name, it's convenient! • Useful for getting initial ideas, such as for a pilot study.	• Major risk that your sample is not representative of your target population. • Results probably cannot be used to draw accurate inferences about the population.
Quota sampling *Selecting a convenience sample but within the bounds of predetermined quotas (e.g., 50% men, 50% women)*	• Only a little harder to do than convenience sampling. • Quotas ensure that you have enough people from different categories relevant to your research in your sample.	• Unlikely to produce a more representative sample than convenience sampling, which means you still have a major risk of sampling bias.
Snowball sampling *Technique where participants in your research or 'gatekeepers' are used to find new participants*	• A useful means of locating participants among stigmatized or otherwise hard-to-access groups (e.g., commercial sex workers and intravenous drug users). • Helps establish some trust and credibility that can help you gain participation in your research. • This option can be the only feasible option sometimes, which makes it your best means of conducting research with hard-to-access groups.	• Major risk your sample won't be representative of your target population. • Can mean that your participants all have similar perspectives or characteristics because people are likely to know and recommend other participants who are like them.
Purposive/theoretical sampling *Uses the researcher's judgement to select participants who will offer valuable insights*	• Can gain insights that are useful for developing theoretical explanations by targeting specific individuals or groups within a population. • Researcher can exercise explicit judgement in identifying who would be most interesting to include in the sample, thus the sampling process benefits from the knowledge and experience of the researcher.	• The participants are unlikely to represent the broader target population. • The researcher's judgement may inadvertently skew the selection of participants, and therefore the data, in ways that are not fully acknowledged.

QUOTA SAMPLING

Quota sampling is the selection of a sample according to a predetermined quota (or number) on a non-random basis. Quota sampling is often compared with stratified random sampling, because both control the sample based upon variables of interest. They differ in cost (quota samples are much less expensive), and in their abilities to accurately represent the population of interest: stratified random sampling is able to deliver a probability sample while quota sampling is not.

There are two ways to use quotas: proportionally and non-proportionally. Proportional quota sampling involves selecting participants for your sample in proportion to some characteristic of the population as a whole. For example, if 10 per cent of the population you are interested in have no educational qualifications and your sample size is 100 people, then you would sample no more than 10 people without qualifications. Once you have reached this quota, you would stop sampling this category of participant. This method allows you to generate a sample that is on the surface reflective of the distribution of some characteristic across the population (e.g., 51 per cent female, 49 per cent male). However, there is no way to ensure that the sample is representative of the population. For example, while you may use quotas for gender, age and education, there are no further controls beyond these demographic categories. Thus, the particular individuals selected may be highly unrepresentative of the broader demographic category they have been selected to represent.

SNOWBALL SAMPLING

Snowball sampling is a technique where participants in your research are used to find additional participants. It relies on discovering what Henn et al. (2013, p. 337) describe as a 'strategically important contact'. This contact introduces you to other contacts that fit the characteristics of your population. This is particularly useful for 'selecting cases where no obvious lists of [relevant] cases exists'. As Hennink, Hutter and Bailey (2011, p. 100) point out, the technique is 'particularly suitable for identifying study participants with very specific characteristics, rare experiences or "hidden" population groups who may be difficult to identify with other recruitment methods', such as intravenous drug users or commercial sex workers. While this technique almost guarantees your sample won't be representative, it's used when there may be no other way to access your population other than through personal introductions.

REAL WORLD EXAMPLE

Snowball sampling mineworkers

When researching a project on the experiences of Norwegian oil workers who had worked abroad, Ellen initially found it hard to gather a sample of the population. There was no central record system such as a census, electoral register or health records from which to generate a sample. Scouring the internet for retired oil workers who had written about their own experiences provided only a small number of contacts.

(Continued)

(Continued)

Using snowball sampling, Ellen's participant pool mushroomed from this initial set of contacts. From the first few interviews, it became clear that these oil workers had formed a tightly knit group who had kept in touch with each other as they moved around the world. This meant that each participant knew a large number of other former oil workers. Thus, Ellen soon had several hundred people expressing interest in participating in the research.

PURPOSIVE/THEORETICAL SAMPLING

Purposive or theoretical sampling uses the researcher's judgement to select participants who are likely to offer particularly valuable insights. This type of sampling is 'directed and re-cast by reflexive researchers towards the purpose of developing and testing theory into an intellectual puzzle about the social world' (Emmel, 2013, p. 46). To undertake purposive sampling you will to need to use 'special knowledge or expertise about some group to select subjects who represent this population' (Berg, 1995, p. 179). The selection process can be guided by earlier data collection within the project, prior research or theory, as well as the researcher's instincts. This technique may involve selecting for the extremes in a population, or selecting individuals to represent categories that are of interest.

 **REAL WORLD EXAMPLE**

Purposively sampling those affected by political violence

During Charles's qualitative research on political violence in Zimbabwe, he was looking for perspectives from a range of stakeholders across the political spectrum. Doing this kind of research posed major challenges in locating participants willing to take the risk of discussing contentious political issues with a researcher. For this reason, a probability sample would not have been feasible or appropriate.

Instead, Charles relied on purposive sampling so he could deliberately select specific participants to give insights into the range of perspectives on political violence in Zimbabwe. He sought out people who had initiated violence in order to understand their motivations, policy-makers to shed light on the objectives of politically motivated conflict and a range of different types of victims in order to assess the consequences of political violence for people in different positions in society. Within all of these groups he tried to gain as many different viewpoints as possible, for example by interviewing violence practitioners from the military, police and various militia groups.

By relying on purposive sampling Charles could seek out specific participants who were the most likely to have deep insights to offer based on a varied range of experiences and backgrounds relevant to his topic.

5•2•4 CHOOSING YOUR SAMPLING STRATEGY

To decide on the most appropriate sampling strategy for your project, you need to consider the following:

- The population you're interested in researching.
- The scope of claims you want to be able to make about this population.
- The time and resources you have available.

In the next sections, we discuss a practical approach to sampling in quantitative and qualitative research, issues of sample size and problems you might face. This will help you determine the sample size and sampling system you need to support the type and scope of research claims you want to make.

5 ● 3 WHAT YOU NEED TO KNOW ABOUT QUANTITATIVE SAMPLING

5●3●1 UNDERSTAND THE PRINCIPLES

Quantitative research involves applying inferential statistics to your sample in order to make generalizations about your population as a whole. Often, the goal is to describe your population's characteristics. To support quantitative knowledge claims, your sampling technique should be:

- **Robust.** It should be carried out in ways that are consistent, well justified and clearly spelled out in advance, as well as in the methods section of your research report.
- **Objective.** It should not be dictated by the personal views or pre-existing assumptions of the researcher.
- **Representative.** It should match as closely as possible the characteristics of the population most relevant to your study.

5●3●2 DECIDE ON YOUR QUANTITATIVE SAMPLE SIZE

Decisions about sample size affect your options later on when you conduct your statistical analysis. A larger sample size will increase the sensitivity of your analysis, making it easier to detect patterns that exist within the population. In addition, if you want to make fine-grained statistical comparisons between different subcategories within your data (e.g., comparing across ethnicities), you need to ensure you have at least 20 people in each category (preferably 40). For example, if you're studying patients' satisfaction with their doctors, you might want to analyse levels of satisfaction by the level of severity of a patient's health condition (e.g., minor, moderate or major injury). In this case, you would need to ensure you had at least 20 patients from each of these categories in your sample to allow you to make meaningful statistical comparisons. One thing to keep in mind when choosing a probability sample size is that the smaller your sample, the less likely your sample will reflect your population.

5●3●3 TRACK RESPONSE RATES AND REFUSALS

An important metric in quantitative survey research is the response rate: the percentage of those you invite to complete your surveys that actually do so. You determine the response rate by tracking 'refusals' when someone declines to participate in your survey for whatever reason. In order to determine whether there are obvious biases entering your sample at this stage, you should keep a 'refusals log' where you write down basic information such as:

- Date and time of refusal
- Apparent age of non-respondent
- Apparent gender of non-respondent
- Apparent ethnicity of non-respondent
- Explicit reasons given for the refusal
- Other possible reasons for the refusal.

Depending on your study, other categories may be relevant to include in the refusals log. For example, in research aimed at the public, noting the group size and composition (e.g., two young children) could prove beneficial. In other cases, the type of clothing (e.g., a suit and tie) worn by respondents and non-respondents may be a useful indicator of possible sampling bias. Tracking this refusal information enables you to answer questions about sampling bias in a robust manner. With online surveys, there may be fewer options for tracking refusals. If you have conducted a mixed online and face-to-face survey, you could run analyses to check to see if the online survey respondents' profile is significantly different from the face-to-face respondents' characteristics. You could also use website analysis software such as Google Analytics (http://www.google.com/analytics) to determine how many people, from which countries, etc. visited the survey website and then left without completing the survey.

5 ● 4 WHAT YOU NEED TO KNOW ABOUT QUALITATIVE SAMPLING

As you have read throughout this chapter, qualitative sampling involves different goals and standards than quantitative sampling. Qualitative samples are different from quantitative samples in several key ways. Qualitative samples tend to be:

- Smaller, as they involve more intensive data analysis.
- Selected purposively, rather than randomly.
- Less focused on statistical representativeness, and more on saturation (see below).

Qualitative research involves exploring patterns and processes across a relatively narrow range of cases, rather than the distribution of certain characteristics across a population. When formulating and undertaking a research project, 'qualitative researchers self-consciously draw on their own experiences as a resource in their inquiries', further seeking 'strategies of empirical inquiry that will allow them to make connections among lived experience, larger social and cultural structures, and the here and now' (Denzin & Lincoln, 2011, p. 243). Following this research approach does not require you to be able to accurately account for the prevalence of individuals' characteristics across the population. Indeed, good qualitative research can build up valid explanations that make no mention of the percentage of the population for whom those explanations apply.

Nevertheless, if you are doing a qualitative research project you do need to consider how representative your sample is. The characteristics of your target population can help inform your decision-making about which research participants to recruit for your study. For instance, a study on the effects of divorce on people's careers would be significantly skewed if your sample only contained men or people over the age of 50. You can choose to focus on particular categories of individuals like this, but you need to justify this selection and adjust your analysis and knowledge claims accordingly.

5•4•1 DECIDE ON YOUR QUALITATIVE SAMPLE SIZE

The short answer to the question of how many interviews, focus groups or qualitative observations you should conduct is rather unhelpful: 'it depends'. Patton (1990, p. 184) points out that 'there are no rules for sample size in qualitative inquiry. Sample size depends on what you want to know, the purpose of the inquiry, what's at stake, what will be useful, what will have credibility, and what can be done with available time and resources.'

Before you even start your data collection, qualitative research can require a significant time commitment. For example, it can take more than 10 hours to prepare for each interview. Then there is the amount of time necessary to contact participants and conduct the data collection. A one-hour interview recording, with good-quality audio and the same competent researcher conducting all the tasks, is likely to require about 24–30 hours to prepare the audio recording equipment, organize and conduct the interview, transcribe and analyse the interview, etc. As you can see, the time demands can quickly escalate if you don't limit your sample size. For example, if you only have 20 working days available for your project (assuming eight hours per day) for the analysis phase of your project, you would need to limit your sample to between five and seven hour-long interviews.

USE EMERGENCE, SATURATION AND REPRESENTATIVENESS TO GUIDE YOU THROUGH THE SAMPLING PROCESS

While keeping in mind the practical constraints of time and resources, it's important to stay flexible while conducting qualitative research. You must allow for both emergence and saturation. **Emergence** involves following interesting, often unanticipated lines of inquiry that come up during the qualitative data collection and analysis process. While this practice typically only leads to you asking additional or revised questions (a worthwhile outcome in and of itself), it can also indicate that you need to change your sampling strategy. For example, you may need to focus your interviews on a different set of participants than you had initially planned on.

A uniquely qualitative technique for deciding you can stop collecting data is called **saturation**. You've reached saturation once you reach the point where new cases in your data collection are no longer expanding or modifying the range or depth of relevant ideas that have already come up. Ideally, this saturation point dictates when you can stop collecting and analysing data. What makes this approach feasible in qualitative research is that data collection and analysis phases at least partially overlap.

Qualitative sampling methods don't offer the certainty of precise quantification of the probability that a sample is representative. However, it's far less important if you have under- or overrepresented an element of the population in a qualitative sample than in a quantitative sample. Indeed, as discussed above, you may legitimately target your qualitative sample for theoretical or other reasons. You will be on solid ground if you avoid making claims at the population level, and focus on developing detailed, contextualized knowledge about your participants and their circumstances. For further details on sampling in qualitative research, see Kuzel (1992).

REAL WORLD EXAMPLE

Sampling call centre workers

Hannah was seeking to understand the experiences of call centre workers in Scotland through a series of qualitative interviews with current and former call centre employees. The management of the call centres she focused on were not interested in cooperating with her research, so she could not recruit participants directly at the workplace. However, through a friend who had worked at several different call centres, Hannah was able to make contact with several participants and arrange interviews. They, in turn, introduced her to other call centre workers who were interested in participating in her research (an example of the snowball sampling technique).

While this method allowed Hannah to build up a sample, it also ensured that this sample was biased. The people she interviewed were almost all young graduates unable to find work that is more permanent and they had introduced her to their friends, who had a similar profile. Unwittingly, she had captured the experiences of only one section of the workforce and had to counter this by specifically asking her participants to introduce her to older workers.

5●5 WHAT YOU NEED TO KNOW ABOUT MAKING QUALITATIVE AND QUANTITATIVE KNOWLEDGE CLAIMS BASED ON YOUR SAMPLE

The 'rules of the game' for making claims to knowledge based on your research are markedly different within qualitative and quantitative research. This section walks you through an overview of these differences, but we will return to these issues in more detail later in the book.

5●5●1 DEVELOP QUALITATIVE KNOWLEDGE CLAIMS FROM YOUR RESEARCH

Qualitative researchers are often in an excellent position to develop context-rich, detailed and descriptive accounts. Indeed, it is through a strong understanding of the specific context affecting your participants and your research that you can develop qualitative knowledge. Yet identifying your project's broader implications is also important, both in establishing its value and ensuring its contribution to knowledge beyond the particular case you are researching. One way to develop general knowledge through your qualitative study is to look for processes that may feature in a wider range of cases than the particular one(s) you investigated.

Generalizing in qualitative research can range from explaining the 'how' and 'why' of your particular case to explaining general processes and developing theoretical models. Katz (2001, p. 446) argues that 'an explanation is always a hypothesis'. That is to say, the explanations you develop based on your qualitative research are testing theoretical ideas. Katz and others have suggested that qualitative research should not attempt to offer causal explanations or predictions.

Rather than observing the present to predict future events, qualitative researchers seek to use observations of the present to describe past occurrences that have led to the present situation (Katz, 2001, p. 448).

For example, if you were researching how a particular business team managed conflicts, you would want to identify factors that might also apply to other business teams or general team-based conflict management. While you can't be sure those processes are broadly applicable, you open the potential for your research to be applied in other contexts. Over time, as other studies apply your findings in different contexts, a more general model of team-based conflict management could be developed and its variations across different contexts explored. Thus, the emphasis on the particularities of individual cases in qualitative research need not preclude the development of insights and models explaining processes that apply in different contexts.

Another way of contributing to general knowledge is to use qualitative research findings to build your own theoretical explanation, elaborate or to challenge an existing theory or explanation. You can show what a theoretical concept looks like in practice, and evaluate its strengths and limitations in your research context. For example, to help account for his research findings, Charles explored how theoretical concepts developed to explain practices within the Italian Mafia's organized crime syndicate might apply to his topic of politically motivated seizures of farms in Zimbabwe. Gambetta (1993, 2009a, 2009b) and Varese (2001) explained that in order for a Mafia-like organization to emerge certain factors were required. These necessary factors included an available pool of people with ability and willingness to use targeted violence and a market for extralegal protection, such as when police failed to provide adequate security. Charles found these ideas applied remarkably well in his research context. However, his research highlighted the importance of the type of motivation in the development of such crime syndicates. The violent practices he documented in Zimbabwe were politically motivated, which caused different patterns to emerge when compared to the economically motivated violence within Mafia crime syndicates. Thus, Charles's research showed a key factor – economic versus political motivation – that was not fully developed in the original theory he applied in his study.

You can also use your qualitative study to demonstrate gaps and limitations in an existing theory. For example, Eric's qualitative study of the shifting values and assumptions of professionals involved in communicating science to UK public audiences showed that a prominent theory of practice by sociologist Pierre Bourdieu did not adequately account for the role of social change (Jensen & Holliman, 2015). Eric offered a theoretical explanation to address this gap, using the particular case to show the general principle that Bourdieu's theory needs to be supplemented to address transformations in a professional field.

5•5•2 DEVELOP QUANTITATIVE KNOWLEDGE CLAIMS FROM YOUR RESEARCH

In quantitative research, knowledge claims are often developed using inferential statistics. Here, the goal is to identify statistical patterns and relationships between variables at the population level, using data you've collected in your sample. Inferential statistics use probability theory developed over decades in the fields of mathematics and statistics to test hypotheses, and create quantitative models that can show the probability of a knowledge claim's accuracy.

BE A SAVVY CONSUMER AND USER OF STATISTICAL INFERENCE

Quantitative data, drawn from a representative sample, allows you to make claims about a population's characteristics with a known level of confidence. If you've ever seen a newspaper reporting the results of a political opinion poll, you may have seen how this level of confidence is expressed in practice. For example, you may read that US President Barack Obama has a 46 per cent approval rating, plus or minus 3 per cent. What this means is that the paper is confident that there is a high likelihood (95 per cent confidence or better) that Obama's approval rating is somewhere between 43 per cent and 49 per cent.

Another area where confidence comes into play is in reporting differences between two groups in your sample. For example, you may conduct a study and find that the incomes of men and women in your sample are different from each other at a 'statistically significant' level. A difference that is 'statistically significant' is one that is very likely (again, with 95 per cent confidence or better) to apply to the larger population. That is, a statistically significant result is unlikely to result from chance or from the random variation that occurs whenever you draw a sample from a larger population. It is a real difference that should be observable in the larger population, if you were able to collect data from all members of the population.

Statistical significance and confidence intervals both come from inferential statistics, statistics which generalize the results of a sample to the population.

USE STATISTICAL CONCEPTS TO THINK ABOUT QUANTITATIVE SAMPLING AND GENERALIZABILITY

Whenever you draw a sample to represent a larger population, there will be differences between the sample and the population. This difference is known as **sampling error**. When making inferences based on quantitative data, there are two main types of inferential error that you can make. These are summarized below.

- **Sampling frame.** A **sampling frame** is a summary list of all members of a population who can be sampled (i.e., those who can be identified, located and contacted), which forms the basis of your sampling activity.
- **Type I error. Type I errors** are alternatively known as 'false positives'. This error involves the rejection of a null hypothesis that is actually true. For example, if you were to conclude that a new medical treatment helps to cure cancer, when it does not, the results would be tragic.
- **Type II error. Type II errors** can be referred to as 'false negatives'. This error is the failure to reject a null hypothesis that is actually false. For instance, it would be a very serious error if you were to dismiss a potential cure for cancer as ineffective when it actually cures the disease.

A great deal of the focus in social research statistics is on Type I error. This is generally considered the most important type of error to control. Imagine a new design for an aircraft has been proposed. Before we accept that the design should be used, we would want to be reasonably sure that it would work as intended (i.e., it won't crash). Therefore, we would want to reduce the risk of a 'false positive', by convention, to less than a 1 per cent probability before accepting that further development should be undertaken using the prototype design.

This is a precautionary position: things stay as they are until there is a sufficient level of evidence to show a change is needed.

EXPLAIN STATISTICAL INFERENCE TO YOUR READERS USING CONFIDENCE INTERVALS AND P-VALUES

'Confidence intervals' are used to indicate the level of Type I error (risk of false positives) that would apply if you were generalizing a finding from a sample to a population. Generalization within explicitly identified confidence intervals is informed by probability theory, which has been developed out of decades of mathematical research. It provides a robust basis for making inferences about populations based on samples and for analysing relationships between variables.

By convention, less than a 1 in 20 chance of making an inaccurate generalization has been set as a tolerable level of Type I error within quantitative social science research. This is expressed in statistical notation as $p < 0.05$ (p stands for the risk of making a Type I error; 0.05 stands for a 5 per cent or 1 in 20 probability of occurrence). If a result is found to be statistically significant in this way, that doesn't necessarily mean it's an important finding. As discussed in Chapter 12, you would still need to determine the 'effect size' to establish how much is explained by the statistically significant difference. If only a small amount is explained, then the finding could be statistically significant (i.e., there is a 95 per cent or better chance that there is a real effect in the population) but relatively unimportant for answering your research question.

In general, social research focuses on the overall or typical patterns (aggregate level) rather than the unique or unusual aspects of individuals' views and lives. In quantitative research, particulars from people's lives are conceptualized as variables that can be investigated statistically across your sample. This can reveal patterns that apply at the population level, but it is important not to overstate what can be concluded from such aggregate research. Indeed, you have to be careful about making claims at the individual level based on statistics that apply to the whole population. For example, if you found that male teachers in the UK earn an average or 'mean' of £40,000 per year, while female teachers earn an average of £30,000 per year, you could say that 'male teachers earn more *on average* than female teachers'. However, it would be inaccurate to simply say 'female teachers make less money than male teachers'. A mean is obtained by adding up all the values in a sample and dividing by the number of individuals in that sample. In the example above, both male and female teachers are likely to earn a wide range of income. Some men would probably earn less than women. For example, it may be that there are a small number of very highly paid male teachers at elite boys' schools who are dragging the average upwards. It's even possible with this aggregate result that more male teachers earned less than £30,000 per year than female teachers. The flawed reasoning that a sample or population average would apply at the level of individual teachers is unfortunately quite common: it's an example of the ecological fallacy we met earlier in this chapter. A better way to phrase the above finding would be: 'Male teachers in the UK earned an overall average of £40,000, while the average of all wages for female teachers was £30,000.' However, the average is simply a poor measure of central tendency for unequally distributed characteristics such as income: the median income would be a more valid comparison (for more detail, see Chapter 12).

━━ REAL WORLD EXAMPLE ━━━━━━━━━━━━━

Drawing inferences about 'average happiness'

Mitchell, Frank, Harris, Dodds and Danforth (2013) used automated analysis of words used in tweets to draw inferences about 'average happiness' levels across the 50 American states. For example, Mitchell et al. offer answers to such questions as 'Is California happier than New York?' While the prospect of being able to compare happiness levels across US states is exciting, this claim deserves scrutiny. Firstly, the validity of this concept of 'average happiness' is highly questionable. For these average scores to be accurate the following would have to hold true:

1　Twitter content would have to provide an accurate window into individuals' offline, real-life happiness.
2　The automated tool analysing words used in tweets would have to be able to accurately identify happiness and sadness in Twitter content.
3　Twitter users (i.e., the sample in this case) would have to be representative of the general population at a state level.
4　The concept of 'average happiness' would have to be meaningful in principle. That is, there would have to be a real world phenomenon of 'average happiness' that was valid (i.e., real) at the individual level.

In fact, none of the above facts were established by the researchers, thereby casting doubt on the study's knowledge claims.

---

5 ⬤ 6　CONCLUSION

This chapter shows you how to develop reliable knowledge about the group you are studying without gathering data from all members. To do this, you will need to look for patterns, identify deviant cases and avoid the fallacy of presuming that trends at the group level apply to the individual level. As you decide what kind of sampling strategy is right for your study, consider:

1　The scope of claims you want to make at the end of your study.
2　The strengths and limitations of your proposed methods for getting at the relevant evidence.
3　Whether there are any discrepancies between (1) and (2).

We highlight that you can narrow the gap between research claims and available evidence by taking steps such as reducing your research scope, using representative sampling and relying on existing research knowledge through your literature review. These steps will help you develop reliable conclusions from your research evidence.

　　The chapter guides you through the sampling process, explaining the practical limits and key advantages of probability and non-probability sampling techniques. We explain that bias in sampling occurs when the participants you've selected for your sample are not representative of the population as a whole. This is an issue no matter what sampling technique you use.

Gathering a truly representative sample of a population is very difficult – and in some cases may be impossible – so there will always be the risk of some sampling error. You should acknowledge this risk and attempt to minimize sources of bias. Be open and self-critical about such limitations and keep in mind how they affect your analysis and knowledge claims. While probability samples are the gold standard, they will sometimes be unachievable within the practical constraints of a particular project. In such cases, the most important principle is to be systematic in order to avoid accidentally introducing sampling bias, for example, by selecting people who look friendly and likely to participate.

In research projects where time and resources are in scarce supply, cutting back on the sample size is often the best option for immediately reducing costs. You may need to use existing data sources rather than doing your own original data collection (see Chapter 9) or take a different, less costly sampling approach. In some cases, such changes to your research plan would mean reducing the scope of your research question.

In the case of in-depth qualitative research we've suggested determining a sample size for your project by taking into account how much time you'll need versus how much time you have available for the project. You should consider how long it would take you to collect, transcribe (if necessary) and analyse your data, as well as writing it up in your research report. In addition to taking available time into account, you should be prepared to adjust your plans based on the emerging findings from your research and avoid sampling past the point of saturation.

In the quantitative tradition, your sample size and approach directly affect your statistical analysis. Having a larger sample size and robust sampling methods will give you the basis for making generalizations that are more likely to be accurate. But you should always avoid overstating your findings. We explain the statistical concepts tied to sampling and generalizability and why so much focus is placed on Type I error. Moreover, understanding common pitfalls in the process of making **statistical inferences** about a population can help you develop accurate knowledge claims. Finally, keep in mind that all knowledge is provisional and open to change when new and better evidence is presented. Keep your research on a solid footing by only making claims that you can support with your data and references to existing research.

━━━ SUGGESTIONS FOR FURTHER READING ━━━

- Henry, G. T. (1990). *Practical sampling.* Newbury Park, CA: Sage. This book goes into greater detail about the practical issues that arise during the sampling process than we have been able to here. The book offers further guidance about how to approach sample selection, design your sample, develop a sampling frame and decide what sample size you need.
- Hoffmann, W. & Patel, P. V. (2015). SurveySignal: A convenient solution for experience sampling research using participants' own smartphones. *Social Science Computer Review,* 33(2): 235-253. This article discusses how 'experience sampling' (gathering data at multiple time points from the same individuals) can be conducted using your respondents' smartphones to yield more accurate data with higher response rates than would otherwise be possible.
- Katz, J. (2001). From how to why: On luminous description and causal inference in ethnography (Part 1). *Ethnography, 2*(4), 443-473. Katz, J. (2002). From how to why: On luminous description and causal inference in ethnography (Part 2). *Ethnography, 3*(1), 63-90.

These two linked articles by Katz offer an extended discussion of generalization in ethnography with valuable insights that apply to qualitative interview studies in particular.

- **Daniel, J. (2012). Choosing between nonprobability sampling and probability sampling. In** *Sampling essentials: Practical guidelines for making sampling choices. (pp. 66–81).* **Thousand Oaks, CA: Sage.** This chapter outlines the strengths and weakness of probability versus non-probability sampling in more detail than we've been able to here. It also offers useful guidelines for deciding between these two categories of sampling.

Visit the companion website at **https://study.sagepub.com/jensenandlaurie** to gain access to a wide range of online resources to support your learning, including editable research documents, weblinks, free access SAGE journal articles and book chapters, and flashcards.

GLOSSARY

Ecological fallacy – The commonly held, but wrong, idea that group-level patterns apply to all the individuals in the group.

Emergence – A feature of qualitative sampling and data collection defined by following relevant but unexpected patterns that crop up during qualitative data collection or analysis.

Generalization – The process of making evidence-based knowledge claims that apply to people and situations that were not captured in your data set.

Inference – The logical process of drawing conclusions and generalizations from available evidence.

Population – The group of people that your research is designed to generate knowledge about.

Purposive sampling – A non-probability sampling technique for selecting participants based on theory or the researcher's judgement and prior research.

Representative sample – A sample that has characteristics closely matching those of the population from which it is drawn.

Sample – A subset of the population you are wishing to study that is manageable in size and accessibility, given the constraints of your project.

Sampling error – The gap between your population's characteristics and your sample's characteristics. It's impossible to have a sample that perfectly reflects the population, no matter how robust your sampling method. Probability sampling ensures that you can know the likelihood of error, but it will always be present.

Sampling frame – A list of all the members of a population who can be sampled. That is, the group of people from which a sample can be drawn.

Saturation – A technique used in qualitative research to determine when data collection can stop. The saturation point is when new cases you collect (e.g. newly conducted interviews) are not broadening or deepening the information you have already gathered from previous participants or observations. This saturation point signals that you can stop your qualitative data collection.

Snowball sampling – A non-probability sampling technique that involves using existing respondents to identify more respondents.

Statistical inference – The process of drawing conclusions about a larger population based on statistical data from a smaller sample.

Type I error – This is a false positive, when a null hypothesis is accepted that should be rejected.

Type II error – This is a false negative, when a null hypothesis that should be rejected fails to be rejected.

REFERENCES

Berg, B. L. (1995). *Qualitative research methods for the social sciences* (2nd ed.). London: Allyn & Bacon.

Denzin, N. K., & Lincoln, Y. S. (2011). *The SAGE handbook of qualitative research* (4th ed.). Thousand Oaks, CA: Sage.

Emmel, N. (2013). *Sampling and choosing cases in qualitative research: A realist approach.* London: Sage

Gambetta, D. (1993). *The Sicilian Mafia.* Cambridge, MA: Harvard University Press.

Gambetta, D. (2009a). *Codes of the underworld.* Princeton, NJ: Princeton University Press.

Gambetta, D. (2009b). Signaling. In P. Hedström & P. Bearman (Eds.), *Oxford Handbook of Analytical Sociology.* Oxford: Oxford University Press.

Henn, M., Weinstein, M., & Foard, N. (2013). *A critical introduction to social research* (2nd ed.). London: Sage.

Hennink, M., Hutter, I., & Bailey, A. (2011). *Qualitative research methods.* London: Sage.

Jensen, E., & Holliman, R. (2015). Norms and values in UK science engagement practice. *International Journal of Science Education, Part B: Communication and Public Engagement.* doi: 10.1080/21548455.2014.995743

Katz, J. (2001). From how to why: On luminous description and causal inference in ethnography (Part 1). *Ethnography, 2*(4), 443–473.

Kuzel, A. J. (1992). Sampling in qualitative inquiry. In B. F. Crabtree & W. I. Miller (Eds.), *Doing qualitative research* (pp. 31–44). Newbury Park, CA: Sage.

Mitchell, L., Frank, M. R., Harris, K. D., Dodds, P. S., & Danforth, C. M. (2013). The geography of happiness: Connecting Twitter sentiment and expression, demographics, and objective characteristics of place. *PLoS ONE, 8*(5), e64417.

Moss, A., Jensen, E., & Gusset, M. (2015). Evaluating the contribution of zoos and aquariums to Aichi Biodiversity Target 1. *Conservation Biology, 29*(2), 537–544.

Patton, M. Q. (1990). *Qualitative evaluation and research.* Beverly Hills, CA: Sage.

Somekh, B., & Lewin, C. (2011). *Theory and methods in social research* (2nd ed.). London: Sage.

Tracy, K., & Tracy, S. (1998). Rudeness at 911: Reconceptualizing face and face attack. *Human Communication Research, 25*(2), 225–251.

Varese, F. (2001). *The Russian Mafia.* Oxford: Oxford University Press.

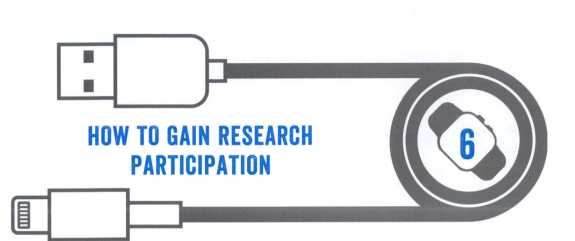

HOW TO GAIN RESEARCH PARTICIPATION

- Why gaining participation in research is essential.
- Why people can be reluctant to engage in research.
- How to gain participation from research subjects who are useful for your study.
- What kinds of ethical considerations you should keep in mind during the process of gaining participation.

6●1 INTRODUCTION

Most social research requires individuals to participate. **Surveys**, **interviews**, **focus groups**, **participant observation** and other research methods depend on participation. You need people to complete your surveys, agree to be interviewed or join a focus group. Therefore, strategies and procedures for gaining participation form the foundation of successful projects involving primary research. Participation also directly affects the quality of your sample and therefore the type of knowledge you can develop (see Chapter 5).

You may believe your research project is important, but how can you persuade other people of this? How can you convince your respondents that it is worthwhile for them to contribute their time and perhaps disclose confidential information to you?

6●2 STRATEGIES TO IMPROVE RESEARCH PARTICIPATION

Some researchers may be lucky enough to encounter scores of willing participants. However, there are a number of good reasons why people may be reluctant to participate in your research. Potential respondents might not be interested in your research project, they might not immediately trust you or they might be wary of participating due to cultural sensitivities. You are often approaching people with whom you have no prior relationship. A normal relationship might only progress to the stage of asking personal questions after a long period of time (if ever). Yet, you may be asking participants about their income, health or drug use after only knowing them for a few minutes. The fact that any personal information can be gathered in such a situation is remarkable – but it *is* possible to achieve with effective communication.

6●2●1 GAINING ACCESS, ATTENTION AND INTEREST

FINDING PARTICIPANTS

The most common difficulties in persuading people to participate in your research are the simplest. Before you even move on to the more complex aspects of gaining participation, you must first locate your potential participants, make contact with them and garner their interest in your project. People lead busy lives. Between family, work and social activities, it can be difficult to find an appropriate time and place to get in touch with potential respondents and get your participation request in front of them. Given the background noise of daily life, your first challenge is to find where and how to reach your targeted participants.

Locate potential participants where they live, work and play. To find people in your target population to include in your sample, you should start by considering:

- Where your participants may be found
- Where they might be most receptive to participation requests.

REAL WORLD EXAMPLE

Go where potential participants are likely to be receptive to an invitation

Stella was looking to understand patterns of illicit drug use in Stockholm. She decided that seeking participants in community centres or rehabilitation clinics would be a sensible starting point. She found that potential participants were more open to an approach from a stranger in these contexts than on streets known for drug use or near a local police station.

KEY TIPS

Gaining participation through social media

Social media sites can be a great way to find key people to invite to participate in your research. In addition, for a qualitative study, social media sites can help you develop a **snowball sample**, as one useful participant is likely to be connected to others via social media. For example, if you are interested in researching migration policy and successfully establish contact with a relevant participant on LinkedIn, you can probably identify others involved in migration policy through that person's contacts. The following are useful social media sites to consider:

- **LinkedIn** – widely used for 'professional' contacts
- **Facebook** – has a major focus on social networks, but many companies and key figures have public profiles on the website
- **Twitter** – not everyone has a Twitter account, but it can be a useful means of approaching people who do

In other cases persistent and creative internet searches can get you contact details for key people. For example, you may not have Katarina Pavlovka's email address, but if you are able to find her colleague's email address (e.g., joseph.smith@eurobank.com), then you could guess at Katarina's (e.g., katarina.pavlovka@eurobank.com). Keep in mind that different research populations may have different levels of visibility online, so this technique is likely to be most appropriate for professional populations where a publicly visible digital presence is common. See the suggestions for further reading at the end of this chapter for more information on online sampling techniques.

PERSUADING PEOPLE TO PARTICIPATE

Gaining attention for your request for research participation requires an understanding of what is likely to matter to people in your target population. The presence of requests for participation in market research in cafés, supermarkets, restaurants and websites means that prospective participants are often faced with a deluge of requests. Against this background, how can you make your request stand out? And how can you convince respondents that they should take to time to participate?

Connect the research to a higher goal. In many cases, your participants are unlikely to directly benefit from your research. In order to convince them to take part, you will need to think of reasons why their participation will help to achieve a broader pro-social goal. Think about how your relatively narrowly focused project contributes to larger, more universally recognized objectives. Most people are far more likely to participate in an activity if they feel that their time and effort will help achieve a greater good (see Table 6.1).

 **REAL WORLD EXAMPLE**

Connect your research to a higher goal

Ryan was researching the use of social networking websites among Yorkshire pig farmers, but struggled to convince participants of his work's importance. Farmers were initially sceptical of Ryan's motives and suspected that his research may be critical of the commercial meat industry by highlighting apparent cruelty to animals.

Ryan eventually had more success in finding participants when he explained that his study was intended to improve the quality and safety of the nation's meat supply by assessing social networks' capacity for spreading information about innovative farming practices. By thoroughly explaining his research and showing examples of some of the evidence he had already collected, Ryan connected his research to higher goals that his participants viewed as valuable. When farmers recognized that his research could contribute to improving the quality and productivity of their businesses while promoting health standards in the national food supply, they were much more willing to participate.

To help you brainstorm ways to appeal to altruistic motivations, here are some questions you can ask yourself about your research:

- Is it likely to **improve quality of life or health**? If so, in what ways? (For example, will it improve health services or customer service practices?)
- Will it **contribute to improvements in socially desirable institutions** such as governments or charities?
- Will it contribute to efforts to **reduce something socially undesirable** such as abuse, conflict or drug use?
- Does it **shed light on an important, contentious social issue** such as food poverty?
- Will it **address some kind of injustice**? Perhaps it will help to 'expose what happened' in an incident, or offer some kind of recognition of suffering.
- Could it **contribute to greater understanding** between groups or improve relationships between those who have a history of conflict?

Consider using appropriate compensation to increase participation. It is legitimate to use incentives to improve your research participation rate. Your participants are

Table 6.1 Strategies and tactics for gaining participation

Issue	Strategies	Tactics
Where can I find participants?	• Target places where you know participants live, work or play. • Consider approaching participants online.	• Think about locations where participants will be most receptive. • Build relationships with **gatekeepers** you can use to gain entry into communities or groups. • Consider if all of your target population has an active online presence to avoid sampling bias.
How can I persuade people to participate?	• Connect research to a higher goal. • Offer reasonable compensation.	• Give prospective participants a reason to believe in your research, such as benefits to a wider community. • Consider different types of incentives.
How can I make sure they stay committed to participating?	• Establish **credibility**. • Gain trust. • Be organized. • Be sensitive to cultural differences and minority perspectives. • Build **rapport**.	• Be knowledgeable about your research topic, but avoid jargon. • Connect research to a trusted and respected institution. • Provide clear details of how **anonymity** and **confidentiality** will be achieved. • Respect your participants: treat them with courtesy and **professionalism**. • Seek guidance from gatekeepers or others who understand the community to ensure you are well prepared to deal with cultural or socio-economic differences. • Consider the way you interact with participants, including your external appearance (e.g., clothing, hygiene).

offering you their time and thoughts, and it is reasonable to expect that they should receive something in return.

There are two main modes of offering compensation for participation:

- Offering incentives to **everyone who participates** means that from the participant's point of view there is a guaranteed gain.
- On the other hand, offering incentives to only a few people – such as with **a prize draw** – will allow you to offer a more substantial potential benefit, but also lowers the likelihood of gain to the respondent.

People are generally divided on whether they prefer the chance of a larger prize or the certainty of a smaller one. If you have extensive resources, it will usually be preferable to offer the same incentive to all participants. However, there are often practical reasons for using a prize draw as your method of compensation. Most notably, if you can only afford, for example, a £50 incentive budget for a study that is likely to have 300 respondents, you have no choice but to use a prize draw approach (as a 16 pence incentive for each person is not going to persuade anyone). If you think creatively and strategically about what kind of prize to use, you can stretch such a small incentive into something that many of your potential participants will find appealing.

Keep your incentives proportionate. For most participants, incentives are seen as an 'acknowledging of the respondent's contribution, rather than payment for her time', so offering appropriate incentives is important (Ornstein, 2013, p. 139). The general rule of thumb is that the level of compensation should depend on:

- **How much your participants will directly benefit from the research.** For example, if you want to convene a focus group on public attitudes about a particular brand, your aim of improving the brand's public relations strategy is not going to benefit the participants. As a result, substantial compensation would be expected.
- **How much they will indirectly benefit from the research.** Perhaps your research will improve services for people they care about?
- **How much of your participants' time you are taking up.** A three-hour focus group meeting will usually require compensation. On the other hand, asking someone in an informal setting if they could answer three or four questions may not require any incentive beyond your friendly demeanour and gratitude. This proportional approach to compensation makes sense on both a cost and credibility basis. If you offer everyone who participates in a brief interview a free MP3 player you will soon run out of research funds.
- **How costly your participants' time is.** There is a point at which participants' time is too valuable to attempt compensation at all. If you are trying to interview a chief executive or a politician you are better off appealing to their sense of generosity or interest in your topic than trying to provide compensation.

Think about different types of incentives. You should evaluate the pros and cons of incentives based on the characteristics and preferences of your particular target sample. Gaining input from a high-powered business executive will require a different incentive than you would need for an unemployed person.

Here are some ideas:

- **Give respondents access to your research findings.** This incentive should be an ethical requirement, when the results would benefit participants. It prevents your research from becoming a one-way, exploitative relationship in which data are harvested from participants and never returned in any form. It is inexpensive and easy to give this access, and reasonable for the respondent to request. It will also help the respondent to feel part of the research, and encourage them to participate more fully and consistently. The downside of this incentive is that it only works if the respondent is interested in your findings. (For further discussion of ethical principles and techniques, see Chapter 3.)
- **Offer a meal, tea and coffee when you meet with participants.** If you are looking for incentives for participation in a focus group meeting, providing refreshments could encourage people to take part. You could provide pastries for a morning session, a sandwich-based lunch for a midday session or biscuits and fruit for an afternoon session. This can be a bargain option as you could self-cater. You can add a personal touch by stressing that you are making pastries or cookies for the session yourself (rather than buying them). This kind of incentive is rather small, and some people may not find the offer very appealing. However, it may be just enough to make some people feel like they are getting something back for their time.

- **Offer vouchers, tickets or gift certificates.** Respondents will see immediate value and appeal in this incentive. The benefit for participation is clear and it is also easy for you to prepare these incentives well in advance. It is sensible to select something with broad appeal. Vouchers to a local comedy club may not appeal to everyone, whereas an Amazon gift certificate has much broader applicability.

- **Think twice before offering small amounts of money.** Cash incentives have clear, nearly universal value. However, some people are not likely to be attracted by small amounts of money. Another major downside of this incentive is that it overtly monetizes the experience, potentially undermining any altruistic motivations for participation.

- **Offer charitable donations.** This incentive has an appealing altruistic side to it, but it only works if the respondents like the charity or generally value charitable donation. In order to maximize the likely success of this strategy, select a charity that has a personal connection to the people from whom you are seeking assistance. For example, if you are looking to interview members of the Bangladeshi community then offering a donation to a Bangladeshi charity may be appealing. This incentive is useful for wealthier participants, who may not be interested in a free meal or a small amount of money. Given that this approach could be viewed as imposing your charitable values, this incentive may work best when you provide participants with a choice about whether to keep the money or donate it to a charity.

- **Reimburse travel costs.** Participants typically expect to be reimbursed for travel costs. However, always communicate an exact maximum amount that you are willing to reimburse, because some respondents may interpret phrases such as 'reasonable costs' too generously. Even people who seem perfectly reasonable may send you a massive travel bill. You will also need to specify that receipts are required. This is necessary so you can track your research costs and will also likely be required if you are claiming reimbursement from a funder. Be sure to send all the necessary details and claim forms to the participant in advance of their travel.

When preparing your incentives, always ensure you have enough to meet your commitments to participants. See Table 6.2 for an incentives chart.

Table 6.2   Incentives chart

Incentive categories

Individual incentives	Direct compensation	• Vouchers • Tickets • Gift certificates • Prize draw • Cash (fair market value)
	Reimbursing expenses	• Travel costs • Stipend for meals (e.g., lunch) or alternatively provide refreshments
Social incentives	Charitable	• Donation to charity of researcher's choice • Donation to charity of participant's choice
	Community/ Society	• Details of how findings will benefit the participant's community or society
Ethical incentives	Access	• Give respondents access to the research findings

It is also worth noting that incentives should not be withheld if someone ultimately decides not to participate.

When thinking about these incentives, you also want to think about how you frame them in your initial approach to the participant. For example, if you are approaching strangers in the street then explicitly identifying your incentives will likely be necessary. By contrast, if you are seeking to interview a high-level professional, it may be more appropriate to suggest meeting 'over lunch or a coffee' at a time that suits them.

Remember that incentives are not always appropriate. Incentives can be unhelpful for some research topics and target populations. For example, if you are research-ing depression in new mothers, it would be inappropriate to tout free theatre tickets or a raffle draw as an incentive. Indeed, when researching topics that hold deep emotional meaning for your participants, such as wartime experiences or family conflict, you will often find incentives are not helpful. Participants may even be repulsed at the prospect of exchanging their emotionally charged stories for a 'prize'. For such participants, you should use the other strategies discussed above, such as demonstrating that your research will offer general benefits to society, help others in a similar position to themselves or allow them to document their experiences. Finally, be sure to always allow people to opt out of incentives as they may, for example, face a tax liability that they might not want to deal with.

 **KEY TIPS**

The wrong incentive can bias your research

Make sure that the particular incentive you choose does not make it more likely that you will get one kind of participant and not others. For example, if you were conducting research on public views about the ethics of zoos, then offering free zoo tickets would be a problematic incentive to offer. Only those who enjoy visiting zoos would be attracted to such an incentive. As such, the incentive could introduce systematic sampling bias against those who dislike zoos. You can avoid this kind of bias by choosing widely desirable and inoffensive incentives that do not hold any direct relevance to your research topic.

Finally, if you use incentives, they will be part of your self-presentation as a researcher. Moreover, you should think about whether the particular incentives you are using could affect the kind of people who participate or what people say. For example, when Eric studied people attending the UK's Cambridge Science Festival, the festival organizers wanted to use 'science kits' as an incentive. Eric advised against using this because people interested in a science kit for their children could be expected to be systematically different from the larger population of event attendees. This meant that the incentive could introduce systematic bias, with consistently lower participation from those less interested in science. Avoid this type of scenario by thinking critically about the appropriateness of your incentives, given your research population and goals.

━━━━━━━━━━ **KEY TIPS** ━━━━━━━━━━

Safeguarding your research from incentive bias

Offering incentives that are disproportionate or favour one social group over another can bias your sample and research findings. The following safeguards, adapted from Alderson and Morrow (2011, p. 68), aim to reduce the possibility that people will participate in your study purely because of the incentives:

1   Distinguish between the types of payment: **reimbursement** (e.g., of travel costs incurred), **compensation** (e.g., payment for time), **appreciation** (this is free!) and **incentives** (e.g., prize draw for gift certificate).
2   Be prepared to justify your selection of research incentives.
3   Ensure you still make payments to people who pull out of participating in your project.
4   Develop a clear, open way of describing your incentives in consent forms, in conjunction with your supervisor or ethics committee.
5   Make direct payments to the person who has participated in the research, not via an employer or other gatekeeper.
6   Normally avoid lump-sum payments to participants, except when reimbursing expenses.
7   Think about using deferred or non-cash payments.

Build bridges with gatekeepers. Gatekeepers are 'sponsors or individuals who smooth access to the group. They are the key people who let us in, give us permission, or grant access' (O'Reilly, 2009, p. 132). Having individuals who are known and trusted by your potential participants vouch for you can be very helpful when you are seeking to gain participation. Gatekeepers can save you time and headaches by helping to convince a large pool of people that your research is valid and participation is worthwhile. Gatekeepers can also give you insights into the knowledge and habits of your target population to guide your strategy for gaining participation. Gatekeepers might include:

- Local leaders such as members of the clergy.
- Members of a city or town council.
- Leaders within clubs and social organizations.
- Politicians.
- Schoolteachers or administrators.
- Executives or managers in a company.
- Activists from NGOs.

Gatekeepers may be able to bridge language and cultural barriers between you and your participants.

Just as gatekeepers have the power to grant you access, they can also restrict your access to a particular group (O'Reilly, 2009, p. 134). O'Reilly uses the example of a gang leader seeking 'commitment from the ethnographer' in order for them to continue enjoying access to the community. For a real life example of such an instance, see Venkatesh (2009).

In the case of research with children or vulnerable adults, gatekeepers are mandatory in almost all cases. You will need to approach the professionals or parents who are responsible for protecting these individuals. Approaching these guardians minimizes the risk of upsetting either your prospective participants or their gatekeepers. You will still need to ensure that you get some kind of **informed consent** for research participation directly from the children or vulnerable people you are conducting your research with. This may need to be given verbally, and the gatekeeper could then sign a paper consent form. In UK law, for instance, the only people who can give legally valid consent for research are those with parental responsibility or the (competent) children themselves. Teachers, social workers or other gatekeepers do not have parental responsibility and therefore 'can grant researchers access to children, but cannot consent to the research' (Alderson & Morrow, 2011, p. 105). See Chapter 3 for more information on the ethical issues of doing research with children.

 REAL WORLD EXAMPLE

Access participants through a gatekeeper

Olivia was hoping to conduct a verbal survey of children at a local primary school about their dietary habits. She knew that it would be unethical to contact the children directly, so she contacted the head teacher of the school and explained the objectives of the research. Olivia was able to convince the head teacher that her research would be contributing to the valuable social objective of combating childhood obesity.

The head teacher then agreed to contact the parents of children in one class to ask for their written consent for participation in the study. After this was granted, Olivia was careful to fully explain her study to the schoolchildren and to obtain their consent before conducting the survey.

Create an effective contact letter. This letter is your key means of persuading people to participate in your research (see Figure 6.1). It should contain the following details:

- **Describe yourself and your role.**
- **Describe the purpose(s) of the research.**
- **Identify how personal information will be used.** For example, you might say 'Your data will be kept confidential and used only for research purposes. Any quotations will be anonymized and your name will not be used in the report.'
- **Provide appropriate justification for the importance of the research** (e.g., connect the research to a higher goal).
- **Indicate any incentives being offered.**
- **Explain how the participant was selected** (e.g., through gatekeeper).

6•2•2 GAINING PARTICIPANT TRUST

An essential first step as you seek to build a new research relationship is to show your participants that you are friendly, likeable, credible and trustworthy. Consider the situation from the

22 October 2015

Dear Mr. Hernandez,

   I was given your name by Julio Velasquez, the pastor from Holy Trinity church. He suggested that you might be interested in participating in a research study. I am a postgraduate student carrying out research at the University of Berkeley on homelessness in the San Francisco area. More specifically, I am investigating which groups of people are most at risk of long-term homelessness.

   I am looking to interview key professionals like you for this research project. In particular, I would like to better understand your experience as a community outreach officer working for the State of California in order to gain insights into reasons why individuals are vulnerable to homelessness.

   I can confirm the following for your participation in this study:

- Your anonymity will be maintained and no comments will be directly attributed to you or will be provided to any third party.
- You are free to withdraw from the study at any point.
- I will send you a copy of the interview transcript within one month of the interview.
- I will notify you once the study is complete and the final research report will be made available to you.

   I would be happy to arrange a convenient meeting time and location for you should you be willing to participate in this research. I would also be pleased to meet you over lunch or coffee if that was more convenient for you.

   Thank you very much for considering this request to participate in the study. Please do not hesitate to contact me by email (duane.alvarez@stateuniversity.edu) or by phone (123-456-7891) if you are willing to participate or if you require any additional information.

Yours sincerely,
Duane Alvarez

Figure 6.1 Contact letter

perspective of your potential participants. You are a stranger who is asking for a favour, or at least some assistance. If you behave in a professional and courteous manner, you will maximize the possibility of your potential participant respecting you, trusting you and agreeing to your request for participation.

   Assure participants of privacy. One important factor that needs to be managed in the process of building participant trust is concern over privacy. Why should people give information to strangers about anything from their food preferences to their sexual behaviour or illegal drug use?

   People may be dissuaded from participating in your research owing to concern over the security of any data they provide. There are regular news stories about breaches of privacy by companies and organizations. These breaches can be inadvertent, such as when laptops and memory sticks containing private data are lost. However, they also include deliberate efforts by hackers to breach data systems in order to gather personal information.

   While not all research contains highly confidential personal information, many people are concerned about being targeted by marketing companies if they disclose even basic information. For example, filling in your address on a survey form for market research can often result in a barrage of junk mail from the company concerned, as well as third parties who are sold this information.

Even more critically, many participants may be reluctant to provide more sensitive information in case there are negative consequences later on. For example, a participant may fear at least embarrassment or even loss of employment or prosecution if they answer questions on psychological conditions or criminal behaviour. Indeed, studies examining any kind of socially undesirable activity carry risks for the participant and will make it difficult for you to carry out your research. Chapter 3 demonstrates the importance of maintaining participant privacy throughout your research.

KEY TIPS

Manage concerns over privacy

Given concerns over privacy, many potential participants may either refuse to participate or withhold details that could be vital to your research (for instance, on socially undesirable activities). Although you should never force anyone to participate in your research, you can help to assuage concerns about privacy in a number of ways. The following list is adapted from James and Busher (2009, p. 5):

- Indicate to your participant that:
  - Their information will not be passed to third parties under any circumstances.
  - There is no reason to believe that anyone would be specifically hacking your computer system.
  - Every reasonable precaution (such as using password-protected computers and never talking about personal information over email or on the phone) would be used to maintain privacy.
  - Collected data will be assigned a unique identifying number and the correlating respondent names will be stored on a medium not connected to the internet.
  - Data will only be used for the original purpose and unnecessary data will not be collected.
- Establish your credibility as a researcher.
- Take time to build up trust between you and the participant, especially if the topic is particularly personal.

Establish your credibility as a researcher. In order to overcome these potential concerns, you will need to convince participants that your research is credible. This will help to reassure participants that their private information is in safe hands and will not be misused.

KEY TIPS

Reassure online respondents of your credibility

When you make a research participation request online, establishing your credibility is even more important. Specifically, your prospective respondents need to feel assured that they are not opening themselves up to an onslaught of spam when they click on a link to answer your online survey or register their interest in participating in a focus group.

There are a number of steps that you can take to assuage any concerns that your potential participants might have:

1 Thoroughly check for typos or other errors in your message, as these can indicate a lack of credibility.
2 Post some kind of information about yourself and the research you are conducting on your institution's website if possible. If you send a web link, keep the address as simple as possible so prospective respondents can type it into their web browser themselves, rather than having to click on the link.
3 Do not be surprised to receive queries from prospective respondents emailing you to confirm the research is legitimate. This means you need to keep a particularly close eye on your email inbox in the first 48 hours after you send out an online request for participation in your research.
4 Use an institutional email address. This will offer the reassurance that you are part of a respectable institution.

Connect the research to a trusted or respected institution. A good strategy for establishing your credibility is to link yourself to an established brand that the respondent will

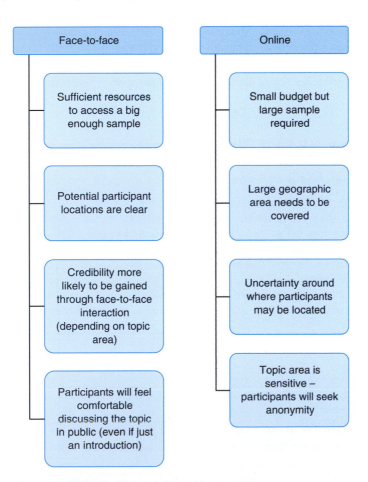

Figure 6.2   Soliciting participants: a decision matrix

already be familiar with. This may make your research seem more important and credible. For example, if you approach an individual and indicate that your research is being conducted through the Kennedy School of Government at Harvard University, your association with this major research institution helps to implicitly validate the quality and value of your research. It is as if the institution is vouching for you. This is particularly important at the early stages of building a research relationship, when prospective participants have very little else they can use as a basis for judging your credibility as a researcher. Your institutional affiliation does not need to be famous or nationally known to benefit your credibility. It just needs to have an established place in the minds of your participants. Tying your research to a local community college or business also suggests that you are credible. This strategy is particularly important when you are approaching potential participants online, as other non-verbal cues are not available to indicate your credibility. So, if you have an institutional email account (e.g., johnsmith@institution.edu), be sure to use it. If you don't have an institutional email account, then make sure your email address lends credibility (so not 'donutsforever24@hotmail.com' or ' bieberfever4ever360@gmail.com').

Of course, some institutions have reputational baggage. If you are conducting research for BP or McDonald's, you may find a positive reception from some and immediate rejection from others. Think carefully about how an institution is perceived before you make a final decision about whether to emphasize your association with it. This also means that researchers using an institutional email address have to be particularly careful to uphold high standards of professionalism throughout their research process so as not to harm the reputation of the institution they are representing. See Figure 6.2 for a decision matrix when soliciting participation.

 **REAL WORLD EXAMPLE**

Tie your research to a well-known institution

Tying your research to a well-known institution can be the determining factor in gaining participation. When Fiona was seeking interviews with respondents on the topic of hepatitis C and intravenous drug use, she knew people might be hesitant to participate due to the personal nature of the topic and possible legal consequences for using illegal drugs.

Fiona found that emphasizing that the research was connected to the International Committee of the Red Cross pre-empted many concerns such as Fiona's identity and trustworthiness and the purpose and value of her research. Indeed, numerous respondents stated that they would take part in the research if it was for the Red Cross, but they may not have been so willing if it was only for Fiona.

Even after you establish that your research is credible and participants' data will not be misused, there is still more you can do to show that you are someone who can be trusted and taken seriously.

Be knowledgeable about your research. In some cases, you may not know very much about your research topic at the time that you are collecting data. For example, you may be researching how social media sites such as Facebook influence the music buying behaviour of 18–25-year-olds. As the growth of social media has occurred relatively recently, you may not know very much about the topic. However, you do need to be able to demonstrate mastery of the details of your own research and what you are seeking to achieve with it. Prepare answers for questions about what your research topic is, why you are doing the research and how you will ensure that your participants' data will be kept secure. You may also be asked about whether, how and when the participant can view the results.

You should be able to answer the following common questions from participants:

- What is your research about?
- Why do you need my participation?
- How will my information be used?
- How long will it take?
- What's in it for me?
- Can I see the final research product?
- When will the research be completed?
- What if I don't know the answer to a question you ask me?
- Can a friend help me complete the survey?
- I feel uncomfortable knowing I will be recorded. Does the interview have to be recorded?
- What if I change my mind and decide I don't want my data to be used at a later date?
- Will my contribution be kept confidential? How can I trust that my personal details will be kept private?

At the same time, you should also be able to speak easily and knowledgably about more in-depth aspects of the research project. The following points are some possible detailed questions you might encounter:

- *Your research objective sounds ambitious, but is your small study really going to have any effect at all on this issue?* One response to this question is that there have been many major advances built on ideas and findings from smaller studies, and that you intend to widely publicize your findings to achieve the greatest impact.
- *Who is funding your research? How do I know they will not influence your research findings?* In responding to this type of question, you would need to provide a full and honest account of who is supporting your research financially. To reassure participants, you could, for example, indicate that your funder does not require you to hand over any confidential information and will only see the final version of your report.
- *All I am doing is talking about myself. How are you going to be able to do anything with this discussion?* One response is to indicate that you will be carefully analysing each interview/ questionnaire to look for patterns that shed light on your topic.

Even well-prepared and experienced researchers can be surprised by participants' questions. When you encounter questions like those listed above, you should make a note of them so you can prepare good answers in case they come up again. Even if you don't end up getting asked questions you prepared for, having sharp, concise and knowledgeable answers about your research will be useful to you, no matter where you end up presenting your research.

Avoid using jargon or appearing unapproachable. Use clear and concise language that is appropriate for someone who is not an expert in your field when you explain your research. One way of quickly spoiling an interaction with a participant is to sound like you are talking down to someone. You may feel that using fancy or theoretical language and jargon may help to establish your reputation in your research community, but it will make you appear out of touch and unapproachable to a respondent. Indeed, your research topic may sound dull, overly complex and generally unappealing if framed in academic or obscure terms.

🔑 KEY TIPS

Translate your topic for prospective participants

Be sure that you are expressing your research interests in terms that will make sense to your prospective participants. Consider the following example for this kind of translation.

Pre-translation: 'I am investigating the provision of holistic palliative care programmes for acquired immunodeficiency syndrome patients with a CD4 count below 100 who are beyond treatment.'

Post-translation. 'I am researching ways to reduce the suffering of AIDS patients who are in the last stages of life.'

Build rapport. A strong rapport will almost certainly improve both the rate of participation and the quality of your interactions. This will be especially important if you are engaging in research that will require longer-term participation, such as interviews, focus groups or longitudinal studies. The key to building rapport is to create understanding and establish common ground.

Meeting over a cup of coffee or a meal will help to establish a more meaningful relationship with prospective participants because it personalizes the meetings and gives depth to the interaction. Another strong means of building rapport is to meet people in locations that are comfortable for them, like religious or community centres. This will help respondents to relax, which will in turn encourage them to participate more fully in your research.

Here is a brief checklist to go over as you prepare to meet prospective participants:

- **Clothing**. Dress appropriately. In covert observational or ethnographic research, blending into your surroundings is the priority. Therefore, you should wear clothing that is similar to other people in your research setting. When conducting a survey in a public space such as a museum or hospital lobby, you need to use the non-verbal cue of being reasonably well dressed (though not excessively so) to help establish your credibility. In most cases, it is essential that you have clean, unstained clothing that would match or slightly exceed the level of formality of most of your respondents' clothing. For example, if you were interviewing bankers, you would need to wear formal business attire. On the other hand, partygoers at a chaotic and muddy music festival are unlikely to want to be interviewed by somebody wearing a suit.
- **State of mind**. You have done your preparations. You have your materials in hand. You should turn off your mobile phone and be 100 per cent focused on your research.
- **Demeanour**. Introduce yourself with a smile and exude calm and confidence. If you seem nervous and uncertain, it may shake your participants' confidence in you.

Keep appointments and provide promised incentives. Convey professionalism by getting the basics right. Remember that your participants are helping you, so you need to ensure that you accommodate their needs as much as possible.

- Always hold to your end of any agreements or commitments to your participants.
- Arrive early at appointments so you are organized and prepared when the respondent arrives. Even being a few minutes late can really annoy people and hurt your standing with them. Perfectly reasonable explanations (e.g. you encountered traffic or genuinely got lost) are of little use in this situation, so be sure you are in position well in advance of the agreed meeting time.

These may seem like obvious points, but they can greatly affect participants' impressions of you, and by extension, their willingness to fully participate in your research.

Be organized when scheduling meetings. Arranging interviews or focus groups requires you to be well prepared, organized and diligent in following up with your participants:

- **Know your own availability and be flexible.** Avoid giving the impression that your time is more important than the participant's. You are more likely to secure an interview if you say that you can meet any time the following week except on Tuesday from 2pm to 4pm, than if you say that you can only meet on Wednesday at 9am. From a practical point of view, if you genuinely do have limited weekday availability then you can try offering early evening and weekend times as well when you might have more flexibility.
- **Be sure the participant commits to a particular day, time and location.** If you receive a vague or uncertain response, gently press for a specific date, time and location. A meeting is much less likely to materialize if your potential participant only makes a vague promise to call you at some unspecified point in the future. Often people will ask you to email them details as a way of avoiding committing to something. Never force people if they don't want to participate, but also remember that friendly, courteous persistence can be persuasive!
- **Always confirm the date and time of meetings.** You should always confirm the details of an interview or focus group by email or telephone the day before. If there are more than a couple of weeks between the point when you first seek research participation and the day of the data collection, you should also confirm several days in advance (unless you are concerned about bothering the participant with too many messages). These confirmations will enhance your credibility and serve as a polite reminder of the meeting, thereby reducing 'no-shows'.
- **Provide a realistic estimate of the time commitment** required from the participant. Test this out in advance. Participants can become irritated if you underestimate the time required from them. For example, if you tell a respondent that your interview will only take 15 minutes when in fact you know it will take an hour, the respondent would be entitled to feel deceived. If during the interview, new topics arise and the interview looks like it will last longer than you expected, you should make this clear to the participant and check that they are willing to continue.
- **Research appropriate places where you can meet.** Be flexible and be prepared to offer your participant a range of meeting places. Given you will most likely be recording the interview, the quieter the setting the better in most cases. Make sure that you know

how to get to the place where you have agreed to meet. If you have problems finding the participant, you are both likely to feel stressed and distracted.

- **Choose convenient meeting locations.** You need to prioritize the needs of your participant and choose a meeting place that is close to their home or place of work. In general, you should travel to your participant, not the other way around. Your own home could be a particularly poor choice if you share housing where roommates might interrupt or behave inappropriately. Moreover, inviting people to your home could set off alarm bells for the participant from a safety point of view, and lower their trust in you as a researcher.
- **Select locations your participants are likely to feel comfortable in.** For example, if you are seeking input from skateboarders, asking them to do an interview at a skate park would probably be a more sensible than suggesting that you meet in a library. Similarly, if you are studying investment bankers, choosing a setting in an office block may provide a comfortable and familiar location for the research.
- **Ensure that you have everything you need to conduct the interview.** Don't forget to bring pens, clipboards, and fully charged recording devices. Also be sure you know how to access the room or area where you will meet the participants. Imagine the embarrassment of being stuck outside the locked room in which you were supposed to hold your focus group or interview, or the awkwardness of having to interrupt an interview when the battery dies on your audio recorder. Such practical failings can undermine your credibility.

6•2•3 ACCOUNT FOR SOCIAL AND CULTURAL DIFFERENCES

Consider potential cultural sensitivities regarding your research. It is important to be culturally inclusive. The results of your research will be skewed if you fail to ensure that your sample reflects the population that you are studying. For example, it could be unwise to assume that prospective participants from ethnic minorities (e.g., recent immigrants) speak English, have internet access, or are aware of certain local historical events. If you don't recognize these sensitivities, you are likely to struggle to communicate the ideas behind your research and your efforts to gain participation will prove fruitless. Moreover, unrealistic assumptions can make your research appear irrelevant or disconnected from the social reality of the group you are trying to sample.

Note that subcultures within your culture can require just as much sensitivity as immigrant populations with which you are unfamiliar or research participants you encounter outside of your home country. Before you approach a target population, make sure that you consider a range of variables including local languages, educational backgrounds and levels of social marginalization.

REAL WORLD EXAMPLE

Be sensitive to your research context

Jens was conducting research on how residents of a low-income housing estate in London access information about their local area. He began his verbally administered survey by asking which digital device residents used to access information about local public services: iPad/tablet, desktop computer, laptop computer, smartphone or 'other'. He was taken aback when the first respondent rejected the question, saying 'We don't have iPads: we have pencils!'.

Jens had made an inappropriate assumption that participants in low-income areas accessed information by some kind of digital technology when in fact a number of residents gained such information using other, non-digital means. Appearing out of touch like this reduces the likelihood of gaining and maintaining participation. With a self-administered survey, a respondent might stop participating if they came across an unrealistic assumption suggesting the researcher did not understand the situation.

Minority groups may also be reluctant to participate in research for reasons stemming from historical discrimination. Immigrant communities may feel vulnerable and could be reluctant to participate in research for fear of negative repercussions from the state, such as from immigration officials. Other communities may have a history of being exploited that has led them to mistrust research and research institutions. Being aware of these histories can help you understand that you may need a more careful approach to build rapport with some communities, including ethnic minorities.

REAL WORLD EXAMPLE

Tuskegee syphilis experiment

Between 1932 and 1972 a clinical study was conducted in which African-American men were unwittingly part of a major research project studying syphilis. Individuals who had previously, but unknowingly, contracted the disease were told that they were receiving free medical care. However, their syphilis was deliberately left untreated so that researchers could track how the debilitating effects of the disease progressed differently amongst African-Americans.

The project has rightly become notorious as an extreme example of unethical research. The fact that it continued for nearly 40 years highlights the pervasive racism against African-Americans at the time. Ethnic minorities are often treated poorly worldwide by authorities, which can make them reluctant to engage in research.

Be sensitive to minority perspectives. Where applicable, you should try to get input from people representing the different minorities within your target population when you are planning how to carry out your research. Furthermore, you may need to take ethnicity and other minority categories into account when you are seeking out gatekeepers. For example, if you are carrying out a survey among a population of recent immigrants, it would make sense to be accompanied by someone who is respected within the particular minority ethnic community you are working with and is able to act as an interpreter if necessary. This will help to ease community members' concerns about participating in your research.

6●3 CONCLUSION

In this chapter we have highlighted strategies you can use to secure participation in your research. You should be prepared to demonstrate basic mastery of information about your research topic to assure your participants of your credibility as a researcher. You should also avoid terms and phrases that may make you sound condescending, pompous or unapproachable. For example, you should normally avoid using theory or jargon when describing your research.

We also discussed the role of incentives in research. The greater the time commitment, inconvenience and risk faced by your respondent, the more you will need to offer incentives for participation. A five-minute survey will require less of an incentive than a two-hour-long focus group. Regardless of incentives, you may need to work through gatekeepers in order to reach your participants effectively. For instance, you will need to approach a parent or guardian if you want children to participate in your research.

In this chapter we have also discussed the importance of getting the fundamentals right: dress appropriately, keep your appointments, arrive early and ensure that both you and the participants are absolutely clear about where and when you will meet. Finally, regardless of your particular strategy for gaining participation, you should always follow the core ethical principles discussed in Chapter 3. These principles include your duty to produce quality research, to get informed consent, to respect your participants' right to refuse and to keep your promises of confidentiality or anonymity. Finally, despite all your efforts, there will be no guarantee that potential participants will trust you enough to take part in your research. Be prepared for rejection and take it gracefully, expressing thanks for considering your participation request. But if you follow the steps outlined in this chapter, you will be well on your way to gaining (and maintaining!) participants for your research project.

▬ SUGGESTIONS FOR FURTHER READING ▬

- **Alderson, P., & Morrow, V. (2011). Money matters: Contracts, funding, projects and paying participants. In P. Alderson & V. Morrow, *The ethics of research with children and young people: A practical handbook* (2nd ed., pp. 63–73). London: Sage.** This entire text is a useful guide for doing research with young children, but this chapter in particular provides guidance on the financial side of research. While the chapter comes from the perspective of research with children or young people, the messages are applicable to research with any demographic.
- **Fricker, R. D. (2008). Sampling methods for web and e-mail surveys. In N. Fielding, R. M. Lee & G. Blank (Eds.), *The SAGE handbook of online research methods* (pp. 195–217). London: Sage.** This is a useful text that discusses the advantages and shortfalls of various sampling methods for online research, either through email or web-based platforms such as Survey Monkey. The chapter also includes a broader discussion of sampling methods outside of internet-specific research.
- **McNamara, P. (2009). Feminist ethnography: Storytelling that makes a difference. In P. Atkinson & S. Delamont (Eds.), *SAGE qualitative research methods* (pp. 162–197). London: Sage.** This chapter provides a useful real world example on the importance of establishing researcher credibility and gaining participant trust.
- **Ornstein, M. (2013). Survey data collection (pp. 115–140). In *A companion to survey research.* London: Sage.** This chapter contains a good discussion on the use of incentives to improve survey responses.

- **Silverman, D. (2013).** *Doing qualitative research: A practical handbook* **(4th ed.). London: Sage.** Silverman offers a well-written perspective on conducting qualitative research. Of particular interest for this chapter is his brief but useful discussion in Chapter 17 of 'impression management' and gaining access in the field.
- **Venkatesh, S. (2009).** *Gang leader for a day: A rogue sociologist crosses the line.* **London: Penguin.** This book provides a very readable, entertaining, popularized account of an ethnographic study of a gang in Chicago. If you are thinking about doing an ethnographic study with a challenging population, this extended real world example can help you prepare as it reveals some challenging issues involved in gaining participation. However, this book describes some very problematic research practices, so don't look to it for solutions to these issues!

Visit the companion website at **https://study.sagepub.com/jensenandlaurie** to gain access to a wide range of online resources to support your learning, including editable research documents, weblinks, free access SAGE journal articles and book chapters, and flashcards.

GLOSSARY

Anonymity – Not identifying an individual by name in your research to ensure their privacy. Anonymity typically means the researcher doesn't know the participant's identity.

Confidentiality – If you offer participants confidentiality, that means you know who they are but you promise to keep their information private and not to publish their names or associate them with what they have said when you write up your research report.

Credibility – This refers to the combination of qualities such as being trustworthy, reliable and honest.

Focus groups – This is a method of research in which three or more participants take part in an extended group discussion about a given issue.

Gatekeepers – Individuals who know and have influence over a pool of potential respondents.

Informed consent – The process of ensuring that respondents know all the necessary information about your research before agreeing to take part.

Interviews – A method of research whereby you have an extended, somewhat structured face-to-face conversation with an individual, during which you ask them questions.

Participant observation – A method of research in which you observe individuals in a setting from the position of someone participating in whatever activities are taking place in that setting.

Professionalism – Establishing yourself as competent and knowledgeable when approaching individuals.

Rapport – A trusting relationship you can develop with an individual.

Snowball sampling – A non-probability method of sampling in which you recruit new participants from the acquaintances of individuals who have already taken part in your research.

Surveys – A method of research in which participants answer a series of questions, either through filling out a paper survey or being asked by an interviewer.

REFERENCES

Alderson, P., & Morrow, V. (2011). *The Ethics of Research with Children and Young People: A Practical Handbook* (2nd ed.). London: Sage.

James, N., & Busher, H. (2009). Curating and disseminating online qualitative data. In *Online interviewing* (pp. 115–128). London: Sage.

O'Reilly, K. (2009). *Key concepts in ethnography*. London: Sage.

Ornstein, M. (2013). Survey data collection (pp. 115–140). In *A Companion to Survey Research*. London: Sage.

Venkatesh, S. (2009). *Gang leader for a day: A rogue sociologist crosses the line*. London: Penguin.

PART III

DATA COLLECTION METHODS

HOW TO DO SURVEY RESEARCH

—— **THIS CHAPTER COVERS THE FOLLOWING TOPICS** ——————

- How to develop a well-designed survey plan.
- How to design survey questions that can validly collect information about people's thoughts, feelings, attitudes and behaviours.
- How sources of survey bias can be avoided.
- How to test your survey questions in advance to save resources in the long term.

7.1 INTRODUCTION

This chapter is a guide to the process of designing and conducting survey research. It will show you how to efficiently gather valid survey data, even under tight budget and time constraints, in order to help you steer a course through the survey research process. Equipped with an understanding of the principles of good survey practice discussed in this chapter, you will find that the many challenges of survey design can be overcome with good planning and critical thinking.

Figure 7.1 provides a visual overview of the survey process from start to finish. Note how this process involves constant refinement and adjustment in order to be as efficient and robust as possible.

Surveys (also called questionnaires) offer a standardized method of collecting both quantitative and qualitative data from individuals (not groups or institutions). A survey can be an excellent tool for gathering information about memories, knowledge, personal experiences, attitudes and behaviour, as long as the survey measures are both *reliable* and *valid* (quality criteria we'll return to later on). Surveys are particularly good for research topics focusing on the details of a person's recent actions and experiences or their current thoughts, opinions, interests, intentions or values. Survey data can be used to address research goals such as describing patterns in a large population (e.g., national public opinion or customer satisfaction across an entire business) or determining individuals' characteristics within a population (e.g., how much do people earn? How healthy do they feel? Are there variations across different cities, institutions or ethnicities?). Survey data are also useful for assessing current social and political conditions from individuals' perspectives within a population (e.g., is the nation moving in a positive direction? What are the consequences of unemployment? What are the dimensions of current anti-immigrant sentiment?) and comparing the perspectives of different groups of individuals within a population (e.g., how do people in differing economic classes feel about their healthcare provision? How do individuals from different ethnicities living in the same community view crime?).

However, if your research question requires data collection during an event, activity or social practice (e.g., a religious ritual), surveys *can* limit the validity and depth of the data collected in such settings. This may occur either by breaking the normal flow of the activity (on-the-spot surveys) or by requiring respondents to reconstruct the activity in their memory at a later point. Therefore, surveys may not be the right choice if your goal is to directly measure or observe people's practices as they develop. For such topics, instead consider ethnographic methods (Chapter 8).

As surveys often require respondents to reflect on and self-report their knowledge, attitudes or behaviour, they should sometimes be avoided (see Table 7.1).

This chapter doesn't go into detail on every aspect of the survey process because the book covers some aspects in other chapters, such as ethics (Chapter 3) and analysis considerations

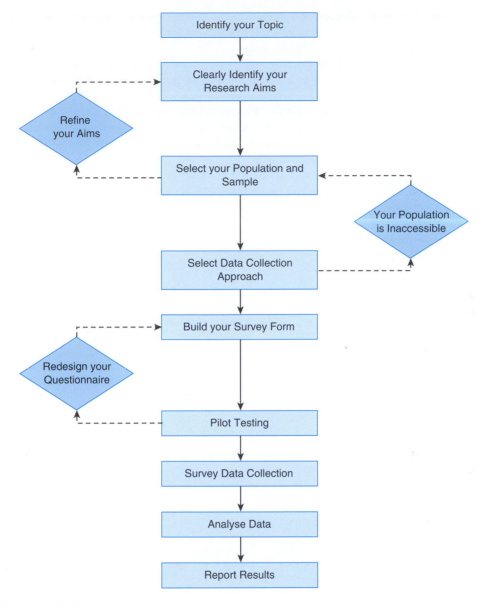

Figure 7.1 Overview of survey process

(Chapters 11 and 12). This chapter pays particular attention to how to translate your research aims and constraints into workable survey designs, data collection plans and procedures.

This chapter takes you through the decision-making process for survey design and data collection, addressing key challenges along the way:

1 **Define the goals for your survey.** What are you trying to discover? Do you simply want to be able to describe a population, or are you trying to discover causal factors? Sometimes these questions are harder to define than you might think.

2 **Prepare a data collection plan.** Where are the data coming from?

3   **Avoid the pitfalls of question design.** Do not make needless work for yourself later in the research process, or worse, generate unusable or biased data. Mistakes can easily arise that are harder to resolve at later stages.

4   **Test your survey in advance.** This chapter guides you through the process of pilot testing and survey redesign. This is a good way to save resources by avoiding wasted data collection effort.

5   **Develop strategies and procedures to effectively conduct the survey data collection.** Specific plans with clear procedures can make the data collection process more efficient. Describing these procedures in your report also reassures your readers that you have been systematic in your approach.

6   **Plan ahead for survey data analysis.** What resources and skills can you draw on to make sense of the information you have collected? It is easy to feel overwhelmed by the amount of information a survey can generate. Therefore, it is important to ensure you can effectively analyse the data you collect. This chapter shows how you can take your later data analysis into account during the survey design process.

Table 7.1   When a survey is an inappropriate method

Research focus	Research example	Why a survey is inappropriate	Alternative method
Causal factors and events beyond the scope of respondents' knowledge or experience	Surveying the general public about what factors are negatively affecting the national economy	Most people are unlikely to be aware of many details about the national economy	Semi-structured interviews
Behaviour that respondents are unable to accurately recall	Researching public behaviour in a museum – the number of times someone stopped to look at a particular sculpture	It would be unreasonable to assume that most people could accurately recall details of a one-time abstract event	Systematic observation – counting the number of times someone stopped to look at a particular sculpture
Behaviour that people are unlikely to disclose	Consumption of illegal substances (e.g., cocaine)	Respondents may be unwilling to accurately report behaviour within a survey due to concerns over legality, disclosing socially undesirable behaviour, and protecting their own privacy	Ethnography of a particular group/persons of interest

7•1•1 PLAN YOUR SURVEY PROJECT STEP BY STEP

Begin asking yourself questions to set the boundaries for your topic, aims, target population and survey design. What time and resources do you have available for data collection and analysis? Given your available time/resources and external support, how feasible is your ideal sample size? What is the scope of the research claim you want to be able to make using the survey results? (For example, do you want to be able to generalize to your target population?) The answers to such practical questions feed into the process of designing survey research; this effectively balances the need for accurate measurement against your available resources and capabilities. Maintaining a tight focus on your research question, as well as only collecting survey data that help you address it, can save you significant time and resources.

As discussed in the introduction, all social research involves compromises between ideal research procedures and what is actually possible in practice. Navigating the key survey challenges outlined above with limited resources often requires compromises. For example, you may need to limit your sample size and the quantity of survey questions. Subsequent sections will help guide you through such options and highlight where in the survey process you may need to make practical decisions.

7●2 DEVELOP YOUR SURVEY RESEARCH DESIGN

7●2●1 SHOULD YOU USE SURVEYS FOR YOUR PROJECT?

This section guides you through the benefits and challenges of choosing different types of surveys as data collection methods. Surveys are often thought of as a quantitative method, but can be qualitative as well. **Qualitative surveys** enable you to collect data from a larger number of people than other qualitative methods in the same amount of time. Moreover, you can use surveys to collect qualitative data in settings that make other forms of qualitative data collection difficult (e.g., where people are in a hurry or are unable to stop for an interview at that moment). In such cases, a small amount of contact information can be collected at the time. You can then follow up with an online or telephone-based survey to be completed at a more convenient time and location. In addition, a survey can be used to collect a combination of quantitative and qualitative data to simultaneously address different dimensions of your research topic.

From a practical perspective, surveys can be an especially useful option if you are going to need other people to administer some of your data collection for you. Most data collection methods require formal social research training to conduct. However, it is often possible to have novice researchers, whom you train yourself, assist with data collection for surveys. Having novice helpers distribute and collect self-administered surveys for you is much simpler and cheaper than trying to prepare them to conduct in-depth, semi-structured interviews or focus groups (see Chapter 8 for details about these methods).

───── **REAL WORLD EXAMPLE** ─────

Large-scale survey research on a tight budget

A large festival wanted to know how satisfied its audience was with their festival experiences. To make the most of a small research budget, the festival recruited volunteers to conduct its audience satisfaction survey. The volunteers did not have any prior research skills. After a quick briefing,

(Continued)

(Continued)

however, they were able to distribute, collect and enter data from survey forms prepared by a social scientist acting as an external research consultant. This approach meant the festival could limit its use of a (costly) social scientist consultant to the survey design and analysis phases. Therefore, the festival got the information it wanted without compromising research quality or its budget.

Maintain efficiency in survey data processing and analysis. Surveys can be designed in ways that minimize the amount of time required to collect and analyse data. First, the type of survey questions you use affects the amount of time required for data analysis. The broadest way of distinguishing question types is **open-ended** (respondents generate their own responses) and **closed-ended** (respondents choose from a limited range of pre-specified response options); see Table 7.2.

Closed-ended survey questions produce quantitative data, which is faster to process and analyse. However, closed-ended quantitative survey research is particularly sensitive to mistakes in survey and question design that can undermine the accuracy of your data (thereby eliminating the value of any time savings). In contrast, qualitative data gathered with open-ended survey responses generally require a much slower and more in-depth analysis. Open-ended surveys also take significantly longer to administer and can be harder and more time-consuming to analyse, especially if only a handful of respondents give a particular response (American Association for Public Opinion Research (AAPOR), 2015b). The general rule is: the larger your sample size, the more time you save overall by using closed-ended questions.

Maintaining standardization. From a quantitative perspective, surveys offer the great advantage of ensuring that every respondent is asked exactly the same questions in exactly the same way. Such **standardization** makes valid generalizations about your target research population possible. Without standardization, differences in question phrasing can make data from different respondents impossible to compare and combine statistically (Beatty, 1995).

Table 7.2 Strengths and weaknesses of closed- and open-ended questions

Survey question type	Response type	Strengths	Weaknesses
Closed-ended	Choice of pre-selected options	• Easy to administer and complete • Easy to process and analyse • Enhance comparability of responses	• Generate limited detail • Sensitive to design errors • Time-consuming to design • Can make respondents feel constrained if they can't give their preferred response
Open-ended	Respondents generate their own responses	• Respondents can answer in their own terms • Limited researcher bias • Useful for exploring areas of limited researcher knowledge	• Time-consuming analysis (see Chapters 11–12) • Require greater effort from respondents

The highest degree of standardization comes from survey forms that respondents complete by themselves. Self-completion is the norm online, but face-to-face survey data collection can require verbally administering your questions, depending on the context. If you're verbally administering your survey, you must ask the exact same question to each respondent in the same way. Try to anticipate any aspects of the survey respondents might find unclear and make sure you have a pre-prepared standardized list of definitions or elaborated explanations (Conrad & Schober, 2000). You can include follow-up questions or 'probes' in your design of a verbally administered survey to elicit more detailed responses, but this also requires advance planning to standardize your procedures. If anybody is going to help you conduct your survey data collection, they need to be at least minimally trained in following such procedures, reading questions verbatim and ensuring they don't accidentally bias respondents' answers (AAPOR, 2015a).

Once you have considered these issues and decided that survey methods are right for your topic, you will face the issue of what makes a 'good' survey.

7•2•2 DESIGNING A GOOD SURVEY

Validity and reliability. When designing a survey, you must always consider the **validity** and **reliability** of your methods and measures. Validity refers to the extent to which the information you gather from your survey respondents accurately represents the concept you are studying. For example, you may be interested in whether intelligence predicts income. Often, researchers will use educational attainment as a substitute measure of intelligence, because it is easy to measure and often correlates well with 'actual' intelligence. While this is a valid substitute measure for many research questions, it would not be valid for predicting income because there are many things that influence educational attainment beyond simple intelligence. Instead, you may choose to use an IQ test, or something similar. While an IQ test only measures one 'type' of intelligence, it may still provide more validity than educational attainment because it more accurately reflects the underlying concept (i.e., intelligence).

Reliability is a quality criterion that refers to the extent to which the measures you use, and the data you collect, provide consistent results. A useful way to think about the distinction between validity and reliability is in terms of different kinds of *survey error*. Reliability, in these terms, would refer to *random error*, or the extent to which responses to a question randomly diverge from each other. This contrasts with validity, which can be seen as *systematic error*, or error that affects all responses to the question in a similar way. It is worth noting that it is impossible to have a valid measure that is not also reliable, although a reliable measure is not necessarily a valid measure.

A perfectly reliable survey would be completely free of random error; for example, if you read the same questions twice to the same person, in exactly the same way, the answers would be exactly the same. While it is impossible to remove all random error from a survey (and thus impossible for your survey to be perfectly reliable), you can usually increase the reliability of your survey findings by simply taking more measurements (e.g., increasing your sample size, or asking respondents numerous questions that are designed to measure the same concept). For more on creating valid and reliable measures, see Chaffee (1991).

The basics of survey preparation. Use surveys to access thoughts, feelings, attitudes and values that would normally be difficult to access systematically through external observation alone. Survey design involves multiple (and sometimes competing) goals. In your survey you are seeking to:

- Ask questions that allow you to shed as much light as possible on your area of research.
- Ask no more questions than you need to address your research question.
- Ask standardized, focused questions that are likely to be relevant and understandable for your respondents.
- Avoid the many possible forms of bias, such as leading questions.

Putting these and other goals into practice in your particular project typically requires a balance. When designing a survey form, you should ask enough questions to thoroughly address your research question. But if you take this too far and ask too many questions, then your respondents may feel inconvenienced or fatigued and become unwilling to finish your survey (Dillman, Sinclair, & Clark, 1993). In order to design a good survey, you must understand how surveys work from the perspective of respondents and prepare accordingly.

Survey preparation stage 1: Gaining your respondents' attention and understanding. Respondents must pay attention to your survey instructions and questions. They must also understand the survey questions' guidance or instructions, any terms or concepts embedded within the question, as well as what information the survey is seeking (Jabine, Straf, & Tourangeau, 1984). To achieve this, you must ensure your survey questions and instructions are clear, while avoiding jargon and complicated wording.

Survey preparation stage 2: Ensure that your questions are clear. In order to ensure that your respondents' answer as accurately as possible, ensure that the framing and context of your questions do not give unintended cues. Respondents formulate opinions and thoughts – positive and negative – from a range of cues. Such cues include how the survey questions are written and framed (Tversky & Kahneman, 1974), the data collector's appearance and demeanour and the location in which the survey is being conducted (Godden & Baddeley, 1975), among many other factors. For example, it could be problematic for a uniformed shop employee to verbally survey customers about their experiences at a store. Respondents (customers) in this situation might give answers the employee would want to hear rather than accurately reporting their actual experiences in order to avoid offending the employee (and thereby causing themselves psychological discomfort). Your survey design must account for such social norms (Holtgraves, 2004).

Think also about how your questions might be misinterpreted, and phrase questions so that respondents do not feel compelled to guess. We'll discuss this issue later on in this chapter in the sections on writing survey questions (Section 7.3.1) and piloting surveys (Section 7.3.3). However, it's worth pausing here to think about the complexity of answering a survey question. If respondents can only partially recall their memories, they may fill in the gaps with inaccurate guesses or assumptions to provide a survey response (Menon, 1993). For example, a recent global survey asking zoo visitors to indicate how many times they had been to the zoo in the last 12 months yielded responses including '50' and '300' (Jensen, 2014). Such large round numbers are immediately recognizable as estimates (or guesses) rather than precise reporting of past behaviour.

Survey preparation stage 3: Align your survey response options to cultural norms. It is important that response options align with respondents' normal language and the information they are likely to know to the greatest extent possible. For example, if you were researching the use of computer technology by IT professionals, it would make sense to refer to equipment by the terms IT professionals would use (e.g., perhaps use 'laptop' instead of 'portable computer'). If the response options do not closely match the respondents' existing knowledge (e.g., if they are too technical), respondents may make a guess, select a neutral or 'don't know' response option, or leave the question unanswered. In all of these cases, respondents are likely to experience a degree of frustration, and this may affect the accuracy of your data (AAPOR, 2015a, 2015b).

Even with a carefully considered survey design, you can only make reasonable guesses about what kinds of responses your survey questions will elicit. For example, if you are asking patrons at a restaurant about how much they enjoyed their meal, you may feel that it is perfectly clear that you are asking about the food. However, some respondents may think you are also asking about the quality of table service, the décor in the restaurant and a host of other variables. This kind of confusion can lead to poor-quality survey data (Suessbrick, Schober, & Conrad, 2000).

This means you will need to carry out a pilot test to refine your survey design. **Pilot testing** involves trialling your test survey on a group of people from a similar demographic background to your intended respondents. A first step is to have your supervisor or someone else experienced in survey design review your questions and give feedback: do your questions make sense? Are they phrased appropriately? Are they grouped in a logical manner?

Then ask your test respondents to actually do the survey. Make this a process of open dialogue where you not only review the answers they give to ensure that responses match your questions, but also ask how they felt and what they thought when completing it. Did they find the questions clear? What was confusing and why? Take this feedback seriously and refine your questions. You may decide that you need to do another round of pilot testing if you needed to make a lot of changes. Remember – it is much easier to find and eliminate errors in pilot testing than down the road!

Therefore, the survey process involves a cycle of writing draft instructions, survey questions and survey responses for respondents, critically evaluating what you have written, revising those questions, pilot testing and continued revision and so on.

The process of refining your survey could go on indefinitely. However, time is always limited and, ultimately, you have to make the judgement about when a survey design is 'good enough'. Ideally you make this judgement in consultation with others who can offer you advice and feedback, such as a tutor, colleague or supervisor. Our advice is that some pilot testing is better than none. So go ahead and collect whatever feedback you can get (even if that means resorting to using friends and family). Plan your survey design phase carefully, so as to leave enough time for pilot testing and revision of your survey questions (for more information, see Oksenberg, Cannell, & Kalton, 1991).

7•2•3 MAKING SURVEY DESIGN DECISIONS: FORKS IN THE ROAD

As you develop your survey design, you will come across a number of forks in the road. This section guides you through these crossroads, highlighting the implications of the different survey design decisions you will have to make.

Combine methods or use a survey only? As you consider your survey design, you will need to decide on appropriate questions to ask, how to phrase them, and what sort of response options are appropriate. You can obtain this information from published research on your topic (if it is available), informal conversations with members of your target population or colleagues familiar with the topic, or by drawing on your own informal experience with your research context and target population. If these sources of information are unavailable or inadequate, you should strongly consider employing an additional data collection method to fill in the knowledge gap.

Combining surveys with another method, such as a preliminary small-scale ethnography or small focus group study, can give you crucial insights about the context or conditions for your research topic. Hypotheses, variables and contextual knowledge about the target population developed from preliminary small-scale qualitative research can feed directly into survey design, enhancing research quality and validity. You can also follow up on survey results using a depth-oriented qualitative method.

REAL WORLD EXAMPLE

Combining surveys and other research methods

Eric conducted a combined qualitative and quantitative pre- and post-visit survey investigating whether zoo visits promoted children's learning about animals. His research showed that children who attended a zoo-delivered presentation during their visits learned much more than children guided only by their regular schoolteachers. However, the survey didn't reveal *why* the schoolteacher-guided zoo visits resulted in significantly less learning. To address this key question and explain the survey findings, Eric conducted a small-scale follow-up ethnographic study of schoolteacher-guided zoo visits. The follow-up study revealed that these schoolteachers had relatively poor knowledge about zoo animals, which they passed along to their school pupils (rather than looking up correct answers or admitting they didn't know an answer). Therefore, the combined survey and ethnographic study were able to provide a more complete result than either single method could achieve on its own.

Qualitative, quantitative or mixed methods? Within your survey research, you can use any combination of closed-ended or open-ended questions. Both types of question can complement each other within a single survey. You can use the quantitative data generated by closed-ended survey questions to identify general patterns. These patterns can then be further explored and deeper explanations identified using the qualitative data generated by open-ended questions. Closed-ended survey questions require the least time and resources to analyse, and tend to be the most reliable if designed well. The great advantage of open-ended survey questions is that they can gather data on emotions, interests and attitudes that you were not able to anticipate when first designing the study, and tend to be more valid. A mixed methods survey enables both kinds of questions to be used together to support and reinforce each other.

Cross-sectional or longitudinal design? You will need to decide whether to run your survey at a single point in time (**cross-sectional survey**) or to conduct multiple linked surveys focused on investigating change over time (**longitudinal survey**). Researchers choose cross-sectional surveys because they are the simplest and lowest-cost option. Often, survey researchers use cross-sectional survey data to measure change over time (e.g., by asking about attitudes, interests or behaviour in the past, in the present and projected into the future). While these data can provide interesting insights, there is substantial risk of bias stemming from the reporting of distant memories (Menon, 1993; Sánchez, Koskinen, & Plewis, 2014). This risk of bias (and therefore inaccuracy) is also present when respondents are being asked to speculate about their future behaviour. Therefore, it is important to be cautious when using data collected at a single point in time to make claims about events in people's past or future, or any changes that might have occurred over time.

Depending on your research question and your available time and resources, you may want to consider the option of longitudinal survey research. A longitudinal survey involves at least two separate data collection points, separated by a period of time (which could be from as little as a couple hours to as much as 10 or more years, depending on the research topic). While the limitations of self-report still apply, such data can provide unique and valid insights about change in a phenomenon over a period of time.

In practice, the challenging logistics and high costs involved in conducting longitudinal survey research make it an impractical research choice for many people. In addition, the analysis of longitudinal data (known as 'time series analysis') is much more advanced than anything covered in this book (for an accessible overview of time series analysis, and for a list of additional resources for conducting time series analysis, see Williams & Monge, 2001). However, if your research topic focuses on change over time, it may be worth facing the downsides in order to conduct a small-sample longitudinal study, perhaps using an online survey to lower costs.

Self-administered or verbally administered surveys? **Self-administered survey** forms require respondents to read the survey instructions and questions for themselves and respond on paper or screen without a researcher's active participation. If there is verbal interaction between respondent and researcher in this mode, it is generally limited to an initial invitation to join the study. Once respondents agree to participate, they may also be verbally advised of the survey's purpose, ethical conditions (e.g., 'you can withdraw from this study at any time'), and any standard instructions.

For online surveys, self-completion is the norm. It is also common, however, for self-administered surveys to be distributed face-to-face by researchers, a gatekeeper or volunteers on the researchers' behalf. Respondents given survey forms in face-to-face research encounters can complete the survey either immediately or later at a time and place that is more convenient. Locations for distributing self-administered surveys are typically selected based on where the target population can be most easily accessed. This kind of data collection can occur in public places, businesses, people's homes and anywhere else; potential respondents can be reached by mail, email or online surveys.

Self-administered survey instructions and questions require the highest level of clarity. If respondents become frustrated with confusing instructions, they may decide to stop completing the survey, and you might never know why. Moreover, securing an adequate response rate can be more challenging with self-administered surveys. Statistically, anything less than a 100 per cent response rate could technically be considered problematic. In practice, however, if 50 per cent or more of those you select for your sample actually complete surveys, this is usually viewed as a satisfactory response rate. With online surveys or hard-to-reach populations, even this level of response rate is very difficult, if not impossible, to achieve in many cases. The important thing is to be transparent about your sample selection procedures and to be sure to send reminder messages for any survey forms distributed online or by post (AAPOR, 2015a).

The other option you have at this fork in the road is to **verbally administer** your survey. In this option, you (or trained assistants) talk through all aspects of the survey. Respondents give their answers verbally or by pointing to a survey response option. Verbally administered surveys can be done over the phone (with or without a computerized survey form) or face-to-face. As with self-administered forms, verbal data collection can occur in a wide range of locations.

Table 7.3 Self-administered vs. verbally administered surveys

Type	Strengths	Weaknesses
Self-administered	• Allows for data collection from multiple individuals in different locations simultaneously • Can offer respondents full anonymity • Respondents may be more likely to provide honest answers on sensitive topics • Allows survey to be completed in the respondent's own time (useful for lengthy open-ended questions) • Saves researcher time and resources	• No opportunity to clarify any unclear phrasing from the survey instructions or questions • Achieving adequate response rates can be challenging (especially with postal and web surveys) • Cannot probe for further details about a respondent's answer • Requires extra up-front time investment to refine survey design
Verbally administered	• Opportunity to clarify aspects of the survey for respondent • Easy for respondents to complete (little effort on their part) • Possible to gain further depth by asking 'probe' questions (e.g., 'could you tell me more about that?')	• More expensive and time-consuming; requires data collectors to conduct • Risk of misquoting respondents when writing down responses • If survey is recorded, a lengthy transcription process for open-ended questions is required

If you are conducting a relatively brief survey with closed-ended questions, a verbally administered survey can make participation easy for respondents. This is especially true in a busy setting where your potential respondents are walking around.

However, a verbally administered survey has downsides, especially when you ask open-ended questions. If you are *not* recording the interaction, you then risk missing some of your respondents' words when you attempt to write down their answers. If you *do* record, then the amount of time and effort required to process and transcribe the responses can be substantial if you have a medium to large sample size.

Self-administered and verbally administered surveys are compared and contrasted in Table 7.3.

REAL WORLD EXAMPLE

Using response cards for verbally administered surveys to reduce bias

If you are asking any potentially sensitive questions (e.g., anything a person might not want to state about themselves out loud: personal income, sexual orientation, drug or alcohol use) in a verbally administered survey, it is good practice to use response cards with the different response options for a given question so respondents can point rather than verbalizing their answer. Alternatively, you can designate the response options with numbers or letters.

For example, Safia was conducting research on sexual minorities in Nigeria. She knew that homosexuality was a taboo subject in the country and had to find a way to allow her respondents to answer honestly. She decided to ask 'Which of the following most closely matches your sexual orientation?", but held up a set of response options on cards: A – Heterosexual, B – Homosexual,

C – Bisexual, D – Other. The respondent would answer by saying 'A', 'B', 'C' or 'D' (or pointing), thereby avoiding the need to state their sexual orientation verbally and increasing the likelihood that they would be truthful.

Plan a few steps ahead: Consider available time for data analysis. At this stage of the survey design process, you should also consider your data analysis. How much time do you have available for the analysis? Do you have the skills to analyse qualitative and/or quantitative data? These factors need to be taken into account at the level of overall survey design as well as the selection of particular questions. For example, you may need to use closed-ended response options if you do not have the time or skills to do the qualitative data analysis. Indeed, question design is the next stage in the survey process.

7●3 DEVELOP YOUR QUESTION DESIGN

7●3●1 DESIGNING GOOD SURVEY QUESTIONS AND FORMS

Developing good survey questions requires a degree of ingenuity and knowledge about your topic. As you begin to fill in the details of your survey form, you will have to make a number of key decisions about the:

1 focus of your questions (i.e., what variables you are going to measure);
2 type of question response (e.g., Likert, multiple-choice, open-ended);
3 content and phrasing of your questions;
4 sequence of questions and overall layout of the survey form.

Before starting any survey data collection, consult the existing research literature on your topic to see if there are relevant survey questions that have been used in previous published studies. There may even be an entire set of survey questions that you could reuse as published or with some adaptation. It is entirely consistent with good practice in survey research to use and adapt previously published questions for your research project as long as you cite the author(s) of the original study.

You can also turn to web services that compile the questions and results from large-scale social surveys. Two in particular stand out: SDA and iPOLL. SDA is a service based at the University of California, Berkeley, that provides detailed documentation for a vast set of surveys, including the General Social Survey (GSS) and the American National Election Study (ANES), and programs for web-based analysis of survey data. You can find out more by visiting their website: http://sda.berkeley.edu.

iPOLL, a service of the Roper Center at the University of Connecticut, provides a comprehensive and easily searchable database that includes over 650,000 survey questions (and answers) dating back all the way to 1935. Updated every week, iPOLL is a key survey archive for every major polling organization in America. You can find out more by visiting http://www.ropercenter.uconn.edu.

Table 7.4　Structuring your survey form

Task	Strengths
Title your survey form	Give your survey form a *title* at the top of the first page (e.g., 'Cheltenham Festivals Visitor Survey').
Note the version number	Include the *version number* (e.g., 'v.3') on the survey form in the headnote or footnote. This will help you track drafts and prevent you sending the incorrect version to respondents.
Provide a brief introduction	Include a research project description (usually from one sentence to one paragraph in length), summary of research aims, researcher identification and sources of funding.
Number individual questions	To speed up the data entry and analysis process later on, you should number individual questions, with subquestions indicated as follows: 12a, 12b, etc.
Include contact information	Provide contact and address information, as well as your email address. It is preferable to use your institutional email address (if you have one) rather than a personal email account in order to identify your institution and to give you more credibility.
Offer thanks for participation	Finish with a concluding statement thanking respondents for participating and, if appropriate, ask for permission to contact them again in future.

Structuring the survey form. Regardless of the topic, survey forms require a number of standard features. To begin building your survey form, you need to complete the tasks in Table 7.4.

In addition to these basic structural features, there are principles of good survey design that apply widely:

- **Be consistent in phrasing**. For example, don't use 'job', 'employment' and 'work' if just one of these terms would function just as well.
- **Avoid using too many different question types** (e.g., Likert scale, multiple-choice response, ranked response). It takes time and effort to get used to a question type; you don't want to make your respondents expend this extra effort unnecessarily.
- **Ensure questions are as brief as possible**. This avoids tiring out or confusing your respondents.
- **Use plain language.** Avoid jargon and assumptions of specialist knowledge unless surveying a specialist population. Try to account for the likely language capabilities, age and vocabulary of your target population. If respondents read words they don't understand or come across unusual terms, they may lose interest in participating or provide invalid or irrelevant responses.
- **Minimize ambiguity** in the questions and response options.
- **Use a clear, legible font,** such as Times New Roman or Arial that is no smaller than 11 point in size but preferably 12 point.
- **Format your survey consistently**, for example in the use of *italics* and **bold** (e.g., for instructions and for the question or category headings).

Survey form layout. Effective layout of your survey form also helps to keep the survey data collection process as simple and straightforward as possible for your respondents.

- **Don't put too many questions on any one survey page.** Avoid overloading respondents by making the page appear like 'too much work' or too intimidating.
- **Don't let your survey get too long.** Ideally, you should keep a survey form down to two or three pages while still addressing your research question, to avoid hurting your response rate. You may be able to get away with a slighter longer survey form online, particularly if you divide the survey form into separate pages focusing on different aspects of the topic.

Question sequence. The order in which the respondent encounters your survey questions can affect the readability and effectiveness of a survey. Keep these general principles in mind:

- **Structure your survey to go from general to specific questions, and from easy/simple to more difficult/complicated questions.** This way the reader can be gradually introduced to your research area and their thinking will be 'warmed up' before more challenging questions arise.
- **Save the demographic questions for the end** so that the respondent does not become fatigued early in the survey from the questions they can answer most easily.

These principles help to pave the way for your substantive survey questions, by making the process as easy as possible for respondents. Continue to consider the flow of your survey form as you select your question types. For example, you don't want closed-ended response options too early in a survey form to bias answers to open-ended questions.

Question types. As you build your survey form, you will need to choose from a range of well-established question types. You should make this selection based on what you are trying to discover from a particular question and what kind of analysis you are able to complete. The list in Table 7.5 offers advice on when to use the most common survey question types.

Open-ended questions allow respondents to tell you about their experiences, thoughts, attitudes and values without the constraint of a limited number of response options. However, many respondents find it burdensome to have to answer too many open-ended items.

Table 7.5 Common survey question types with examples

Question Type	Example
Open-ended	What interested you in visiting the store today?
Classification or demographic	Please select the category below that matches your household's income.
Ranked-response	Rank your preference from among the following options.
Multiple-choice ('select one')	Select the best answer among the following statements which matches your opinion.
Multiple-choice ('tick all that apply')	How did you hear about this event? Tick all that apply.
Likert scale	Please indicate your level of agreement with the following statement.

Also, beware of the much larger challenge that open-ended survey data pose at the data entry (if using a paper survey) and data analysis stages.

Classification or **demographic questions** about the objective characteristics of respondents (e.g., gender, ethnicity, religious affiliation) can take different forms. For example, a question about the respondent's age could request the individual's exact age, date of birth or an age category to be selected from a list provided by the researcher. Exact age keeps more statistical analysis options open, date of birth provides very precise information, but a respondent may feel that an age category question is a less intrusive one than exact age (thereby making it more likely that they give an answer).

Ranked-response questions should be used when you need to know your respondents' relative preferences, when compared to a limited set of alternatives. This can be an effective question type for researching comparisons between different commercial products, political candidates, preferred medical treatment options or other finite sets of choices in a particular domain.

REAL WORLD EXAMPLE

Using the ranked response question type

When Melissa was conducting an employee survey for a company making cutbacks to avoid redundancies, she tried to determine employees' relative support for a range of possible undesirable actions: (1) reduced pay by 5 per cent for everyone; (2) forced unpaid leave of an additional two weeks in every three-month period; (3) reduced holiday leave entitlement; or (4) reduced employer contribution to employee retirement accounts. By asking for ranked responses, she was able to determine which of these unpleasant options would be resisted least by employees.

Multiple-choice questions require respondents to 'select one response' from a set of options that you devise. This question type can be used when there are established (from previous research) or obvious answers that different respondents might give. By pre-specifying these response options, you save yourself the time-consuming task of converting a wide diversity of open-ended responses into a smaller set of categories during the data analysis phase. When you are designing survey response options for multiple choice questions, the response options need to be:

- **Exhaustive** – everyone fits into at least one response category
- **Exclusive** – everyone fits into only one response category (unless specifically required to 'tick all that apply').
- **Unambiguous** – response categories hold the same meaning for everyone so that all responses are comparable.

In order to capture any unforeseen answers a respondent might wish to give, 'Other (please specify): _____' is often included as one of the multiple-choice response options. An additional way to mitigate the risk of your multiple-choice response options failing to match a respondent's desired answer is to qualify the instruction within your question, saying 'select the best answer among the following statements' or 'the option that is closest to your view'. Finally, it is wise to provide a response option that allows respondents to get out of a question if they do not have an opinion, view or other relevant response to offer (e.g., 'don't know/no opinion'). For example, if your question related to views about becoming pregnant, the 'don't know/no opinion' option would allow male respondents to indicate a valid response. Forcing a response in such cases would increase non-response levels at best, and introduce bias at worst.

Multiple-choice questions that ask respondents to 'select all response options that apply' require extra time for you to process and analyse, when compared to single-response multiple-choice questions. However, this is sometimes the only viable question type (e.g., for the question 'How did you hear about this event', a 'tick all that apply' question listing a range of possible sources such as television broadcasts, newspaper and word of mouth would typically be the best choice). If you limit your analysis to descriptive statistics (e.g., identifying the percentages selecting each response option), then this question type should not substantially delay your data analysis.

REAL WORLD EXAMPLE

Multiple-choice question

The following multiple-choice (select one) question was asked during an NBC News Poll (2014) on crime, values, religion, economics and equality: 'Whether you oppose the death penalty or not, which of the following do you feel is the strongest argument in opposition to the death penalty? ...'

The researchers listed five common statements given by advocacy organizations and politicians in opposition to the death penalty. Importantly, the polling organization also allowed respondents to say that all of options were equally strong (i.e., all of these), that all of the questions were equally weak (i.e., none of these), that they knew of a different reason that they thought was stronger than any that was listed (i.e., some other reason), or that they couldn't decide (i.e., not sure). In total, 10 per cent of respondents gave one of those options, showing how important it is to cover all possible response options.

The poll found the following results:

35% – It carries the risk of killing someone who was wrongly convicted

18% – It is not applied fairly or uniformly across the country

13% – It is against my religious or moral beliefs

12% – It costs taxpayers more than life imprisonment

12% – It does not deter murder any more than long prison sentences

1% – Some other reason

2% – All of these

3% – None of these

4% – Not sure

Likert scale questions are best employed when the variable you are measuring has multiple levels (i.e., not a yes/no variable). The response scales should normally be 1–5, 1–7 or 1–9. This allows for a neutral response to be included in the middle of the scale. The standard Likert scale options are (for a five-point scale): strongly disagree, disagree, neutral, agree, strongly agree. These options can be stretched for seven-point scales by adding 'somewhat' to the list, as follows: strongly disagree, disagree, somewhat disagree, neutral, somewhat agree, agree, strongly agree.

You can also use **Likert-type** scales, which use concepts other than 'agreement' to anchor the scale. For example, you might have a scale that captures 'level of concern' about different political or social issues or 'level of confidence' in different types of information or professions. Normally, you should simplify your Likert scale statement (level-of-agreement questions) by using positive phrasing (i.e., avoiding negation). For example, 'I enjoy learning about survey research' (strongly agree – strongly disagree) would be simpler for respondents to interpret and respond to than 'I do not enjoy learning about survey research'. To cover the negative possibilities, you could use a framing such as: 'I find survey research difficult to understand' (strongly agree – strongly disagree). There are some great online resources for finding well-tested Likert-type scale response anchors. We especially recommend Vagias (2006).

 **REAL WORLD EXAMPLE**

Likert-type question

The following Likert-type question was asked during a Harvard Institute of Politics (2014) survey on Americans' attitudes toward politics and public service: 'How much do you agree or disagree with the following statement? ... "Religious values should play a more important role in government".'

The question was measured using a five-point scale, ranging from 1 (strongly agree) to 5 (strongly disagree). Importantly, the survey did not give a 'don't know' response. The results are listed below:

- 08% – Strongly agree
- 13% – Somewhat agree
- 34% – Neither agree or disagree
- 13% – Somewhat disagree
- 31% – Strongly disagree
- 2% – Decline to answer

Over a third of respondents stated that they neither agreed nor disagreed, with only 13 per cent somewhat agreeing, and 13 per cent somewhat disagreeing. This is an unusually high number of respondents reporting that their opinion falls in between agree and disagree. Because there was not a 'don't know' response, it's impossible to know how many of these individuals didn't have an opinion versus how many had an opinion that actually fell in the middle.

The big advantage to the closed-ended survey question types described above is that the data can be entered (paper form) or imported (online form or tablet) into a spreadsheet in a numerical format ready to be used in statistical analyses.

Table 7.6 summarizes the uses and benefits of and possible issues with the above survey question types.

Address errors in your survey questions when you spot them. What do you do when you realize part of the way through your data collection that there is an error in one or more of your questions? Whether or not you are stuck with your mistake until data collection finishes depends on what kind of error it is. If it is a typographical mistake (e.g., a gender response option, 'femele') or grammatical error that is irrelevant to the meaning of the question (e.g., 'Please select which of the following best describes you're experience at the museum'), then fix it immediately.

You might make a mistake (e.g., a grammatical error or an incorrectly named response option) that could affect the meaning of the question/response. For instance, if you were to ask 'Regarding your pet's interaction with the veterinary surgeon, how do you feel she responded to him?', the pronouns 'she' and 'him' make it unclear what information the question is seeking. In this case, you have two possible pathways:

1   If the flawed version is not useful for addressing your research questions (as in the case of the preceding example), you should make the change as soon as possible and exclude all the data you collected up to that time for that survey question. If you are throwing out a closed-ended response option for a multiple-choice question, you will need to exclude data for that entire question. This is because respondents' choices could have been affected by the flawed response option, meaning that the pre- and post-change data are not comparable.

    If, however, the flawed response option was on a 'tick all that apply' survey question that included a 'don't know/not applicable/no opinion' option, then you can still use those data with a 'methodological limitations' note describing the nature, timing and rationale for the change you made.

2   If the flawed version is still meaningful for answering your research question (but not what you ideally wanted), then you may want to simply carry on with the flawed version so that you can still use all of the data you have collected up to that point.

If you have included unnecessary additional response options that you wish you had not, you will probably have to live with this mistake (and acknowledge it as a limitation in your write-up – see Chapter 13). If you have failed to include a response option (that you now realize you should have), you should consider two main criteria based on how essential the response is to answering your research question:

- If **it is not essential**, then make a note to yourself for future research purposes and move on.
- If **it is essential**, then ask yourself how far into the data collection process you are. If this is a multiple-choice question, you will have to throw out any data you have already collected on this question. So the further you are into the data collection process, the more likely your best course of action is to keep the flawed question/response as it is. You would then acknowledge this limitation in the methods section of your research report.

Table 7.6 Uses and benefits of survey question types

Question type	Uses and benefits	Possible issues
Open-ended	• Allows the respondent to give any response they choose, without any constraints • Great for exploratory research, where you don't know what the responses will be • Allows you to capture 'rare' responses, i.e., things you may not expect to find	• Lengthy coding process • Can be burdensome for survey respondents • Can be more difficult to analyse and to interpret
Classification or demographic	• Captures information about who the respondent is • Can be used to validate the representativeness of your sample • Allows you to check for any systematic differences between segments of the population	• Can feel invasive to the survey respondent • Can significantly increase the overall length of the survey
Ranked-response	• Good for understanding relative preferences • Especially useful when survey choices reflect real-world choices (e.g., ranking political candidates or vacuum cleaners)	• Impossible to know whether the difference between option 1 and option 2 is the same as the difference between option 2 and option 3 • Can be frustrating when the respondent sees no difference between options
Multiple-choice ('select one')	• Useful if you already know what the most common responses are going to be, either from prior research or experience • Easier to code than open-ended • Easier to analyse than multiple-choice ('tick all that apply')	• Not as much depth as open-ended questions • Not as valid as multiple-choice ('tick all that apply'), especially if respondents see more than one option as their top choice
Multiple-choice ('tick all that apply')	• Useful if you already know what the most common responses are going to be, either from prior research or experience • More valid than multiple-choice ('select one'), especially if respondents see more than one option as their top choice • Especially useful for sensitive demographic questions (e.g., race/ethnicity)	• Not as much depth as open-ended questions • Not as easy to analyse as multiple-choice ('select one'), and may require complicated statistics
Likert scale	• Allows you to capture multiple levels (i.e., not a yes/no variable) • Used to capture attitudes, beliefs, and/or perceptions • Easily used with most inferential statistics • Easy to analyse	• Not useful for capturing preferences or classifications • Impossible to know why an individual gave a certain response without follow-up questions • Impossible to know how important the attitude, belief, etc. is without follow-up questions

For errors on qualitative survey questions, it is generally less problematic to make changes during the data collection process because qualitative research does not necessarily require standardization. If the change affects the question's meaning, you may also need to analyse the data from the pre- and post-change versions of the question separately (at least initially) to assess whether the change has affected the data.

Finally, be careful about pre-categorizing your data (e.g., by asking for age ranges rather than current age or year of birth). This can limit your data analysis options. Categories can always be applied later, but pre-categorized data cannot later be converted back into continuous data that would allow for a greater range of statistical analyses. (For more information on designing an effective questionnaire, see Bradburn, Sudman, & Wansink, 2004.)

7•3•2 AVOID SURVEY BIAS

Reducing bias in its many forms (see Table 7.7) improves the reliability and validity of your survey research. Designing survey forms that avoid or minimize bias can sometimes feel like running an obstacle course. It is easy to make a potentially hazardous mistake on your first attempt at designing a survey form. This risk of making mistakes is why it is so important to edit, get feedback from others and ideally pilot test your survey forms.

In addition to the common survey biases listed above, it is also important to only ask for information that respondents could reasonably be expected to know. For example, you could reasonably ask hospital patients to report their level of satisfaction with hospital services. However, posing the same question to randomly selected individuals on the street could be problematic, since many of them might have little or no experience with the hospital services that are the focus of the research.

Also, ensure you don't have *double-barrelled questions*, that is, two questions in one (see Forth, Bewley, Bryson, Dixon, & Oxenbridge, 2010). According to the AAPOR (2015b), in this type of question 'It is not possible to determine whether the respondent is indicating one response or the other, or both.' For example, the question 'Do you support the death penalty and lifetime imprisonment as criminal punishments for rape?' is actually two separate questions (possibly with two completely different answers!).

Equally, you should avoid *leading questions* that reveal what the researcher is expecting the results to be, such as 'Do you agree that Durrell Wildlife Conservation Trust is doing important work to save animals from extinction?' There are two forms of leading question: those that suggest which position or stance is preferred (as in the example above), and those that provide only information about one side of an issue. An example of the second type might be 'If it would result in increased opportunities for education New Jersey citizens, would you favour or oppose building a new TV transmitter at liberty science center?' (AAPOR, 2015b). Avoiding such possible sources of bias is the key to good survey question design.

Self-report: A key potential source of bias. Many survey questions involve requests for respondents to 'self-report' information. For example:

1   How satisfied are you with the event you just attended?
2   Please indicate your level of agreement with the following statement: 'Politically, I tend to identify with the Conservative Party.'

Table 7.7 Types of survey bias to avoid

Type of Bias	What is it?	Example
Researcher expectancy effect	Researchers unintentionally introduce bias by using survey questions and response options based on their existing assumptions about the topic they are researching, the person they are interviewing, or the 'treatment' (i.e., experimental condition) the respondent is in (Dutton et al., 2015).	A business's customer service team expecting positive feedback might unintentionally bias their survey by asking leading questions. For example, the team might ask 'What was the best part of your store visit' and not ask about the 'worst part' because it is assumed that customers would not have a 'worst part' of their experience.
Acquiescence bias	All things being equal, respondents tend to agree with Likert scale (level of agreement) statements (Kam & Meyer, 2015).	If all such Likert scale statements ('I am fairly compensated for the work I do') are framed positively, the results may skew towards agreement purely due to acquiescence bias. Address this bias by reverse-coding half of the questions. For example, 'I usually feel appreciated at work' could be reversed to 'I rarely feel appreciated at work'.
Demand characteristics	Respondents tend to alter their answers based on what they believe to be the expectations of the situation or the researcher's preferred result (Orne, 1962).	If respondents are asked by a uniformed hospital employee for their verbal feedback on their hospital stay while still in the hospital, they may give responses that are more positive than they really feel because of the implicit demands of the situation.
Social desirability bias	Respondents try to hide their true views or behaviours to make themselves look better (to both themselves and the researcher) by overreporting views and behaviours that are widely praised in their culture and underreporting those that are not (He et al., 2015).	Inaccurately reporting higher levels of recycling or charitable donations in order to appear more caring is typical of this bias. Likewise, people tend to underreport such socially undesirable behaviours as overeating, pornography viewing and binge drinking.

These self-report questions are appropriate because a respondent could be expected to have existing views to report.

Self-report questions can also be problematic when they require respondents to be highly self-aware and undergo a complicated internal editing process. For example, questions asking 'Did you learn anything during your visit to the museum today? ("Yes" or "No")' would require museum visitors to:

- call up memories of the entire visit;
- identify moments from that visit in which new information was acquired;
- identify that acquired information as 'learning'.

This may be an unrealistic expectation of the respondent, inflating the likelihood of deviation between what actually happened and its representation in survey data (Sánchez et al., 2014).

Similarly, you should avoid questions that ask respondents to predict their future behaviour (e.g., 'How will your exercise routine change over the next five years?') or go far into the past to recall details of behaviour or thinking (e.g., 'How have your movie preferences changed over the last five years?'). Likewise, asking about how someone behaves in a 'typical week' is likely to introduce bias: how are they supposed to accurately assess what constitutes a 'typical' week? It is best to ask about specific recent periods of time, such as asking how someone behaved in the last seven days.

REAL WORLD EXAMPLE

Bad survey question design: Overreaching with self-report

To illustrate the challenges involved in using self-report, let us consider a recent study that used a self-report measure as its main outcome variable:

> Respondent self-reported knowledge of science and technology was measured by asking 'how much would you say that you know about science and technology.' Answers were close-ended and contained four response options: 'nothing at all,' 'a little,' 'a moderate amount,' and 'a great deal.' (Falk & Needham, 2013, p. 436)

This survey question is problematic for a number of reasons. First, it is double-barrelled, requiring a single response from the respondent regarding two different general topics (science and technology). Secondly, the intervals between response options are not equal; that is, there is no reason to believe the space between 'nothing at all' and 'a little' is the same as between 'a moderate amount' and 'a great deal'. Other important limitations affecting this question stem from the fact that it is using a self-report measure as a proxy for directly evaluating science knowledge:

- **Low in validity.** While this question does measure something (e.g., perhaps self-confidence relating to science and technology topics), it does not measure its intended concept of actual knowledge about science and technology.
- **Low in reliability.** Science and technology are multi-faceted domains, encompassing thousands of different sub-domains, fields of practice and particular technologies. When one person thinks of 'science', they might be thinking of human cloning or neuroscience. Another person's mental representation of 'science' might focus on earthquake detection or climate change (or simply a man with white hair in a lab coat!). This means that respondents are each essentially answering different questions, depending on which aspects of science and technology are most prominent for them.
- **Risks overestimating knowledge.** Social desirability (and ego) may drive some respondents to overestimate their knowledge.
- **Risks underestimating knowledge**. Some respondents may not recognize their knowledge as 'knowing something' (e.g., it may just be taken for granted as 'the way it is') or being about 'science and technology'. For example, they might have in-depth knowledge about why and how their heating unit works at home, but not recognize such knowledge as relating to 'science and technology'.

The above limitations exemplify the risks of producing inaccurate data by using self-report when a direct measurement would be more appropriate.

A related, but worse, practice is to ask respondents to report on another person's knowledge, feelings or values. An even more problematic variant of the museum learning question above might be one aimed at parents saying 'Did your child learn anything during your visit to the museum today? ("Yes" or "No")'. You can avoid such flaws by thinking through whether your respondents could reasonably be expected to have direct knowledge on the topics you are asking them about.

It is easy to miss something important in your survey or just to make a mistake, so take every available opportunity to get feedback. Feedback from people who know your topic can be particularly good at pointing out variables or response options you may have forgotten to include. This is not a replacement for pilot testing, but it can be a useful tool later in the survey design process.

Once you are confident you have thought through the potential sources of bias for your survey, you can turn to pilot testing to evaluate whether your survey questions and formats need further development.

7•3•3 PILOT TEST YOUR SURVEY

No matter how experienced you are, there will always be small mistakes that creep into your survey forms. These mistakes can cause problems later on if they aren't identified and eliminated in the early phases of your survey design. Pilot tests can help you to confirm that the intended meaning of your survey questions is clear to your respondents and that any directions you provide can be easily and accurately followed.

In this section, we go into detail about the different dimensions of the pilot testing process. Of course, in practice you may not have the time or the research budget to employ every pilot testing procedure described below. As we discuss these two main steps in pilot testing, keep in mind that any effort you can put towards pilot testing will improve your survey research.

There are two main steps to pilot testing: seeking up-front feedback as you develop your questions and then testing your near-final draft questions.

Formative pilot testing, step 1: Gaining up-front feedback as you craft your questions. It can be challenging to develop survey questions when you are not yet very familiar with the research topic. This means that during the survey design phase it makes a lot of sense to get feedback from the kinds of people who will ultimately take your survey. This way, you can be sure that you are adequately covering key issues, and that the questions you are asking are clear.

There are two main ways that you can go about developing your questions during this formative phase:

- **Ask open-ended survey questions to inform your closed-ended question design.** By asking open-ended questions on the points you would like to explore with your survey research, you allow your pilot testing respondents to show you the range of responses you need to account for with your closed-ended questions. These answers may include responses you haven't yet thought of, and indications of how your question phrasing can be improved. They may also highlight when a single, general question should be asked as multiple, specific questions.
- **Engage your pilot testers in an open discussion.** Engaging in an open discussion about your questions and topic areas is particularly useful when you are not sure what

questions to ask, what possible answers may be forthcoming, or how to phrase questions. This method is most helpful when you are in the early stages of designing your survey and are 'exploring' questions and topic areas. If you are doing this at a later stage in the survey design process, you can also invite critical comments about whether your draft response options (for closed-ended questions) make sense and seem reasonable.

Once you receive this feedback, you then return to your draft questions and refine them before either engaging with pilot testers again to further improve the questions or moving on to test the near-final questions.

Summative pilot testing, step 2: Pilot testing near-final draft questions. Once you have refined your individual questions, phrasing and terminology, the survey in its entirety should be administered to respondents for pilot testing. You can then analyse responses to open-ended questions and respondents' feedback to refine all aspects of the survey form before committing to a set of final survey questions. For more information on pilot testing, see Oksenberg et al. (1991).

7•3•4 DESIGN ROBUST DATA COLLECTION PLANS AND PROCEDURES

After pilot testing, you need to develop a plan to put your survey into the field and begin collecting data using standardized procedures. For example, if a person is invited to participate in a study, they could either agree to participate, decline to participate, or express uncertainty or some other response. You need pre-defined procedures in place for all of these outcomes. For example, in the case of rejection or expressions of uncertainty, you could either:

- Thank the individual for their consideration and note any of their visible demographic characteristics in your refusal log (see below).
- Provide additional information and request participation using different phrasing.

You should always carefully prepare for all possible reactions from potential respondents you approach.

Maintain a refusals log. Individuals declining to participate are a normal part of the survey data collection process. When it is possible to know something about the individuals who decline to participate (usually in face-to-face data collection), it is essential that you systematically capture such information. Refusals have to be captured systematically and reported in survey research because they can indicate the representativeness of your survey sample. Complete an entry into your **refusal log** immediately after each refusal. Each entry should note the date/time of refusal, any observable characteristics of the individual who refused (e.g., ethnicity, age, gender, accompanying individuals such as children) and any reasons they offer for refusal.

A high refusal rate raises the risk that your selected sample differs significantly from the target population. This means you must be more cautious in making any generalizations. However, you should not have unrealistic expectations of participation rates: the frequency of refusals is on a long-term increase worldwide as the total number of surveys people are exposed to continues to rise. Response rates as low as 30 per cent are not unusual in published survey research. You can analyse the refusals log entries to see if there are any categories of individuals being systematically lost from the sample (e.g., disproportionately high numbers of women or ethnic minorities declining to participate).

While you want to capture refusal information, be sure you don't pressure respondents into giving reasons for refusing. Always treat your respondents with courtesy. If they don't want to give explanations for refusing, then just thank them for their time and move onto the next potential respondent. For more information on refusals and refusal logs, see AAPOR (2015a, 2015b).

REAL WORLD EXAMPLE

Boosting response rates using a supplemental online survey

Eric often conducts research in the hustle and bustle of festivals, zoos or museums. From past experience, he knows that visitors in such settings frequently refuse participation because it keeps family members waiting or because they want to go to their next destination. Therefore, to increase the response rate he implemented a new system for responding to refusals. If respondents indicated that their refusals were due to such time-related reasons, then they were offered the secondary option of providing their email addresses so they could be sent an online version of the survey for completion when it was more convenient for them (e.g., at home). This additional procedure increased response rates by about 35 per cent.

INTRODUCING WEB-BASED SURVEYS

Conducting your survey using an online system can offer great advantages, helping to make surveys possible on a limited budget. Web-based surveys also enhance efficiency in data transcription and management. Instead of entering data by hand from paper forms, online survey systems allow you to automatically download your data into Excel or.csv spreadsheets, ready for data cleansing and analysis.

REAL WORLD EXAMPLE

Doing survey research with limited resources

Matthias wanted to do research during his undergraduate studies comparing the views of aid agency workers on the controversial topic of giving food aid to groups accused of war crimes. He had no assistance for the study (it was only him!) and financial resources were limited to exactly $0.00. Conducting interviews was one possibility, but travelling around the world to meet each participant would have been expensive. Instead, he used a web-based survey and conducted interviews via Skype to gather his data. This offered a no-cost means of collecting data, allowing him to complete the research within budget.

Assess appropriateness for your target population. Online surveys can be the most appropriate choice for data collection with certain populations, such as white-collar professionals who tend to already have good computer access. University students are also a good population to survey online because in most parts of the world they have at least basic access to an email account and computers. Online surveys can be especially useful when your desired respondents are geographically dispersed. They can open up new global research questions by allowing you to gather data from individuals around the world at no additional cost.

At the same time, it is important to keep in mind that not everyone has access to the internet or the technical ability to participate online. If your target population is poor, under the age of 12, over the age of 65, or located in a developing nation, you will need to be cautious when choosing an online survey approach. For an in-depth discussion of the pros and cons of using online survey methods, see Baker et al. (2010).

Choose a web-based survey system. Online survey data collection can be conducted using both paid and free services. Some of the prominent free online survey options are:

1 **Google Docs/forms:** Not designed for survey use, so requires some effort to get the survey form into a suitable format. This option should only be used for internal surveys, as it is difficult to make it look professional. However, this option is free, regardless of the number of forms or survey respondents you have.
2 **Lime Survey:** Requires technical proficiency, including knowledge of the Linux operating system and computer coding.

A number of online survey websites offer free use of their service for a small number of survey forms:

1 **Wufoo.com:** An easy-to-use website for creating web survey forms without any computer coding knowledge. It offers a small number of survey forms on a free account. Alternatively, you can upgrade to a paid account for a monthly fee to allow you to create more survey forms and receive a larger number of survey responses.
2 **Surveymonkey.com** A very popular website because of its simple set-up. It also does not require computer coding skills and allows you to start with a limited free account, or upgrade to a pay account for more capacity.
3 **Qualtrics.com** This service has become the go-to online survey platform for university researchers and major corporations alike. Qualtrics is great for both novices and experts, merging the ease of pre-formatted questions and survey designs with the ability to go 'under the hood' to change any aspect of the survey you want. Perhaps the best feature of Qualtrics is its incredible randomization features, allowing you to test for question order effects, question wording, etc.

The number of survey responses you are allowed with these websites is unlikely to be enough for most projects. Therefore, you will likely need at least a small amount of money and a credit or debit card available for the duration of the data collection if you use these services. However, the advantage of using specialized survey sites is their provision of the tools you need to conduct an effective online survey. Furthermore, because they are designed specifically for surveys they are more likely to connect to other applications that can allow you, for example, to conduct part or all of your data collection using a tablet. Moreover, surveys on wufoo.com can be synched with Android or Apple tablets or smartphones using a second service called 'Device Magic'. A number of other companies offer additional services that sync with both Wufoo and Survey Monkey.

Build your online survey form. When you design your online survey you can easily identify tools to enable you to ask a range of different question types. For example, for multiple choice questions, you use radio buttons so respondents can only choose one response option. For 'tick all that apply' survey questions, you would use check boxes so respondents could choose multiple response options. Be very careful about setting any questions so responses are 'required'. Required fields can easily create problems for respondents, causing them to become frustrated and exit your survey prematurely. You should only require answers for those questions that are absolutely essential (e.g., you may need an email address from respondents to send them a follow-up survey later on).

SURVEY DATA COLLECTION USING TABLETS OR SMARTPHONES

An app on your tablet or smartphone can sync with online survey forms, allowing you to collect data face-to-face which automatically upload to the online survey system. This option holds great advantages (see Table 7.8). However, if you are using tablets or smartphones as your main data collection mode, you should be prepared with backup paper forms, just in case.

Table 7.8 Advantages and disadvantages of survey data collection using tablets or smartphones

Advantages	Disadvantages
• No need to pay someone to enter the data, which also reduces data entry errors. • Automatically captures certain information such as time, date and/or location of survey completion. • Data available for instant secure download, allowing data analysis to commence without delay. • In the case of larger sample sizes, avoids the logistical problem of transporting large volumes of paper. • Limits risk of transcription errors due to illegible handwriting or sloppy data entry. • No printing costs or risk of losing paper survey forms.	• You need access to Wi-Fi (or mobile data) at some point. • You may need to buy one or more tablets or other electronic devices. This can be a particularly important problem if you lack sufficient funding. • Some respondents may not be comfortable using the technology, thereby making them less likely to participate in your research. • Technology problems can cause major delays and be challenging to resolve. • Dependence on having fully charged data collection device batteries. • An extra layer of pilot testing is needed to ensure the technology works as intended.

Data collection using paper survey forms usually imposes greater pressure on time and resources. Consider your budget, level of comfort with (and access to) technology and your target population when deciding whether to use online or tablet-based surveys. The most obvious opportunity to use an online survey is when your research topic focuses on activity taking place online (e.g., political discourse in online news comment websites; use of Facebook profile pages for self-presentation and other purposes; online health advice websites as a replacement for doctor visits). Of course, there are times when paper-only or a hybrid of paper and electronic survey forms is the only viable option (e.g., self-completion survey of political views of low-income elderly citizens in care homes).

Making the most of your survey design

- Keep focused on the outcome variables that are most important for your research. Avoid the temptation to stock your survey with extra questions 'just in case' you might need them.
- Once you have created a first version of your survey, critically review each question to ensure it has a clear connection to your research question.
- Keep your analysis firmly in mind when deciding on the type and quantity of questions. Avoid overloading yourself with data you won't have time to process and analyse.
- Ensure your survey questions and response options are as clear and concise as possible. If possible, use pilot testing to check this.
- Use plain language. Avoid jargon and assumptions of specialist knowledge.
- Generally phrase questions/statements in the positive to minimize any confusion.
- Be careful about pre-categorizing your data (e.g., by asking for age ranges rather than current age or year of birth). This can limit your analysis options later in the research process. You can always convert the more detailed data to categories later, but pre-categorized data can't be turned back into continuous data.
- Ensure you don't have any double-barrelled questions (e.g., 'What interested you in visiting the festival this year and last year?').
- Finally, be realistic about what your respondents can reasonably be expected to know and to report to you. For example, ask about current views, rather than past or future views, to limit the risk of error.

7.4 CONCLUSION

This chapter has addressed the key elements of the survey design and data collection process. We began with the question of whether surveys are the right choice for your research project. We then discussed the guiding principle for survey design: balance a consistent focus on your research question with the practical constraints you are facing. Issues of sampling were taken up in an earlier chapter, but you may need to re-evaluate your sampling plans in light of your survey design choices (e.g., selecting open-ended versus closed-ended survey questions). Indeed, the chapter highlights the rule of thumb that closed-ended questions require more time and planning at the earlier design phase of the research process, while open-ended questions lead to much greater demands for time and resources in the data analysis phase. Moreover, this distinction becomes stronger as sample size increases.

We then described the survey process as a whole before going into detail about the principles of good practice in question selection and design. We showed how pilot research is often necessary to effectively design survey questions, forms and procedures, and avoid unnecessary work in the long term. Finally, we highlighted the importance of survey data collection plans and procedures, with a particular focus on the use of refusal logs.

This chapter has highlighted the detailed considerations involved in designing and conducting survey research while facing resource limitations. In sum, if survey design seems too easy, then you are probably doing something wrong! While there are straightforward rules for surveys that have been worked out through decades of methodological research, survey design does take careful thought, editing and (ideally) pilot testing. From surveys, we now turn to the more resource-intensive data collection methods of qualitative interviewing, focus groups and ethnography. These methods have very different strengths and weaknesses, which we will elaborate in the next two chapters. As you read on, continue to consider which method of data collection would be most beneficial for accurately addressing your research question.

SUGGESTIONS FOR FURTHER READING

- **American Association for Public Opinion Research (2015).** Retrieved 4 July 2015, from http://www.aapor.org. The American Association for Public Opinion Research. As the leading association of public opinion and survey research professionals, the AAPOR provides a huge body of resources for both experts and lay public alike. In addition to providing links to the journals the organization sponsors, the AAPOR website has an entire section dedicated to survey education and resources. There are guides to reading surveys, fielding surveys, writing about surveys, and much more.
- **de Leeuw, E. D., Hox, J., & Dillman, D. (Eds.) (2008)** *International handbook of survey methodology.* **New York: Lawrence Erlbaum.** If you're wanting a more in-depth look at the entire survey process, this edited volume is a great resource. There are 25 chapters covering every step in the survey process, taking you from conception to data analysis.
- **De Vaus, D. A. (2002).** *Surveys in social research.* **London: George Allen & Unwin.** If you know that surveys are your chosen research method, this readable book offers a useful starting point. It offers useful insights across the whole survey process, but the sections on survey data analysis and interpretation are especially helpful.
- **Link, M. W., Murphy, J., Schober, M. F., Buskirk, T. D., Childs, J. H., & Tesfaye, C. L. (2014). Mobile technologies for conducting, augmenting and potentially replacing surveys: Executive summary of the AAPOR Task Force on Emerging Technologies in Public Opinion Research,** *Public Opinion Quarterly,* **78(4), 779–787.** The field of survey research is moving quickly, with a number of important cultural and economic factors quickly reshaping how surveys are done. This article gives an overview of how new and emerging technology may be able to fundamentally change (and hopefully improve) survey research of the future, while also giving guidance about how to embrace mobile technology in an ethical and effective way.
- **Tourangeau, R., Rips, L. & Rasinski, K. (2000). The psychology of survey response. Cambridge: Cambridge University Press.** This book is slightly dated, but draws together a clear and concise summary of key methodological research relevant to surveys. The book helpfully provides the details of studies that were used to test different kinds of survey bias. This allows you to draw your own conclusions about adjustments you should make to your survey designs in light of known survey response biases.

Visit the companion website at **https://study.sagepub.com/jensenandlaurie** to gain access to a wide range of online resources to support your learning, including editable research documents, weblinks, free access SAGE journal articles and book chapters, and flashcards.

GLOSSARY

Acquiescence bias – All things being equal, respondents tend to agree with Likert scale (level-of-agreement) statements.

Closed-ended question – A survey question where respondents choose from a limited range of pre-specified response options.

Cross-sectional survey – A survey that collects information reflecting a single point in time.

Demand characteristics – Respondents tend to alter their answers based on what they believe to be the expectations of the situation or the researcher's preferred result.

Demographic question – A question about the objective characteristics of the respondents (e.g., gender, ethnicity, religious affiliation).

Likert scale – The sum of responses to several Likert-type items, reflecting the direction and intensity of attitudes, beliefs, etc.

Likert-type item – A statement that a respondent is asked to evaluate on any subjective or objective dimension ranging from one extreme to another (e.g., from 1 – strongly disagree to 7 – strongly agree).

Longitudinal survey – Multiple surveys with the same or similar questions, focused on investigating change over time.

Multiple choice ('select one') question – A closed-ended survey question that only allows for one response.

Multiple choice ('tick all that apply') question – A closed-ended survey question that allows for multiple responses.

Open-ended question – A survey question where respondents generate their own responses.

Pilot testing – The process of administering, and gaining feedback on, all or part of your survey prior to the main survey, in order to confirm that the intended meaning of your survey questions are clear to your respondents and that any directions you provide can be easily and accurately followed.

Ranked-response question – A survey question where respondents are asked to rank a finite series of items according to some stated criteria, from highest to lowest.

Refusals logging – The systematic capturing and reporting of information about who refused to participate in your survey and why.

Reliability – A prerequisite to validity; refers to the extent to which the measures you use, and the data you collect, provide consistent results.

Researcher expectancy effect – Researchers unintentionally introduce bias by using survey questions and response options based on their existing assumptions about the topic they are researching.

Self-administered survey – A survey where respondents are required to read the survey instructions and questions for themselves and respond on paper or screen without a researcher's active participation.

Social desirability bias – Respondents try to hide their true views or behaviours to make themselves look better (to both themselves and the researcher) by overreporting views and behaviours that are widely praised in society and underreporting those that are not.

Standardization, survey – Every respondent is asked the exact same questions in exactly the same way.

Validity – The extent to which the information you gather from your survey respondents accurately represents the concept you are studying.

Verbally administered survey – The individual administering the survey talk through all aspects of the survey, including both direction, questions and response choices.

REFERENCES

American Association for Public Opinion Research (2015a). Best practices for research. Retrieved 4 July 2015, from http://www.aapor.org/AAPORKentico/Standards-Ethics/Best-Practices.aspx

American Association for Public Opinion Research (2015b). Question wording. Retrieved 4 July 2015, from https://www.aapor.org/AAPORKentico/Education-Resources/For-Researchers/Poll-Survey-FAQ/Question-Wording.aspx

Baker, R., Blumberg, S. J., Brick, J. M. et al. (2010). Research synthesis: AAPOR report on online panels. *Public Opinion Quarterly, 74*(4), 711–781.

Beatty, P. (1995). Understanding the standardized/non-standardized interviewing controversy. *Journal of Official Statistics, 11*(2), 147–160.

Bradburn, N. M., Sudman, S., & Wansink, B. (2004). *Asking questions: The definitive guide to questionnaire design – For market research, political polls, and social and health questionnaires* (revised ed.). San Francisco: Jossey-Bass.

Chaffee, S. H. (1991). *Explication*. Newbury Park, CA: SAGE.

Conrad, F. G., & Schober, M. F. (2000). Clarifying question meaning in a household telephone survey. *Public Opinion Quarterly, 64*(1), 1–28.

Dillman, D. A., Sinclair, M. D., & Clark, J. R. (1993). Effects of questionnaire length, respondent-friendly design, and a difficult question on response rates for occupant-addressed census mail surveys. *Public Opinion Quarterly, 57*(3), 289–304.

Dutton, G. R., Fontaine, K. R., Alcorn, A. S., Dawson, J., Capers, P. L., & Allison, D. B. (2015). Randomized controlled trial examining expectancy effects on the accuracy of weight measurement. *Clinical Obesity, 5*(1), 38–41.

Falk, J. H., & Needham, M. D. (2013). Factors contributing to adult knowledge of science and technology. *Journal of Research in Science Teaching, 50*(4), 431–452.

Forth, J., Bewley, H., Bryson, A., Dixon, G., & Oxenbridge, S. (2010). Survey errors and survey costs: A response to Timming's critique of the Survey of Employees Questionnaire in WERS 2004. *Work, Employment and Society, 24*(3), 578–590.

Godden, D. R., & Baddeley, A. D. (1975). Context-dependent memory in two natural environments: On land and underwater. *British Journal of Psychology, 66*(3), 325–331.

Harvard Institute of Politics (2014). Survey of young Americans' attitudes toward politics and public service, 25th edition. Retrieved 18 July 2015, from http://www.iop.harvard.edu/sites/default/files_new/Harvard_ToplineSpring2014.pdf

He, J., van de Vijver, F. J. R., Dominguez Espinosa, A. et al. (2015). Socially desirable responding: Enhancement and denial in 20 countries. *Cross-Cultural Research, 49*(3), 227–249.

Holtgraves, T. (2004). Social desirability and self-reports: Testing models of socially desirable responding. *Personality & Social Psychology Bulletin, 30*(2), 161–172.

Jabine, T. B., Straf, M. L., & Tourangeau, R. (Eds.) (1984). *Cognitive aspects of survey methodology: Building a bridge between disciplines. Report of the advanced research seminar on cognitive aspects of survey methodology.* Washington, DC: National Academy Press.

Jensen, E. (2014). Evaluating children's conservation biology learning at the zoo. *Conservation Biology, 28*(4), 1004–1011.

Kam, C. C. S., & Meyer, J. P. (2015). How careless responding and acquiescence response bias can influence construct dimensionality: The case of job satisfaction. *Organizational Research Methods, 18*(3), 512–541.

Menon, G. (1993). The effects of accessibility of information in memory on judgments of behavioral frequencies. *Journal of Consumer Research*, *20*(3), 431–440.

NBC News (2014). Americans weigh in on lethal injections. Retrieved 18 July 2015, from http://www.nbcnews.com/storyline/lethal-injection/americans-weigh-lethal-injections-n105501

Oksenberg, L., Cannell, C., & Kalton, G. (1991). New strategies for pretesting survey questions. *Journal of Offical Statistics*, *7*(3), 349–365.

Orne, M. (1962). On the social-psychology of the psychological experiment – with particular reference to demand characteristics and their implications. *American Psychologist*, *17*(11), 776–783.

Sánchez, J. P., Koskinen, J., & Plewis, I. (2014). Measurement error in retrospective work histories. *Survey Research Methods*, *8*(1), 43–55.

Suessbrick, A., Schober, M. F., & Conrad, F. G. (2000). Different respondents interpret ordinary questions quite differently. *Proceedings of the American Statistical Association*, 907–912.

Tversky, A., & Kahneman, D. (1974). Judgment under uncertainty: Heuristics and biases. *Science*, *185*(4157), 1124–1131.

Vagias, W. M. (2006). Likert-type scale response anchors. Retrieved 18 July 2015, from https://www.clemson.edu/centers-institutes/tourism/documents/sample-scales.pdf

Williams, F., & Monge, P. (2001). Time series analysis. In *Reasoning with statistics: How to read quantitative research* (5th ed., pp. 195–215). Boston: Wadsworth Cengage Learning.

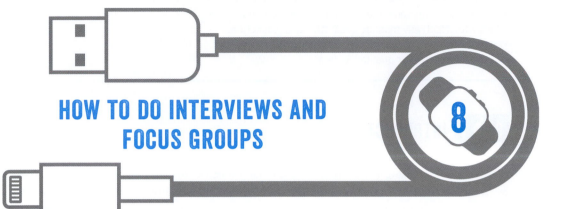

HOW TO DO INTERVIEWS AND FOCUS GROUPS

8

━━ **THIS CHAPTER COVERS THE FOLLOWING TOPICS** ━━━━━━━━━

- How interviews and focus groups can benefit your research.
- How to structure your qualitative interview and focus group data collection.
- How to develop good interview and focus group questions.
- How to effectively manage qualitative data collection.
- Where to do your qualitative data collection.
- How to record your qualitative data.

8 ● 1 INTRODUCTION

Why does society associate university students with binge drinking, when their alcohol consumption is decreasing (e.g., Office for National Statistics, 2015)? How do pupils perceive teachers' interactions with ethnic minority children in predominantly white neighbourhoods? These are the kinds of questions that are best answered through qualitative data. **Qualitative research** prioritizes personal interpretations and meaning over such quantitative ideals as objectivity and standardization (see Chapter 11). While qualitative data takes many forms (see, for example, Bergold & Thomas, 2012), this chapter focuses on the general principles of generating qualitative data, with a detailed focus on qualitative interviewing and focus groups.

Qualitative research offers unique opportunities for gaining insights into your participants' social lives, experiences and the underpinnings of their worldviews. Through *interviews* and **focus groups**, you can gain direct, detailed insights into people's thinking, behaviour and relationships. You can ask questions, such as why do certain ideas or distinctions seem natural to a reasonable person? Why would this be considered appropriate to act on? (Becker, 1998, p. 134). However, there are also a number of common pitfalls that can undermine the quality of qualitative research. Getting the most out of qualitative research requires a step-by-step approach that accounts for the strengths and weaknesses of different ways of generating your data.

You'll need detailed plans, including interview or focus group guides, templates for taking **field notes** (see Chapters 8 and 10) and strategies for how best to interact with your participants, as well as a plan for your research ethics practices (see Chapter 3). Yet, you also need to be flexible when developing your research plans. Good qualitative research allows for 'emergence' in which new information that comes to light during the process of generating data can trigger changes in the focus, approach and content of subsequent data gathering (see also Chapters 5 and 8 for discussion of 'emergent research design'). This flexibility makes qualitative methods particularly well suited to exploratory studies about new or underresearched topics. For instance, these methods may be better suited to accessing small populations or traditionally hard-to-access, 'closed' communities. For example, if you wanted to gain insights into prison cultures at maximum security facilities in the UK, then qualitative interviews with prison officers and inmates may help you identify the depth of insights and richness of individual experiences needed to understand the issue.

Section 8.2 explains why semi-structured interviewing is such an appealing method. It shows you how to design and plan your interviews. We walk you through the important skills involved in managing a qualitative interview. We also discuss how many interviews you should conduct for a range of research needs. Section 8.3 outlines how focus groups can benefit your research. We note what topics you should cover, what kind of venues to choose and how to select your participants. Finally, Section 8.4 discusses the process of recording your qualitative research, a common feature of interview and focus groups studies. We explain why recording is important, when not to do it, how to select the right equipment and how to get effective recordings.

8●2 CONDUCT QUALITATIVE INTERVIEWS

This section focuses on a particular kind of qualitative interviewing, which is widely used in the social sciences. Semi-structured qualitative interviewing relies on a list of open-ended questions that include follow-ups. The list identifies topics you'd like to cover, but you don't need to ask these questions in order. Rather, you want to strike a natural, conversational tone that addresses your research interests as gently as possible. You ask probing questions to explore what participants tell you in more detail (see, for example, Hoets, 2012). By minimizing restrictions on the scope of the conversation, **semi-structured interviewing** allows your participants to answer freely based on personal reflection, knowledge and experience. This approach also embraces the collaborative nature of the interview: through the interview process, interviewer and participant work together to develop a shared understanding of the topic under discussion. Semi-structured qualitative interviewing is the most appropriate method of data collection when you're looking to understand individuals' perspectives on a specific topic in depth while maintaining the flexibility of exploring interesting threads in the interview as it unfolds (e.g., Jensen & Holliman, 2009). If you would like to read more about the theoretical underpinnings of this method, a classic text on this topic is Kvale (1996); see also Kvale (2006) for a critical perspective on interviewing.

8●2●1 USE QUALITATIVE INTERVIEWS TO UNDERSTAND THE 'WHAT', 'HOW', 'WHY', 'WHEN' AND 'WHO'

What assumptions, needs, stereotypes, desires and hopes are underpinning the issues you're researching? For example, if a participant says she is opposed to government-mandated vaccination programmes for children, qualitative data collection would probe how and why she has arrived at this perspective (not the surface-level opinion itself). Qualitative interviews enable you to unearth what lies beneath the surface of a personal experience, political opinion, issue, situation or process. This depth means that qualitative data collection tends to take a long time (around one hour for an interview and three hours for a focus group). Interviews can be conducted on just about any subject with a broad range of different types of participants (different ages, ethnic background, education levels, etc.).

8●2●2 DESIGN YOUR INTERVIEW

There are many different types of interview. Each has strengths and weaknesses for different research questions and types of available participants. Semi-structured qualitative interviews are the most common type of interview because you get the best of both worlds: you get a somewhat structured list of questions so you cover your topic in a coherent manner, while maintaining the flexibility to adapt as issues come to light during the interview. This interview type is particularly useful when you're exploring a little-known topic because you can (and should) follow up interesting issues as they arise. However, semi-structured interviews have the drawback of potentially resulting in long and detailed audio data, which require a major effort to organize, transcribe and analyse. Table 8.1 lists the strengths and weaknesses of semi-structured interviews.

Structured interviews rely on a fixed list of questions that all participants are asked in the same order and phrasing; they select answers from a pre-defined group of responses. This style is useful if you want all your participants to address the same questions. The obvious problem with this interview type is its inflexibility; it doesn't let you dynamically explore new issues as they emerge. Likewise, participants may feel constrained if they can't fully elaborate their responses. Structured qualitative interviews are best suited for the following circumstances:

1   Working in a field of research you know quite well, so that you know what is and isn't important to ask about, and so you can come up with good **structured interview** questions.
2   A situation when you're very short on time and need to keep the interviews tightly focused to avoid gathering any extra data beyond the bare essentials – again, it is always important to keep your original research question in mind (see Chapter 1).

Table 8.1   Strengths and weaknesses of semi-structured interviews

Strengths	Weaknesses
• Enable very detailed understanding of basis for your participants' thinking, feelings, memories and behaviours. • Allow for intensive focus on one individual's perspective. This allows you to probe and follow up on any interesting points emerging in the interview. • You can adjust the direction of the interview as it unfolds in response to what is said. • You can clarify and explain aspects of the research without affecting other participants. • Relatively high participation rates are possible. • The interviewer can develop initial analytic thinking about participants' answers as they are given, potentially ask follow-up questions to clarify unclear or underdeveloped responses. • The relative privacy of one-to-one interviews may encourage participants to be more open and honest. • Can be a positive experience for participants to be intently listened to in an affirming manner for a significant period of time.	• Face-to-face interviews can be expensive and time-consuming to conduct (online interviews take much less effort and cost usually, but are still a significant investment of time). • Depends on your skills as an interviewer to think of good questions, probe participants' views during the interview and maintain a positive relationship. • Interview samples are usually relatively small, raising the risk of not gathering perspectives from a key segment of the population. However, this risk can be mitigated through purposive sampling (Chapter 5). • Your identity, demeanour and way of framing the interview will affect the replies participants give. This method of data collection intertwines your behaviour as the researcher with the data that you collect. • Can be challenging to directly compare data from interviews, as each one is different.

Informational interviews are directed towards a general interest area but almost entirely unstructured. Using your original research question for guidance, you select participants who are likely to be able to point you in the right direction for your research, with minimal expectations or assumptions about what issues would be useful to discuss. This interview type can be valuable at an early stage of research when you don't know much about your topic.

8•2•3 PLAN FOR YOUR INTERVIEW

You need to think clearly about what you're trying to find out before you start writing your interview questions. Always keep in mind what overarching research question you're addressing, and then think about what specific questions would help you develop a detailed answer.

The following is a basic overview of how you will arrive at your interview questions:

1 **Follow your research question.** You obviously need to start with a clear research focus – what are you looking to understand? (This is discussed in detail in Chapter 1.)
2 **Know the research field.** You should have read the key literature in your area of study (see Chapter 2). Know the prevailing arguments and areas where leading scholars are in disagreement. You should also be clear on where your research lies in this space – and therefore where you want to focus your interview questions. This way your interview questions will benefit from existing research while adding to knowledge.
3 **Consider your participants.** Who could they be? What special insights would they be in a position to provide? For example, if you were looking to research the pharmaceutical industry, then you would need a different set of interview questions depending on whether you were interviewing executives, scientists, sales people, marketing staff or product users. Be realistic about what kinds of information people will give you and for how long they will be interviewed. For example, the head of a major company probably won't agree to a three-hour interview or give you sensitive company information.
4 **Begin crafting your interview questions.** Developing interview questions is an ongoing process: getting exactly the right phrasing and set of questions on your first draft is nearly impossible. You'll need to adjust your questions multiple times during your project. As you come across new information and get a feel for how the questions work with your participants, you can refine them to ensure they are helping you get the most valuable data for your research.
5 **Test the questions.** Ask your supervisor and other experts in your field to review your questions and give you advance feedback. You can also try out questions on friends or family to see how clear or awkward they sound in practice. Update your questions based on this feedback.

As you start crafting your interview questions make sure you cluster them by major groups and subgroups, according to some kind of logical categorization. By clustering your questions logically you can help maintain a smoothly flowing conversation during the interview, which allows responses from one question to feed into and inform others.

REAL WORLD EXAMPLE

Structuring interview questions about organized crime in Bulgaria

Francesca wanted to understand how trust is established among members of criminal groups in Bulgaria. She knew that high-ranking members of organized crime groups, such as the Mafia, were unlikely to speak to her. However, during her early research on the illegal drug trade she had established contacts with less prominent criminal groups that would agree to interviews.

The following is an abbreviated list of her interview questions to demonstrate clustering and the inclusion of sub-questions:

A. Recruitment to organized crime [*example of clustering of question*]

1 Can you walk me through how members of your organization are first selected to join? [*primary interview question*]

- What are their typical backgrounds? [*sub-question*]
- Do you always have a set of people under consideration for membership? [*sub-question*]

2 What kind of people are you seeking?

- Why are these types of people preferred?
- Do you seek people with criminal backgrounds? (Why or why not?)
- Do you seek people with previous experience of violence? (Why or why not?)

B. Period of 'trials'

1 Can you explain the process of integrating new people into the group once they have met your basic requirements?

- Who decides which candidates are chosen?
- How long does this process take?
- Is there a 'probation' period when the candidate is tested?

In the above example, clusters are structured using an outline format. This enables you to see at a glance where you are in the interview. In practice, however, a participant may well address questions out of sequence in the normal flow of the interview conversation. Therefore, you would typically make a tick mark or some other kind of notation when an interview (sub-question) has been addressed. This makes it easy for you to see towards the end of the interview if there are any issues that you still need to bring up.

You should pay careful attention to how you phrase your questions and ensure that they are clear and concise. Don't use complex vocabulary or jargon that may not be easily understood. You also want to make sure that you ask one question at a time so that you don't confuse your participants.

Example of a poorly phrased question

'Can you walk me through why your museum visitors seem to prefer dinosaur exhibits over the insect exhibit, and why men aged 18–34 had higher levels of spending in the gift shop?'

In this example, the subject is unclear and there are multiple questions for the participant to deal with, and try to remember, while formulating a response.

Example of how to fix the poorly phrased question

It would be better to divide the question into two or three separate questions:

1 'Can you help me understand why your visitors might prefer dinosaur exhibits?'
2 'Is there anything about your insect exhibit that you think visitors might not like?'
3 [to be introduced in a different part of the interview when it fits with a set of other questions] 'What do you think affects how much people spend in the gift shop?'

- Sub-question: 'Do you think there is anything that might be causing men to spend more in the gift shop than women?'
- Sub-question: 'Why do you think young men age 18–34 are spending so much in the gift shop?'

Here are some additional tips for when you write your interview questions, some of which were already mentioned in the discussion of survey question design in Chapter 7:

- **Avoid jargon or slang.** Using slang terms or jargon in interview questions can confuse participants if they are unfamiliar with the terminology. Normally, it's not worth taking the risk that the participant won't know what the words mean. Instead, use plain, clear language to state your questions.
- **Keep your language neutral or aligned with your participants.** Use professional and neutral language rather than emotional, biased or loaded terms. It is important that you and your research appear impartial. Where you must use loaded or controversial terms, it is best to use the terms that would be recognized by the people you're interviewing. For example, if you were interviewing anti-abortion activists, you should refer to them as 'pro-life' (their preferred terminology). Likewise, if you were interviewing pro-abortion rights activists, you should call them 'pro-choice' (their preferred terminology). This is in keeping with the principles of qualitative research, maintaining a focus on what the world looks like from the vantage point of your participants. It is also the right move on a practical level, as people will be more likely to speak freely when they don't feel judged. Mimicking their terminology therefore will make for a smoother and more effective interview.
- **Ask open-ended questions.** They are far more likely to generate useful data than yes/no questions. For instance, the question 'When you went for the bar exam, did you pass on your first attempt?' is unlikely to prompt an elaborated response. The following alternative question framing would be more likely to generate a full response: 'Tell me about your experience taking the bar exam. What was it like?'

The following nine types of interview questions have been adapted from Kvale (1996). These encompass both pre-planned questions you design for your interview guide and questions that you develop spontaneously during the interview itself:

- **Introducing questions** are useful for kick-starting conversations. Here are some examples: 'Walk me through why …', 'Can you think of a time when …', 'Could you help me understand how …', 'Tell me about …', 'Can you give me an insight into why …'.
- **Follow-up questions** help you to extend discussion on a topic. For instance: 'Can you provide other examples of that kind of situation?'

- **Probing questions** allow you to dig deeper into a specific claim or reported experience. For example: 'You mentioned that patients tend to prefer it when nurses wear formal uniforms. Can explain more why this might be the case?'
- **Specifying questions** help you gain greater precision about a particular claim or reported experience. For example: 'How exactly did you respond to that situation?' or 'Have you ever seen this kind of event yourself?'
- **Direct questions** help you clarify a point of fact that emerges during the interview. For example: 'When you said that you had been an educator for 22 years, was all that time spent at the school in Lakewood, California?'
- **Indirect questions** can help you explore issues that may be too sensitive to bring up explicitly. For example, rather than asking whether a participant has done something illegal or dishonest, you might ask a more general question, such as whether they have heard of that behaviour happening in their organization or neighbourhood.
- **Structuring questions** redirect the flow of the interview, such as when you move from one cluster of questions to another. For example: 'Now that we have discussed early education programmes, I would like to ask you about …' A smooth transition like this can help maintain the natural feel of the interview conversation.
- **Interpreting questions** are used when you're unsure whether you understand a point made by the participant. For example: 'Did you mean that …' or 'Am I understanding you correctly that …' Such questions provide participants the opportunity to clarify their view and correct your interpretation of their statements.
- **Silence.** While of course not really a question, a pause is often an effective means of prompting further discussion. It prevents you from having to ask one question after another, and gives space to the participant to reflect on what has just been said in order to contribute more points. Learn to be patient and wait a couple of seconds to allow participants to continue with an explanation.

AVOID LEADING QUESTIONS

Leading questions are those that imply that one answer is more correct than another or that point the participant towards a certain expected answer. They may skew your research findings and can limit the chances that you will discover previously unknown explanations for events. For example, the following is leading the participant towards a certain answer rather than keeping the discussion open: 'Do you agree that the decision to disrespect trade unions by failing to listen to their concerns was wrong?' This could be rephrased in a more neutral way, such as: 'How do you feel management has responded to your union's concerns?'

 **KEY TIPS**

Practice makes perfect when developing interviewing skills

There is much more to interviewing than having a casual conversation with your participant. The trick is to make the interview feel as natural as possible, while ensuring that you cover all the topics you want to get to and explore the participant's views in detail. The more you rehearse your questions, understand the context around your questions and are familiar with the field you're investigating, the more likely you are to make a positive impression and get the most out of the research encounter. Struggling with your questions and looking confused as you search up and down a poorly prepared list thinking about what you should ask next can show incompetence and undermine the quality of the interview.

Practise, practise, practise! It is a good idea to practise interviewing with friends and colleagues so you have a 'live' audience that can give feedback and suggest improvements for your questions and interview style. You should also practise organizing the practical elements of the interview. Make sure you have a well-organized bag that contains all the interview material you'll need, such as pens and notepads, and that you know how to quickly set up your recording equipment. This can help you avoid looking disorganized and ensure you don't forget a crucial piece of equipment.

Giving a positive impression of your competence, responsibility and professionalism is important. It can make continued participation and cooperation more likely. Think about what kind of person you would trust your personal or sensitive data with, and try to live up to that image.

CHOOSE YOUR INTERVIEW MODE

You will also need to consider four main interview modes: face-to-face, telephone or online.

1   **Face-to-face.** This is generally the preferred interview mode for numerous reasons. In-person contact helps you build **rapport** with the participant and draw on non-verbal cues when interpreting their words. Establishing a personal connection through a face-to-face interview will often yield more and better information.

    The obvious downside of this mode is that you (or a trained research assistant) have to meet up with the participant, leading to a greater time and cost commitment (how great depends on the physical distance between you and your participants).

2   **Telephone.** While you and your participant don't get to see each other in telephone interviews, this mode still allows you to benefit from cues in the participant's tone and to develop a dynamic conversation. This mode also has the advantage of being relatively easy to conduct, inexpensive and enabling you to connect to people in remote places or who are otherwise unable or unwilling to meet in person. For participants used to conversing over the telephone, this mode might actually be preferable to face-to-face. For example, when Eric was interviewing journalists, he found that many of them were just as comfortable (or more so) on the phone: this was a comfortable mode for them because they conducted most of their daily work over the phone.

3   **Online.** Online communication through audio-visual programs such as Skype, FaceTime or Google Hangout can be an efficient option for qualitative interviewing. Each of these programs is free to download and use with others on the same program. This can make such programs a much more cost-effective option than the telephone. The major benefit for research quality is being able to see and speak to participants, so both you and the participant can pick up on non-verbal cues within a dynamic conversation. However, online communication programs are not the same as face-to-face discussions. The interaction can seem less natural because of the technology and physical distance. Moreover, problems such as a poor-quality internet connection can interfere with the flow and quality of the interview. Also, ensure you are completely comfortable with the program you would like to use and have practised with more than one person before conducting your main data collection.

4   **Email and instant messaging**. It is possible to conduct an interview over a period of time via email, by sending an open-ended question to your participant and following up on their response. This option is rarely used because it is a rather stilted way of conducting a full conversation – you cannot reply to each other's comments in real time. In contrast, online instant message services can be very useful when you need to conduct an interview with someone at a distance. This is a particularly useful option when your participant does not want their verbal responses to be overheard, or when the internet connection is not strong enough to support video or audio conversations.

In sum, while face-to-face interviewing is generally preferable, the other modes provide workable alternatives and cost-effective access to far away participants if used appropriately.

8•2•4 ACTIVELY MANAGE THE INTERVIEW PROCESS

You are responsible for managing the interview. Interviews evolve based on what you communicate prior to the interview, the questions you ask, the participant's willingness to speak and depth of knowledge and experience, and the rapport between you and the participant.

 **KEY TIPS** ━━━━━━━━━━━━━━━━━━━━━

Prepare the interview basics in advance

The strongest interviews are usually those that have been carefully prepared. Make sure that you have scheduled your interviews in advance, requested enough time with your participant to conduct a complete interview and selected the right venue to minimize disruptions:

- Schedule interviews two-three months in advance if possible for most professional participants, so you have time to prepare and can ensure the participant will be available. For those working in lower-level positions in an organization or participating in your study on their personal time, two-four weeks may be sufficient notice. Be aware that as it gets nearer to the planned interview time, the participant may need to reschedule, but it is always better to give them as much notice as you can, so that participants don't feel rushed or surprised by your request.
- Ask the participant to set aside sufficient time for the interview. Add at least 30 minutes to the longest time you think the interview will take to allow for small talk when you first meet, setting up your equipment, and ethics procedures. If your participant says they can't spare that much time, ask how much time would be feasible and reduce your number of questions accordingly.
- Choose the interview venue in advance so you aren't forced to meet or conduct your Skype interview in a noisy or distracting setting that might interfere with the dialogue.
- For face-to-face interviews, normally find a quiet and somewhat secluded location. A private office is usually ideal. Meeting at the participant's home may be necessary, but be careful about committing to a setting you can't easily control. There could be a range of interruptions in someone's home, from children or pets to loud television in the background. Locations like a café may be necessary, but try for one that is relatively quiet at the time of day you will be there and ideally one with spaces off to the side you can use. Beware of background noise that can spoil your interview recording.

HOW TO APPROACH THE INTERVIEW PROCESS

How you set up the interaction and carry it out plays a very big part in the ultimate success of the interview. Keep the following in mind:

Don't rush. Make sure that the pace of your interview is relaxed. No one likes to be hurried, but you also don't want too many long pauses. Ask your questions in a clear, understandable manner, giving participants time to think through their answers.

Maintain focus and relevance. Keep the discussion focused on topics relevant to your main research question. It's fine if the discussion drifts away from what you initially asked, as long as it's still useful for addressing your overall research interest. While you don't want to interrupt someone, it is permissible to briefly and politely interject if a participant is straying far off course. Often the participant won't be aware that they are doing this. Use the following phrases to redirect the conversation:

- 'Going back to my earlier question about …'
- 'Looking once again at …'
- 'Your comment made me think of …'

Do this redirection carefully. If you shut down a line of discussion too harshly, it can undermine the free-flowing nature of the interview.

Probe for depth and detail. You will need to start with relatively broad questions. So it's up to you to probe and use follow-up questions to get down to the level of detail needed for your project.

Keep it natural. The more you make the engagement natural and comfortable the more likely you are to have a successful interview. Don't just fire off a barrage of questions, or robotically read them off your interview guide. Instead, frame the interview as a conversation and allow the discussion to evolve naturally. Ensure you know your interview questions well enough that you can steer the conversation towards your interests without constantly consulting your interview guide.

Ask sensitive questions after establishing rapport. Hold back the particularly personal or difficult questions for a later stage of the interview when rapport and trust are established and the participant is feeling more comfortable. If you start with sensitive questions, the participant may become defensive and closed off to further discussion.

STRUCTURE YOUR INTERVIEW

The following is a basic overview of how the interview process generally unfolds:

1   **Introduction.** Begin by introducing yourself. Thank the participant for coming to the interview: it's essential that you show that you value their participation. It's a nice touch to ask the participant if they need anything, such as a drink of water, before carrying on with the interview.

2   **Describe your research**. If you are using a verbal informed consent procedure (see Chapters 3 and 6), then ask the participant if you can start recording at this point. Use a script or bullet points to provide a brief description of your research so you don't forget anything. Be sure to include the following:

- State the title of your research and an overview of your research goals. Explain how the research is funded, how results will be used and who will have access to the data and the results.
- Give the expected completion date.
- Explain that participation is voluntary and that the participant should feel under no obligation to answer any of the questions. The participant is also free to end the interview at any point (see Chapter 3 for more details).
- If using written consent procedures, ask the participant to review the informed consent document, and if the participant agrees, then ask for it to be signed. If you are using verbal consent, then ask them if they can briefly summarize their understanding of what their participation in the research involves and whether they are willing to participate.

3   **Brief overview of the forthcoming interview.** Explain how the interview will be structured so the participant can be put at ease. Emphasize that you are only having a conversation; it is not a test and there are no 'right' or 'wrong' answers. Also discuss what kinds of questions you will be asking and how long you think the interview will take. Be sure you confirm that the participant has enough time.

4   **Interview questions.** Start off gradually with basic questions the participant can easily answer so the participant can feel comfortable and gain confidence. For example, you might ask demographic or background questions, only working up to the more challenging questions when the participant seems secure and confident in the interview conversation. Also remember our advice above about clustering your questions.

5   **Closure.** It is important to end the interview with a genuine and gracious 'thank you' and an expression of how valuable their contribution has been. Ask the participant if you can follow up at a later time with other questions – even if you currently think you have all the information you need. If you're using the snowball sampling technique (see Chapter 5), then you can ask the participant for additional people who may be willing to participate in your research at this point.

 **KEY TIPS**

Display appropriate emotions and empathy during the interview

Even though you need to be professional during interviews, you should still be warm and emotionally responsive. You're discussing issues that often have deep personal significance for your participants, and you should show appropriate emotions and empathy broadly in line with how you would respond in a normal conversation. For example, if a participant is discussing an experience they found very funny, then you can show some appreciation of the humour.

Likewise, if a participant is discussing the death of a loved one, then displaying some empathy is appropriate. In both cases, having a human response to your participant's account helps build trust. In both examples, remaining emotionless could make the participant feel that you are cold and uncaring.

GAIN MORE DEPTH AND INSIGHTS DURING INTERVIEWS BY USING 'DIGGING' STRATEGIES

As your interview develops, be prepared to follow up to seek a fuller and more in-depth explanation. For example, if your participant has just said she distrusts state-sponsored health programmes, you might ask 'what is it about state-sponsored health programmes that you find problematic?' By actively following up like this, you can get to the underlying factors that affect people's surface-level claims, opinions and descriptions of events. Knowledge gained from compiling your literature review (see Chapter 2) can help you decide when to keep asking more questions about a statement by a participant. You don't need to worry about noting down everything you're told, as all interviews should be recorded (this is covered in more detail later in the chapter).

Qualitative interviews are designed to enable you to dig deeper and dig wider. You dig deeper when the participant has given you an informative response but you want more details. You dig wider when the participant has given a vague or shallow response and you are seeking more basic information about the context. For example:

Digging deeper

Interviewer: Can you describe any instances in your life where you have experienced homophobia?

Participant: Well, when I was a teenager … [participant provides a complete response].

Interviewer [digging deeper into the answer given by the participant]: How did this affect your relationships with your friends?

Digging wider

Interviewer: Can you describe any instances in your life where you have experienced homophobia?

Participant: No, I've actually been very lucky and never had a tough time [participant is unable to indicate a personal experience].

Interviewer [digging wider by providing additional information in order to understand the participant's perspective of homophobia]: Can you describe any instances where you have witnessed homophobia that targeted your friends or family? (If yes, how did this affect you?)

If the participant does not provide a sufficient answer you may attempt to dig wider again, but the participant may not know or have the answer to the question.

A related issue is deciding when you should stop digging. If the participant appears exasperated or uncomfortable, then you should not ask further questions. Likewise, if the questions seem to be upsetting the participant, then politely ask if you may continue, but be prepared to stop asking further questions if the participant is too distressed. If the participant is happy to continue but the answers are getting shorter, less detailed or less useful, then it's time to shift to a new interview question.

KEY TIPS

Be a good listener!

Non-verbal cues such as good eye contact and slight head nods to show that you're hearing and understanding the participant show that you are a good listener. The occasional brief affirming comment or minimal verbal response such as 'mmm hmm' will also communicate your interest in the interview. Avoid appearing too rigid or robotic; participating in a genuine and natural manner will draw out the best responses and create the most positive experience for your participant.

Similarly, avoid the temptation to interrupt – unless the participant misunderstood the question or is going down the wrong track – and even then interject politely and gently. People almost always find interruptions annoying and disrespectful. Interruptions can also prevent thoughts from evolving and can give the impression that the interview is based more on right/wrong answers, making the participant reluctant to give elaborated responses.

Table 8.2, adapted from William Marsiglio's (2013) guide to conducting qualitative interviews, identifies some of the challenges you might encounter when trying to gain detail and insights from a participant.

Table 8.2 **Interview challenges and resolution strategies**

Issue	Challenge	Resolution strategies
Non-talker	Some participants will be reluctant to provide detailed responses, and may tend to give yes/no answers or say just a few words.	Try to get such participants to reflect further on their experiences by using different prompts: 'Could you explain more about ...' or 'Could you elaborate on that point'.
Discomfort	Some of your questions may cause discomfort in participants, for example, when discussing an upsetting situation, socially undesirable behaviour, illegal activities or very personal matters such as sexual behaviour.	Be clear in recognizing the discomfort. Don't pretend you haven't noticed it. Empower such participants by reminding them that participation in all parts of the interview is voluntary. Ask if there is a particular aspect of the question they would prefer not to discuss. If the participant is too upset to continue or wishes to end the interview, then don't try to ask more questions. End the interview politely and graciously.

Issue	Challenge	Resolution strategies
Contradictory	The participant says something that contradicts a point they made earlier in the interview.	Don't ignore contradictions because when you go to analyse the interview you will be left in a bind. When you notice the contradiction, try not to interrupt immediately; allow the participant to reach a natural pause or stopping point and then ask a clarifying question, such as 'I am not quite understanding the situation. Earlier you mentioned .... Could you help me understand why this situation is different?'
Confused	The participant doesn't understand your question and either asks for clarification or gives an answer that does not address the question.	Ensure that your questions are perfectly clear and test them to make sure a range of potential participants find them easy to understand. If a participant doesn't understand then rephrase the question when you try again to get a relevant response.
Personal	A participant asks you a personal question. This situation can occur when the participant feels defensive. For example, 'Don't *you* sometimes like to have a drink or two after a stressful day?'	Recognize that the participant perceives the question or situation in a negative light. You shouldn't ignore it or become defensive. Instead recognize that you need to reassure the participant to get the interview back on a productive track. In the example given, you could provide this affirmation by responding in general terms so you are not providing personal information. For example, 'Many people choose to have a drink at the end of their day'. The situation can also be handled more explicitly by emphasizing that you're only trying to understand the participant's point of view.
Flirt	Occasionally a participant might flirt with you.	If you feel it is reaching an awkward level, you can briefly stop the interview and say that you're not comfortable with flirtatious comments. Handling the situation with a smile, but firmly and politely, will usually allow the interview to resume on a more professional footing.
Inquisitive	The participant may be curious about your perspective on the issue being discussed. Be cautious about expressing your personal views because your response could skew the discussion towards your views, when the point is supposed to be learning about your participant's perspective. For example, if the participant asks which political party you support in the United States and you say 'I always vote Republican', then this may influence the participant's answers.	If the question is not relevant to the interview questions you'll be asking, then there is usually no problem providing a brief answer and then refocusing the discussion. If the question relates more directly to the interview and your response could affect the participant's future discussion, then – politely and with a smile – give a brief, general answer that is as neutral as possible while still being truthful, and then redirect the focus back to the participant. For example, 'I do like to take the train, but I would really be more interested in hearing your views about public transport'. If the question is more sensitive then avoid answering it and redirect: 'I am happy to discuss this with you in more detail after the interview, but for now I would be interested to hear more about your thoughts on ...'

Facing unwanted romantic attention during qualitative research

Sarah's research included in-depth interviews with food-insecure individuals using a UK food aid charity. As part of her research, Sarah ate meals with these individuals, and then asked for their contact details in order to conduct in-depth qualitative interviews with them later. She encountered a range of individuals from different backgrounds, who were all vulnerable emotionally, physically and/or financially. Sarah was 22 years old, and at times during the research she encountered indications of romantic interest among male participants. Some of these men tried to initiate conversations relating to this romantic interest such as asking whether she was single. In one case, when Sarah was gathering a male participant's contact details to arrange a follow-up in-depth interview, another woman warned her that she should be careful about meeting with him. This made Sarah feel worried about her safety.

Clearly this is a difficult situation with no perfect solution, given that Sarah could not afford to abandon these potential participants. Sarah dealt with this situation by arranging for her interviews to be conducted in public places, such as cafés. She conducted all of her follow-up interviews with male participants in this study over the phone. Other options could include asking a friend to come along for face-to-face interviews in a public place, asking someone else to conduct the interview if you feel uncomfortable or making a polite excuse to cancel the interview entirely. (For further advice on dealing with unwanted sexual advances during data collection, see Chapter 4.)

8 ● 3 CONDUCT FOCUS GROUPS

Focus groups bring sets of participants together for a structured or semi-structured discussion about a chosen topic. This section discusses why you might use focus groups in your qualitative research, the practicalities of organizing such groups and examples of the kind of research that will benefit most from focus groups.

8●3●1 WHY CHOOSE FOCUS GROUPS?

Focus groups provide a social setting and opportunity for participants to discuss specific topics, such as a new product or patient experiences in hospitals, in an informal and supportive setting, using their own concepts, frames of reference and vocabulary (Kitzinger & Barbour, 1999). The group interaction, which focus groups facilitate, can help bring out new perspectives on issues as participants challenge, persuade and influence each other. You still guide the discussion, but ideally by intervening as little as possible. You let the group take charge as much as possible (Kitzinger, 1994b), so that the issues discussed are based on what participants think is most important or relevant.

Sociologist Erving Goffman (1961, p. 18) explained the methodology of focus groups using the term 'focused gatherings', defining them in terms of their 'single cognitive focus of attention; a mutual and preferential openness to verbal communication … an eye-to-eye ecological huddle'. Kitzinger and Barbour (1999, pp. 4–5) extend this definition:

Focus groups are group discussions exploring a specific set of issues. The group is 'focused' in that it involves some kind of collective activity – such as viewing a video, examining a single health promotion message, or simply debating a set of questions. Crucially, focus groups are distinguished from the broader category of group interviews by the explicit use of interaction to generate data. ... Focus group researchers encourage respondents to talk to one another: asking questions, exchanging anecdotes, and commenting on each others' experiences and points of view.

If the structure and purpose of focus groups are carefully designed, they have the potential to facilitate analysis of the similarity and diversity of opinions on a particular issue from a variety of research respondents (Kitzinger, 1994a). Moreover, the practical value of focus groups is illustrated by their use beyond social science research. For instance, focus groups are often used by political parties to test reactions to proposed policy changes and in market research to get potential customers' views on a product. If you would like to learn more about the theoretical underpinnings of focus group research, a good starting point is Stewart and Shamdasani (2015).

While the vast majority of focus group studies only bring participants together once, it can be beneficial to get the same group's perspective on an evolving phenomenon (e.g., a follow-up session six months later), or a series of linked groups over a defined period (e.g., once per month for a year). This allows you to see how people's views evolve over time. For example, Dania convened a set of focus groups, first to inform an interactive science centre's redevelopment plans, and later to get feedback on how those plans were developing. This helped to ensure that the plans were not drifting too far from what the initial focus group discussions had suggested.

Your decision about whether to use interviews and focus groups should be determined by your research question (see Chapter 1 for detailed discussion of research question development). Table 8.3 summarizes the strengths and weaknesses of focus groups.

Beyond the characteristics that distinguish interviews and focus group research, they also share some important features:

- **Valuing the knowledge of our participants**. Becker (1998, p. 98) offers a helpful summary of the shared perspective of qualitative researchers: 'People know a lot about the world they live and work in. They have to know a lot to make their way through its complexities. They have to adjust to all its contradictions and conflicts, solve all the problems it throws their way.' This is usually addressed through paying close attention to the 'common knowledge and routine practice' of our participants.
- **Limited replication**. It's difficult for the structure of an interview or focus group to be replicated exactly because they follow the flow of conversation directed by participants. This can make them difficult to use in 'repeated measures' research where you collect data from the same individuals over a period of time. Such 'repeated measures' research is usually done with surveys so that each person receives the same question in the same way at each time point (see Chapter 7). In particular, the array of different individuals can make a focus group discussion go in any number of directions. But it can still be valuable to see how such a discussion unfolds about the same topic at different points in time.
- **Constructive remembering**. When you are asking people to remember things that happened in the past, you must be aware that this remembering process isn't like a computer accessing an exact file of what was stored (also see Chapter 7 discussion of self-report survey questions). All kinds of factors affect the way people remember and

Table 8.3   Strengths and weaknesses of focus groups

Strengths	Weaknesses
• Possible to gain further depth and breadth by having participants ask each other questions (which you might not have thought to ask), and build on each other's statements. • Allow disagreements to be identified and discussed. • To some extent, you can see the process of developing, changing and reframing views in action during focus group discussions and debates. • Can be a rewarding intellectual and social experience for participants. • Can offer a more natural setting for discussing issues in the sense that we normally talk about our ideas in a social context. • May bring about intensive interactions in which participants persuade and influence each other. The way this plays out can offer interesting findings and be more realistic than a one-to-one interview where confrontations are less likely.	• Requires much greater preparation to coordinate a meeting of several people and to ensure that the setting and structure for the focus group will be conducive to a good discussion. • Focus groups are more complicated to conduct than one-to-one interviews. You're responsible for a broad range of activities, including practical issues such as welcoming people as they arrive and ensuring they have food and drink as needed, as well as the research tasks of managing the group dynamics and drawing out useful research insights. • Having participants persuade each other could be viewed as transforming the views of participants through the process of gathering them. While this concern applies to all intrusive methods of generating data, it can be a particularly acute issue with focus groups because of the range of people exerting mutual influence on one another. • Due to the fast-moving nature of a multi-person conversation, you may be unable to follow-up on some points to get them fully clarified. This can lead to ambiguity during analysis. • Some participants may be relatively quiet, for example, because they are uncomfortable expressing their views with a group of people they don't know. • It can be hard to follow up on the details of individuals' expressed views without disrupting the natural flow of the conversation. Similarly, the views of the individual can become submerged or altered by the group discussion. • Focus group **transcriptions** can be particularly challenging as you have multiple voices speaking, sometimes in a rapid and overlapping manner.

describe events in their lives (see Wagoner, 2012). So you must be cautious in how you frame the qualitative data you get from interviews and focus groups, acknowledging that it is a story presented from a particular vantage point. That doesn't mean the data aren't valuable: just that they can't be treated as an innocent record of objective reality.

• **Over-disclosure**. Because of the dynamic flow of qualitative data collection methods, participants can end up disclosing things they wish they hadn't. If you think this may have happened, you should provide them with an opportunity either at the time, or at the end of the interview, to withdraw their consent for you to use such personal disclosure in your research (see Chapter 3 for further discussion).

8•3•2 ORGANIZE YOUR FOCUS GROUPS

Gathering a group of people together for a discussion that you will be facilitating can be a daunting prospect. In addition to the normal research issues, there are also practical challenges that do not apply to one-to-one interviews. Advanced planning for focus groups is important for a number of reasons. You should have training in facilitating group discussions before organizing your own focus groups. Ideally, you should attend other focus groups, either as an observer or as a participant, before moderating one yourself. Your supervisor or other more experienced researchers in your department may be able to help you find such opportunities. Make sure that you factor in this need for training well in advance of organizing your first focus group.

Your role within the focus group is to act as the 'moderator', also known as a 'facilitator'. As moderator, you provide the topic or specific questions for the participants to discuss. You then facilitate the discussion to ensure that all participants have an opportunity to speak. This is a role that requires good judgement, knowing when to intervene in the discussion as well as when to recede into the background and allow a discussion to unfold. A reasonable target would be to have the **moderator** represent less than 5 per cent of the total words appearing in the focus group transcript.

Focus groups are most useful for topics that can be discussed openly with strangers, and where multiple individual experiences of the same or similar issues can be discussed. While focus groups have been used for very challenging topics such as child sexual abuse or cancer survivor coping strategies, you should approach such topics with caution. Controversial issues (e.g., abortion or animal experimentation) or sensitive issues (e.g., sexual health or recreational drug use) should only be introduced after you and your supervisor have thought through all the challenges and alternative approaches. If you go ahead, ensure that your participants are effectively briefed before agreeing to come to the focus group. Controversial topics should also be discussed under the moderation of experienced **facilitators** and with a clear set of ground rules put in place at the outset of the discussion. This is particularly important as participants may disclose personal information and feel vulnerable in the context of the semi-public focus group setting.

Focus groups can also be challenging in terms of ensuring confidentiality, therefore you may need to adjust the kinds of **confidentiality** guarantees you offer participants while at the same time asking all participants to respect the privacy and confidentiality of other participants (see Chapters 3 and 6 for further discussion of how you communicate guarantees of confidentiality to participants).

It is also important to ensure that you have enough time to secure your desired venue and allow time for advertising, and recruiting and briefing of participants. Give some thought to your target sample and be realistic about the time needed to locate them to ensure you have the best opportunity to recruit high-quality participants for your focus group.

Just as with interviews, you select focus group participants based on criteria that indicate their particular relevance for the study. You should think well in advance of your planned focus group date about what kinds of participants should participate. You generally want to choose individuals who did not previously know each other but who share some relevant characteristic for your study. However, some social science research will involve the need for a discussion with people who are acquainted with one another in a specific capacity. For example, if you were exploring the impact of a new piece of legislation on the charitable sector, then your focus group may include people who work for different organizations, but who may have met one another in their field of work. Therefore, using complete strangers in focus groups is not always a prerequisite, or even desirable. A common question is how many participants you should have in your focus group. You can run a focus group with between 3 and 12 participants.

If you are moderating a focus group for the first time, you should work with a group that is at the small end of this spectrum (e.g., three–six). It can be challenging to keep everyone focused and listening to each other if they have to wait too long for their turn to speak. A focus group of five or six people is likely to be the most straightforward to moderate.

Decide on the number of participants you want for your focus group, then invite two more to account for people not showing up on the day of the focus group. It's much better to have one or two more people than you need than to have too few.

8•3•3 CHOOSE AN APPROPRIATE VENUE FOR THE FOCUS GROUP

Where you hold your focus group is very important. You need a location that is quiet and conveniently located for your participants. Think about other convenience and costs issues, such as the availability and cost of parking or public transport, when choosing your venue. The venue should have:

- Physical accessibility for your participants.
- Childcare facilities.
- A single large table or a group of tables that can be put together so all participants can sit together and face each other.
- A room that allows everyone to easily hear each other and that will be free from interruptions.
- Water, and preferably also hot drinks, available as well as snacks such as pastries and fruit. Avoid crunchy snacks (e.g. bananas are preferable to apples or carrots) or those in noisy packets that will potentially interfere with the audio recording.
- Toilet facilities.

Focus groups typically last two–three hours from the time participants first arrive until they leave, so remember that the provision of adequate bathroom facilities and some basic food and drink is both a courtesy and a practical necessity.

A focus group could also be usefully conducted in a more familiar and social setting such as the back room of a pub, a side room in a café or a family home. Such locations lend a natural feel to the meeting, encouraging a relaxed conversational. However, they also carry more risks, such as interaction between participants and non-participants, as well as a broader range of possible distractions and background noise. Our advice is to only use these kinds of venues when there is a good reason, for example, if this is the most convenient location for your participants, or they are likely to feel uncomfortable in the more formal venue options available.

Focus groups can be held online, although there are many barriers to conducting focus groups effectively in this way. For example, you must ensure all your participants have the necessary equipment, software and computer literacy. There are risks relating to technology, software or internet connectivity failures that could easily cause interruptions. However, as free or low-cost options for group video phone calls, such as Google Hangouts, FaceTime and Skype, have become more widespread and reliable, conducting focus groups online is becoming an increasingly viable option. These options are especially useful when participants are located in different cities or countries, are not physically mobile or have busy schedules. If you and your participants are comfortable with the relevant technology (e.g., if you are researching computer scientists or IT consultants), then such an approach may be particularly justifiable for you. However, given other downsides such as the risk of a more stilted discussion and less opportunity to develop interpersonal rapport, online focus groups should normally be a backup option that you only use when face-to-face focus groups are not feasible.

8•3•4 CONDUCT YOUR FOCUS GROUP

As with semi-structured qualitative interviews, you'll need to develop a list of open-ended questions that you can use to steer the discussion. You don't need to hold rigidly to this list, but rather follow the flow of the conversation, as long as it's relevant to your overarching research question. You may well find that subsequent questions are addressed in the natural flow of conversation without your having to bring them up.

Develop a plan that contains a detailed outline of your focus group structure. Table 8.4 gives an example of a plan for a focus group lasting approximately two hours.

Table 8.4 Sample structure of the focus group

Stage	Task	Organization
1	**Initial briefing** This is the initial briefing when the moderator convenes the focus group. It reiterates information provided during the recruitment process and delivers any further details.	Moderator-led (~ 5 minutes)
2	**General discussion** This stage is facilitated by the moderator through a series of open-ended questions that probe the participants' views. For example, if your research is on campus experiences you may want to structure this section as follows: *Giving feedback* The main focus of this project is to find effective mechanisms for people to be able to provide feedback about campus services, which can be used to improve them over time. (a) What feedback, if any, have you given on any aspect of campus services (e.g., food, retail, IT services)? (b) What led you to provide that feedback? Why? (c) What methods have you used to provide feedback? (d) How did you feel about these methods? (e) What do you think would be a good way to provide feedback? (f) How much feedback do you think you would be willing to offer?	Moderator-led using pre-selected open-ended questions (~ 30 minutes)
3	**Group activity** At this stage, you as the moderator may ask the group to work together on a shared project. For example, you might say: 'I would like to hand over the reins of this discussion to you. I have a "tip sheet" here that explains what I would like you to discuss. I want to emphasize that this part is led by you. I am going to leave the room. I look forward to seeing what you come up with.'	Participant-led (~ 35 minutes)

(Continued)

Table 8.4 (Continued)

Stage	Task	Organization
	Participants will then be asked to work together to produce, for example, a storyboard relating to a specific aspect of your research. Ensure that they will have all the materials they need and that the directions you give are completely clear.	
4	**Presentation of group activity output** Participants should present the results from their group activity to the moderator, describing the content, and allowing comments from other participants. This is the product of the focus group, allowing the participant-led discussion to come to a point of closure, but not necessarily consensus.	Participant-led (~ 15 minutes)
5	**Follow-up questions** The moderator may want to ask follow-up questions about the output from the group activity: What kind of information would it be useful to have about campus services in an app for your phone or tablet?	Moderator-led (~ 25 minutes)
6	**Final questionnaire** Participants complete a final questionnaire, where they list any issues that they feel have been missed, and reflect on their experiences of taking part in the research.	Completed as individuals (~ 5 minutes)
7	**Final debrief** The researcher invites questions from participants and provides them with any relevant information about the research.	Moderator-led (~ 5 minutes)

8●3●5 USE ACTIVITIES IN YOUR FOCUS GROUP

Consider using a focused activity to foster collaboration among participants and inject energy into the group discussion (Holliman, 2005). This involves participants in addressing a relevant issue with minimal intervention from the researcher. Stimulus materials are important to facilitate this process. These can include instructions (usually written so participants can refer back to them on their own) and resources (e.g., pens, paper, cards, images from media coverage). This kind of activity can work well at the very start of the focus group to act as an 'ice-breaker' to get your participants talking to each other (while also generating valuable data) or further into the focus group to provide a more detailed treatment of a topic. In addition, having each group do the same activity can give you an anchor point when you start to analyse the discussions in the different groups.

One example of a focused activity that has been used successfully in the past to research media audiences is the 'news game'. Participants are given 20–30 minutes to generate either a television news bulletin (including a script and image montage) or a newspaper article (including the headline, text and images) using images selected to represent media coverage of the specific issue under discussion.

Regardless of the specific task, focused activities require a sufficiently directive structure to encourage interaction between participants with minimal intervention from the researcher.

For example, the focused activity needs to be free-standing, in that participants are given all the information, equipment and instructions for the entire activity before they begin work. Most importantly, each participant should be given a 'tip sheet' of one or two pages with a list of considerations relevant to the focus group topic that they should address through group discussion. It is also useful to have the participants construct some kind of output that visually represents the results of their discussion in a manner that makes sense to the group. The figure below is an example of the kind of handout you can leave for participants to enable them to self-guide.

REAL WORLD EXAMPLE

Focused activity handout

The following example is of a focused activity handout that could be given to members of a focus group to work on together.

We would like to understand the kinds of resources desired by Warwick University campus users, and the optimal ways in which these resources can be framed and delivered. To this end, we would like to invite you to work with the other participants in this focus group to plan your own information-oriented app, populated with useful and accessible resources for people like you.

Please use the blank sheets of paper provided and design your own app as a group, including as many screens and functions as you see fit. You will have about 20 minutes. At the end of this activity, you will be asked to present your app design to the moderator. If possible, it would useful to have sketches of your app's pages on individual A4 sheets.

Some preliminary questions to consider in designing your prototype app:

- What functions should be available to app users?
- What different screens should be part of this app?
- What structure would make sense for the app?
- What kind of introduction should be provided to users?
- Which options are available to different kinds of users?
- How are the options laid out on the screen?
- From a visual/aesthetic perspective, what should the app look like?
- How might you be able to evaluate the effectiveness of this app? (What would count as 'success' for this app?)

Participants will justify their proposed plans to each other as they develop their group output, and this provides a window into their thought processes. Such activities can be used to form the basis of the entire focus group discussion. This kind of structured activity can enable some degree of comparability across focus groups. The comparison then becomes about how group A approached the stimulus task and how their discussion evolved, compared to group B.

8•3•6 EVALUATE YOUR FOCUS GROUP

Evaluating how your participants found the focus group experience can help you make improvements over time, so it's especially important if you'll be conducting more than one focus group for your project. This evaluation does not need to be overly formal or onerous, but it's useful to assess whether participants felt the focus group was well organized, worth their time and that they were able to actively participate.

There are a number of options for evaluating the effectiveness of your focus group. Here, we discuss three of the most useful and straightforward methods. First, the moderator or observer's impressions and observations of the focus group can be used to evaluate the process (see below). Second, a brief **questionnaire** can offer valuable insight into participants' perceptions and what they feel they have gained from the experience. Third, if the focus group is recorded (as it generally should be), then the moderator can review the recording and/or transcript to assess the quality of the focus group dynamic.

MODERATOR OBSERVATIONS

It is important for moderators and/or observers to take 'field notes' about any potentially relevant non-verbal activity during the focus group (which would not be picked up by the audio recording), as well as noting points in the discussion to which they would like to give special attention, during the data analysis. This enables you to capture impressions and items of interest from the focus group session. This might include body language, participant gestures, discussion points that spark heightened passions or debate, side discussions and emerging subgroupings amongst participants, and thoughts offered during the breaks or after the session is complete. These field notes can also be used by the moderator to spark further discussion on the day, or in a future focus group on the same topic.

PARTICIPANT QUESTIONNAIRE

Giving participants a questionnaire (or sending them a link to an online questionnaire later that day) asking them to reflect on their experiences of taking part in the research is a simple and cheap way of evaluating the session. You could use a Likert scale measure (see Chapter 7), such as: 'Please indicate your level of agreement with the following statements: I found it difficult to have my views heard during the focus group; I was able to actively participate in the focus group discussion; etc.' Or you could ask open-ended questions, such as 'how could the focus group have been improved?' Such participant feedback can inform the structure of subsequent focus groups. It is worth noting that this form of feedback need not be considered a 'mixed methods' research design, but rather a form of quality assurance for your qualitative study.

8•3•7 DEBRIEF YOUR FOCUS GROUP PARTICIPANTS

Save time in your focus group plan to have a final wrap-up discussion with your participants in which you explain what is going to happen next with their data, the timeline for project write-up and any further communication they can expect from you. Meanwhile, invite questions and comments from your participants and encourage them to get in touch at any point if they have further questions, comments and concerns (ensuring they have your contact details). Debriefing from the focus group experience in this way helps to ensure you maintain a positive relationship with your participants (see Chapter 6 for an extended discussion of the participant–researcher relationship).

━━━━━━━━━━ **KEY TIPS** ━━━━━━━━━━

Focus group supplies list

Essential

- Paper and pens for each participant
- Sticky notes spread out on tables
- Large marker pens (at least two or three, ideally different colours)
- Rulers (two or three)
- Coffee and/or tea and cups
- Bottled water
- Pastries, biscuits, pre-prepared vegetable tray or other snack food. (It is important to have something that is healthy and vegetarian included in the food you provide, if possible.)
- Audio recording equipment (see Section 8.4.2).

Optional

- Projector and screen if playing a video clip or displaying some other information
- Materials for the focused activity – printouts of the focused activity tip sheet, any written materials required (e.g., newspaper stories) and possibly some informational materials for the participants to take home with them about the topic under discussion. Be sure to have enough copies for each participant and for the moderator in case she or he is asked a question about them.
- Video recording equipment – it may be desirable to record some of the focus group discussions for additional forms of analysis. Good video recording equipment can be expensive, especially when seeking high-quality audio as well. The video recording function on a standard digital camera is unlikely to provide a usable recording.
- Some organizers pay incentives for participation: these should be on hand to distribute at the focus group if possible (see Chapters 3 and 6).
- If you are gathering feedback about the focus group, you will need printed questionnaires or have prepared a web-based questionnaire.

8 ● 4 RECORD YOUR QUALITATIVE DATA GATHERING

Recording interviews and focus groups should be standard practice for researchers for a number of reasons. Recordings will increase the accuracy of analysed qualitative data, reduce the risk of biased memory and biased selection of which elements are noted down and allow you to focus more fully on engaging with participants. You will not be worried that you are missing information, have forgotten something, that your participants are being misquoted. Moreover, you can avoid feeling the need to interrupt participants to have them repeat something they said earlier. Thus, as long as the participant is protected, you should try to record all the qualitative data you collect.

8•4•1 WHEN YOU SHOULD NOT RECORD YOUR QUALITATIVE DATA GATHERING

Recording is very important for maintaining the quality of your interview and focus group research data. However, there are occasions when you may need to forgo recording. Do not record if a participant explicitly asks you not to or if you have not specifically sought permission from the participant to record. It is never acceptable in academic research to secretly record your participants. Secret recordings are ethically wrong as you are undermining the participant's ability to make autonomous decisions about how their data are gathered and used. It can even be illegal in some cases, but even if it's not, it would undermine the crucial relationship of trust between participant and researcher (see Chapter 6 for further discussion of the participant–researcher relationship).

Your research objectives are always secondary to participants' well-being (see Chapter 3). If recording your qualitative research is likely to cause psychological or physical harm to your participants, then you should not record. You might not know with any certainty whether recording will harm your participants. Therefore, the following questions can help you determine whether you should record your interviews:

- Are participants sufficiently informed about how you will use the recordings?
- Are participants sufficiently informed about potential risks from third parties (e.g., the news media, government) accessing the recordings?
- Are you capable of protecting the participants' privacy and maintaining confidentiality?
- Have other researchers in your field encountered problems with participants having negative experiences because qualitative research was recorded, or problems arising over the existence of the recorded interviews?

Although participant well-being is the primary concern, it is also important to recognize that your research will benefit enormously from recording qualitative data (see next subsection). There is also an ethical rationale for recording, as it enables you to present an account of your participants' words that directly corresponds to what they said (limiting the risk of accidentally misrepresenting their statements).

8•4•2 RECORD QUALITATIVE RESEARCH

Audio recording is the most common mode of capturing qualitative data. Video recording can be useful if non-verbal communication will be included in the analysis, but participants will be more likely to object to video recordings, especially if personal or controversial topics are being discussed. Audio recording will usually be sufficient to capture the data you need, is easier to set up than video, and will not raise as many privacy concerns for participants.

Prepare for and conduct the recording of your interviews or focus groups using the following steps:

1 **Preparation** (before you meet the participant). You'll need a primary and backup recording device along with backup power supply. Make sure that your recording equipment is of high quality and try to keep the amount of equipment to a minimum, sufficient to do the job. Masses of complicated and cumbersome equipment will take

time to set up and can distract from the interview process. You also need to ensure that participants are informed in advance of the interview or focus group that you are intending to record.

2   **Setting up** (when you meet the participant). Set up your equipment quickly and discretely. If the participant is there, this is a good time for light conversation and rapport building.

3   **During process of generating qualitative data.** Your equipment needs to be visible so you can ensure it's running properly. While the interview or focus group is progressing, discreetly check the devices from time to time to ensure they are running, but don't become preoccupied or fiddle with them, because it would be distracting.

4   **After data gathering.** Once you have completed the interview or focus group, immediately make a backup copy of the recording. This way if one device is lost, stolen or damaged you can rely on the backup. If you're encrypting your data, do this soon after your data gathering. Unencrypted data should be kept in a secure location.

WAYS TO MAKE RECORDING LESS INTRUSIVE

Make the recording of qualitative research as unobtrusive as possible. There are three way to do this.

1   **Be familiar with the recording equipment.** Fumbling with cables, adjusting settings, checking if the batteries are charged – all while the participant waits – can make you appear less professional. Practice with the equipment beforehand and learn all the settings before you do any interviews so you can set up quickly.

2   **Use the right equipment.** Be sure you have a purpose-built recorder and microphone of good quality. A simple device built specifically to record audio is preferable to a complex device with features you will rarely use. Especially when recording in stressful, emotional or volatile situations, you want to avoid being intrusive with your equipment. For example, if a participant was providing an emotionally sensitive account you don't want to be preoccupied with equipment or having to place the microphone in an uncomfortably close proximity to the participant. Good-quality equipment that can record from a moderate distance will enable you to be more flexible in establishing a comfortable interview environment.

3   **Use less recording equipment.** Keep the size and quantity of equipment to a minimum. You will have fewer items to set up, keep powered and monitor during the data gathering process and later when such items can be lost or stolen.

Further guidance on selecting the right recording equipment for your project and budget is on the companion website, at https://study.sagepub.com/jensenandlaurie.

8•4•3 PROTECT YOUR RECORDED DATA

Storage of recorded data poses potential issues for confidentiality (see also Chapter 10). Your research participants need to be made aware of who else will have access to their transcriptions; if you promise them that only you will have this access, then you need to ensure that this will be the case.

There are three main ways of protecting recorded data from unauthorized use. First, you can copy your recorded data to an external storage device that is not permanently connected to a computer, is kept in a secure location and is password-protected. This is sufficiently safe for most researchers. It is unwise to leave the storage device connected to a computer because it can still be accessed by others and is vulnerable to viruses and other hazards such as physical damage and theft.

The second method – which can be used in addition to the first – is to encrypt the data. Software encryption uses a process of scrambling information so only the intended user can access it by using a passcode. Encryption software makes this process relatively easy, so don't think you need to be an IT wizard to securely protect your data using this method. With encryption you can have much higher confidence that recordings containing confidential research data can be protected from unauthorized access if they are lost or stolen.

There are many different types of encryption, and the technology is constantly evolving. You will want to carefully investigate each before choosing which is best for you. Keep in mind that for all types you will ultimately need a password and that your data will become very difficult, if not impossible, to access if you forget your password.

The third method is to copy your data to third-party servers, such as Dropbox or iCloud, or other cloud-based data storage options. This method is more secure than keeping data in a non-password-protected environment but less secure than storing your encrypted data on an external storage device that is not connected to the internet. This is because third-party servers are far more easily accessed by unauthorized users such as hackers seeking passwords, data, or private information. If data will be stored on third-party servers, this should be acknowledged if possible in your communication with your participant because they are generally less secure (for further details on issues relating to participant confidentiality and data protection, see Chapters 3, 6 and 10).

Staffordshire University (2015) has useful additional information on data storage, disposal and transfer. For information on national-level data protection requirements and useful guidance on general data storage considerations, see the Gov.uk (2015) site on data protection and the Information Commissioner's Office (2015) guidelines on data protection.

8●5 CONCLUSION

If you establish that a qualitative study is your most appropriate option, you still need to select the particular methods of data collection that would work best for addressing your research question. The main methods of qualitative data collection used across the spectrum of social science disciplines are interviews and focus groups, which is why we have focused on these methods in this chapter. Another important qualitative research method that you may wish to explore is ethnography, a method which combines observations and interviews that are conducted where the relevant action is taking place for your topic. A good jumping-off point for exploring how to do ethnographic research is O'Reilly (2009). If you are interested in considering doing ethnographic research online, the now classic text on this topic is Miller and Slater (2001).

We have assessed the kind of insights that can be gained using qualitative research methods and how best to go about obtaining these insights from your participants through interviews and focus groups. We have stressed the importance of preparation and remaining flexible when planning your interviews and focus groups. The best qualitative research allows for emergence, where information gained during the initial stages of data collection can hone, alter or otherwise influence your research focus. You need to be able to adapt your data collection to incoming information and to do at least some analysis while you are still collecting more data.

This chapter has provided details on the practicalities of conducting interviews and organizing focus groups. We've covered different types of interviews, interview techniques, the kind of equipment you should have and how to deal with challenging interview scenarios. We also provide strategies for gaining in-depth information from your participants by preparing probing questions in advance but keeping the interview questions flexible, all while ensuring that participants feel comfortable and valued in the interview context. We have also described the mechanics of planning, designing and moderating focus groups. This should give you a solid grounding in how to conduct your own qualitative research, what preparations you need to make beforehand and what issues you're likely to face. Finally, we have provided detailed information about recording your qualitative data. We explain why recording is so important, but also when not to record. We have detailed what equipment to use and the importance of backing up your data and keeping it secure.

You should be realistic when choosing qualitative data collection methods. Done right, qualitative research is not an 'easy option' for your project. It involves a substantial investment of time, energy and specialized skill in question design, carrying out the interviews or focus groups and analysing the data. However, the insights that emerge from such research can more than justify this investment, providing you with a real window into the lives and thinking of others.

■■ SUGGESTIONS FOR FURTHER READING ■■

- **Layder, D. (2013). Qualitative data & mixed strategies. In *Doing excellent small-scale research* (pp. 70-94). Thousand Oaks, CA: Sage.** Following a practical approach akin to the present book, this chapter offers you further discussion of the options you can consider for generating qualitative data.

Interviews

- **Ekman, S. (2014). Critical and compassionate interviewing: Asking until it makes sense. In E. Jeanes & T. Huzzard (Eds.), *Critical management research: Reflections from the field* (pp. 119-135). London: Sage.** This chapter engages with emotional and identity challenges you may encounter during the process of qualitative interviewing. It will help you reflect on your role as interviewer and how you are approaching your participants.
- **Beck, C. T. (2005). Benefits of participating in internet interviews: Women helping women. *Qualitative Health Research, 15*(3): 411-422.** This article uses a study of 40 women from an internet-based study of birth trauma to demonstrate the potential of qualitative email interviews.

- **James, N., & Busher, H. (2006). Credibility, authenticity and voice: Dilemmas in online interviewing.** *Qualitative Research, 6*(3): 403–420. This article reflects on the key challenges in conducting qualitative interviews by email, focusing on issues such as establishing credibility and gaining valid responses through this medium.

Focus Groups

- **Morgan, D. L. (1997).** *The focus group as qualitative research.* **Thousand Oaks, CA: Sage.** This now classic book provides a comprehensive introduction to focus groups as a social research method, including planning, design, moderating and analysing focus groups. This is the clearest and most practical book you will find on this topic to date.
- **Morgan, D. L., & Spanish, M. T. (1984). Focus groups: A new tool for qualitative research.** *Qualitative Sociology, 7,* 253–270. This classic article compares focus groups to individual interviews and participant observation, and also provides discussion on the value of focus groups as a tool for data triangulation.
- **Holliman, R. (2005). Reception analyses of science news: Evaluating focus groups as a research method.** *Sociologia e Ricerca Sociale, 26*(76–77), 1–13. This open access article provides detailed analysis of the benefits and limitations of using focus groups.
- **Fox, F. E., Morris, M., & Rumsey, N. (2007). Doing synchronous online focus groups with young people: Methodological reflections.** *Qualitative Health Research, 17*(4). 539–547. This article discusses some of the challenges and opportunities involved in conducting focus groups online, with a specific emphasis on research with young people.

Visit the companion website at **https://study.sagepub.com/jensenandlaurie** to gain access to a wide range of online resources to support your learning, including editable research documents, weblinks, free access SAGE journal articles and book chapters, and flashcards.

▬ GLOSSARY ▬

Confidentiality – Research data are often confidential, meaning participants share their experiences on the condition that their personal information and knowledge will remain anonymous. Research methods like focus groups make confidentiality harder.

Facilitator – See moderator.

Field notes – Notes taken by a researcher during research. These notes may refer to interesting points identified during research, relevant body language or participant gestures and general thoughts made throughout the process of data collection. Field notes can also be used to initiate further discussion or expand on points, or used later on in a follow-up focus group.

Focus group – A research method that involves sets of participants interacting in a group discussion or activity concerning a chosen topic. Focus groups can be both structured and semi-structured. Focus groups should be mediated by a moderator or group of moderators to ensure content discussed is relevant to the research topic.

Informational interview – This interview type is almost entirely unstructured and is loosely based around the research area. Participants are selected because they are likely to be able to point you in the right direction for your research. This interview type can be valuable at an early stage of research when you don't know much about your topic.

Leading question – A question that has a biased structure and implies that one answer is the correct or expected response to the given question. Leading questions can skew your research findings and are considered to produce very poor data.

Moderator (or facilitator) – A moderator leads interview or focus group discussions. This role includes providing topics and questions for the participants to discuss and guiding group discussions to ensure all participants have an opportunity to speak. Although an important role, moderators must judge when to intervene and when to allow the discussion to unfold.

Rapport – A close, open relationship developed between the moderator and participants in an interview or between participants in a focus group. Moderators should always try and establish a rapport with participants as it makes the research process seem more natural and is likely to yield richer and more valuable data.

Qualitative research – Qualitative research prioritizes personal interpretations and meaning over such quantitative ideals as objectivity and standardization. Quantitative research is more focused on gaining insights into participant's thoughts, behaviours and experiences.

Questionnaire – A research method involving participants answering a number of questions in a written format. Questionnaires can be self-completed or can be completed with the assistance of a researcher.

Semi-structured interview – Interviews structured around a list of unordered open-ended questions and follow-ups. These interviews are more natural and conversational, and open-ended questions allow participants to answer more freely and openly based on their own knowledge and experiences.

Structured interview – Interviews that rely on a fixed list of questions that have identical phrasing and are asked in the same order, and where participants select answers from a pre-defined group of responses.

Transcription (or transcript) – The written-out version of recorded interviews or focus group discussions. Researchers often translate their research into a textual form to make data analysis easier.

▬▬ REFERENCES ▬▬▬▬▬▬

Becker, H. S. (1998). *Tricks of the trade: How to think about your research while you're doing it.* Chicago: University of Chicago Press.

Bergold, J., & Thomas, S. (2012). Participatory research methods: A methodological approach in motion. *Forum: Qualitative Social Research, 13*(1).

Goffman, E. (1961). *Asylums: Essays on the social situation of mental patients and other inmates.* New York: Doubleday Anchor.

Gov.uk (2015). Data protection. Retrieved 20 July 2015, from https://www.gov.uk/data-protection/the-data-protection-act

Hoets, H. (2012). Focus group questionnaire fundamentals – basic questions. Retrieved 19 July 2015, from http://www.focusgrouptips.com/focus-group-questionnaire.html

Holliman, R. (2005). Reception analyses of science news: Evaluating focus groups as a research method. *Sociologia e Ricerca Sociale, 26*(76–77), 1–13.

Information Commissioner's Office (2015). *Data protection principles.* Retrieved 20 July 2015, from https://ico.org.uk/for-organisations/guide-to-data-protection/data-protection-principles/

Jensen, E., & Holliman, R. (2009). Investigating science communication to inform science outreach and public engagement. In R. Holliman, E. Whitelegg, E. Scanlon, S. Smidt, & J. Thomas (Eds.), *Investigating science communication in the information age: Implications for public engagement and popular media* (pp. 55–71). Oxford: Oxford University Press.

Kitzinger, J. (1994a). Focus groups: Method or madness? In M. Boulton (Ed.), *Challenge and innovation: Methodological advances in social research on HIV/AIDS* (pp. 159-175). London: Taylor & Francis.

Kitzinger, J. (1994b). The methodology of focus groups: The importance of interactions between research participants. *Sociology of Health and Illness, 16*(1), 103-121.

Kitzinger, J., & Barbour, R. S. (1999). Introduction: The challenge and promise of focus groups. In J. Kitzinger & R. S. Barbour (Eds.), *Developing focus group research: Politics, theory and practice* (pp. 1-20). London: Sage.

Kvale, S. (1996). *Interviews: An introduction to qualitative research interviewing.* London Sage.

Kvale, S. (2006). Dominance through interviews and dialogues. *Qualitative Inquiry, 12*(3), 480-500.

Marsiglio, W. (2013). *Conducting qualitative in-depth interviews.* Gainesville: University of Florida. Retrieved 7 September 2015, from http://users.clas.ufl.edu/marsig/conducting.qual.interviews.pdf

Miller, D., & Slater, D. (2001). *The internet: An ethnographic approach.* Oxford: Berg.

O'Reilly, K. (2009). *Key concepts in ethnography.* London: Sage.

Office for National Statistics (2015). *Adult drinking habits in Great Britain, 2013.* Retrieved from http://www.ons.gov.uk/ons/dcp171778_395191.pdf

Staffordshire University (2015). *Ten rules for data protection compliance.* Retrieved 20 July 2015, from http://www.staffs.ac.uk/legal/privacy/10_rules/

Stewart, D. W., & Shamdasani, P. N. (2015). *Focus groups: Theory and practice.* Thousand Oaks, CA: Sage.

Wagoner, B. (2012). Culture in constructive remembering. In J. Valsiner (Ed.), *Oxford handbook of culture and psychology.* Oxford: Oxford University Press.

HOW TO USE EXISTING DATA

CHALLENGES AND OPPORTUNITIES

9

9●1 INTRODUCTION

This chapter aims to help you save time and resources and learn from other people's research by using existing data to inform your own research. Using existing data collected by other people can be an efficient and effective way to conduct social research. This kind of social research is known as **secondary analysis** because the data were collected by someone else, that is, by the **primary researcher(s)**.

The major advantages of a secondary research approach include the possibility of avoiding long hours of data collection and data entry, and the possibility of having a larger sample size than you would feasibly be able to gather yourself. This can free up more time for other aspects of your project, while saving you the financial cost of collecting data yourself. Another consideration favouring the use of existing data is that new data collection can be impractical or impossible in some contexts, such as historical research. In sum, using existing data can provide insights that it would not be possible to achieve in any other way.

Yet relying on such data also raises the same questions of **research design** and **validity** that apply to data you collect yourself. Using existing data requires you to:

- **Creatively identify promising data sources**. There are many sources of interesting data for most fields of study. However, you may have to think creatively in order to spot opportunities and find ways of integrating data on different topics into your specific research area.
- **Adapt your research to existing data**. Existing data will only be available for certain topics and will often be context-specific. You may need to shape your research around these data by reversing the normal order of the research process, for example by first identifying available data and then finding a viable research question for those data.
- **Ensure quality**. Mistakes may have been made in existing research, making the data completely or partially unusable. You will need to critically evaluate the quality of this research to determine whether the data are suitable for your project.
- **Format the data**. The way that the data are categorized or formatted may make them difficult to use, for example, with data analysis software. You'll need to make an assessment and, if necessary, identify the steps required to convert the data into a usable format.

These challenges involve a **cost–benefit analysis**, where you must weigh research quality concerns against the benefits of using existing data. For instance, data gathered by NGOs in high-risk environments may be the only data available on a particular event, yet the data collection methods may be unknown or severely flawed.

This chapter addresses these and other challenges involved in secondary research, providing step-by-step guidance on how you can identify and evaluate existing sources of data for your project. The chapter also provides practical solutions you can use if your planned data sources are problematic, including collapsing categories to form new and more useful variables.

In the first segment of this chapter, we will help you think through the process of identifying potential data sources. We then discuss the challenge of reverse-engineering your research question once you've spotted a useful data source. You'll learn how to evaluate the quality of your selected data before deciding to take on any strengths and limitations as your own. Finally, we will explain the practical challenges that arise when using different kinds of existing data.

9●2 CREATIVELY IDENTIFY PROMISING EXISTING DATA SOURCES

The types and amount of publicly available data are vast. Governments, research institutions, aid organizations and businesses generate an increasing amount of data on a broad range of topics that researchers can tap into. Recently, government policy in places like the UK and USA has supported increased and improved archiving of both qualitative and quantitative social research data for public use. Publicly funded research data are often made readily available online. For example, in order to receive government social science research funding in the UK, researchers are required to **archive data** so that they can be reused by others. Thanks to policies like this and the improved technical means of making data available, the opportunities for reusing data are greater than ever before.

9●2●1 LOCATING AND ACCESSING PUBLIC OR OPEN-SOURCE DATA

By far the most straightforward option for accessing existing data is to use *publicly funded sources* that have already been specifically prepared for public use. Table 9.1 identifies a number of example sources for readily available data. You can also find sources by searching online, and at your university library.

These sources, like the Mass Observation website pictured in Figure 9.1, provide ready access to data sets that would otherwise take an enormous amount of time and resources to gather.

If you have a topic you're interested in researching, it would be wise to do a search through these and other sources to look for any data you could use before investing your own time and resources in primary data collection.

9●2●2 ACCESSING ORGANIZATIONAL DATA

Many organizations – including businesses, government departments and NGOs – collect data for their own non-research purposes. These kinds of data are rarely publicly available. They tend to require working with organizational gatekeepers to negotiate access.

To identify available and accessible data held by organizations, think about which organizations have a stake in the topic you're researching. It's important to cast your net wide when thinking about these kinds of **stakeholders** so you understand the broadest possible extent of available data. Who are the major stakeholders in your field, and who are the smaller players that may also have relevant data? What kind of information might they be collecting?

Table 9.1 Examples of **publicly available social research data sources**

Cornell Institute for Social and Economic Research	• Social survey and administrative data sets • Quantitative, qualitative and mixed methods, raw data sets http://ciser.cornell.edu/ASPs/search.asp
FedStats	• Dissemination of statistics from US federal government • Directory of federal data since 1997 http://fedstats.sites.usa.gov
Mass Observation Archive	• Social research of everyday life in Britain. Data include diaries, questionnaires and observations • Qualitative, raw data set http://www.massobs.org.uk
Pew Research	• Conducts public opinion polling, demographic research, media content analysis of social issues • Quantitatives and qualitative, raw data sets www.pewresearch.org/data/download-datasets
Statistics South Africa	• Census figures, including causes of death, work and labour force • Quantitative and qualitative, data summaries http://beta2.statssa.gov.za
UK Data Service	• UK surveys, cross-national surveys, longitudinal studies, international macrodata, census data, business microdata. • Qualitative and mixed method raw data sets http://ukdataservice.ac.uk/get-data/key-data
US Census Bureau	• Decennial census conducted by United States Census Bureau • Raw census data http://www.census.gov/data.html

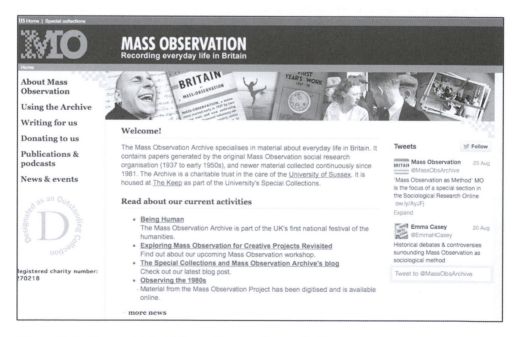

Figure 9.1 Screenshot of Mass Observation website

REAL WORLD EXAMPLE

Do zoo visitors prefer mammals?

Andy Moss, Conservation Social Scientist at Chester Zoo in the UK, is interested in the apparent bias among zoo visitors in favour of mammals (as compared to, for example, fishes or reptiles). He found a way of reusing organizational data gathered by Chester Zoo over the last several years to investigate this topic. The zoo's organizational data set on 'animal adoptions', that is, zoo animals people select to make a donation to support, allowed Andy to infer Chester Zoo visitors' animal preferences.

Andy's research showed that 81 per cent of visitors adopted mammals, while just 14 per cent adopted birds, 4 per cent reptiles, 0.5 per cent amphibians and invertebrates (each), and 0.5 per cent adopted fishes. Andy could use these data to show that visitors to Chester Zoo do tend to prefer mammals more than other types of animals.

However, before leaping to conclusions, Andy would need to consider whether this is a good measure of people's preferences. For example, how many mammals are advertised for adoption compared to other animal types? If around 80 per cent of the animals available for adoption are mammals, then the results above don't really show anything significant. He would also need to consider whether there are any other factors that might bias the data he is using. For example, what is the ratio of mammals to other animal types in the zoo? If there are more mammals in the zoo than other types of animals, this might make it more likely for children to develop an attachment and want to adopt that kind of animal. In addition, how are the animal adoptions advertised? Are mammals such as polar bears and tigers given a privileged position in the advertising? If so, this is another alternative explanation for the results, and throws into question the idea that these data represent visitors' authentic preferences.

Like Andy, you must go through this process of evaluating existing data and identifying possible alternative explanations for your results to avoid coming to **false conclusions**. While this is true for all research, it's especially important for data you didn't collect yourself.

Once you have worked up a list of organizations that might hold useful data for your topic, you can begin to make contact with them. Making contact with large, well-established organizations with major data operations often takes place through official routes, normally made clear on their websites. Other organizations may not regularly share information, requiring you to make initial contact using general phone numbers or email addresses before you locate the specific person or department within the organization who might be able to help you.

KEY TIPS

Find an inside source

Keep in mind that organizations may be just as interested in having research done as you are in having access to their data. For this reason, it may also be helpful to make contact with individuals within the organization who might have a special interest in your research, for example, because

(Continued)

(Continued)

of their work responsibilities or personal interests. One way to find such individuals is to look for authors or those cited or acknowledged in publications from the organization you are interested in. Support from such individuals can help facilitate your access. Gatekeepers and decision-makers in the organization are more likely to cooperate with your request when their colleague is serving as your advocate. Inside sources can also help you locate information that may not yet be publicly available or easy to find.

When you gain access to someone at one of these organizations, your next task is to develop an inventory of all the information that is currently being collected at the organization relevant to your topic. You will then need to review the strengths and limitations of each option for your project. Once useful data have been identified, you then need to reach an agreement with the organization about your access to the data.

Persuading organizations to agree to access can sometimes be difficult. Your explanation of how you intend to use the data may not be sufficient to persuade sceptical data gatekeepers. If offering to share your research findings with the organization is insufficient, you could propose running a few extra forms of analysis to address internal research interests alongside your social research goals. Another strategy is to anonymize the organization, referring to it in generic terms in your report such as 'a small non-governmental organization specializing in African refugee support'. This can reduce the reputational risks of participation, which may be a concern for some organizations with valuable existing data.

9●3 GENERAL CHALLENGES INVOLVED IN REUSING DATA

While all research methods have their strengths and limitations, there are particular challenges involved in working with existing data. While most of these are technical issues regarding data cleaning, there can also be challenges in deciphering how, where and when data were collected. Details regarding the primary researcher's methodological decision-making and data collection procedures are essential ingredients affecting the quality and limitations of the data you are analysing; these are often unknown when accessing existing data. If there were flaws in the design of the primary research, these flaws may persist in the secondary analysis.

Therefore, you must undertake a detailed review of the available information about the existing data that you are contemplating using. Some flaws in existing data can't be retrospectively repaired. For example, mistakes that were made in the phrasing and structure of particular survey questions and response options are permanently inscribed in the data those questions generated. However, other flaws can be mitigated using strategies discussed in this chapter.

9●3●1 FILL IN MISSING INFORMATION ABOUT THE PRIMARY RESEARCH

Once you review the available details about the data you're interested in using, you may find that there are key pieces of information that the primary researchers failed to include when they deposited the data in the archive. As Moore (2007) points out, there are parts of research design and analysis that researchers may be reluctant to acknowledge, let alone write down and store in an archive. In this case, the most straightforward solution is to make a direct enquiry, asking the primary researchers about the additional details you need to know to assess the quality of the data you're considering using.

For example, Eric recently conducted an analysis of existing data gathered through a UK government-commissioned survey (Smith & Jensen, 2016). Once Eric started digging into the details of the publicly available data, he realized there was some important information missing. He sent an email to the relevant government contact, who then forwarded it onto the primary research organization. The letter is reproduced in Figure 9.2 to show the kinds of issues that are often left unanswered when primary data are archived. The example

Dear Ms. Smith,

I am currently working on an article for the journal *Public Understanding of Science* reviewing the report by Ipsos MORI entitled Public Attitudes to Science 2014. I am really impressed by the move to a probability-based survey, and feel that the multi-clustered sampling technique and corresponding weighting system added a lot of credibility to this year's report. Still, looking through the technical reports, I was left with a number of questions I am hoping you could help address (or know who else I should ask). Could you possibly get us information on any of the following issues (all pages are cited from the technical report):

- On pg. 3, it says "Where a household contained more than one adult, one was randomly selected". Could we get a description of that process? What was the method of randomly selecting the participant? The same questions apply to the selection of dwellings, discussed on pg. 3.
- Could you provide a breakdown on when the surveys were conducted? It says on pg. 10 that the time, date and outcome of all calls were recorded; it would be great if we could get access to that information. If not, a breakdown of the percent obtained by week or month would still be useful.
- Given that the number one reason for refusal to participate in the survey was "lack of knowledge about science", could you provide some details on if/how you adjusted your findings to account for the self-selection bias this implies? The report says that attempts were made to contact these individuals again, but other than that, I could find no details.
- On pg. 14, it discusses the weighting model for non-response: "the explanatory variables in the model were Government Office Region and the proportion of adults in the PSU SOC grade AB". Could we get some details on why these two factors were considered the most appropriate predictor variables? Were other variables tested, and if so, why were they excluded from the report?
- Finally, pg. 17 says that post-interview coding took place, but offers no details on how it was conducted. Could we get information on what is and is not included in each code, and how the codes were developed? For example, on Q43. the possible risks reported include "not properly tested" and "don't understand the long term effects". How was it decided to include these particular codes? Was there ever any overlap etc.? It would be especially useful if there were any raw qualitative data on these items we could look at (currently there is only pre-coded data in the published spreadsheet).

I know this is a rather lengthy set of questions, and you may or may not be able to answer all of them. If you know a better person to contact, I would greatly appreciate an introduction.

Thank you very much for your time and effort in helping us track down the answers to these queries.

Best wishes,
Eric Jensen

Figure 9.2 Sample letter seeking further information from primary researchers

showcases how such a letter should be clear and provide relevant detail, such as page numbers. However, it must also be kept as short as possible to minimize its demands on the reader's time and improve the odds of obtaining a favourable response. The example also shows that your tone should be courteous and understanding.

When it's impossible to ask follow-up questions, you can find yourself with interesting data you'd like to analyse but no way of knowing essential information about how they were collected or managed. However, you may still be able to use the data. All research has limitations. If the data would still offer useful insights, you could go ahead with your secondary analysis. Just be explicit in acknowledging the limitation that you don't know key methodological information. You also have the option of adding to the data you're using with new primary data collection to gain a more robust angle on your research topic.

9•3•2 MITIGATE PROBLEMS WITH THE PRIMARY RESEARCH DESIGN

You may come across a flawed research design that casts doubt on the quality of the existing data you want to work with. Primary researchers may not always be quick to acknowledge such problems (if they are aware of them at all), so it's up to you to ask critical questions about the data:

- Do the numbers and approach make sense?
- Is this how this kind of research is normally done?
- Are key steps that would normally be reported left out of the report (possibly signalling that they haven't been addressed)?

You can also contact the researchers themselves. Be careful when contacting researchers regarding potential problems with their research methodology. They may feel their reputation is under threat, or that you are trying to corner them into admitting mistakes. Secondary data are the product of potentially hundreds of hours of labour, and so researchers may take offence and be unwilling to help if they feel you are criticizing them. Approach them in a kind and understanding way, stating clearly that you want to use their data because you think they hold valuable insights for your topic. Thus, you'd like to know if there are any words of caution or issues the primary researcher(s) would like to point out. You may be surprised how many researcher(s) will be quick to help you understand their work and its limitations if you contact them directly.

 **REAL WORLD EXAMPLE**

Knowing when to walk away from flawed existing data

Anje was asked to evaluate the potential research value of existing data that had been collected over many years by the Senckenberg Natural History Museum in Frankfurt am Main. The questionnaires that had been used to gather these data originally used some survey items that were flawed. For example, there was a Likert-type 'level of agreement' question that used an imbalanced scale: 'excellent', 'very good', 'good', 'average', 'needs improvement'.

The badly flawed Likert-type scale item meant it was invalid to use it as a continuous variable. However, it would still be statistically valid to use the individual responses as categories (although their may still be response bias). That is, you could report the percentages of people that gave the different responses as separate categories, but not present an average level of satisfaction.

9•3•3 ADDRESS THE SPECIAL CHALLENGES OF REUSING QUALITATIVE DATA

The rapid expansion in the quantity of research data available for reuse includes qualitative data. This goldmine of ready-to-access qualitative data holds obvious appeal to researchers interested in saving time and resources, while still developing useful social research knowledge.

Yet, there are unique pitfalls affecting the reuse of qualitative data:

- Lack of sufficient contextual information to develop a valid understanding of the data
- Going against the grain of traditions in qualitative research where primary data collection is prioritized (although this is changing)
- Ethical considerations, particularly those regarding consent, which cannot be presumed to have been given for secondary analysis.

Some argue that secondary analysis of qualitative data is an entirely different scenario than recycling statistical information. In principle, there is no reason why you can't use existing qualitative data. However, because qualitative researchers often pride themselves on developing a deep understanding of their participants through full immersion in their social and cultural context, the idea of using data gathered by someone else can face resistance. Yet, good primary qualitative research practice should involve extensive documentation of the data gathering process and environment. Therefore, reusing existing qualitative data shouldn't require major sacrifices in research quality.

As for 'going against the grain' of qualitative research traditions that prioritize primary data collection, some researchers' attitudes towards secondary analysis appear to be changing. Bishop (2011) argues that secondary analysis of qualitative data merely suffers from an image problem:

> It's what I call the 'poor relation' problem, and that is that somehow, maybe because of the name 'secondary analysis', it's also thought of as second class … second tier in some way. There is a little bit … of a bias that would say that somehow primary [research] is privileged, that primary data is always better. I just don't think it's true.

Indeed, secondary analysis of qualitative data is prized for its numerous advantages. Firstly, geographical and longitudinal comparisons become possible, where you as a researcher may not have the resources to do research in foreign countries, or you wish to use historical data to compare your contemporary findings (Bishop, 2011; Thorne, 2004, p. 1007). Secondly, reading through someone else's data can give you a deeper understanding of their methodology, of the processes they went through to reach the conclusions they drew, and also of the flow of participant–researcher interaction, in an interview for example (Bishop, 2011). In a similar vein, when using someone else's data, taking a second look at such data can lead to a more accurate representation of a given phenomenon, which takes into account 'the implications of the original inquiry approaches' (Thorne, 2004, p. 1007). In short, combining your own data with someone else's on the same phenomenon acts as a form of **triangulation** and also allows a new perspective or conceptual focus to form (Heaton, 2003, p. 282).

Finally, the use of recent secondary qualitative data avoids overburdening vulnerable populations, such as the elderly or the ill. Such groups may find extensive surveys or interviews stressful and time-consuming, and minimizing this burden is a part of ensuring no harm comes to your participants (Bishop, 2011).

The reuse of data is becoming increasingly popular among qualitative researchers and the growing interest is reflected in the establishment of Qualidata in Britain (Heaton, 2003, p. 282). Qualidata is a national service that collects and stores qualitative data for reuse (to find out more, visit http://www.esds.ac.uk).

9•3•4 THINK CAREFULLY ABOUT ETHICAL REQUIREMENTS

Another issue concerns consent (see also Chapter 3). Even if informed consent was given for the primary research, this does not necessarily extend to secondary research. The reasons for this are numerous. For example, participants might not have consented to use of their data if they had known about the subsequent research purposes associated with your secondary analysis study. On a practical level, with more researchers accessing data, the number of people handling their confidential information and risk of breaches in confidentiality may increase.

Ideally the *primary researcher* would contact participants to acquire further consent. This may be feasible in qualitative research where sample sizes tend to be much smaller than in quantitative research. However, in practice the primary researcher may be reluctant to undertake this task. It may also be impractical or impossible to contact participants due to their large number, out-of-date contact details or for a host of other reasons. Therefore, a judgement must be made about whether secondary analysis violates the terms of the original consent between participants and primary researchers. This difficult ethical judgement should be made by those who have primary responsibility for, or ownership of, the primary data, you as the researcher and representatives of relevant ethics committees.

9•3•5 USE ONLINE CONTENT AS DATA

As people use the internet, they leave all kinds of **digital footprints**. Because these footprints are already electronic, they can easily be rounded up and analysed for patterns. There are all kinds of interesting social and cultural activities playing out online. Some of these online activities can even be used as indicators of offline behaviour, attitudes and other social variables. For example, researchers have increasingly become interested in using people's conversations on Twitter to detect their mood and satisfaction with particular services or events, social and professional networks, and even to identify whether someone is likely to be suffering from clinical depression.

Given the internet's influence on economic, social and cultural practices, you can also conduct social research on activities that are primarily online phenomena. For example, online gaming, internet gambling, and new currencies such as Bitcoin only exist online in virtual environments, with the users never having met each other in the physical world. While these activities are undoubtedly affected by the offline physical world, they can be effectively researched using a primarily, or even completely, online approach. While the same issues of sampling and representativeness discussed earlier in the book still apply to web-based research, there are new analytic options that are more feasible due to the digital nature of online data.

LOOK FOR INTERESTING DATA IN WEBSITES

The internet plays host to a wide range of political and social debates. The representations of, and debates over, issues in social media, discussion sites, blogs, news comments and many other online locations offer ready sources of data about many domains of life. Think broadly when seeking relevant online data:

- **Interested in how patients talk about their experiences with their doctors?** You can analyse patterns in their online reviews of hospitals, clinics and specific doctors. You could also look up forums on diseases, support groups and treatments.
- **Want to know about the concerns people have when choosing a university?** You can analyse conversations on discussion forums about universities or comments on university admissions Facebook pages.
- **Curious about what people are looking for in a romantic partner?** You can analyse online dating profiles from large internet dating websites such as http://www. match.com, or websites catering to specific types of partner seeking, such as ethnic and religious dating websites.

In each of these, and a vast array of other topics, you can find online data that offer interesting insights into topics that are of general interest to social researchers.

Online content often features both dominant and dissident voices, offering you an excellent insight into the range of responses that a particular issue can stir up. In the case of the climate change debate, for example, online discussions were used to challenge the work of scientists seeking to form and maintain a consensus about anthropogenic climate change (Holliman, 2012). The opportunity to access both the pebble that is thrown into the pond (e.g., a news story) and the ripples it creates (e.g., a range of responses to that news story) makes online discourse a particularly useful reservoir for social research data.

KNOW WHERE TO LOOK FOR GOOD ONLINE DATA

Discussion forums, comment pages on mainstream news stories, Twitter feeds and Facebook pages can all be good places to look for existing social research data. Start by thinking about where online conversations relevant to your topic are most likely to take place. Don't forget to account for the need to develop representative sampling (see Chapter 5) and justify your selected focus when you're gathering existing online data for your research.

With the rapid global proliferation of social media, there has been growing interest in using the internet as an existing source of easily accessible data to develop social science knowledge. The extraordinarily large sample sizes that are made possible by social media-based research have made such **big data** studies particularly alluring options. Big data research is associated with very large sample sizes (e.g., hundreds of thousands or even millions of tweets or Facebook posts). Setting aside ethical issues such as uncertainty over whether participants have consented to the use of their data for your specific research purposes (see Chapter 3), the primary advantage of big data analyses is obvious: enormous data sets can be amassed at minimal cost. Big data analysts are using social media data from platforms such as Twitter to address major social research questions that have been traditionally investigated using social surveys or other more costly methods. However, amidst the big data gold rush, long-established principles of good social research mustn't been ignored. It is important to recognize that the physical world has not simply been 'virtualized' by the transfer of actions and emotions online (cf. Ågren, 1999). While affected by similar issues, online social life is distinguishable from offline social reality. We can see distinctive cultural patterns arise in online communities, which have their own characteristics that don't necessarily map directly onto the offline reality of the individuals participating in those communities (Boellstorff, 2008; Miller & Slater, 2001). As Boyd and Crawford (2012, pp. 669–670) argue, 'When researchers approach a data set, they need to understand – and publicly account for – not only the limits of the data set, but also the limits of which questions they can ask of a data set and what interpretations are appropriate'. This means that, just as in the offline world where you must deeply consider how to apply principles of good social research to the range of contexts you encounter, you should take the same approach with the online world by understanding the context you are researching.

Some kinds of social media data may be unique to the online setting. This is still interesting and valuable to explore for social research purposes. Indeed, all of the factors that affect social reality offline also play out online: power, voice, symbolic representation, identity, leadership, struggles over scarce resources and visual representations continue to exert strong influence on the internet. This means there is a great deal of scope for conducting valuable social scientific research with social media data, big or small.

9•3•6 BE OPEN TO OTHER DATA SOURCES

Beyond the categories of data sources discussed so far, you can also access data on a personal basis (e.g., someone has been keeping records to which they allow you access), or even a professional basis (e.g., a researcher working on a topic you find interesting opens their data for you to use). It is worth contacting established researchers in your field of study, especially if you have the capacity to take on a research project but don't have a ready source of data. You may find that someone has data they have already collected and processed but not found the time to analyse and write up. You may be able to make an arrangement whereby you give them an acknowledgement or perhaps even co-authorship (assuming they have further input) in exchange for access to their data.

9●4 FINDING A WORKABLE RESEARCH QUESTION

Once you identify a data source that is of sufficient quality, you need to determine the research question(s) you can effectively address with your data. You don't have an unlimited range of options in terms of the questions you ask, so you might as well focus your attention on the aspects of your topic for which you now have data. This can be an awkward process that reverses the normal order in social research, where you first establish your research question and then find data to shed light on it. When reversing the process, you first sift through the available data and identify interesting variables. Once you establish that you have a workable amount of data to address an interesting research question, you can then shift back into a deductive mode for your statistical analysis. However, before beginning statistical analysis on existing data, you need to return to the standard model of having a research question, positing hypotheses and testing whether they hold true.

REAL WORLD EXAMPLE

Supplementing existing data in a media effects study

Lana was interested in how news media affect public attitudes towards science. In exploring possible research avenues, she ran across a survey conducted on behalf of the UK government that measured public attitudes toward science. In particular, part of the study looked at the perceived risks and benefits associated with genetically modified crops. In addition, she noticed that the study asked individuals about which newspapers they regularly read. Based on these data, Lana formulated the following research question: 'Does the way British newspapers write about genetically modified crops influence the perceived risks and benefits mentioned by that newspaper's readers?'

Using a content analysis of British papers to supplement the secondary data analysis, Lana found that there was little correlation between the risks and benefits mentioned in each newspaper and the risks and benefits cited by each newspaper's readers. However, she did find that the average tone of the coverage in each newspaper was highly correlated with the number of risks and benefits mentioned by readers.

9•4•1 TRIANGULATE YOUR DATA

When using existing data sources, you may find yourself with an imperfect way of addressing your research question. For example, the data source may shed light on only one aspect of your research question. In such cases, it is useful to identify a second data source that sheds different light on the same topic. This approach is known as 'triangulation'. This is a way of providing greater assurance in the validity of your findings, even when the data are imperfect or partial indicators of the variable(s) you are interested in.

Developing interesting secondary analysis insights by combining two or more forms of data is a long-standing practice. In a classic study, Émile Durkheim examined the relationship between existing data on the number of suicides taking place each year and economic conditions at the societal level. By comparing these two data sources, he could see that the expected pattern of suicides decreasing in boom times and increasing during busts was not occurring. Instead, suicides increased whenever there were sudden changes in economic conditions, whether positive or negative. He used this observation to build up his explanation that any form of sudden change at the societal level could send individuals' expectations into a tailspin. With their ability to self-regulate compromised, they were then prone to extremes, most clearly seen in suicides.

9•4•2 SUPPLEMENT YOUR DATA

Sometimes you can access a large and robust data source, but the significance of your data is not entirely clear. You can collect some primary data yourself in order to help you understand what the larger set of data can tell you about your research question. For example, imagine you have access to a large data set showing how long people spend waiting for the bus in different parts of a city. You might conduct a small amount of ethnographic data collection or qualitative interviews with people who wait for buses at different points around the city where wait times are particularly long or short. This could help you understand what it means to have to wait a long time for the bus. Are waiting times a big or small problem? Are there obvious demographic patterns, such as the long waits concentrating in economically disadvantaged parts of the city? You might be able to identify interesting possible explanations that you can then test statistically: for example, you could compare postcode data on income or ethnicity to your bus wait times data. This kind of supplementary data collection can make the difference between a boring set of statistics and being able to develop an important social science insight.

9●5 TAKE INTO ACCOUNT COMMON SECONDARY ANALYSIS CHALLENGES

To sum up this discussion, we would like to highlight some threats to the quality of data you will need to navigate when performing your secondary analysis:

- **Some individuals may have contributed more to the data set than others.** For example, if you were using reviews of particular doctors on a healthcare website, prolific website users will have a much greater representation. This means prolific users could be overrepresented in the data.
- **Some individuals may have been excluded from the sample in ways that are not fully known or understood.** For example, those who don't use Facebook would be entirely absent from a study using existing data on Facebook. You would need to be careful about using Facebook data to make claims about populations beyond the universe of Facebook users.
- **It may be not be feasible to source information about the data creators, and their intentions or rationales.** This limitation brings with it the risk of developing knowledge claims that inadvertently ignore key information about the individuals from whom data have been collected or the context within which data were collected. For example, a study that only used content on Twitter would be missing details about the Twitter users who produced the sampled tweets, which may have provided valuable explanations.
- **Reliance on by-products of social action rather than direct observation or questioning individuals can result in plausible but inaccurate interpretations.** For example, the foundational assumption that some researchers using existing data have made about Twitter is that tweets provide a reliable index of real human thought, emotions, attitudes or behaviour occurring offline. This assumption is not evidenced (nor has it been demonstrated empirically to date). Thus, there is likely to be error in such

studies introduced in the gap between social reality (e.g., happiness) and the easily observable by-product (i.e., the words in a tweet).

- **When analysing existing data, you have to make the best of what is available.** You can easily end up with data that do not include all relevant factors that could explain the outcomes you are measuring. This can lead to developing claims about the causes of a given outcome, which is in fact mediated by other factors outside your view. For example, if media researchers used a simple analysis looking at the number of negative or positive words used in comments left by online news readers after opinion articles by politically conservative activists, a lot of negative words in their sample might lead them to conclude that people are feeling negative about the Conservative Party. However, people may have been expressing their outrage about a terrorist incident or some other event unknown to the researchers (or at least unaccounted for in the analysis).

9.6 CONCLUSION

As you will be using existing data for a different purpose or context than what was originally planned by the primary researcher, you are essentially giving such data new life. While this process can be challenging, the potential benefits are substantial, in terms of both saving time and being able to address topics that would otherwise require far more resources than you have available.

The process of conducting secondary analysis involves a reframing of the existing data in light of your own particular research interest. Using existing data limits your options in terms of the scope of your investigation. However, the extra time it gives you can expand your options in terms of the scope of the analysis you are able to conduct. Achieving the best fit between your research interests and the available data sources can require creative thinking and compromise. You might need to investigate a somewhat different research question than the one you set out to study. Indeed, using existing data often means working backwards in places to identify a good research question that you can address with your data.

The extensive social and political action playing out online every day helps to make this ready source of data an excellent option for social researchers to consider (see Chapter 3 for discussion of ethical issues involved in using such data). You need to make the data work for addressing the research question that you are interested in exploring. This may require you to alter your research question, or supplement the data with original analysis or analysis of other existing data sources.

While there is very little guidance in the methods literature on how to go about reusing qualitative data, and some sceptics suggest it cannot be done validly, there is every reason to go ahead and do it. As Moore (2007) argues, 'eschewing our comfort zones, and developing a more creative, and even messy, approach may be the key to opening up the full potential of qualitative data reuse'.

Finally, when researchers find themselves with easily accessible data, there is a temptation to 'make it work'. When you are unable to gather your data directly, you are more likely to rely on data that do not perfectly address your research question. It can be very tempting to draw inferences that are not fully justified by your available data. Always be sure to face up to the limitations of your data and avoid overstating your findings.

SUGGESTIONS FOR FURTHER READING

- Brooker, P., Barnett, J., Cribbin, T., Lang, A. R., & Martin, J. (2014). *User-driven data capture: Locating and analysing Twitter conversation about cystic fibrosis without keywords.* Sage Cases in Methodology. London: Sage. This paper uses a case study in the medical context to discuss the practicalities and methodology of using Twitter data to develop new knowledge.
- Goodwin, John (Ed.). *SAGE secondary data analysis.* London: Sage. [http://srmo.sagepub.com/view/sage-secondary-data-analysis/SAGE.xml]. This Sage collection includes chapters discussing the use of secondary data sources to conduct both qualitative and quantitative secondary analysis. It also addresses ethical, methodological and practical issues raised by this type of social research.
- Heaton, J. (2014) *Growing up with Chronic Illness: A Secondary Analysis of Archived Qualitative Data.* SAGE Research Methods Cases. London: Sage. This study considers young adults' experiences of growing up with a chronic illness, but also gives a good insight into the use of secondary analysis of archived qualitative data. As well as a reflection on the method, the paper also discusses how to minimize poor research design and how to involve participants in secondary qualitative studies.
- Hinds, P. S., Vogel, R. J., & Clarke-Steffen, L. (1997). The possibilities and pitfalls of doing a secondary analysis of a qualitative data set. *Qualitative Health Research*, 7(3), 408–424. This article helpfully highlights the special concerns associated with using existing qualitative data.
- Howell, D. C. (2007). The treatment of missing data. In W. Outhwaite & S. Turner (Eds.), *The SAGE Handbook of Social Science Methodology* (pp. 208–224). London: Sage. This chapter highlights key methodological issues that arise when you have missing data in a quantitative research project. The advice is also applicable to the context of secondary analysis when the material you are accessing has missing data.

Visit the companion website at **https://study.sagepub.com/jensenandlaurie** to gain access to a wide range of online resources to support your learning, including editable research documents, weblinks, free access SAGE journal articles and book chapters, and flashcards.

GLOSSARY

Archived data – Information that is stored in a central location, either online and downloadable, or in a library. In the UK, a condition of securing government funding for research is that the data is made available to all.

Big data – Big data research involves very large sample sizes. For example, you may be analysing thousands of tweets sent as a result of a breaking news event.

Cost-benefit analysis – The weighing up of research quality against the benefits you will gain by using such research.

Digital footprint – The trail your activity leaves online, for instance all the websites you have visited in a given day.

False conclusion – When a summary or research findings are reached through flawed logic or faulty methods.

Primary researcher – The researcher who initially collects the data.

Public or open-source data – Data freely available to anyone.

Research design – The structure and planning required before you start collecting any data. Your research design asks 'how will I try to answer my research question?' This will involve assessing what data or information already exists on the topic and how to make sure your research will be of a high quality.

Secondary analysis – this is when you use data collected by another researcher to inform your own work. For example, you may use data collected by the Office for National Statistics in a report you write, as the sample size is likely to be far greater than anything you could collect on your own.

Stakeholders – People or organizations who have an interest in a certain topic. For instance, if you wish to conduct research on the automotive industry, key stakeholders would include manufacturers and engineers, amongst others.

Triangulation – The use of several research methods or several pieces of data to give a more complete and deep answer to your research question.

Validity – Essentially this is the social scientific term for 'accuracy'. Valid research findings are those that closely correspond to the objective or subjective reality (depending on your research question) of the situation you are studying.

■ REFERENCES ■

Ågren, P. (1999). Virtual community life: A disappearance to third places for social capital. In K. Braa & E. Monteiro (Eds.), *Proceedings of IRIS 20: Social Informatics*. Oslo: Department of Informatics, University of Oslo.

Bishop, L. (2011). *What is Secondary Analysis of Qualitative Data?* Sage Research Methods. Thousand Oaks, CA: Sage.

Boellstorff, T. (2008). *Coming of age in Second Life: An anthropologist explores the virtually human*. Princeton, NJ: Princeton University Press.

Boyd, D., & Crawford, K. (2012). Critical questions for big data. *Information, Communication and Society*, *15*(5), 662–679.

Heaton, J. (2003). Secondary analysis of qualitative data. In R. L. Miller & J. D. Brewer (Eds.), *The A-Z of Social Research* (pp. 281–286). London: Sage.

Holliman, R. (2012). The struggle for scientific consensus: Communicating climate science around COP-15. In B. Wagoner, E. Jensen & J. Oldmeadow (Eds.), *Culture and social change: Transforming society through the power of ideas* (pp. 185–207). Charlotte, NC: Information Age Publishers.

Miller, D., & Slater, D. (2001). *The internet: An ethnographic approach*. Oxford: Berg 3PL.

Moore, N. (2007). (Re)using qualitative data? *Sociological Research Online*, *12*(3).

Smith, K. & Jensen, E. (2016) Critical review of the United Kingdom's 'gold standard' survey of public attitudes to science, *Public Understanding of Science*, 25(2): 154–170.

Thorne, S. (2004). Secondary analysis of qualitative data. In M. S. Lewis-Beck, A. Bryman & T. Futing Liao (Eds.), *The SAGE Encyclopedia of Social Science Research Methods*. Thousand Oaks, CA: Sage.

MANAGING AND ANALYSING DATA

PART IV

HOW TO MANAGE YOUR DATA

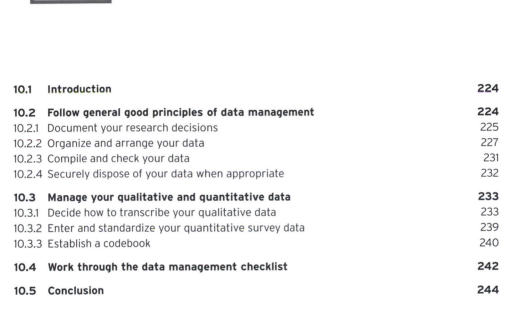

- What data management is and why it is fundamental for your research.
- How you can best organize and store your data.
- How to transcribe audio-recorded data.
- How to translate survey responses into standardized numerical data ready for analysis.

10●1 INTRODUCTION

Developing and implementing a robust **data management** system is fundamental to any successful research project. Data management is about keeping track of the information you collect, storing it efficiently and organizing it for easy retrieval. MacQueen and Milstein (1999, p. 29) highlight the pitfalls that sound data management can help you avoid: 'Seemingly small errors early in the process can snowball into major problems that require considerable time and effort to locate, undo, and then redo correctly. The end result is lost productivity [and] difficulties in maintaining error-free analyses.' Indeed, successful data management keeps your research on track by enabling you to move smoothly from one project phase to the next, while keeping your data safe and accessible.

This chapter guides you through the process of establishing systematic and standardized data management. Data management requires the following:

- A detailed and comprehensive **accounting of your data**.
- Tracking the reasons behind **data collection and organization decisions**.
- Systems that enable **centralized, consistent and easy data retrieval**.
- Robust and **simple data organization** that allows you to cope with even large, unwieldy or complex data sets.

This chapter begins with general advice on data management, then addresses more specific issues you will encounter when doing qualitative and quantitative research.

10●2 FOLLOW GENERAL GOOD PRINCIPLES OF DATA MANAGEMENT

Any research project you do will normally take place over a period of weeks, months or even years. You will therefore find yourself holding data that you can only vaguely remember collecting and saving. Data management enables you to trust that your data has been systematically recorded and organized so that you can develop your data analysis with confidence. Without a systematic approach to data management, many problems can crop up as you transition from data collection to data analysis, including mislabelling of data, data entry errors, and misplacing of data. Here are some indicators of effective data management:

- You **can easily tell how many interviews or focus groups you have completed**, or how many questionnaires you have sent to participants.
- You are **sure what version of your survey** you sent to respondents.

- You can **easily find your participants' contact details** when you go to send them a follow-up survey or thank-you message for their participation.
- Your **file names** **on documents, recordings and other research files do not cause confusion** and do not require you to open the file to determine basic information.
- Your **data sources are collected together.** Data are not scattered between various computers and storage devices, requiring you to check multiple places to find what you need.
- You **keep multiple copies of your important data files**, such as audio recordings, spreadsheets and text documents, in a well-organized manner. Keeping multiple copies ensures that if you make a mistake you do not accidentally save over your only copy of a file. Also, ensuring you have backups saved in other physical locations (e.g., online storage and a USB backup copy stored safely in a different building) gives you piece of mind knowing your data files are safe even if you encounter a total catastrophe (e.g., your computer catches fire and your building burns down).
- You save time and money by **only transcribing or entering the data you actually need**.

REAL WORLD EXAMPLE

Questionnaires

Chi Chi was sending questionnaire participation requests by email to three different categories of respondents, keeping each category on different spreadsheets. She soon realized that her contact lists had duplicate entries, resulting in some respondents receiving multiple requests. This created confusion, and in some cases annoyance, for the respondents. The problem could have been solved if the three samples were managed and checked in a centralized spreadsheet, before questionnaires were sent to respondents. Using a centralized spreadsheet, you can easily check for duplicate names, email addresses and telephone numbers to minimize errors. This would have saved Chi Chi the wasted time dealing with respondent complaints and potential damage to participation rates due to respondent frustration.

10•2•1 DOCUMENT YOUR RESEARCH DECISIONS

Over the course of a research project, you will face many decisions, large and small. Documenting your decisions and the reasons behind them is essential, as you will need to be able to defend your decisions later in the research process. You may have a range of good reasons at the time you are making a **research decision**. However, these reasons may not be obvious or easy to recall later in the research process when you are writing up or responding to criticisms.

Suppose that you are trying to understand how much time participants spend feeding their pets each day. You first ask the respondents how many pets they have. If a respondent

Table 10.1 Steps to manage your data

	Timing and frequency
Document your research decisions For example, which sampling approach, data collection method and analytic framework to use and why	**Timing:** Begin at the outset of your research project **Frequency:** Ongoing
Establish a planned timeline for your research project Account for the major steps and milestones for your project – from the very first stage until the last – so you don't run out of time before everything is finished	**Timing:** Begin at the outset of your research project **Frequency:** Ongoing
Organizing, storing and arranging your data Ensure you know the location of your data, what you have ready and what is missing	**Timing:** As you collect data **Frequency:** Ongoing
Compile your data Gather all your data from various sources and keep them in a centralized location	**Timing:** As you near the end of data collection **Frequency:** During the data collection phase
Prepare your data for analysis Make sure your data are ready for coding and analysis. For qualitative data, ensure all necessary transcription is complete. For quantitative data, ensure data have been entered/imported into the appropriate computer program (e.g., SPSS, SAS or Excel)	**Timing:** After data collection has begun (qualitative) or completed (quantitative) **Frequency:** Once you have completed data collection

answers, '6 goldfish', should this be coded as '1 pet' since the goldfish are fed collectively in one act of feeding (assuming they are in the same bowl), or as six individual pets? Whatever you decide, you would need to keep records to be able to remember and justify the decision later on (see Table 10.1 for guidance on the timing and frequency for data management steps).

Start taking **research notes** from the earliest stages in your research. Be detailed and include the following:

- The date, as this will help you track your decisions.
- An explanation of how you arrived at your final decision.
- What other options you considered.
- Why you decided that other options were not as appropriate or feasible.
- Other considerations or any uncertainties you might still feel about the decision.

These notes help provide 'an audit trail of [your] methodological decisions and analytical hypotheses for the research' and can also 'improve the reliability of the study should another researcher wish to replicate it' (Bloor & Wood, 2006, p. 151). You are unlikely to regret taking too many notes explaining your decisions. Remember, a few moments of note-taking could possibly save you days or weeks of work further down the line!

REAL WORLD EXAMPLE

Studying teenage slang

Isabelle was conducting research on the interaction of female teenagers on an online forum. The teens used slang regularly in their conversations. Some of these slang words used the same spelling but alternative meanings of conventional English words, while others were newly invented and do not have standard definitions. Isabelle kept a separate document with each of the words, describing what they mean in her research and how she defined the terms. By keeping a record, Isabelle could easily remember and justify her decision if she were questioned on a term's meaning.

Documenting your research decision-making will help you achieve the following:

1   You will have an **audit trail of your reasoning that you can consult** later on when:

   a   You feel uncertain about why decisions were made
   b   You are queried by a colleague or supervisor
   c   You need to write up your decisions and procedures in the methods section of your research report.

2   You **avoid the risk that your memory of a prior decision shifts or fades** over time, potentially introducing inaccuracies and inconsistencies into your explanations of research decisions.

3   You can **free up your mind to focus** on other research issues.

Documenting your research decisions by hand in a notebook – your 'research diary' – may seem to have old-world charm, but what is more appropriate is an easily updatable and searchable electronic system. An electronic format lets you share your notes, send them to colleagues, amend them, adjust the layout and use them as a starting point for writing the relevant parts of your report's methods section. Spreadsheet programs, such as Excel or Numbers, are ideal for this purpose because they will allow you to create tables for your data to keep your research organized in a single place.

10•2•2 ORGANIZE AND ARRANGE YOUR DATA

Keep a 'raw' copy and multiple working copies of your data. It is very important that you keep a copy of your **raw data** – information that comes directly from the respondent and is unaltered in any substantive way, such as by editing or file format conversion. Keeping a copy of the raw version is crucial because mistakes are easy to make during data preparation and analysis. If problems arise, you always want to be able to refer back to a raw version to check if data preparation activities are responsible. At the same time, ensure all data are stored securely and in compliance with your discipline's ethical guidelines and your country's laws (see Chapter 3 for further details).

What do I do if I realise part-way through the project that I made data management errors early on?

If you end up making a mistake during data handling, it is sometimes easier to go back, make a new copy from your raw data, and begin data preparation again. Having a fresh start means that you can be assured you are working from a complete and unaltered data set. This way you can make judgements about your data without having to doubt whether errors are affecting your data.

KEY TIPS

Keep multiple copies of your key files

Make two copies of your raw files and store them in separate locations using two different methods – to be absolutely sure you have something to fall back on in the event of serious data loss. Flash drives are commonly used for data storage, but they are prone to sudden failure after they have been used a lot. So make sure you have at least one copy stored using another method, such as cloud memory or a DVD. For files that are small enough to email, sending yourself a copy by email can be a good, extra safeguard as large email providers, such as Google, back up their data on multiple servers. In a similar vein, consider using a cloud storage service such as Dropbox, Google Drive or iCloud, as these services automatically back up the files they hold. You may even be able to access files you deleted through these services. To ensure confidentiality, all digitally stored documents should be password-protected.

Ensure you have a good naming system for easy data identification. You should be able to tell from looking at a file name the 'when, where and how' of that piece of data and whether it is the most recent version you worked on. Having good naming conventions in place will save you a lot of time – and potential headaches – at later stages of the research project.

REAL WORLD EXAMPLE

Keeping good file naming systems

Jimena gathered over 200 survey responses and a dozen qualitative interviews (which she transcribed) in a rural village in Argentina during her research project on attitudes to road safety. When she began the analysis stage of her project, she found that the file names she had chosen to record these data did not adequately explain what each file contained. Her computer was filled with vague file names, such as '5 August – updated version'. It was impossible for her to distinguish between the survey responses, various field notes and the qualitative interviews without opening each file. Jimena eventually spent an entire day going through her data, opening and relabelling each file one at a time until her data were in an intelligible form.

Especially for longer-term research projects, set up a file naming convention at the beginning of your research and stick to it as your project progresses. Thinking you'll remember the contents of a file days, months and sometimes years down the road means you are needlessly risking your data and wasting your valuable research time.

Ensure you add identifying information to your file names for all your research data, including documents, photographs, video files and audio recordings. For extra assurance, you can embed identifying information within the data file as well in a subtle and unobtrusive (and easily changeable) manner, such as in the footer of a document. Establish **identifiers** that relate to key characteristics of the data, such as:

- **Part of study** (e.g., interview, focus group)
- **Type of data** (e.g., interview audio, interview **transcript**)
- **Detail tag** (provides further detail for type of data tag)
- **Data subcategory** (e.g., if you are researching schools this might be the school name and/or particular classes in that school)
- **Date of data collection** (e.g., date of interview)
- **Site of data collection** (e.g., town name)
- **Sample category** (e.g., teachers, students or administrators)
- **Unique participant identifier** (keep in mind that in some cases using names raises confidentiality issues)
- **Data collector identifier** (e.g., interviewer initials)
- **Transcriber identifier** (e.g., transcriber initials)
- **Version** (e.g., numbered sequentially with the highest number being the most recent draft)

For example, you might use the following formula for your electronic file names: Interview – Data Type – Sample – Respondent – Date [of data collection] – Location [of data collection] – Data Collector – Version. This could be written as 'IntTranS1 Chris Jones 5Aug14–SmithHospital–EJ–3'. Make sure your formula is noted down and consistently followed throughout. Finally, ensure you have a straightforward folder structure within which you can put these files. Your folders should also have meaningful names, such as '2013 Healthcare Attitudes–Interviews–Audio–as of 5Aug14'.

Store your data in a centralized and simple manner. Whether you are storing files on your computer or in a filing cabinet, a centralized and simple storage approach is essential. Ensure all your data are in one central place, and then create backup copies from there. For example, avoid keeping some of your primary files in your email, others in your main documents folder and others on an external storage device. The same applies for hard copies of research documents, such as photographs and letters: keep them well labelled and centrally organized at all times.

Develop an organization system to track your data. This system will depend on what data you are storing, but it will usually involve developing a tracking system that uses an Excel spreadsheet divided into 'tabs' (such as by data type, including interviews, surveys and focus groups – see Table 10.2). This approach ensures that you can quickly identify the status and location of your data at all times, including maps, recordings, surveys and interviews. Table 10.2 shows an extract from a spreadsheet for tracking data.

Table 10.2 Example of a spreadsheet for keeping track of your data

Type	Description	Respondent key contact	Storage location	Backup?	Status	Notes
Interview	Interview with school superintendent in Cincinnati, Ohio, USA	Anderson, Kevin	Main hard drive	Yes	Transcribed	Interview recorded in two parts, now combined into one recording
Interview	Interview with Principal of Franklin High School, Ohio, USA	Peters, Andrew	Main hard drive	Yes	Transcription scheduled for 4 August 2013	
Document	Map of Midwest United States, dated 1978	Cincinnati Museum of Pioneer History	Copy in filing cabinet	Yes	Not yet analysed	Some city names not easily discernible
Focus group	Focus group – high school principals, Shelby country	Andreesen, Stefan	Main hard drive	Yes	Not yet analysed	Would like to view results before publication
Focus group	Focus group – high school principals, Logan country	Alvarez, Kelly	Main hard drive	Yes	Not yet analysed	
Document	Map of Cincinnati	Loaned by J. Mark Everson	Copy in filing cabinet. Original returned on 3 January 2014	Yes	Not yet analysed	

Assign unique identifiers to your questionnaires

Adding unique identifiers to questionnaires will give you an easy means of retrieving your survey data. This is particularly useful if you are surveying large numbers of people. Think about adding additional value to your unique identifier that can aid in data retrieval. For example, you could simply number your questionnaires sequentially, or you could come up with a code that adds additional information, such as:

- Sample name
- Name of the person administering the survey (or their initials)
- Date that the survey was conducted

For example, you could use the following formula to number your questionnaires: London [sample name] - KL [initials of person administering the survey] - 3Aug2013 [date of survey] - 5 [sequential number].

10•2•3 COMPILE AND CHECK YOUR DATA

Once you have established your **research timeline** and started data collection, it is time to begin the process of **compiling** and checking your data. This process allows you to see what data you have gathered, whether they are of sufficient quality and what (if any) additional data need to be collected.

Take stock of the data you have collected. Consider the following steps during the process of taking stock of your data:

1   **Bring the data you have collected into one place.** The first step in compiling and checking your data is to gather them together in a centralized location. If you have any handwritten notes, these can be scanned. This allows you to systematically and comprehensively assess what you have and what is missing.

2   **Track your progress towards a completed data set.** When looking at your data, are there missing pieces, sections or components? For example, if you plan on completing 60 interviews, how many have you conducted and transcribed so far? What tasks do you still need to complete and when will you be doing them?

3   **Ensure your data have been accurately recorded.** Have your survey data been entered correctly? Have your qualitative data recordings been accurately transcribed? Through careful checks at each stage of the data entry and preparation process, you should be absolutely certain that problems, inconsistencies, anomalies and anything that may cast doubt on the accuracy of your data have been addressed *before* you begin data analysis. For example, for your research you have three trained data collectors helping to administer your survey but you need to be absolutely sure of the quality of their data. Therefore, a quality check before combining the three data sets together is vital in addition to the regular checks that should be undertaken. In the long run it will be much

more beneficial to correct the problems at this stage than trying to disentangle the good data from the bad later.

4   **Be sure that you clean or prepare your data to maintain consistency**. Your raw data may have inconsistencies or otherwise need **cleaning** in order to analyse them systematically. For instance, some survey respondents might have written their birth year in the format '1987' while others wrote '87'. Cleaning eliminates these discrepancies by making the format consistent across your entire data set. All of your data need to be in a consistent, systematic and uniform format in order to undertake your analysis effectively. This is particularly vital for quantitative analysis, which relies entirely on the assumption of uniform data in order to meaningfully aggregate and compare across categories in your data.

5   **Store your data properly.** Treat your data as your research 'treasure', something that is really valuable to you, impossible to replace and deserving of special attention. You are making a major investment of time and resources, as well as depending on the goodwill of many respondents, to obtain your data, so it is worth putting in the effort to store them properly in a secure location to avoid their corruption or loss.

As you work through the steps outlined above, keep your timeline firmly in mind to check whether your project is on schedule, and make adjustments as necessary. For example, if you find it is taking longer than you expected to conduct your data collection, consider cutting back on your sample size immediately so that your entire project is not pulled further and further off schedule (see also Chapter 1).

10•2•4 SECURELY DISPOSE OF YOUR DATA WHEN APPROPRIATE

You are also responsible for securely removing your data from all places you have them stored when you have reached the appropriate point in time. How long you need to store your data depends on your institution's rules and your discipline or relevant professional association's guidelines. Generally speaking, the length of time you need to store data and how to dispose of data will vary from project to project, from institution to institution, and among data types. For example, the University of Reading (201–) in the UK specifies that consent forms must be kept for a minimum of five years, starting from the project's completion date. Meanwhile, your institution's ethics committee may have a different policy for how long to keep documents.

Research sponsors also may impose their own guidelines on data storage and disposal. The Economic and Social Research Council (ESRC) makes compliance with data inspection a condition of its grant funding and requires all funded researchers to provide copies of their work to both the UK Data Archive and ESDS Qualidata within three months of the end of the project (JISC, 2007, p. 10). Meanwhile, the Wellcome Trust, a research funder in the charitable sector, expects institutions to have their own guidelines on the storage and disposal of data, but suggests that a period of 10 years is a suitable time to store data before destruction (JISC, 2007, p. 22).

As can be seen from the examples above, there are no universal rules about how long data should be kept before they are deleted. Data protection laws and ethical guidelines state that information should not be stored beyond what is reasonably necessary, or beyond the purposes of the research; however, many institutions and sponsors will insist on data being available for a given time for auditing and peer-review purposes. It is therefore always best practice to consult with your institution's ethics committee and any funders for advice on how long to store your data. For a useful guide on the disposal process, including who to consult with and how to dispose of data securely, see National Archives (2011).

10●3 MANAGE YOUR QUALITATIVE AND QUANTITATIVE DATA

Having discussed how to protect your data and ensure their quality, we now turn to tasks that lie between the immediate collection of data (e.g., administering a survey or recording an interview) and data analysis. For all kinds of research, sound data management is primarily about deciding on basic principles of gathering, storing and preparing your data for analysis. However, there are distinctive considerations for qualitative and quantitative data, which we address below.

In qualitative research, transcribing and quality-checking audio or video recordings requires a major time commitment to arrive at finalized data ready for analysis. With quantitative survey research, responses are often gathered in formats that require **data coding** to turn raw data into standardized numbers that can be used in a statistical analysis (see Section 12.3 on content analysis). The present section offers detailed advice about how to manage these essential processes in qualitative and quantitative research.

10●3●1 DECIDE HOW TO TRANSCRIBE YOUR QUALITATIVE DATA

Transcribing audio can be enormously time-consuming, particularly when you have poor-quality recordings, multiple speakers and challenging accents or speech patterns. Therefore, in practice the need for high-quality transcripts must be balanced against the total time you have available for your project. Many books and research methods teachers will only countenance ideal transcription practices, viewing any time-saving strategies as 'sloppy research'. If you have time to do ideal transcription then such advice is feasible. However, we recognize that you may find you have to take shortcuts somewhere in the research process to complete your project on time. Therefore, this section is designed to help you understand where you can save time while limiting any negative consequences for the quality of your research.

What do transcribed data look like? Forthcoming sections will give you detailed insights into how detailed your transcriptions should be. A standard transcription should contain the following elements:

- **Date and label** of the interview.
- **Identification of the interviewer** (normally abbreviated as 'Int'); keep in mind any anonymity agreements made with the participant.
- **Unique identification of each speaker**, usually by gender. For example, 'M1' would mean 'male participant number 1'.
- **A key to identify each speaker** (provided you aren't anonymizing the transcript).
- **Timestamps at least every five minutes** (e.g., normally shown as '<3:20>' to indicate 3 minutes and 20 seconds into the interview).
- Make sure **each page is numbered**. Transcripts will often run to multiple pages.
- **Add a space after each speaker** so it is easy to see who is speaking.

Your completed transcript should look something like this:

Sample Interview Title – 7 August 2014

Int: Why do you think that?

M1:   Because I am a man

F1:   But I think that and I am a woman

How much do you need to transcribe? While many researchers would tell you that you have to transcribe every word of your recorded interviews and focus groups, we believe this is often unrealistic. You are likely to find that some parts of your recorded interviews or focus groups drifted away from your primary research focus, that is, these segments are not relevant to your research question. In our experience, these elements of the recordings are usually non-essential and unlikely to feature in your data analysis and write-up. As such, you can normally skip such parts in the transcription without damaging research quality. However, be honest with yourself when you evaluate the relevance of different parts of your interview recordings, ensuring you are not skipping segments just because you don't like or agree with what your participant is saying. Never start with an opinion and then skip through your recorded interviews until you find confirming evidence (this is discussed further in Chapter 11).

A second related question you will need to ask yourself is how much of the recording, beyond the actual words used, needs to be transcribed. The following examples illustrate the difference between a more detailed **verbatim** (exact) **transcription** and a **standardized** (paraphrased) **transcription**:

- **Example of verbatim transcription that includes non-verbal speech elements:** 'Well [2 second pause], it's, um, um, no- I suppose- it's hard to say [clears throat for 2 seconds]. No, actually it's more, yes, it's more a matter of who, who is prescribing the medications.'
- **Example of standardized transcription without non-verbal speech elements (content only):** 'I suppose it's hard to say. No actually it's more a matter of who is prescribing the medications.'

As Kowal and O'Connell (2014, p. 65) note, 'the appropriate use of transcription entails an awareness of problems related to the tasks of both the transcriber and the reader of the transcript'. That is, the transcription method you choose will affect how different people interpret the contents of your transcription. For example, the verbatim approach may be preferable for helping a person who was not present when the interview was conducted get a more accurate picture of the respondents' ways of expressing themselves.

To enhance this kind of use of transcripts, you can also rely on a method known as the **Jefferson technique**. The Jefferson technique employs symbols in the transcription to indicate mannerisms or physical characteristics (Table 10.3). This helps capture more accurately the interaction between the participant and the researcher, and the participant's reactions to certain questions. As an example, consider the question and response shown below:

Interviewer: Could you tell me how you feel about the legalization of same-sex marriage?

Respondent: Um … I don't really have an opinion, I guess. Yeah, it's not really my business, is it? They can do what they like.

Without any notes provided from the interviewer and only the verbatim transcription to go on, the respondent may appear disinterested, as if she has no particular opinion on the issue of same-sex marriage. However, her intonation or body language may give a different impression. For instance, if she was rushing her speech, or not making eye contact, this might suggest that she was trying to conceal her opposition to same-sex marriage, and give a 'socially desirable' answer.

Table 10.3   The Jefferson technique

(.)	This indicates a micro pause - a pause that is notable, but not of a significant or extended length
(0.2s)	This denotes a timed pause (in seconds) - one that is long enough to be timed and then be shown in transcription
[	This is used when overlapping speech occurs; e.g., Person A might be saying one thing then person B might interrupt to mention something else
> <	These arrows are used to enclose speech where the pace of the speech has quickened
< >	These arrows are used to enclose speech where the pace of the speech has slowed
( )	These brackets, with a space in between, are used to denote that transcription was not possible due to unclear speech
(( ))	These double brackets are used for including a description providing contextual information
Underline	Any words, or part of a word, can be underlined to show a rise in volume or emphasis
↑	An upward arrow is used to denote a rise in intonation
↓	A downward arrow is used to denote a drop in intonation
→	A sideways arrow is used to show that a sentence is of particular importance or interest to the analyst
CAPITALS	Capital letters can be used to show that something was said loudly or shouted
(h)	Shows that the respondent laughed while they were talking, e.g. We were walking along the river and my father fell in (h)! It was very funny
=	This is used to show latched speech, where answers are given continuously from questions, without a pause, e.g: *Interviewer:* So would it be fair to say that the introduction of pupil premium has made a noticeable difference to your students? *Respondent:* = Oh yes, it has made such a difference […]
::	These are used to show elongated speech, or a stretched sound, e.g. ::Yes might sound a bit like 'Yeeeeees'

Source: adapted from University of Leicester (n.d.)

When people speak, their words are punctuated with silent and vocalized (e.g., 'um', 'ah') pauses and other sounds, such as throat-clearing, coughing, laughing or crying. These non-verbal speech elements can implicitly communicate information (e.g., uncertainty) that may be relevant to your research questions, for example, when people are less like to explicitly articulate all of their relevant feelings and thoughts. The more controversial, personal, secretive, emotional or socially undesirable your research topic is, the more you are likely to find non-verbal speech elements to be a valuable source of information. So, if you are asking a respondent about patterns of shopping at a grocery store, the non-verbal elements are likely to be less important than if you are asking about extramarital affairs (when a pause or throat-clearing may be more important).

Whatever you decide, you should establish a consistent transcription method. Achieving this consistency requires developing a guide for transcribers (including yourself) that clearly defines how different non-verbal features of speech are to be represented.

KEY TIPS

Use dictation software to save time when you transcribe

The following strategy is the only effective timesaver we have found when doing our own transcriptions, while avoiding high error rates. First, listen to your recorded data on headphones, then repeat what you hear back into a microphone connected to dictation software, which in turn types out what you say. Since dictation software requires clear speaking at a consistent pace, this method is far more effective than playing a recorded interview directly into the microphone.

Be patient with this strategy! It will take a little time to get comfortable with it – but if you persevere you could save a lot of time.

You will need the following:

- Headphones.
- Microphone (an inexpensive headset that keeps your hands free and can be placed over your headphones works well).
- **Dictation software** (Google's dictation software is free and works well. Dragon Naturally Speaking is purpose-built and works even better, although it can be expensive).
- Software to slow down the audio recording, such as Transcribe! (there are also free alternatives).

Here is the transcription procedure (note that the following may need to be adjusted based on your computer set-up):

1 If your recording includes multiple participants, you will need to develop familiarity with their different voices so you can identify who is speaking.
2 Open the software that will slow down your recorded interview and open the interview file from that software. Become familiar with how to slow down the playback speed.
3 Connect your microphone to your computer and make sure that your dictation software is able to record what you are saying. Take a bit of time to become familiar with the software. Learn how it works and get comfortable with the speed and clarity of your speech required to achieve high-quality transcription of what you dictate. You will need to speak slowly and clearly, which is why you need to simultaneously slow down the audio playback. You may

need to add additional notation verbally along the way, for example, you would need to specify when a different speaker is talking in a focus group recording.

4   Put on your headphones and orient yourself so you can easily hear the recording while repeating what you hear into the microphone. You will need to adjust the playback speed to a comfortable pace.

5   Begin playing back the recorded interview in short bursts, for example about 5-10 seconds at a time. Pause the interview, then clearly and slowly repeat back into the microphone what you just heard. Repeat the process until you have completed the transcription and are certain that your transcription is accurate.

You will undoubtedly find that errors appear in your transcription where the software has not understood you or has had trouble with technical or foreign words, places or names. The software can also get confused with similar sounding words such as 'their' and 'there' or 'your' and 'you're'. We strongly recommend that you don't waste time trying to get it exactly right the first time. Aim to get a thorough – although probably imperfect - first round completed. You can read through the whole transcription while listening to your slowed-down recording, correcting mistakes as you go. This may sound time-consuming (and it is!), but you often need to go through this kind of quality assurance procedure to correct errors even if you use a professional service.

Can you get away with minimal transcription? Many research methods textbooks will tell you that you always need to do complete, verbatim transcriptions, capturing the entire length of the interview or focus group as well as non-verbals. This is sound advice – in an ideal world. However, this ideal is rarely reached beyond PhD dissertations and projects with funding for professional transcription. Capturing non-verbal information and creating complete transcripts takes considerable time and effort, so you should only do so if you really need this level of detail.

In practice, not all information is likely to be necessary to your research. Consider whether content such as the following is necessary for you to transcribe:

• **Background information** about the participant, such as where the individual grew up, was educated or experiences prior to the period you are investigating. For example, you could just note down key biographical information to report in your sample description without a verbatim transcript.

• Any **introductory information** you provide, such as descriptions of your research and details of how you plan to use the data (i.e., any standard project description content). There is no obvious benefit to having such information typed up for each interview or focus group you conducted.

• **Lengthy anecdotal information** from the respondent that is peripheral to the core area of investigation. You can end up with such peripheral information because you don't want to rudely interrupt participants.

However, more complete transcription does allow you to be more rigorous and thorough in your analysis, so you should only contemplate the most minimalist approach (i.e., only transcribing the parts you are quoting) if you honestly don't have time for more complete transcription. In such cases, you should thoroughly and repeatedly listen to your recordings, making basic notes for yourself, to ensure you've taken into account the full context of the data you transcribe.

KEY TIPS

Pay particular attention to planning for phases of your project that may be tedious, repetitive or tiring

Transcribing interviews (or coding and data entry) can be very tiring even at the best of times. If the quality of an audio recording is poor, transcription can be hell. As a general rule, allow at least four-six hours to do a transcription of only the words someone says in a one-hour qualitative interview (at least double this time for a recording with multiple speakers). Allow 10-14 hours to do a fully detailed transcription with speech effects noted for one hour of interview (at the lower end for high audio quality and at the higher end for poor audio quality). Don't assume you will have the stamina to do more than a few hours of transcription at a time! Again, the overriding rule is to be realistic with your expected timeframes for key tasks, erring on the side of caution (and not collecting more data than you can handle!).

WHO SHOULD TRANSCRIBE YOUR QUALITATIVE DATA RECORDINGS?

Option 1: Transcribe your own data. Many researchers do their own transcriptions, particularly when they are students or lack funding. The advantages of this option are that you can set your own pace, control the quality level and avoid spending money you don't have. You also know your research well, so you can more easily transcribe unusual words and phrases. Also, you will know your research data even better once you have spent many hours listening to your recordings and typing them up. The disadvantages are that it can take a long time, may diminish your efforts in other aspects of your research and can be generally exhausting.

Option 2: Use a professional transcription service. Well-funded researchers often use professional transcription services. Their obvious advantage is saving time, which can free you up for other tasks. The equally obvious disadvantage is that they can be expensive. But there can also be quality problems. Even when you pay at the high end for professional transcription, it is very hard to find someone you can trust to know the relevant terminology for your research and care as much as you do about getting it right.

REAL WORLD EXAMPLE

The limitations of professional transcription services

Charles used professional transcription services for several interviews he conducted for his research on Zimbabwe. Rather than an efficient way of handling the transcripts, he found that the combination of Zimbabwean accents, foreign place names, slang and unusual phrasing resulted in unusable transcripts, which he still had to pay for!

Eric used a UK-based service to transcribe focus group audio data featuring different sets of British participants. He found that about 30 per cent of the transcripts were of very poor quality (sometimes unusable), with everyone in the transcript (e.g., eight participants plus the focus group moderator) listed as either 'Unidentified Male' (UM) or 'Unidentified Female' (UF). There were also missing chunks across all the transcripts that were marked as '[unintelligible]'. The transcription service explained both issues by saying that the audio quality of the recordings they were given was 'poor', and added that the UM/UF notation was necessary because the different voices on the recording could not be distinguished. However, when Eric listened to the audio files, he found that it was clear enough to make out nearly all of the elements left out of the transcripts.

What both of these examples illustrate is that professional services are unlikely to be as diligent and persistent as you would be when faced with difficult transcription tasks. You should probably only consider using them if you have very high-quality audio recordings of people discussing topics familiar to an average person in the country where the transcription service is based. Even in the most ideal conditions, be a critical consumer of transcription services: consider having the company provide you with a sample transcript to make sure you are happy with their work before you send them your entire data set.

Option 3: Train others to transcribe your data. This option tends to be used to avoid the problems associated with professional services, while still saving the researcher's time. The strength of this option is that someone else does the actual transcription, but you can be closely involved to monitor quality. For example, you can answer questions about place names or help decipher hard-to-understand phrases. You could also select transcribers with relevant expertise. For instance, interviews with heart surgeons about their decision-making processes are likely to be laden with medical jargon, which medical students may be well placed to understand. Another advantage is that this option tends to be less expensive than professional transcription services, which are prohibitively expensive for most researchers.

A disadvantage is that you need to carefully train and monitor the transcribers, which takes more of your time, especially at the beginning of the process. In practice, however, a motivated group of bright students will learn quickly and often do excellent transcriptions. Overall, this can be a good compromise option if you have some funding to draw on. It can save you money and boost quality compared to professional transcription.

KEY TIPS

Record transcription details for quality assurance

Be sure to keep detailed information about who performed each transcription, who checked it and any problems encountered during the process. To make quality assurance easier, make sure the elapsed time on the audio or video recording is noted periodically in the transcript. For example, at the end of the second paragraph, you could put <1:16> to indicate that the paragraph ends 1 minute, 16 seconds into the recording.

10•3•2 ENTER AND STANDARDIZE YOUR QUANTITATIVE SURVEY DATA

Survey data entry is the process of converting raw quantitative or open-ended response data into a final, standardized quantitative format ready for analysis. To get to this point, you will need to enter data as numbers following a consistent system, sometimes transforming the data as you enter them to achieve this consistency. You will need to decipher what respondents have written, make judgement calls on unusual, complex or difficult-to-understand responses, and become deeply familiar with the range of responses in your survey.

TRANSLATE YOUR DATA INTO USABLE NUMBERS FOR ANALYSIS

Once all your data have been collected, gathered in a centralized location, and prepared for data entry, your next step should be to prepare for data coding. Data coding is a means of making responses to particular survey questions consistent by either assigning standard numbers to each response option or grouping related open-ended responses and then converting them into numerical data. Let's go through an example of the second type of data coding. If an open-ended survey question asks for 'gender', responses could include a range of specific terms, such as 'boy', 'man', 'girl' and 'woman'. You need to have a system for converting these open-ended responses to turn them into standardized data that could be analysed statistically. For instance, you could use the system: 1 = male (including 'boy', 'man', 'male', etc.) and 2 = female (including 'girl', 'woman', 'female', etc.). By systematically replacing the words with numbers (i.e., data coding), you convert your open-ended responses to usable quantitative data that can be processed using SPSS or other analysis software.

10•3•3 ESTABLISH A CODEBOOK

Your **codebook** is your guide for entering and 'decoding' your quantitative data. The codebook contains a list of your research questions followed by the possible answers for each question. For example, if your survey asked for respondents' age, but you wanted to convert raw age to age bands, the codebook would identify the survey question and then age ranges for each band. In this example, there is a two-step process: first, you must convert – code – age into age ranges, then you would need to attach a numerical data code to each age range. So, in step 1 of this process, you might define the following categories: 'under age 20', 'age 20–29', 'age 30–39', 'age 40–49', 'age 50–59', 'age 60–69' and 'age 70+'. Once applied to the data, these categories in turn need to be converted into a single number per category for entry into your spreadsheet for quantitative analysis. For example, you could convert the categories above as follows: 'under age 20' = 1, 'age 20–29' = 2, 'age 30–39' = 3, 'age 40–49' = 4, 'age 50–59' = 5, 'age 60–69' = 6 and 'age 70+' = 7. Your codebook details this translation process for all the questions in your survey, acting as your master guide to interpreting your quantitative data. In this example, only the final set of numbers (1–7) would appear in your statistical analysis under the variable name 'age range'.

 **KEY TIPS**

Use word-processing software to write your codebook

Your codebook will undergo considerable editing, especially in early phases. Microsoft Word (or similar word-processing software) works well for writing your codebook because it allows for flexible and intuitive layouts as well as easy editing. Excel is not appropriate since it is far less flexible for written content. Likewise, a handwritten codebook is insufficiently adaptable.

Your codebook is essential to ensure you enter your survey data consistently and interpret your statistical results accurately. You should develop and fine-tune your codebook before you begin entering your data into a spreadsheet for analysis. Thorough preparation is crucial at this stage; it will save you a lot of time later in your research project.

Develop a detailed codebook. Take the following steps in order to understand your data and then develop a sufficiently detailed codebook that appropriately accounts for your survey responses.

Step 1: **Be familiar with your data.** Spend some time getting a sense of the range of responses to each survey question and the frequency with which they occur. Once you have an overall understanding of the types of responses, you are well positioned to gauge the depth and detail needed for your codebook.

Step 2: **Enter key information into your codebook for each survey question, as follows:**

- Accurately reproduce the survey question.
- Enter a short and unique variable name (e.g., 'Gender' or 'DOB' for date of birth) that does not exceed 16 characters (no spaces), the limit for most statistical analysis software.
- Add a variable label, which is a longer descriptor that makes it easier to differentiate similar questions (e.g., the respondents' gender or date of birth).

Table 10.4 provides a sample of a portion of a codebook for research on farmers. In the sample, three basic survey questions are identified along with corresponding 'codes' for each question. The sample also shows that it is important to have data codes for missing data (e.g., '98' and '99'). 'Variable Number' is a simple way of identifying each variable, such as by how it

Table 10.4   Sample codebook for research on farmers

Across the codebook, the following data codes apply:

99 = *Does not apply to this respondent (to be excluded)*
98 = *Applicable to this respondent, but no response given*
 9 = *Prefer not to say*

Variable Number	Question	Variable Name	Label	Code
1	Please indicate your gender	Gender	Respondent's gender	1 = Male 2 = Female
2	Which of the following categories best describes your ethnic background?	Ethnic	Respondent's ethnic background	1 = White 2 = Black 3 = Indian/Asian 4 = Mixed race 5 = Other
3	What is the main crop you grow on your farm?	Primary crop	Primary crop	1 = Maize 2 = Tobacco 3 = Soya beans 4 = Horticulture 5 = Cotton 6 = Other

corresponds to your survey questions, whereas 'Variable Name' provides a descriptive means of identifying the variable.

Step 3: **Capture the range of responses in your data.** Once you have established a basic structure for your codebook, proceed survey question by survey question (i.e., variable by variable) and assign numerical data codes for the range of responses you see in your data. However, when you find infrequently mentioned response categories, you should consider whether it would be appropriate to exclude them or gather together clusters of responses into a single category.

 **KEY TIPS**

When to begin quantitative coding

You should usually wait to begin data coding for open-ended survey questions until after you complete data collection. Otherwise, you can end up causing trouble for yourself because you may not have a full sense of the range of responses. For example, if you are researching students' weekend social activities, the initial responses you receive could be markedly different from those you receive later in the survey period. If this happens, you might spend time developing your codebook only to find that the later responses substantially change how you would structure your coding.

10 ● 4   WORK THROUGH THE DATA MANAGEMENT CHECKLIST

We present in Table 10.5 an example checklist to help you ensure you have implemented an appropriate data management plan for your own project. You will need to adapt this plan to suit your project's specific needs.

Table 10.5   Data management checklist

☑ **Document all your research decisions (e.g., which sampling approach, data collection method and analytic framework to use and why)**

1   Establish a system to record all your research decisions. Include the following:

- Date
- An explanation of how you arrived at your final decision
- Any other options you considered
- Reasons why other options were not appropriate or feasible
- Any other considerations or uncertainties you felt about the decision

2   Use word-processing software so that your document is easily updatable and searchable electronically.

☑ **Establish a planned timeline for your research project**

1   Account for the major steps and milestones for your project

- Begin with the first stage of your research project
- Add detailed interim stages
- End with the final stage of your project

2   Be sure to update your timeline regularly so it remains accurate

☑ **Organizing, storing and arranging your data**

Ensure you know the location of your data, what you have ready and what is missing

1   Establish a workflow so as you handle data (i.e., newly arrived information, data you recently analysed, etc.) you know where to store them.

- Devise a clearly organized file structure so you can easily find all your data
- Establish a procedure so hard copies of documents can easily be stored and located. Make sure you scan hard copies of data and then organize the digital files.

2   Develop a naming convention for your files so you can track and identify your data more easily. Include the following:

- Part of study (e.g., interview, focus group)
- Type of data (e.g., interview audio, interview transcript)
- Detail tag (provides further detail for type of data tag)
- Data subcategory (e.g., if you are researching schools this might be the school name and/or particular classes in that school)
- Date of data collection (e.g., date of interview)
- Site of data collection (e.g., town name)
- Sample category (e.g., teachers, students or administrators)
- Unique participant identifier (keep in mind that in some cases using names raises confidentiality issues)
- Data collector identifier (e.g., interviewer initials)
- Version (e.g., numbered sequentially with the highest number being the most recent draft)

3   Keep 'raw' copies and multiple versions of your data

☑ **Compile and check your data**

Gather all your data in a centralized location, consistently prepared and ready for analysis

1   Gather together all the data you have collected
2   Decide whether there are gaps in the data
3   Ensure that your data are accurate
4   Clean and prepare your data if necessary, for example checking for missing data
5   Ensure that your data are of sufficient quality for analysis
6   Ensure that your data are stored properly

☑ **Prepare your data for analysis**

Make sure your data are ready for coding and analysis

Qualitative data - ensure your transcriptions are complete

1   Decide how much data you need to transcribe

- Can you get away with minimal transcription?

2   Describe how detailed your transcriptions should be (e.g., whether they should include non-verbal elements)
3   Determine who should transcribe your data

- Yourself
- Professional transcription service
- Train others

Quantitative data

1   Collect all your quantitative data into a centralized location.
2   Translate your data into usable numbers for analysis

- Establish a codebook
- Complete coding

3   Ensure data have been entered/imported into the appropriate computer program (e.g., SPSS, SAS or Excel)

This chapter offers detailed advice for addressing each of the points on this checklist. You can use the checklist during your research project to make sure you have addressed each of the major elements before moving onto data analysis.

10●5 CONCLUSION

This chapter has offered guidance on the steps required to maintain a clear audit trail so you know why you made key research and data management decisions and how you implemented those decisions. Explanations for research decisions can easily be forgotten. Keeping a detailed record of your decision-making is clearly the solution to the research challenge of remembering and justifying your decision-making. This chapter has identified important techniques for keeping such data management information accessible, such as keeping a centralized spreadsheet to track participant, data collection and data preparation details.

Deciding how much of your qualitative data recordings to transcribe has major implications for the limited time and resources you have available to complete your project. Therefore, it may often be prudent to cut some corners on transcription (e.g. only transcribing the parts of an interview that are directly on topic) in order to ensure you have enough time to conduct a thorough data analysis at the next stage of your research project. If you have the funds to have someone else do some transcription for you, consider training someone rather than using a professional service.

Keep careful records as you translate your completed surveys or observation forms into usable quantitative data. You will need to enter your data using standardized categories and ensure that the final polished version of your data has been cleaned of inconsistencies or other errors. These tasks set the stage for your data analysis.

▬ SUGGESTIONS FOR FURTHER READING ▬

- **Bloomer, A., Griffiths, P., & Merrison, A. J. (2005). *Introducing language in use.* New York: Routledge.** Chapter 2 goes into detail on how a fully detailed transcript is developed, covering all the different non-verbal aspects of recorded speech that might occur.
- **MacLean, L. M., Meyer, M., & Estable, A. (2004). Improving accuracy of transcripts in qualitative research. *Qualitative Health Research, 14*(1), 113-123.** This article offers you the benefit of some experienced researchers' struggles with common challenges around transcribing qualitative data. While the advice about using a third-party transcriber may not apply to you because of the major expense this can represent, the issues they discuss will be relevant to anyone transcribing qualitative data.
- **Marston, L. (2010). Data management. In *Introductory statistics for health and nursing using SPSS* (pp. 22-42). London: Sage.** While this chapter is quite specific in its context (it uses data from the student breast cancer awareness study), it provides a useful 'how to' on using SPSS to clean data, rather than doing this manually. The author argues in favour of using SPSS, to avoid making mistakes and ensuring consistency.
- **National Archives (2011). *Disposal checklist.* Retrieved 14 July 2015, from http://www. nationalarchives.gov.uk.** This website explains why some records require disposal, helps you

determine what information you have, shows you the value of this information, and then guides you on how to dispose of information you don't need.

- **Pallant, J. (2007).** *SPSS survival manual* **(3rd ed.). Maidenhead: Open University Press.** This book provides a useful, user-friendly approach and practical guidance on data entry and codebook preparation.
- **Paulus, T., Lester, J. N., & Dempster, P. (2014).** *Digital tools for qualitative research.* **London: Sage.** The coverage in Chapter 6 of how to transcribe video and audio data will be especially useful. The authors detail the digital tools that can be used to transcribe recorded data and they include discussion of four different transcription methods (among them verbatim and Jeffersonian).
- **Silverman, D. (2013).** *Doing qualitative research: A practical handbook* **(4th ed.). London: Sage.** For information on transcripts and research notes, especially on the value of working with recorded interviews, see Chapter 12. Chapter 16 covers record keeping, providing justifications for the use of research diaries.
- **Strauss, A. L. (1987).** *Qualitative analysis for social scientists.* **Cambridge: Cambridge University Press.** Chapters 2 and 3 in this classic research methods text give detailed examples and techniques for coding.

Visit the companion website at **https://study.sagepub.com/jensenandlaurie** to gain access to a wide range of online resources to support your learning, including editable research documents, weblinks, free access SAGE journal articles and book chapters, and flashcards.

■ GLOSSARY ■

Cleaning – Ensures that the format of the data is consistent and makes analysis easier and quicker. For example, you may need to clean your data to ensure that all dates are written in the dd-mm-yy format, as opposed to any other variation.

Codebook – A document that contains a list and associated descriptions of all the codes used in a given research project.

Compile – Gathering data you have collected for your research in a central, organized location so you can see what you have gathered and what is missing before you begin analysis.

Data coding – The process of categorizing data for analysis.

Data management – The process of managing and coordinating data for your research project to ensure that you know what you have collected, what still needs to be gathered, where different information is located, and how best to analyse it.

Dictation software – Technology to assist with transcription; the software enables you to read something into a device which then types it out for you.

File name – The name given to a document saved on a computer. All file names should follow the same format and allow for instant identification as to the contents of the file.

Identifiers – These can be added to all documents, such as survey responses, to aid instant identification of the provenance of the document.

Jefferson transcription – A transcription method that employs symbols to convey changes in intonation, volume and other mannerisms.

Raw data – Information that has come directly from the respondent and has not been altered or edited by anyone else. Keeping copies of raw data is essential, as mistakes can be made during data preparation and analysis. By storing the raw data, you always have the original to check back against.

Research decisions – Choices you make throughout the research project and the reasons behind making them, or abandoning other options.

Research notes – These are essential to any project and will record decisions, categories, shorthand and coding choices. The more notes you make of decisions you take at the time, the easier writing up will be in the future.

Research timeline – Identifies major milestones so you can effectively plan your project, assess the feasibility of your goals, and determine whether you are on schedule.

Standardized transcription – Transcription that removes all the non-verbal speech elements, such as pauses and fillers (e.g., 'um' and 'err').

Transcription – The written form of speech, such as an interview.

Verbatim transcription – Transcription that records the interview word for word and includes non-verbal cues such as pauses and fillers (e.g., 'um' and 'err').

▬ REFERENCES ▬▬▬▬▬▬▬▬▬▬▬▬▬

Bloor, M., & Wood, F. (2006). Research diary. In *Keywords in Qualitative Methods*. London: Sage.

JISC. (2007). *HEI records management: Guidance on managing research records*. Retrieved from http://tools.jiscinfonet.ac.uk/downloads/bcs-rrs/managing-research-records.pdf

Kowal, S., & O'Connell, D. (2014). Transcription as a crucial step of data analysis. In U. Flick (Ed.), *The SAGE handbook of qualitative data analysis* (pp. 64–79). London: Sage.

MacQueen, K. M., & Milstein, B. (1999). A systems approach to qualitative data management and analysis. *Field Methods*, 11(1), 27–39.

National Archives (2011). *Disposal checklist*. Retrieved 14 July 2015, from http://www. nationalarchives.gov.uk.

University of Leicester (n.d.). What is the Jefferson transcription system? Retrieved 17 July 2015, from http://www2.le.ac.uk/departments/psychology/research/child-mental-health/cara-1/faqs/jefferson

University of Reading (n.d.). *Information management and policy services: Data protection guidelines for researchers*. Retrieved 12 July 2015, from http://www.reading.ac.uk/internal/imps/DataProtection/DataProtectionGuidelines/Research/imps-d-p-research-guidelines.aspx#disposing

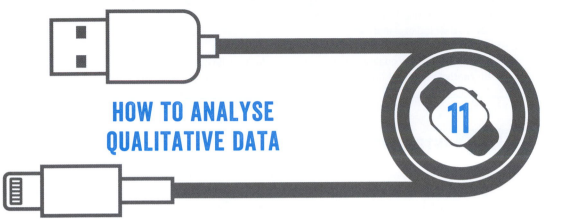

HOW TO ANALYSE
QUALITATIVE DATA

━━ **THIS CHAPTER COVERS THE FOLLOWING TOPICS** ━━━━━━━

- How to account for context in your analysis.
- How to identify and evidence patterns in your data.
- How to use comparisons to understand your data.
- How to develop explanations.
- How to use qualitative data analysis software.
- Ways to ensure the quality of your qualitative data analysis.
- Alternative models of qualitative analysis you can consider.

11●1 INTRODUCTION

Qualitative data analysis is the process of identifying patterns in written information, audio recordings, videos or images. There are no universally accepted rules for this process that define step by step what you must do. You should be thorough and detailed in your approach. But there are different, fully valid pathways to arrive at a good understanding of your **data**.

Qualitative research is open-ended by nature and relies on your judgement to find patterns through the haze of words in your audio recordings or transcripts. While such judgement can be personal and subjective, the techniques specified in this chapter can help ensure your analysis is systematic. Qualitative analysis is not about writing an opinion on a research topic, or selecting a couple of quotes that support an argument you already wanted to make. You must develop a clear analytical route from your data to specific patterns, and ultimately to a written report containing representative examples from your data that show these patterns.

In this chapter, we walk you through how to analyse common types of qualitative data, such as interview transcripts, qualitative survey responses and images (e.g., photographs or drawings). For advice on conducting qualitative analysis of video data, see Heath, Hindmarsh, and Luff (2010). For guidance on full-scale ethnographic analysis, see Atkinson (2015) and Fetterman (2010).

We explain in detail how a close reading of your qualitative data can draw out its nuances in order to reveal:

- How people perceive their world and their place in it.
- How people make sense of their experiences.
- How people interact with each other and their communities.
- How social, political and economic forces affect people's lives.

It's easy to feel overwhelmed when you start your qualitative data analysis, but if you follow this chapter's step-by-step advice you'll find the process manageable and even enjoyable!

11●2 TAKE STOCK OF YOUR QUALITATIVE DATA AND BACKGROUND INFORMATION

Even during your data collection (see, for example, Chapters 7 and 8), you should be thinking critically and analytically about the data you're gathering. Ask yourself questions such as how information collected in an interview aligns with previous interviews you've conducted, and what trends are beginning to emerge. This process can be aided by starting to transcribe recordings of your interviews or focus groups during the data collection phase (transcription often takes longer than you anticipate so it makes sense to start early anyway).

The ideas you have at the early stages of your research can give you a strong head start on your main analysis phase so that you don't feel you have such a steep hill to climb when you reach that phase. There are a number of other benefits to laying down some initial seeds for your data analysis during the data collection phase. First, you can identify gaps in your data that could be filled through your remaining data collection. Second, it gives you a sense of the types of themes and data trends that are emerging from the data so that you can start reflecting on their importance, implications and relevance for your research. These themes and trends can also be further explored in subsequent data collection. Third, starting your data analysis early gives your initial observations and explanations time to mature in the back of your mind before you have to press ahead with full-scale data analysis and write-up. Be sure to write down any initial thoughts you have about the analysis so you know where your ideas developed and so you don't forget them!

Your first step in qualitative analysis is to take stock of the data and contextual information available to you. Written qualitative data can be anything from interview transcripts and field notes to a broad range of other written materials including diaries and meeting minutes. Whatever form your data take, you'll need to organize them to make sense of what you have (see Chapter 10).

KEY TIPS

Always save a new version

Qualitative analysis is an iterative process. It can be easy to go down a promising pathway, only to hit a dead-end. To avoid losing some of your work when this happens, routinely 'save as' a new version at the end of each analysis session. The resulting series of saved versions can create an **audit trail** for you, like slow-motion snapshots of your data analysis as it unfolds. If you later need to retrace the route your analysis has taken, you can refer to these prior saved versions of your analysis. Also, you'll be very thankful you've done this if you change part of your analysis, save it and then change your mind!

When you think of qualitative data, your initial vision might be interview recordings and transcripts. However, you may be surprised at how much additional information you can collect along the way. You can find yourself with information such as diaries, photographs and a range of personal, business or government documents. Such unplanned data is part of the open-ended nature of qualitative research. Just be sure to document how you gathered any new data sources that you may draw on in your analysis.

At this point it is worth distinguishing between **background information** you use to provide context and data that you systematically scrutinize through the data analysis process. Data comprise of information you have defined in your methods section as the focus of your research. Your results will be based on these data. Background information can help you understand the data and provide context. For example, miscellaneous historical information you come across wouldn't necessarily be analysed systemically. However, it can still play a role by providing insights into the broader picture of how your participants' lives are constructed. On a practical level, you will need to add a citation for background information you use in your research report. For *data*, your methods section provides your basis for using them as a source of information.

 REAL WORLD EXPERIENCE

Separating 'data' from 'background information'

Charles used both qualitative interviews and quantitative surveys for his research on politically motivated farm invasions in Zimbabwe. Without being asked, his survey respondents sent Charles numerous pieces of additional information, including photographs, legal documents, letters, emails, personal diaries, ledgers, notes and government documents. Thus, Charles found himself with much more data than expected.

In deciding whether and how to use this unanticipated bonanza of information, Charles first applied the criterion of relevance. That is, he thought carefully about whether this information would help him answer his research question. He also sorted the extra information into the categories of data (to be accounted for in his methods section) and background information (to be cited in his bibliography).

Ultimately, Charles decided not to use any of the extra data, as he didn't think it was directly applicable to his research question. However, he did use the background information, with each element appearing in his bibliography. This additional background information helped to explain the context around Charles's data, thereby giving his research greater depth.

11.3 USE CONTEXT TO LAY THE FOUNDATION FOR YOUR QUALITATIVE DATA ANALYSIS

Once you have separated out your data from background information, you are ready to begin analysis of these data. With a qualitative project, your analysis begins in the methods section. Here you explain who you collected data from and why, in what circumstances and over what period of time. This context orients your analysis and establishes the boundaries of the kinds of knowledge claims you can make. Your data only hold meaning when they can be situated within the context of their collection. For example, if you conducted an interview with an elderly person in a care home in order to understand perceptions of ageing, you would need to take account of the location in which the interview was conducted, that is, within the walls of the home where the participant is cared for by staff. If the participant reported that she felt well cared for by the staff, was this statement influenced by the environment in which it was made, such as the possible presence of staff? Participants may have felt pressure to give certain answers, felt 'guilty' about giving negative feedback while in this setting, or may have felt none of these things and have given a completely frank interview.

Location is just the tip of the iceberg when it comes to the role of context in qualitative research. Because gathering data for qualitative research relies so heavily on the researcher's subjectivity, the analysis often needs to address the way that the researcher influences the results. Indeed, there is an extensive academic literature on how the qualities of the researcher can influence results (see Russel & Mewse, 2009). For example, Ann Stoler (2002), a cultural anthropologist from the United States, conducted interviews with men and women in Indonesia who had been employed as domestic workers in Dutch households during the colonial era. She found that the Indonesian participants were reluctant to criticize their former colonial employers even though there were hints that they had complaints, perhaps because a white American researcher conducted the interviews. How might the interviews have been different if an Indonesian anthropologist had conducted them?

As this example highlights, the identity and demeanour of the person(s) collecting the data can be a key aspect of context, affecting how data are generated. For example, the researcher's perceived social class, ethnicity, gender, accent, clothing or other factors may influence participants. Participants may respond differently based on whether they feel the researcher understands and empathizes with their concerns, or is an uncaring outsider. Female respondents might be uncomfortable discussing certain topics with a male researcher, or vice versa. Imagine a qualitative study on bachelorette parties; the results might be quite different depending on whether the researcher was male or female. Such issues should be openly and thoroughly addressed in your methods section, with the implications also discussed and accounted for in the results and discussion sections. Clearly articulating how your data were collected, why they were gathered that way and contextual factors wrapped up in these data will put you on a good path to accurate qualitative data analysis.

11●4 BUILD FROM DATA TO CODES, TO COMPARISONS, TO CONCEPTS, TO EXPLANATIONS

Now that you've accounted for contextual influences affecting your data, you can begin your focused analysis of the content of your data. There are many possible ways to do this. Here, we take you through a widely used approach we are calling **pattern analysis**. In this stage, you take the words, images, etc. comprising your data and categorize them using codes, which are specific categories for grouping your data that apply across a number of individual quotations. 'Code' can be a confusing piece of qualitative research jargon because 'code' has other meanings (e.g. in the context of computers). In social research, 'coding' simply means making and applying categories to your data. You can use your codes to develop comparisons and connect your data to relevant theoretical concepts you've located in your literature review. Taken together, these codes, comparisons and concepts help you build explanations that address your research question.

11●4●1 ANALYSE THE PATTERNS IN YOUR DATA THROUGH CODING

Once you've accounted for context and taken stock of your available data, you can begin your main qualitative analysis. After refreshing your memory by rereading your field, interview or focus group notes, you begin reading transcripts and other written data, listening to audio or viewing video data. Your aim is to establish a firm grounding in your data by understanding what your participants are saying and why, before you start constructing explanations about what's going on. We advocate following Kelle's (2000, p. 295) six steps when coding with qualitative analysis software:

1 **Format textual data.** Prepare your text for analysis by ensuring it is consistently formatted (see Chapter 10).

2 **Open coding of data.** Categorize your data to arrive at a set of themes that characterize the information in your interviews.

3 **Memo writing.** Record thoughts and ideas that come to mind as you code by **memo writing**. These include interesting connections you are making with other participants, links to theory, ideas for further lines of inquiry or issues you want to highlight in your write-up.

4 **Compare text segments that have been assigned the same code.** Comparisons enable you to situate accounts relative to each other. You can see where the extreme viewpoints of an issue lie and where ideas in this spectrum of viewpoints are clustered.

5 **Integrate codes, and attach memos to codes.** Once you've finished coding you will want to integrate the codes with their relevant memos. This way, as you begin your analysis in earnest, all the relevant information is clustered.

6 **Develop a main theme.** After coding and integrating your memos, and after you've made enough comparisons that you understand the different aspects of your code, you can develop the main theme for that code.

CODE YOUR QUALITATIVE DATA TO UNDERSTAND KEY THEMES

'Coding' is the process of identifying words, phrases or passages of text (or any other unit of meaningful data) and applying labels ('codes') to them. You begin by setting up a series of initial code categories of issues you are expecting to see (this again highlights the value of beginning the analysis, or at least the careful reading, of your data early on so your thinking can be well developed by this stage).

Before beginning coding you should have already formatted all your textual data so that they are uniform (see Chapter 10). Have a consistent and unified electronic format for your content as you start off to avoid confusion and wasted time later on. Open an interview transcript (or other written qualitative data) in your qualitative analysis software (see Section 11.5) and begin applying these codes. As you progress you will quickly see that the codes you initially came up with will need to evolve to capture the new patterns you are identifying. Sometimes you will add an entirely new code to define an emergent category, for example if you discover a new theme. In other instances, you may want to combine codes when the distinction between them is no longer relevant. You may also decide to relabel existing categories to further enhance their meaning. Throughout the process you will want to think constantly about the patterns and connections between the categories. Are the differences in code categories meaningful and distinct? If not, how can you sharpen the differences?

For example, if you had conducted an interview with soldiers returning from war in order to understand the resocialization of former combatants, you might have initial codes for 'Feelings of detachment', 'Pride for serving the nation', 'Positive perceptions of military service' and 'Negative perceptions of military service'. You would begin by applying these codes. But if you find in practice that, for example, 'Positive perceptions of military service' was too vague, you could instead use more specific codes such as 'Public attributions of heroism'. Or, if the participants reported a range of general positive views, you could apply the general code to all instances of 'Positive perceptions of military service' and then develop one or more specific codes such as 'Attributions of heroism' to distinguish a particular type that was very common. In this scenario, you would apply both the general and the specific code to a quotation exemplifying attributions of heroism. Likewise, you may initially think that the code 'Negative perceptions of military service' would include both public perceptions and those of the soldiers, but you may later want to divide the code into 'Negative perceptions of military service – by public' and 'Negative perceptions of military service – by soldiers' (note that if you did this and had already coded some content you would need to reapply these codes to the specific quotations for each of the new codes).

After coding your first transcript and adapting the codes as needed in this first pass, you then move onto the next transcript and continue the process of applying codes until all your transcripts have been coded. Once you've finished a complete first pass, you would then start again doing one pass after another until you are certain that you've captured as much depth as possible for all your transcripts (or until you run out of time allocated to this phase of your research in your research plan).

KEY TIPS

Define your codes

It's important that your codes are clearly defined. As your research progresses and your understanding shifts, it's very easy for your code definitions to shift as well. This can result in your data analysis becoming muddled and hazy. As such, when coding your data, keep a separate, physical copy of your code descriptions with you. This will help you to organize and connect your codes to your data in a coherent, consistent manner. You may find that over time there is a need to create new codes, or split a code into two different codes to accommodate the data you have. Similarly, if you begin a new code, but find you do not have a substantial amount of data to work from within that code, you may consider combining it with another code.

Referring back to the previous topic about soldiers returning from war, you could, for example, start off with the codes 'Pride in serving nation' (summarized as 'Nationalism') and 'Doing one's duty' (summarized as 'Duty'). Over time you may find that the distinction between these two codes is not very clear in your interview transcripts. In this circumstance, you could combine the codes or delete one if it rarely appears in your data.

Having a clear list of your code definitions will make this process of adapting your coding scheme much easier and ensure you have a complete record of definitions used.

Keep noting down analytical thoughts that occur to you during the coding process, however raw or incomplete the thought might seem. Are you finding interesting connections? Have the accounts inspired you to do some additional reading? Are you seeing connections between the data and theory you've been reading about? It's essential to record these thoughts as you go because they are often fleeting and can be easily forgotten. Also, by recording these 'memos' within your qualitative data analysis software they will all be in one place, and you can electronically connect them to the piece of data that sparked the thought within the software. You will be grateful for this easy access to your memos when during the writing-up phase (see Section 11.5).

The following two questions are frequently asked about coding:

- How many coding passes through the data should I undertake?
- How many codes should I end up with at the end of the process?

After you come up with your initial set of codes by drawing upon theory or through your first careful read through your data, you can start applying these codes on your next time going through the data. On this pass, don't feel like you have to apply your codes to every bit of text in your data. Use this pass to make sure your codes are working as you would like them to and not missing anything important. Also, use this opportunity to refine the initial set of codes as needed to suit the data you encounter on this pass. Your second pass through the data with a full set of codes should be much more thorough, applying the codes to all relevant content you encounter in your data. If you still have time, a third, often much lighter, pass with your codes be useful to ensure you have captured everything relevant in your analysis. In sum, if you're short of time, once you have a set of initial codes, two passes through the data can usually suffice.

The number of codes you should end up with largely depends on the depth and richness of your data. You may want only a few codes because you are only searching for a handful of key themes. If you are exploring your transcripts, though, you don't want to end up with only a handful of codes or your 'themes' would be very broad. On the other hand, if you end up with dozens of codes the distinctions you are making between codes may not be very important.

11•4•2 USE COMPARISONS TO DEVELOP YOUR ANALYSIS

As you continue with your coding, start thinking about how you can make more sense of the emerging patterns. This is important from an analytical perspective so your analysis can be thorough and in-depth. But it also helps you tell the story of your qualitative data in order for them to come to life for your readers.

One way you can clarify what is interesting about your results is to present comparisons. Many different types of comparisons can be used to do this. For example, Eric compared what US and UK journalists said about their practices with what actually appeared in print in news media. The gap between word and deed revealed by this comparison became a key part of Eric's results and the focus of the explanations he developed. You can also do this kind of comparison by gathering viewpoints from different stakeholders on the same topic. For example, in Charles's study on political violence during farm seizures in Zimbabwe, he had three main categories of participants: farm workers, farm owners and those associated with the government. Since all three groups were asked about the same issues, he could compare perspectives within and across the three categories. For instance, Charles found that all the farm owners he interviewed believed that the government's farm seizures were illegal and morally wrong. Yet, farm workers' views were more diverse and nuanced, with many expressing regret about the violence but support for the general policy of seizing farms to change the historically white-dominated structure of land ownership.

Use comparisons to develop your qualitative analysis

Vlad Glăveanu's (2010) research on how people understand creativity involved asking different types of professionals whether they think Romanian Easter egg decorating (i.e., traditional forms of wax decoration and printing using leaves) is 'creative'. He describes his research method as a 'multiple feedback methodology that involves the use of different groups of "appropriate assessors" to evaluate the creativity of a certain product or class of products' (p. 342).

His research question was 'How do ethnographers, priests, art teachers and folk artists evaluate the creativity of Easter eggs?' (p. 342). He addressed this research question using semi-structured qualitative interviews with people from each of these four professional backgrounds, analysing the similarities and differences in what they said. His analysis begins with areas of agreement: 'Across the four groups of "evaluators", a high consensus was found in appreciating that there is creativity in Easter egg making' (p. 343). He then explains the main areas of disagreement across the four groups, reporting a 'complex picture of divergent views' (p. 344). The core point Vlad is able to make using this approach is that there are shared cultural expectations about creativity, but different professional groups develop their own more specific account of what it means to be creative. He can present this kind of qualitative research finding by comparing what different participants (and groups of participants) said on the same topic.

11•4•3 CONNECT TO THEORETICAL CONCEPTS

During the coding process, think about how you can connect your findings to theoretical concepts. Go back to concepts in your research question (see Chapter 1) and literature review (see Chapter 2), and look for other related theoretical concepts that you could apply to see if they fit your data. If existing concepts don't help explain your data, then you may need to develop new or adjusted concepts to explain your findings.

For instance, imagine a qualitative researcher is addressing a topic relating to social class. She might start with the idea (or concept) that class identities are passed on from one generation to the next because the richer class oppresses the poorer class (the concept of oppression). If her data show that the poorer class takes pride in its identity and values, she could conclude that the concept of oppression is insufficient to explain the data. In this case, a new explanation might require using a different analytical concept, such as the idea of a 'working-class subculture' (e.g., Willis, 1977). In this way, qualitative analysis can draw on, modify or create theoretical concepts that are useful in developing explanations that may be applicable beyond the immediate context of the project.

11•4•4 USE DATA EXTRACTS TO EVIDENCE YOUR QUALITATIVE RESEARCH CLAIMS

One of the many advantages of coding is that the process allows you to closely engage with the actual words and ideas of your participants. This means that as you code you will be able to use **data extracts** to develop your emerging analysis. Never cherry-pick your data extracts based on what fits your pre-existing assumptions about a topic. This is all too easy to do, but good qualitative research faces up to the uncertainties, contradictions, or unexpected patterns in the data, rather than pretending results are clear and simple. For instance, imagine a comparative analysis of men's and women's attitudes about marriage based on semi-structured interviews. Perhaps the researcher expects that men would display more 'commitment phobia', while women would be more eager to tie the knot, but the results of the analysis indicate that women and men who were interviewed were both equally 'commitment-phobic'. Rather than trying to make the data fit the theory by excluding interviews with 'commitment-phobic' women from the analysis, the best strategy here would be to look for explanations for the unexpected findings. Also, the researcher might seek to clarify the analysis by conducting follow-up interviews or by reading up on the literature about gender roles to find existing explanations that this study might support or challenge.

11●5 SUPPORT YOUR QUALITATIVE ANALYSIS WITH SOFTWARE

11●5●1 HOW QUALITATIVE ANALYSIS SOFTWARE WORKS

There are several qualitative analysis software products (sometimes referred to as **computer-assisted qualitative data analysis software, CAQDAS**) that you can use to help you get from raw qualitative data to results you can use in your research report. Some qualitative researchers have criticized such software for alienating researchers from their data and sometimes causing an overemphasis on coding to exclusion of other aspects of qualitative analysis (Kelle, 2000, p. 294). However, the predominant opinion in the methodological literature indicates that any minor limitations stemming from qualitative analysis software are more than outweighed by increases in productivity, reliability, consistency and transparency (Carmel, 1999, p. 148).

We can't go into all of the qualitative analysis software options, so we've selected one of the most commonly used products, **NVivo**, to demonstrate how this kind of software works. For information on the broader range of qualitative analysis software options, visit http://www.sagepub.com/qdas. Whichever qualitative analysis software you choose, it is generally a good idea to take the time to learn how to use it as it is likely to save you time and improve the quality of your research in the long term.

🔑 ━━━━ **KEY TIPS** ━━━━━━━━━━━━━━━

Get training in qualitative analysis software early in your project

We strongly recommend taking a training course on how to use the qualitative analysis software of your choice before you begin analysing your data. This training can provide you with many handy tools, as well as tips and tricks that will make your data analysis process easier. By taking a training course, such as provided by many universities, you will have the opportunity to 'test-drive' the software you want to use before investing your money and time in obtaining the software (it is always worth checking with the computing services department at your university to see if they provide free or discounted software licences). These courses can also offer expert advice specific to your needs. It also means that when you are ready to begin analysis you can focus all your time on your data and not on fumbling with the software. You can usually find training at a reasonable cost, and this may even be provided free of charge by your research institution. If not, use whatever resources you can find online. A good place to start is http://www.sagepub.com/qdas.

Like the other qualitative software products, NVivo enables both data management and analysis. You can use NVivo to explore and analyse patterns in your data. It can also give you the tools to illustrate your findings in your report. You can use this kind of software for analysing your qualitative data using either a qualitative or quantitative (i.e., content analysis) approach.

First, you need to know five key tips that NVivo uses:

- **Sources** are your data. You can import sources such as PDFs, word processed documents, audio recordings, photos and any other electronic items you want to analyse.
- **Coding** is the focus of the analysis process. It can be conducted by topic or case.
- **Nodes** are sets of codes grouped by category. Nodes assist you in organizing the patterns you've identified in your data.
- **Source classifications** are used to record information about each of your data sources.
- **Node classifications** are used to document information about sets of codes you are grouping together under a higher-level category.

Start by selecting 'new project' from the first screen when NVivo opens. Save the project in a location on your computer or cloud account where you can put all files you will use in your project. For instance, a project evaluating the experience of patients in privately operated hospitals might include 7 GB of video recordings of interviews, 20 MB of audio files and several photographs at 30 MB each. In this scenario, you'd want a minimum of 9 GB of space to be on the safe side. NVivo project files are saved as filename.nvpx.

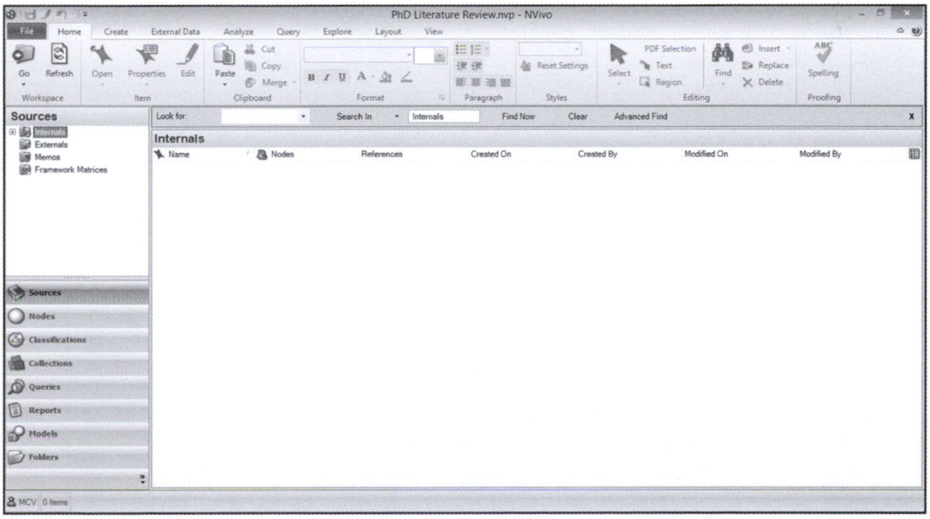

Figure 11.1   NVivo Workspace window
(NVivo version 10, 2013)

The Workspace window (Figure 11.1) is the homepage for all of your data analysis work. It provides access to all the functions you need to conduct your analysis, including importing, coding and editing your data. It has four components: the Ribbon, Navigation View, List View and Detail View.

The Ribbon hosts the commands you'll need to analyse your data. These commands are organized into similar tasks, such as the Media tab, which contains commands to customize the display of audio-visual media data (e.g., video), playback functions (e.g., play/pause) and develop transcripts (Figure 11.2).

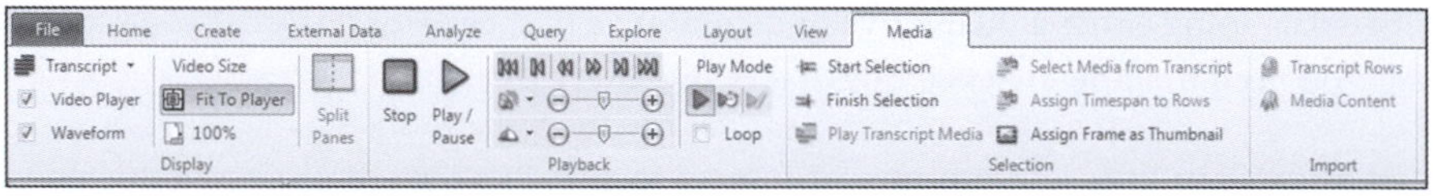

Figure 11.2 Media tab on the Ribbon

The Navigation View provides an organized account of each analytical component of your project. The analytical components include: sources, nodes, classifications, collections, reports, queries, models and folders. The contents of each component are displayed in the List View. In the List View, you can organize items. The List View also displays all of the contents of a component, for example your codes and the number of items in each code (Figure 11.3). The List View is where you can organize your data by their characteristics.

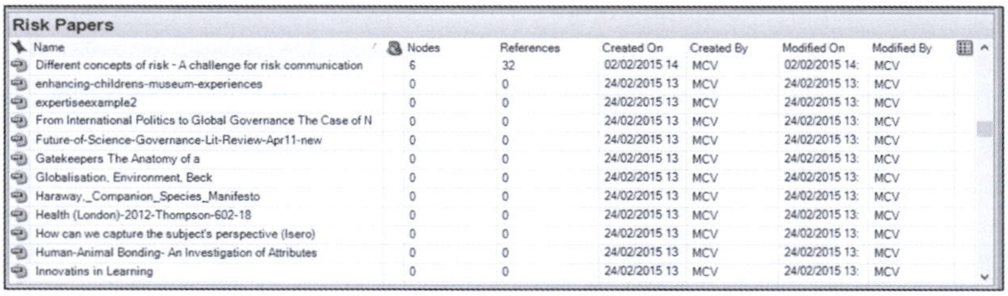

Risk Papers

Name	Nodes	References	Created On	Created By	Modified On	Modified By
Different concepts of risk - A challenge for risk communication	6	32	02/02/2015 14	MCV	02/02/2015 14:	MCV
enhancing-childrens-museum-experiences	0	0	24/02/2015 13	MCV	24/02/2015 13:	MCV
expertiseexample2	0	0	24/02/2015 13	MCV	24/02/2015 13:	MCV
From International Politics to Global Governance The Case of N	0	0	24/02/2015 13	MCV	24/02/2015 13:	MCV
Future-of-Science-Governance-Lit-Review-Apr11-new	0	0	24/02/2015 13	MCV	24/02/2015 13:	MCV
Gatekeepers The Anatomy of a	0	0	24/02/2015 13	MCV	24/02/2015 13:	MCV
Globalisation, Environment, Beck	0	0	24/02/2015 13	MCV	24/02/2015 13:	MCV
Haraway._Companion_Species_Manifesto	0	0	24/02/2015 13	MCV	24/02/2015 13:	MCV
Health (London)-2012-Thompson-602-18	0	0	24/02/2015 13	MCV	24/02/2015 13:	MCV
How can we capture the subject's perspective (Isero)	0	0	24/02/2015 13	MCV	24/02/2015 13:	MCV
Human-Animal Bonding- An Investigation of Attributes	0	0	24/02/2015 13	MCV	24/02/2015 13:	MCV
Innovatins in Learning	0	0	24/02/2015 13	MCV	24/02/2015 13:	MCV

Figure 11.3 List View

The Detail View is where you can explore and analyse each component of your data (Figure 11.4). In this view you can code your data, as well as see all of the content that has been coded at a specific node.

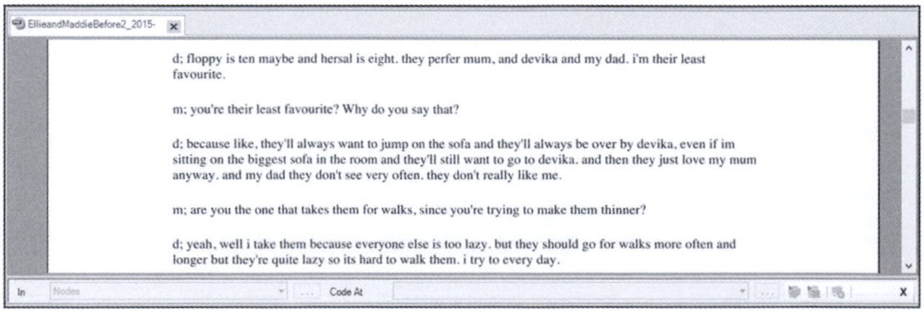

EllieandMaddieBefore2_2015-

d; floppy is ten maybe and hersal is eight. they perfer mum, and devika and my dad. i'm their least favourite.

m; you're their least favourite? Why do you say that?

d; because like, they'll always want to jump on the sofa and they'll always be over by devika, even if im sitting on the biggest sofa in the room and they'll still want to go to devika. and then they just love my mum anyway. and my dad they don't see very often. they don't really like me.

m; are you the one that takes them for walks, since you're trying to make them thinner?

d; yeah, well i take them because everyone else is too lazy. but they should go for walks more often and longer but they're quite lazy so its hard to walk them. i try to every day.

In Nodes Code At

Figure 11.4 Detail View

11•5•2 IMPORT, CREATE AND ORGANIZE YOUR DATA SOURCES

'Sources' is the term NVivo assigns to the materials used in your research. Sources can include most materials, including (but not limited to) transcript documents, videos, photographs, web-pages, handwritten journals, drawings and books.

CREATE NEW FOLDERS

When you import your data, it is best to organize your sources into subfolders. These subfolders help you organize and visualize your data by dividing your data into manageable portions. For instance, if you have carried out a set of qualitative interviews, it's a good idea to have a folder for each participant. To create new folders (Figure 11.5), you need to:

1 Locate the Navigation View, and right-click on the folder in which you would like to add a new subfolder.
2 Select New Folder …. The New Folder dialog box will open.

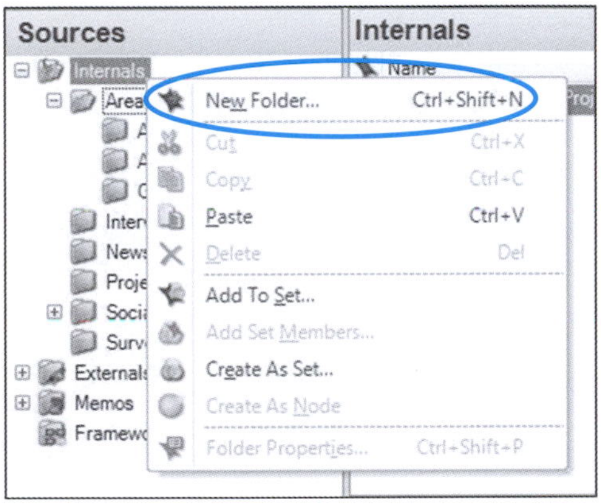

Figure 11.5   Creating a new folder
(NVivo version 10, 2013)

3 Enter a name and description for the new folder.
4 Click OK.

New folders can be created under any folder and reorganized as many times as you need.

USE PRIMARY DATA SOURCES

Primary sources can be organized into one of two folders: Internals and Externals. Internal sources are materials that are imported or created within your project. The file sizes of these sources are small enough to be saved with your project as a package. If you decide you would like to create a source in NVivo, follow these steps:

1 In the Navigation View, click the name of the folder in which you want to create the new document.
2 In the List View, right-click and select New Internal (Figure 1.6).

3   Select the type of file you would like to import.
4   In the Properties dialog box, enter the name and description of the source.
5   Click OK.

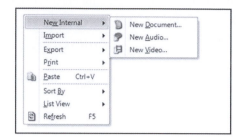

Figure 11.6   Creating a new internal source
(NVivo version 10, 2013)

The most frequently used sources are internal sources imported into NVivo. There are several different file types that can be imported. Each file type must be selected separately, but follows a similar sequence to import the file.

1   In the Navigation View, click the name of the folder into which you want to import the document.
2   In the List View, right-click and select Import.
3   Next, select the type of file you would like to import (Figure 11.7).

Figure 11.7   Import an internal source
(NVivo version 10, 2013)

4   Then select the file you want to import. Click the Open button.
5   In the Document Properties dialog box, change the name and description of the file, as needed (Figure 11.8).
6   Click OK.

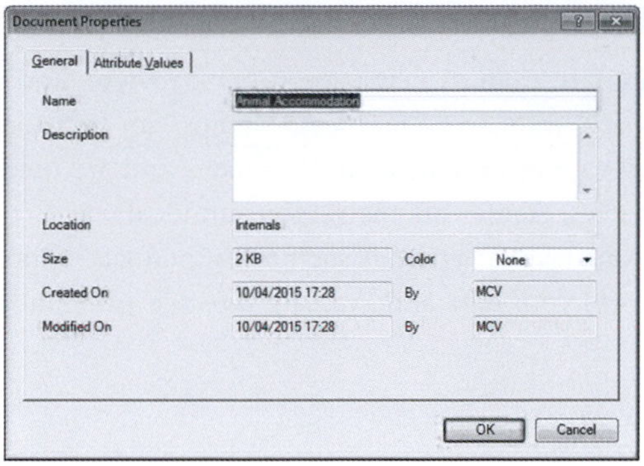

Figure 11.8 Document Properties dialog box for importing an internal source
(NVivo version 10, 2013)

External sources are data files that you link to your project. These sources are too large to be saved within your project or sources that cannot be imported, for example a two-hour film. With external sources, NVivo lets you record notes or summaries about the source, but not directly edit it. Follow these steps to add an external source:

1 In the Navigation View, under Sources, select the Externals folder.
2 In the List View, right-click and select New External.
3 Fill out the External Properties (Figure 11.9). Note that not all property features need to be described. At minimum, fill in the external source's name and a short description.
4 Click OK.

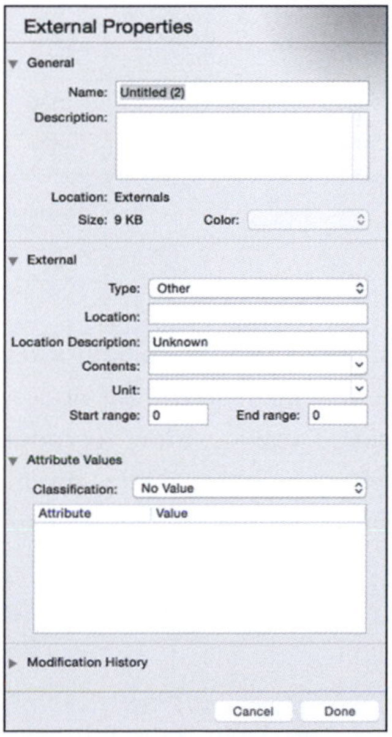

Figure 11.9 External Properties dialog box for an external source
(NVivo version 10, 2013)

USE SECONDARY DATA SOURCES

Secondary research materials, such as newspapers, book reviews and journal articles, can be stored through memos and framework matrices. Memos can be thought of as digital sticky notes. Memos are linked to specific sources and/or nodes and are used to record observations and insights on your sources. Framework matrices are an ideal way to organize your sources by cases. Cases represent your level of analysis such as individuals or organizations. Framework matrices help you organize your data and evaluate possible systematic relationships between different variables.

11•5•3 ASSIGN NODES AND ANNOTATE YOUR DATA SOURCES

Your qualitative analysis involves labelling and coding your data sources to identify patterns. Identifying patterns can be accomplished using what NVivo calls 'nodes' (Figure 11.10). Nodes fulfil one of two functions. They can be used to link codes (ideas, themes or specific attributes) to specific pieces of data or as higher-level codes to encompass a set of more specific codes. In the Nodes category, you can create new folders. You may want to create several folders for different purposes of analysing your data. For instance, you may want to create a folder that will contain your coding scheme and another to represent specific people or organizations.

Nodes

Name	Sources	References	Created On	Created By	Modified On	Modified By
Animal as Risk	1	8	02/02/2015 18:04	MCV	03/02/2015 14:50	MCV
Classifying risk	1	4	03/02/2015 15:11	MCV	03/02/2015 15:25	MCV
Creation of Risk	1	2	02/02/2015 16:45	MCV	03/02/2015 15:01	MCV
Definition of Risk	3	22	02/02/2015 14:36	MCV	03/02/2015 15:28	MCV
Definitions of Communication	2	7	02/02/2015 14:37	MCV	02/02/2015 17:50	MCV
Framing Risk	2	2	02/02/2015 16:49	MCV	02/02/2015 17:02	MCV
Interaction Theories	1	1	02/02/2015 17:52	MCV	02/02/2015 17:52	MCV
Perception of risk	3	25	02/02/2015 15:26	MCV	03/02/2015 15:23	MCV
Precautionary principle - Risk	1	1	02/02/2015 15:08	MCV	02/02/2015 15:08	MCV
Risk and Time	2	4	02/02/2015 15:02	MCV	03/02/2015 15:22	MCV
Risk Communication	1	12	03/02/2015 15:43	MCV	03/02/2015 19:08	MCV
Social Construction of Risk	2	43	02/02/2015 16:39	MCV	03/02/2015 15:30	MCV
Variation between expert and laypeople	4	19	02/02/2015 14:30	MCV	03/02/2015 16:20	MCV

Figure 11.10   List of nodes
(NVivo version 10, 2013)

Nodes primarily act as a basis for linking ideas to points in your NVivo sources. Using nodes in this way often means other training manuals will use nodes, codes, and themes interchangeably. To begin, you need to decide if you are going to conduct your analysis inductively or deductively. There are several options to create nodes, the most basic of which are to either create codes 'as you go' (inductively) or 'prior to analysis' (deductively).

USE DEDUCTIVE CODING

If you have a predetermined set of codes you want to apply to your data, it's easiest to set up the nodes before you begin coding. Enter your codes into your codebook, beginning with one parent code. In Figure 11.11 the first parent code is 'Social Construction of Risk'.

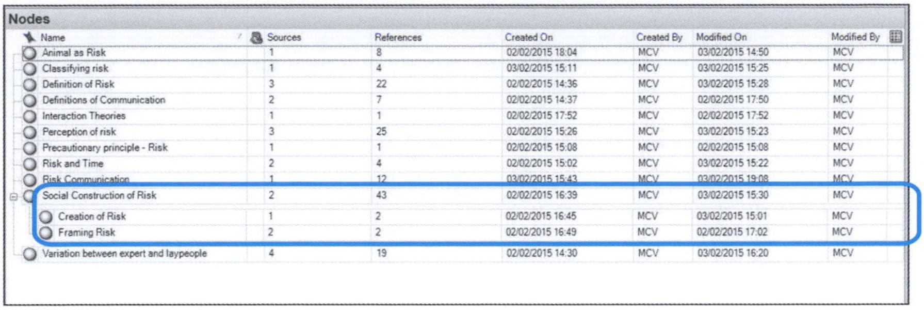

Figure 11.11   Multi-level nodes
(NVivo version 10, 2013)

The way you do this in NVivo is to go to the Nodes category under the Navigation View. In the Nodes category, select the folder that will hold your codes. Then to create a parent (or root-level) code:

1   Click on the Create tab on the Ribbon.
2   Click on Node.
3   A pop-up Nodes Properties window will appear.
4   Enter the name of your code and description. By entering a description you will ensure anyone who works on your project is consistent in their coding and saves you from having to frequently refer to your codebook.
5   Optionally, you can select a colour to correspond with the code.
6   If you will be using sub-codes (also referred to as child or branch nodes) you will most likely want to aggregate your coding from the child nodes. This will include your coding at the child node at the parent node.
7   Click Done.

Repeat this step for each parent code. The next step is to add in your sub-codes. In Figure 11.11, there are four sub-codes ('Mixed', 'Negative', 'Neutral' and 'Positive'). To begin, select the parent code in List View, and then follow the same steps you used to create the parent code. You are now ready to begin coding. To do so, follow the instructions below to code at an existing node.

USE INDUCTIVE CODING

In NVivo, inductive coding is easily accomplished using the functions Code Selection at Existing Node and Code Selection at New Node. When you begin your analysis, you will primarily be coding your data at a new node.

Coding your selection at a new node indicates that you need to code a selected piece of data with a new code. For instance, you may be coding feedback from an event. The first piece of feedback you code is 'Positive'. To create a new code, follow these steps:

1   Select the data you want to code.
2   Right-click the selection, and select Code Selection (Figure 11.12).

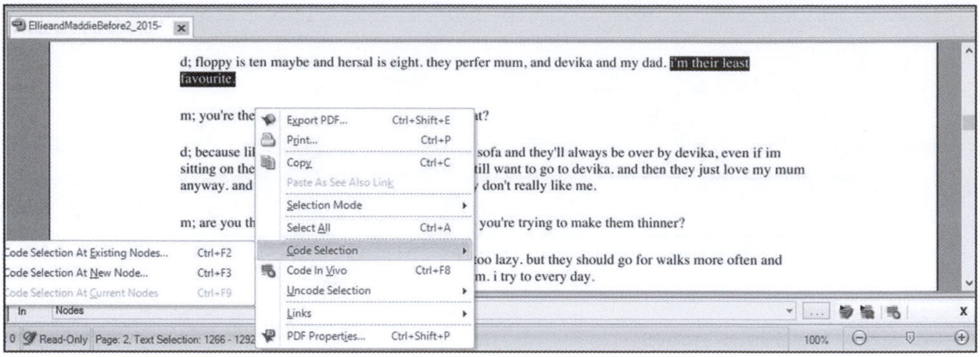

Figure 11.12 Code Selection at New Node
(NVivo version 10, 2013)

3   Select Code Selection at New Node.
4   The New Node dialog box will be displayed (Figure 11.13).

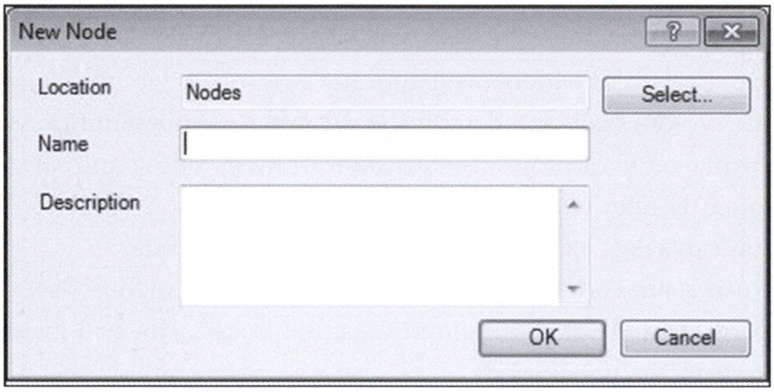

Figure 11.13 New Node dialog box
(NVivo version 10, 2013)

5   You can choose where you want to store the node by changing the location. This is not recommended at this stage. If you need to change the location, you can always drag and drop the node in a new location later.
6   Enter a name and description for the node.
7   Click OK.

The new node will now be stored in your nodes. To use this code again, you will code at an existing node. You will need to repeat this process for each new node you wish to add. For instance, you have just created a node for 'Positive', but you soon discover a 'Negative' comment in your research. You would then need to create a 'Negative' node. However, you will spend most of your time coding with existing nodes.

Once you've created your new nodes, you need to apply those nodes to further analyse your data. In NVivo, this is called 'code selection at an existing node'. To do this, take the following steps:

1   Select the data you want to code.
2   Right-click the selection, and select Code Selection.

3   Select Code Selection at Existing Node.

4   The existing nodes will be displayed (Figure 11.14). Locate the node (or child node) at which you would like to code your data.

5   Click Select.

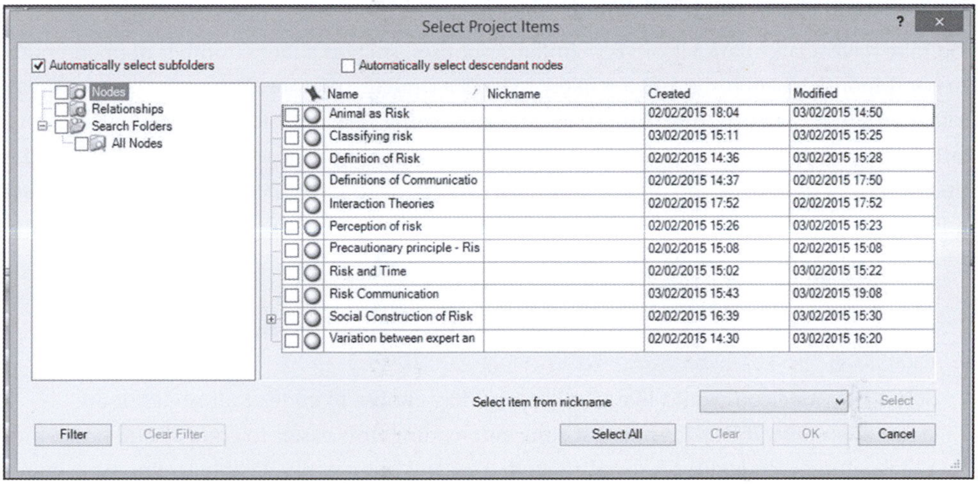

Figure 11.14   **Existing nodes**

VISUALIZE YOUR CODING USING CODING STRIPES

Once you have coded your data it is useful to be able to see what nodes you have coded and where you have coded those nodes. To do so, you simply need to turn on coding stripes (Figure 11.15). Coding stripes are displayed to the right of the source.

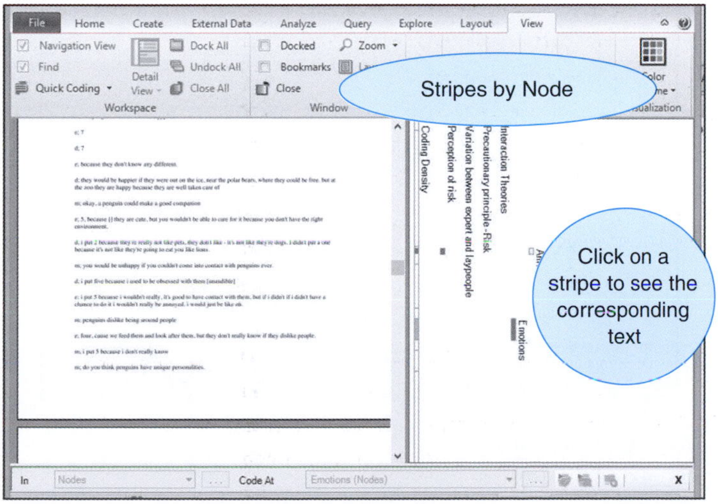

Figure 11.15   **Node stripes**

Each stripe links a section of the source to a corresponding node. Stripes that overlap indicate the data source is coded at multiple nodes. To see which section of data corresponds to which stripe, click on the stripe and the coded data will become highlighted. This view also allows you to see which user coded which section of data.

USE AUTOMATIC CODING FOR LARGE DATA SETS

You may have a large data set of very similar responses, such as a large number of open-ended survey responses. Such responses are likely to have a similar structure. Although they each may hold a different opinion, they still discuss the same thing (e.g., attitudes to the environment). Rather than code all of the interviews individually, you may choose to code a subset of the interviews and auto-code the others. To do this you need to have accurately coded the subset of interviews at that node (in this case attitudes). You then select the Auto Code Wizard from the Analyze tab. To run the wizard, follow these steps:

1   On the first screen select 'Auto code using existing coding patterns'.
2   Click Next.
3   Select the node you would like to code. You may choose to code at all nodes or an individual node. If this is your first time auto-coding, it is easier to code at one node. If the resulting auto-coding is unsatisfactory, you will more easily be able to fine-tune your coding if you have just coded at one node.
4   Adjust the 'How much coding would you like NVivo to create?' slider (see Figure 11.16). If you would like NVivo to be highly discriminatory in its coding, select Less. If you would like NVivo to include a broader definition of your code, select More.
5   Click Next.

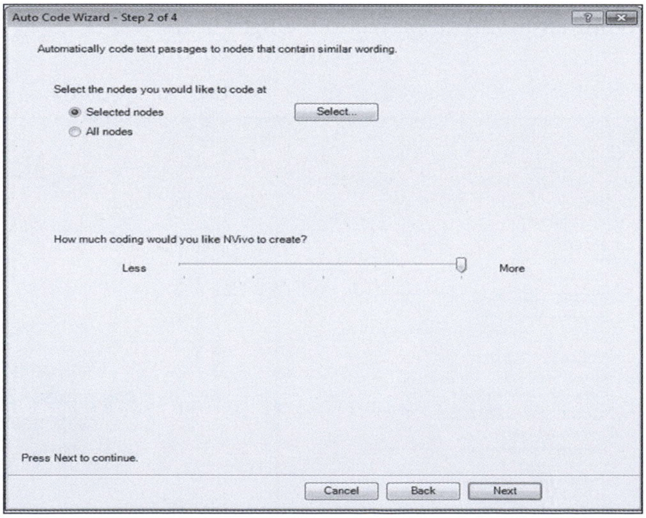

Figure 11.16   Auto Code Wizard
(NVivo version 10, 2013)

6   NVivo will check the existing coding patterns to determine if your selected node is suitable for this function. You may find that your node is unsuitable for auto-coding (this is often due to there being too few codes at that node). If this is the case, you will need to include more sources in your manual coding procedures.

7   Click Next.

8   You now have the option to select how your text sources will be coded. You need to select if you would prefer a fine coding procedure (individual sentences only) or a broader coding procedure (entire paragraphs will be coded).

9   Click Finish.

Automatic coding results are saved as a matrix, which is displayed in the Detail View. You can use this matrix to review the automatic coding. You should always review the results of your automatic coding to detect any problems with the results. Correcting these problems before moving on with your data analysis is essential. As always, try to catch and fix problems as early as possible. In looking at your results you may find they vary from your expectations due to a number of factors, including:

- Quality of your coding. Have you been consistent? Or have you stretched the definitions of your codes to include items that appear to be unrelated?
- Amount of coding you have completed. Have you coded at least 10 per cent of your sources?
- Definitions of words you've coded. Some words have multiple meanings. In these cases, you normally use context to identify the most appropriate meaning. However, automatic coding can't do this for you.
- Whether your codes are distinctive. Do two of your codes contain very similar items? If so, automatic coding will find it difficult to determine differences between them.
- Use of non-standard English. For example, did your participants use slang words or are they using English as a second language?

To review what has been coded, double-click on a cell in the automatic coding matrix to see the content that was coded for that node. If you are satisfied with the results you need not do anything further. However, if you're unsatisfied with the results you can choose to uncode a piece of text by highlighting the coded text, right-clicking on the text and selecting 'uncode'. You can also choose to undo the entire automatic coding action.

11•5•4 USE CLASSIFICATIONS TO DOCUMENT KEY INFORMATION ABOUT SOURCES AND NODES

Use classifications to store information about your sources and nodes (e.g., demographics, authors, dates). Classifications help when you run queries by making it easier to find and sort your sources and elements of your analysis. There are two primary classification types: source classifications and node classifications.

APPLY SOURCE CLASSIFICATIONS

To apply source classifications, begin by selecting Source Classifications from the Navigation View. Once selected, you have the option to choose a predetermined source type (e.g., book or interview) or create your own source type (Figure 11.17).

Classifications	Look for:			Search In	Source Classifica	Find Now	Clear	Advanced Find	
Source Classifications	**Source Classifications**								
Node Classifications	Name				Created On				Created By
Relationship Types	Book				03/05/2014 22:36				MCV
	Book Section				03/05/2014 22:36				MCV
	Interview				03/05/2014 22:36				MCV
	Journal Article				03/05/2014 22:36				MCV
	Newspaper Article				03/05/2014 22:36				MCV
	Reference				03/05/2014 22:36				MCV
	Report				03/05/2014 22:36				MCV
	Thesis				03/05/2014 22:36				MCV
	Web Page				03/05/2014 22:36				MCV

Figure 11.17   Source classifications

Each classification has its own unique set of attributes. For example, if you expand the classification setting for a book (Figure 11.18), you will see attributes such as author, year and title. Classification attributes can be added or deleted to suit your research needs.

Name	Type	Created On
Author	Text	03/06/2010 22:36
Year	Text	03/06/2010 22:36
Title	Text	03/06/2010 22:36
Series Editor	Text	03/06/2010 22:36
Series Title	Text	03/06/2010 22:36
City	Text	03/06/2010 22:36
Publisher	Text	03/06/2010 22:36
Volume	Text	03/06/2010 22:36
Number of Volumes	Text	03/06/2010 22:36
Series Volume	Text	03/06/2010 22:36
Number of Pages	Text	03/06/2010 22:36
Pages	Text	03/06/2010 22:36
Edition	Text	03/06/2010 22:36
Date	Text	03/06/2010 22:36
Type of Work	Text	03/06/2010 22:36
Translator	Text	03/06/2010 22:36
Short Title	Text	03/06/2010 22:36
Abbreviation	Text	03/06/2010 22:36
ISBN	Text	03/06/2010 22:36
DOI	Text	03/06/2010 22:36
Original Publication	Text	03/06/2010 22:36
Reprint Edition	Text	03/06/2010 22:36
Accession Number	Text	03/06/2010 22:36
Call Number	Text	03/06/2010 22:36
Label	Text	03/06/2010 22:36
Keywords	Text	03/06/2010 22:36
URL	Text	03/06/2010 22:36

Figure 11.18   Classification attributes example

APPLY NODE CLASSIFICATIONS

Similarly to source classifications, node classifications describe characteristics of your participants or the places in your research. Node classifications are established in the same manner as source classifications, except that node classifications describe demographic details, such as income level or gender.

11•5•5 USE QUERIES TO EXPLORE YOUR DATA

You can go beyond coding to extract deeper insights from your data using queries. Queries search and analyse your data in several different ways:

- Text Search: the ability to see where terms occur
- Word Frequency: identifies how frequent terms occur
- Coding: searches for content based on how it has been coded
- Matrix Coding: analyses systematic trends in coding

Each of these queries can be run using all of your sources or can be explored by a particular source, node or attribute. To begin queries, you need to locate the Queries component in the Navigation View (Figure 11.19).

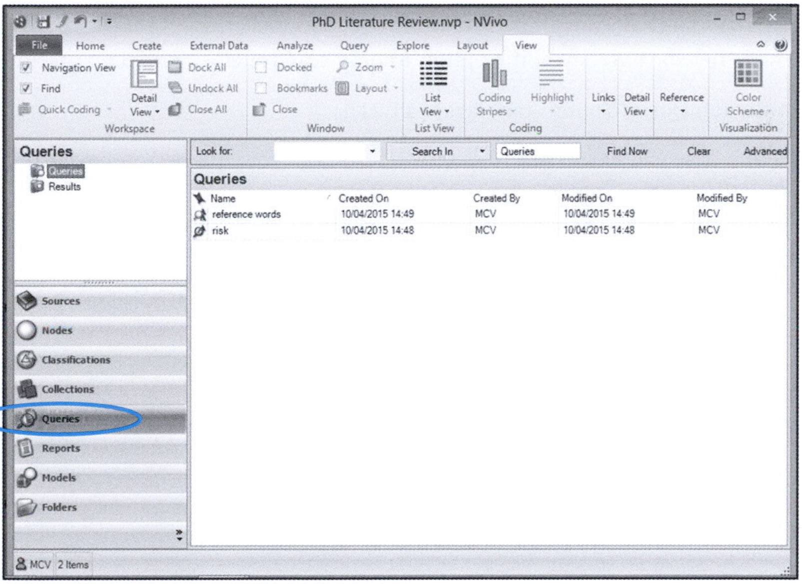

Figure 11.19   Queries component and list

Once selected, a list of queries run will appear in the List View. To open a previously run query double-click on the query, which will appear in the Detail View. You can run new queries by locating the Query tab on the Ribbon (Figure 11.20). Here you can see your query options.

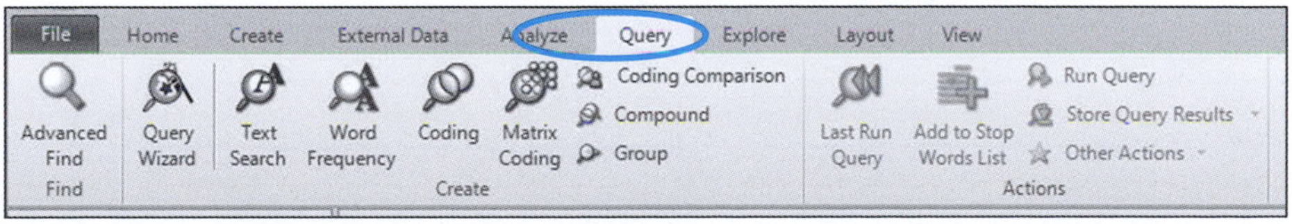

Figure 11.20   Query tab

USE THE TEXT SEARCH QUERY FEATURE

The Text Search Query feature allows you to search for particular words or phrases within your sources. To run the text finder, select the Query tab on the Ribbon, and then select Text Search. From this point you will have the option to choose how you search for text:

1   In the Text Search options Search box, click the first tab, Text Search Criteria, to enter the word or phrase you would like to analyse.
2   Below your search, you have a number of options to adjust the scope of the search:

   a   Select to search text, annotations or both.
   b   In the Of box, you can select which project sources you wish to search. You can search all of your sources or just a single source.
   c   Adjusting the matches slider will adjust your search from an exact match to broad-spectrum synonyms of your word.
   d   The Special option will allow you to combine words, exclude words or include words with special characters.
   e   The Where box gives you the option to only search items created by specific users.

3   Select the tab Query Options tab (Figure 11.21).

   a   Define how you would like to store the results of your query. You have the option to store the query as either a new node or
   b   Define the Spread Coding (i.e., would you like to analyse just the code or a greater space around the code to provide detailed context?).
   c   Click Run.

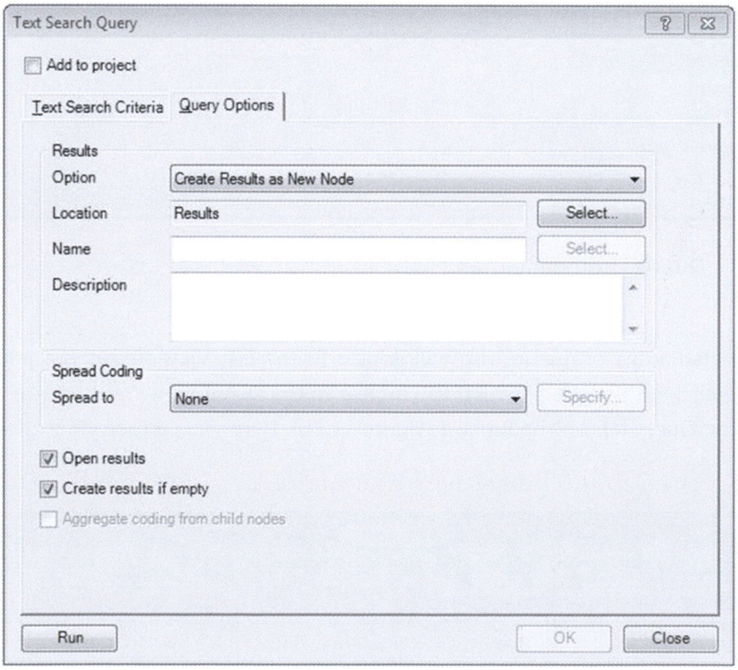

Figure 11.21   Text Search Query property box

The results of your text search query will be displayed in the Detail View (Figure 11.22), including the sources, the number of times the word was referenced in that source and the amount of coverage within that source by that reference. On the far right-hand side of the Detail View, you have the option to view your data in its raw form, from its individual sources (such as in videos or interviews) and as a 'word tree'.

Name	In Folder	References	▽ Coverage
Abstractbook2014	Internals\\Risk Papers	47	0.02%
Gatekeepers The Anatomy of a	Internals\\Risk Papers	36	0.04%
Review_December_2011_Vol9_Nos_1an	Internals\\Risk Papers	30	0.02%
j.1467-954X.2002.tb02807.x	Internals\\Risk Papers	26	0.08%
Future-of-Science-Governance-Lit-Review	Internals\\Risk Papers	25	0.04%
17105107	Internals\\Risk Papers	22	0.05%
PUS	Internals\\Risk Papers	20	0.05%

Figure 11.22 Example text search result

(NVivo version 10, 2013)

A word tree visualizes the words surrounding your search word. For example, in the word tree in Figure 11.23 the word 'penguin' is diagrammed. The most common surrounding words are automatically placed nearest to the focal word (penguin), in this case, for example, the phrase 'can make a good companion'. Similar to concept maps, word trees are useful for illustrating how ideas connect together in your data.

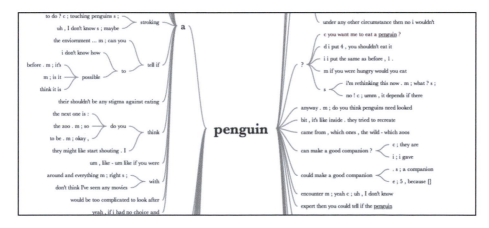

Figure 11.23 Example word tree for 'penguin'

(NVivo version 10, 2013)

You shouldn't expect this kind of automated analysis to provide you with fully satisfying results, but it can provide a useful jumping-off point for your manual analysis.

DETERMINE WORD FREQUENCIES USING QUERIES

Understanding how frequently words, phrases or concepts are used in your sources can give you a sense of the relative importance of certain ideas. NVivo can create such frequency counts while automatically categorizing by source, attribute or node.

To do this, select the Query tab on the Ribbon, and then select Word Frequency. Word Frequency analyses all of the words you specify in your search criteria. To set your search criteria (Figure 11.24):

1   Adjust the matches slider to change your search from an exact match to similar words.
2   In the Of box, select the project sources you wish to search. You can search all of your sources or just a single source.
3   The Where box gives you the option to only search items created by specific users.
4   You can edit Display Words to change the properties of the words displayed:

    a   You can choose how many words to display.
    b   You can choose the minimum length of the words in your results.

5   Select Run.

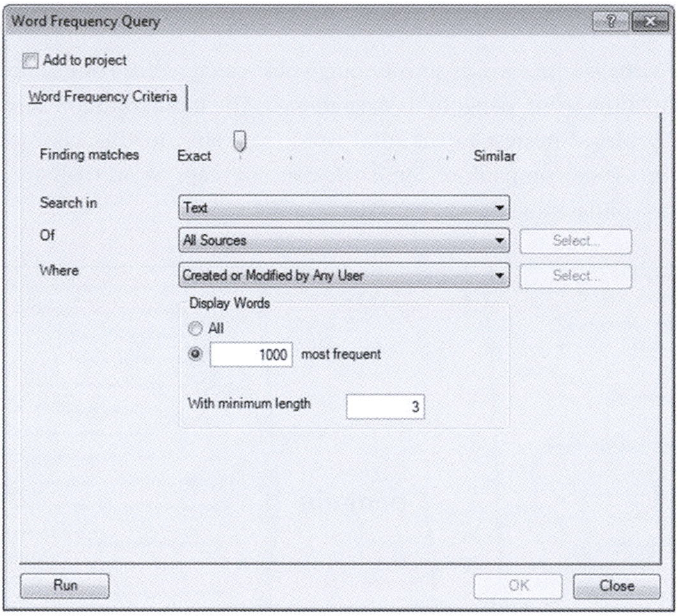

Figure 11.24   Word Frequency Query dialog box

The Data View will list (Figure 11.25), in the leftmost column, in descending order, the most common words. The Count column lists the number of times each word appears. The rightmost column lists the frequency, displayed as a percentage, based on the number of times that word appears in the data. You can also view your results as visual diagrams, such as word clouds, tree maps and cluster analyses.

USE CODING QUERIES

Coding queries show how your data has been coded, and enable you to find intersections between codes. To run a coding query, select the Query tab on the Ribbon, and then select

Word	Length	Count	Weighted Percentage ∨
like	4	327	5.32%
think	5	157	2.56%
yeah	4	126	2.05%
really	6	102	1.66%
penguins	8	73	1.19%
just	4	71	1.16%
penguin	7	51	0.83%
know	4	48	0.78%
people	6	46	0.75%
maybe	5	40	0.65%
animals	7	35	0.57%
around	6	35	0.57%
good	4	35	0.57%
wild	4	35	0.57%

Figure 11.25   Word Frequency results table

Coding. Coding queries can analyse codes by a specific node or nodes by attribute value. To conduct a simple analysis (Figure 11.26):

1   Select to either conduct your query at specific node or analyse nodes by attributes (such as age).
2   In the In box, you can select which project sources you wish to search. You can search all of your sources or just a single source.
3   The Where box gives you the option to only search items created by specific users.
4   Click Run.

Figure 11.26   Coding Query properties box

Coding query results are displayed as individual coded components. Each component can be double-clicked to view in the original source. Viewing the results of the coding query can help you decide where nodes overlap, how they intersect and how they apply to your different sources.

USE MATRIX QUERIES TO IDENTIFY SYSTEMATIC RELATIONSHIPS IN YOUR DATA

Similar to running a chi-square analysis (see Chapter 12) with quantitative data, you may want to evaluate whether there is a systematic relationship between the different variables you've identified in your qualitative data. To do this with NVivo, use matrix coding queries. This type of query produces a contingency table showing the frequencies across two categories. To run this query, select the Query tab on the Ribbon, and then Matrix Coding. Once the Matrix Coding dialog box opens, select your variables (see Figure 11.27).

1 Start with the Rows tab. Under Define More Rows, select the items you would like to compare in rows.
2 Leave the next dropdown at 'by Any User'.
3 Click on Add to List.
4 Select the Columns tab, repeating the Rows tab process described above.
5 On the Node Matrix tab, select the sources you would like included in your query.
6 Click Run.

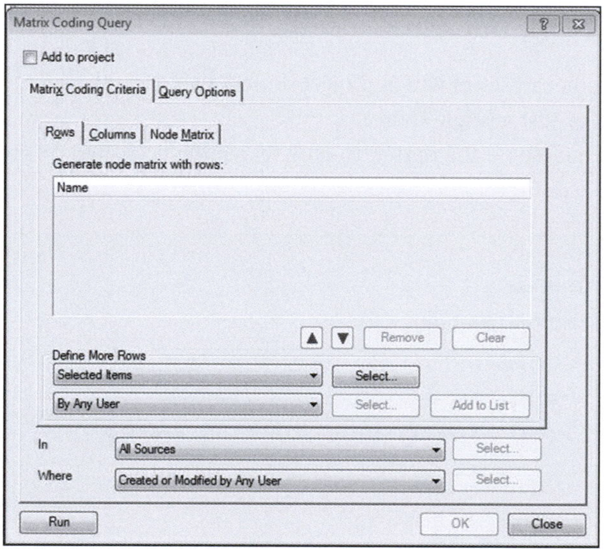

Figure 11.27 Matrix Coding Query dialog box
(NVivo version 10, 2013)

The results will appear as a contingency table (Figure 11.28), which you can use to explore the quantitative relationships in your data.

Attitude about penguins in cap	A : Never Visited Zoo - Pr...	B : Never Visited Zoo - No...	C : Visited Zoo - Previous...	D : Visited Zoo - No Expe...
1 : Positive	25	26	14	70
2 : Mixed	1	1	0	5
3 : Negative	10	5	5	35

Figure 11.28 Matrix Coding Query results table
(NVivo version 10, 2013)

These results can also be displayed as a chart: select Chart from the right-hand side of the Detail View. Such charts can illustrate trends in your data clearly and concisely.

11•5•6 EVALUATE INTER-RATER RELIABILITY FOR QUANTITATIVE ANALYSES

If you follow a content analysis approach to quantify your qualitative findings, you'll need to evaluate the reliability of your analysis to demonstrate its objectivity and quality. This is done using a procedure assessing your project's inter-rater (inter-coder) reliability (see Chapter 12).

To evaluate inter-rater reliability with NVivo, team members must use their individual user accounts for their analysis work. The user account window opens each time you run NVivo. In this window, you need to identify yourself by name and initials. If necessary, users can be added, deleted or edited under Project Properties (Figure 11.29).

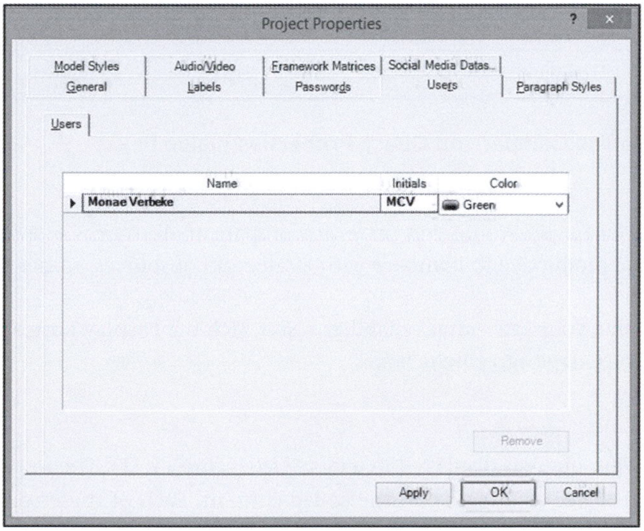

Figure 11.29   User settings
(NVivo version 10, 2013)

The next step is to run a query called Coding Comparison. This evaluates the coding of two or more users, giving a visual illustration of where users differ in their coding. To run this query, follow these steps:

1   From the Query tab, select Coding Comparison.
2   The Coding Comparison Query Properties dialog box will appear (Figure 11.30).

   a   You can set up the query to compare two user groups. This can either be two individual users, or can be two grouping of users. Fill in 'User group A/B' with your selected users.
   b   Choose which nodes you would like to compare your users (under At). You can choose to compare at all nodes; however, it is often more productive to compare one node at a time.

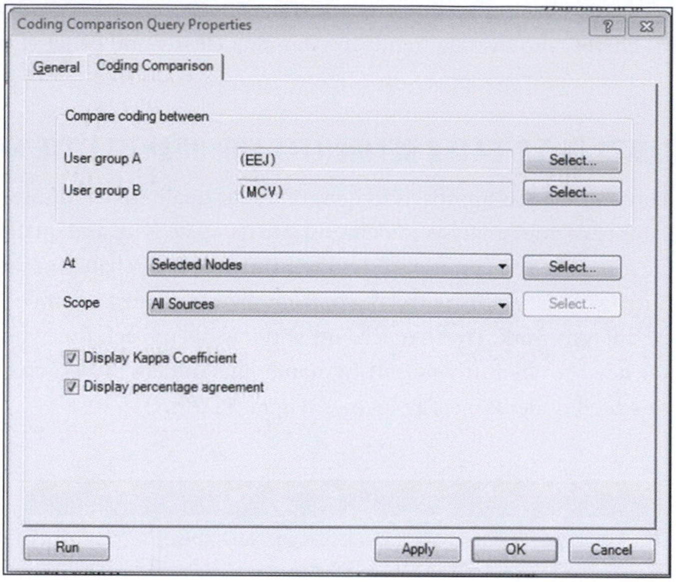

Figure 11.30 Coding Comparison Query Properties dialog box

c Choose your Scope. Would you prefer to compare at all sources or a select few? It's often more productive to compare with a selection of sources, rather than all your sources.

d To determine your inter-rater reliability result, tick the Display Kappa Coefficient and Display percentage agreement boxes.

e Select Run.

The result of your query is displayed in a table (see Figure 11.31). The results illustrate each place where coders agree or disagree on the coded content. Each of these comparisons can be further examined by double-clicking on the line to view individual coding stripes. This provides you with a great tool to discuss your coding as a team, see the differences between users' coding at a glance and dig for further detail.

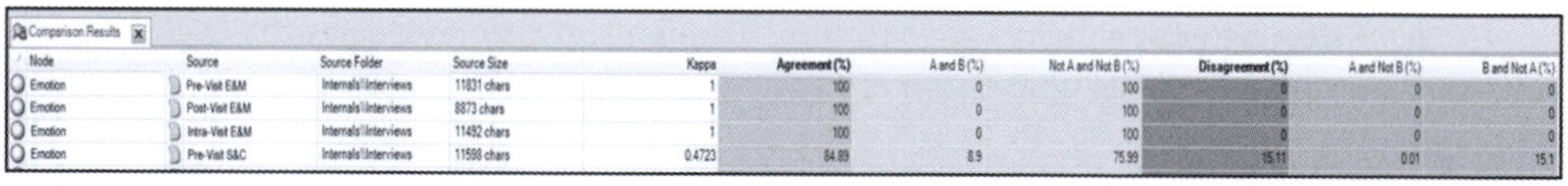

Comparison Results

Node	Source	Source Folder	Source Size	Kappa	Agreement (%)	A and B (%)	Not A and Not B (%)	Disagreement (%)	A and Not B (%)	B and Not A (%)
Emotion	Pre-Visit E&M	Internals\\Interviews	11831 chars	1	100	0	100	0	0	0
Emotion	Post-Visit E&M	Internals\\Interviews	8873 chars	1	100	0	100	0	0	0
Emotion	Intra-Visit E&M	Internals\\Interviews	11492 chars	1	100	0	100	0	0	0
Emotion	Pre-Visit S&C	Internals\\Interviews	11598 chars	0.4723	84.89	8.9	75.99	15.11	0.01	15.1

Figure 11.31 Coding Comparison Query results

11.6 PREPARE YOUR DATA FOR FURTHER ANALYSIS

At this stage you'll have completed your coding passes and ended up with a set of patterns you have identified within your data. You will have combined or adjusted codes along the way and created memos to document any initial ideas you had. You may also have made comparisons between perspectives within each sample (or between samples) to get a clearer sense of the range of views emerging from your data. In addition, you should have started making connections to key ideas from your literature review, especially theoretical concepts that can help you account for your data. These are the first crucial steps in developing a systematic analysis of your data. However, there are still several more steps to take in your qualitative analysis to ensure that it's as robust and insightful as possible.

While qualitative data analysis software is an excellent tool to help you manage and make sense of your data, your analysis extends into the writing-up process (see Chapter 13). Moving your analysis, code by code, into your research report document is an essential step, which can also result in new insights. Lay out your ideas on the page, thinking them through as you write each paragraph and then repeatedly reviewing and rethinking what you have written to deepen your analysis and sharpen your claims. This chapter sets out the basic building blocks of a qualitative analysis, but the real value of your analysis comes through during the writing-up process.

As you begin laying out the elements of your analysis on the page, ensure that you clearly link your reported findings to your data. Provide specific representative examples from the data to illustrate your analysis, using quotes from interviews, descriptions of encounters with research participants and any other relevant material. If you find that you lack the material to support your conclusions, this can be a clue that you need to rethink your analysis or find more data. This is another reason why your analysis does not end with coding.

Concrete qualitative data extracts not only give you a solid basis for your conclusions, but also can breathe life into your analysis by showing your participants' perspectives in their own words. If you're having a hard time deciding which parts of your data to use in your research report, remember that you only need content directly relevant to your reported findings. If you have a lot of similar examples, summarize them and pick only the most interesting to illustrate your key statements (as long as it is representative of the others). You may wish to structure your thesis or article around several sub-points so that each section includes one or more specific examples drawn from your research to illustrate that particular point.

Although your participants' accounts are the primary source of information for your project, don't assume that they offer an unvarnished picture of social reality (see also Silverman, 2007). People are constantly reconstructing their memories of events and developing narratives to present themselves in the moment to you as a researcher. For example, the sociologist Erving Goffman (1990) showed that we are always managing the way we present ourselves to others, and qualitative data collection is no exception to this. When you don't have first-hand observations, video or written documentation and are relying exclusively on your participants' accounts, you should be cautious in how you describe events or activities. In such cases, it is often appropriate to describe your participants' perspective, construction or framing of events, rather than implying you know what actually happened. In qualitative research, the point is usually what participants believe, reported experiences, etc., so what 'really happened' may not be important anyway for answering your research question. Comparisons between different people's perspectives and direct observations can help to reveal the constructive process at play in your participants' accounts.

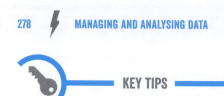

KEY TIPS

Key steps when conducting qualitative data analysis

1 Begin to read through and analyse your data from the moment you complete your first bit of data collection. Your first step should be taking notes about your immediate impressions from the data collection experience, followed by transcribing any audio recordings you gather. Transcription often takes longer than you anticipate (and it can be exhausting), so start on it early in your project. By analysing your data from the start, you can identify gaps in your data collection that you may want to fill during subsequent interviews, focus groups or observations.
2 Pick an analysis method from the outset and stick to it. If you frequently change the method of analysing your data, you will struggle to finish your research or arrive at any conclusions. There is always time to try a new method later!
3 Don't be afraid to experiment with your coding scheme. Remember that codes can easily be merged later, if you find you don't have enough matching data for a code to stand on its own.
4 If you are struggling to analyse a specific set of data, don't be afraid to discuss your struggle with a colleague. A fresh set of eyes can often help you see connections in your data that you're missing.

11 ● 7 ENSURE QUALITY IN YOUR QUALITATIVE ANALYSIS

Many factors can intervene to undermine the quality of your analysis. First, let's consider your role as the decision-maker about how your data will be collected and analysed. You're likely to have some ideas about what you expect to find from your research before you start your project. You need to practise letting go of those ideas and being completely open to where your data will take you. While you won't be able to completely achieve this goal, striving to keep an open mind is valuable in itself.

You can help ensure the quality of your analysis by employing these strategies:

1 Transcribing and reading your qualitative data during the data collection process can put you in a strong position to remember relevant contextual details you can add to your field notes. It can also help create a feedback loop, so that your ongoing analysis feeds back into your data collection in the form of revised or new interview or focus group questions.
2 Read up on methodology in your sub-field. For example, if you're using blogs as your data, delve into articles or books on methodology in web-based research to ensure you're fulfilling quality expectations in this area.
3 Don't try to tie up every loose end or smooth over every rough patch. Qualitative analysis should allow for diversity in people's perspectives and experiences. Also, you don't have to account for every scrap of data you have collected. At some point, you'll have to make a judgement about which aspects of your findings are most relevant to your research question. The patterns relevant to these findings will then become your priority as you prepare the headings in your research report, select example quotations to use, etc.

4   Don't try to do everything. Don't be afraid to make the judgement that something is 'beyond the scope of your analysis'. Just as you must narrow the scope of your project during the research design phase, your qualitative analysis will also need a tight focus so you can complete it on time.

There is a growing body of methodological literature advocating quality assurance techniques to help in 'distinguishing properly from improperly conducted qualitative research' (Thorne, 1997, p. 117). There is agreement in qualitative methodology literature about some of the ways you can ensure quality in a qualitative study. Gaskell and Bauer (2000, p. 342) note that qualitative research requires its own quality assurance criteria, distinct from the long-standing quantitative criteria of validity and reliability. Qualitative research is devoted to developing valid (i.e., accurate) accounts of participants' perspectives, meaning-making processes, etc., but there is no reason to think that even the best qualitative research would achieve reliability (consistent results from applying the same methods of data collection). Each qualitative researcher is different, and every instance of generating qualitative data will develop in different ways due to the dynamic between the researcher, participant, research questions and situation. Therefore, instead of validity and reliability, Gaskell and Bauer (2000) recommend using techniques such as **thick description**, **transparency and procedural clarity**, **deviant-case analysis** and **reflexivity**.

11•7•1 THICK DESCRIPTION

Thick description involves the use of extended verbatim extracts from the data, which empower the reader to either agree with the researcher's conclusions or to come to different interpretations. The idea behind thick description is that it brings the reader 'into the social milieu of the social actors', by providing 'insights into the local colour, the language and the life world' of the people under study (Gaskell & Bauer, 2000, p. 347). To allow the reader to gain this insight, you need to provide longer segments of text rather than brief, isolated quotations (e.g., you should normally provide interview extracts that are closer in length to a paragraph than a single sentence). On a practical level, long data extracts (e.g., a four-paragraph back-and-forth discussion in a focus group) showing the basis for your analysis will need to be broken down into smaller segments that can then be discussed piece by piece. It is your responsibility to walk your readers through the data extracts to show them the patterns you've identified.

11•7•2 TRANSPARENCY AND PROCEDURAL CLARITY: MAINTAIN AN AUDIT TRAIL

In numerous instances in this book we advocate keeping an audit trail of the decisions you make at all key junctures in your research (see, for example, Chapters 1, 5, 7 and 10). This can help you maintain a good record of the rationale behind your decision-making to refer back to in the future. The audit trail also serves as key means of establishing quality in your analysis because it allows you, your supervisor and potentially your readers to follow your analysis process. In this way, an audit trail helps you establish the quality of your qualitative analysis.

Using qualitative data analysis software, such as NVivo, can automate part of the process of creating an audit trail. NVivo stores the steps in the analysis process, and you can add a memo to document your rationale at key decision points in the process. For example, memos can be used to describe a change to your coding structure. Records are date- and time-stamped, allowing you to retrace your steps if necessary. Lincoln and Guba (1985, pp. 382–392) highlight six categories to consider for your audit trail:

1   **Instrument development information**: This includes all materials developed to conduct your research, including pilot data collection tools, preliminary methods and research frameworks.
2   **Raw data**: All internal and external sources, as well as metadata describing the nature of the data and the context of their collection.
3   **Data reduction and analysis products**: What information did you use to conduct your analysis? These details are essential for your audit trail.
4   **Data reconstruction and synthesis products**: For an NVivo-based analysis, this would include descriptions of your node structures (definitions, relationships and themes).
5   **Process notes**: Keep memos documenting your methodological decisions and the associated rationales, including those affecting methodological procedures, research design and strategies.
6   **Materials relating to intentions and dispositions**. Keep personal memos about your personal expectations, motivations and observations during the data collection and analysis processes.

These categories should allow an auditor to easily follow your research decisions, ensuring they stand up to scrutiny.

The audit trail can be straightforwardly demonstrated using NVivo. You are able to assign a category to all of your sources using nodes named with these six categories. You can run a query (see Section 11.5.5) on each node to visualize the records in each category. You can also view previous versions of your project, allowing you to trace the development your folders and subfolders, as they emerged. Qualitative analysis software such as NVivo not only allows you to establish an audit trail, but also assists you in conceptualizing your own thought processes. You can ensure you have a robust audit trail by employing these strategies:

1   **Save a new version of your project file after each working session**. Saving multiple copies of your files ensures you have a copy of your project if NVivo suddenly closes while you are working, and allows you to revisit a previous version if you decide you are unsure of an analysis decision. For instance, if you decide you don't want two codes to be combined after all you can undo the action by revisiting a previously saved version of your project.
2   **Create an organizational system for your memos**. You should record all of your decisions regarding your research and analysis using memos. The memos should be organized systematically for easy access. You may choose to organize memos by the stage of your research or by date. You need to choose a method that works best for you and your project.
3   **Record your decisions as you go along**. You may make physical notes or think of a new idea for your research. To provide an accurate portrayal of your research decisions

you need to record these decisions as soon as possible. If you do not do this, the dates of your decisions will be inconsistent. Remember, the benefit of using NVivo for an audit trail is the aggregation of all your notes and data.

4   **Clarify your nodes from the beginning**. If you need to adjust your nodes, such as what they do or do not include, create a new memo or annotation.

5   **Assign category nodes** to your memos and data to establish an automated audit trail. Once nodes are assigned you can run queries to understand your decisions by over time.

Using these strategies, you can easily visualize your analysis process using NVivo. This software-based capability is invaluable when it comes to maximizing procedural clarity and transparency in the data analysis process, and can save you a lot of time.

11•7•3 DEVIANT-CASE ANALYSIS

To further enhance quality and accountability in your qualitative data analysis, you can use a technique known as deviant-case analysis (also called 'disconfirmatory data cases'). After coming up with your main analysis, this technique involves searching through your data looking for cases that point in the opposite direction to your initial findings. You then use these low-frequency examples to try to improve and refine the interpretations and categories in your main analysis, or to try to disprove them completely (Green, 1998).

If you find opposing cases that you cannot reconcile with your main findings, you should then re-evaluate your initial categories. You may need to recode your data to account for these cases. Accounting for deviant cases can create a stronger explanation by covering the full range of responses within your data.

Alternatively, you can choose to keep your main analysis in place. This means adding into your research report your smaller analysis of a pattern pointing away from your main conclusions. If you follow this approach, you should use the 'deviant cases' to demonstrate the diversity in your data (rather than pretending all your data stack up neatly in, for example, three categories).

Your personal perspective inevitably affects the selection and prioritization of patterns to present as your results. Specifically seeking out and explaining deviant cases can give you a kind of discipline by encouraging you to consider alternative explanations. It is also an important acknowledgement of the fact that any subject of social research can be open to multiple interpretations. In this way, this quality assurance procedure enacts the qualitative research's underpinning assumptions of multiple subjective viewpoints directly affecting social reality in a given situation.

11•7•4 REFLEXIVITY

Reflexivity involves acknowledging your central role in the construction of knowledge (Tindall, 1994, p. 151). Many qualitative researchers view self-reflection as an essential type of quality assurance because it encourages the open acknowledgement of biases that all researchers inevitably bring to a study (Angen, 2000; Flick, 2002; Johnson & Waterfield, 2004). You can achieve this reflexivity by periodically evaluating and writing down your assumptions, feelings and other ways in which your personal response to your research participants and situation might affect how you collect and analyse your data. You can present these personal reflections in your research report, either alongside your results (most likely in ethnographic research) or within your methods section. Reflexive sections in qualitative research reports can take many different forms. However, the main point is to disclose the role of your subjective response to the key aspects of your research, rather than trying to deceive the reader and yourself into believing you are able to take a purely objective stance. For a more extensive discussion of the opportunities and challenges involved in employing reflexivity within your project, see Finlay (2002).

11•7•5 ACCOUNT FOR QUALITY IN YOUR QUALITATIVE WRITE-UP

Researchers specializing in methodology have worked over the last twenty years to define standards for ensuring quality in qualitative analysis. In other words, how can you demonstrate to your readers that you are presenting them with high-quality research? Elliot, Fischer and Rennie (1999) set out guidelines for producing good qualitative research to help researchers improve the rigour of their analysis when writing up findings:

1   **Acknowledge your assumptions.** Your theoretical orientations, biases and expectations always affect the knowledge you create. You should clearly identify these factors and how they may have affected your analysis.

    For example, in Charles's research report on political violence on commercial farms in Zimbabwe he made clear that he comes from a farming background in that country. He explicitly acknowledged how his personal background affected his ability to access certain kinds of participants, as well as his assumptions. If he hadn't, readers later discovering this background may wonder about its effect on Charles's research. Furthermore, they would have been robbed of the opportunity to take this information into account when considering Charles's interpretations of his data.

2   **Situate your sample**. Describe the research participants and their circumstances to help the reader understand where their perspectives are coming from. In addition, you should provide demographic information about your sample such as age, gender and ethnicity and any other information you think could be relevant in interpreting the data.

3   **Ground your analysis in examples**. In presenting your data, always give concrete examples to 'ground' the reader in the basis for your interpretation of events. Providing data extracts is essential for establishing the link between the data and your interpretations in a way that empowers the reader to challenge your interpretations.

4   **Conduct credibility checks**. Don't accept everything your participants tell you at face value. You need to display a probing academic scepticism in your analysis, subjecting your participants' claims to scrutiny and comparing them with other participants' accounts, relevant documents and other sources of evidence (see also Silverman, 2007). In addition to this practice of 'triangulation', demonstrate that you've carefully assessed how participants' backgrounds and social positioning may be shaping their accounts of a situation. Finally, invite alternative viewpoints on your interpretations from your supervisors, colleagues and other students.

For example, if you're studying prison subcultures by interviewing current prisoners, these participants may have an interest in highlighting certain aspects of their social realities, downplaying or hiding other aspects and even intentionally lying to you. You can increase the credibility of your research by:

- Understanding the background of each participant
- Gaining perspectives from other prisoners
- Interviewing prison officials
- Having your interpretations checked by other researchers with experience of studying similar topics.

5 **Establish a coherent structure for your report**. Your qualitative research report needs a coherent structure to avoid confusing the reader with a series of disconnected points. Establish an overarching narrative to bring your research story together for your reader. Integrate and connect individual examples and smaller points within larger issues. Visualizations, such as flowcharts and diagrams, can be very helpful in showing your reader how the different pieces of the story fit together. In your write-up we recommend that you 'dive deep' on an issue and give detailed examples and context, but then 'come back to the surface' to orient the reader with discussion about what it all means and how the pieces are connected.

6 **Align your research claims to your evidence**. All research involves compromises. There are limits on the kinds of research claims you can accurately make based on your data. For example, if you're studying commercial sex workers in Edinburgh you won't be in a position to make valid research claims about sex workers throughout the UK or Europe. This is because your knowledge claims need to be directly supported by your data. However, you could use this kind of localized study to develop a more general theoretical model, for example, of sex worker identity formation. This model could then provide a starting point for future researchers investigating this topic in different locations. Likewise, you could use your research in Edinburgh to call into question or support and elaborate existing models or theories.

7 **Provide vivid, insightful accounts**. When you write up your research, you should vividly bring to life your participants' experiences and perspectives. Use your interview extracts, descriptions of the research setting, photographs, etc. to transport your reader into the social world you're studying. While you do this, remember your focus as a social scientist is on addressing questions such as 'how?' and 'why?', not letting your research report become like a soap opera revelling in emotion for its own sake.

Strategies for maintaining quality in qualitative research are still evolving (e.g., see Yardley, 2007, for further discussion of the role of validity in qualitative research). When thinking about quality in your qualitative analysis, keep in mind that every research project is different. You need to adopt quality assurance strategies selectively based on what seems appropriate for your research topic and context. You don't need to employ all the techniques specified in this section to produce good qualitative research. But you should always be honest with your reader and yourself about your decision-making, data collection and analysis. Identifying and explaining an issue is vastly better than trying to conceal it. This indicates that you are aware of the problem, even if you can't remedy it. Such awareness and acknowledgement of limitations makes a problem with your research much more acceptable as the reader can take it into account when weighing up your knowledge claims.

11●8 LOOK TO QUALITATIVE DATA ANALYSIS OPTIONS BEYOND THIS CHAPTER

This chapter has focused on outlining one commonly used way of conducting qualitative data analysis. However, there is a treasure trove of different options you could choose from within

Table 11.1   Three common approaches to qualitative analysis

Approach	Key literature
Grounded Theory Originally developed by Glaser and Strauss (1967, 2001), the grounded theory tradition is based on the goal of developing theory from the 'ground' up. That is, you start from concrete data and then work up to more abstract ideas. The aim of this approach is to limit the imposition of prior assumptions (whether personal, professional or theoretical) on the data. That is, grounded theory research starts at the descriptive, micro level of the data and then ultimately makes its way to a mid-level 'grounded theory', that is, a theoretical model explaining the social problem or event that is the focus of the research. Grounded theory has very clearly defined steps and is widely accepted in qualitative research methodology. However, it can be problematic if you want to investigate specific theoretical ideas.	• Charmaz (2001) • Glaser and Strauss (1967) • Green (1998) • Strauss and Corbin (1998)
Discourse Analysis In discourse analysis, the goal is to understand the reality constructed in the text (Gill, 2000). Broadly speaking, 'the discourse analyst is after the answers to social or sociological questions rather than to linguistic ones' (Potter & Wetherell, 1994, p. 48). There are as many as 57 varieties of discourse analysis (Gill, 2000, p. 173), so you will need to specify the type you are using when you write up your methods. The discourse-analytic paradigm emphasizes the larger social context surrounding the text, which is revealed through a careful reading of the text. Discourse analysis also considers the functions and consequences of the discourse. Discourse analysis is characterized by the 'Critical stance towards taken-for-granted knowledge' (Gill, 2000, p. 73). Recognition that current understandings of the world are historically and culturally constructed. Belief that knowledge is constructed through social and cultural processes. Commitment to studying the ways in which these social constructions are linked to action.	• Fairclough (2003) • Gill (2000) • Hammersley (2003) • Jupp and Norris (1993) • Potter and Wetherell, M. (1994)
Interpretative Phenomenological Analysis Eatough and Smith (2008, p. 179) define interpretative phenomenological analysis (IPA) as 'the detailed examination of individual lived experience and how individuals make sense of that experience'. This approach draws on the philosophical traditions known as 'phenomenology' and 'hermeneutics'. Researchers in this tradition often emphasize what they call 'lived experience', a term they use to 'encompass the embodied, socio-culturally and historically situated person who inhabits an intentionally interpreted and meaningfully lived world' (Eatough & Smith, 2008, p. 181). While other qualitative analysis approaches have similar underpinnings, IPA stays more closely and explicitly connected to its philosophical roots.	• For a general introduction to IPA, see Eatough and Smith (2008) • For discussion of how it can be applied in the particular context of health, see Biggerstaff and Thompson (2008) • For an example study to see what IPA looks like in practice, see Omari and Wynaden (2014)

the qualitative methods literature. Table 11.1 summarizes three commonly used approaches to help get you started in finding the qualitative analysis approach that's right for your project.

This is just the tip of the iceberg within the diverse landscape of qualitative analysis methods. For example, interpretative phenomenological analysis is one of several traditions of qualitative analysis that focus on the level of the individual case, rather than splitting individuals' data into codes applied across participants. This tradition of 'idiographic' analysis is an important alternative to the mainstream approach to qualitative analysis using coding procedures (Valsiner, 2000; Wagoner, 2009). If you have the time, it is well worth exploring the range of available qualitative analysis options to find one that feels right for you and your project.

11.9 CONCLUSION

Qualitative methods are central to social science disciplines such as sociology or social anthropology, while in other academic disciplines such as economics they are more often used to complement quantitative data. In fact, qualitative methods can be used to identify potential blind spots in quantitative analysis. Either way, qualitative analysis requires both rigorous thinking and open-mindedness at every stage. You have to be sensitive to hidden issues that lurk beneath the surface of what people say and do. Be prepared to modify your focus as you go through the analysis process, following interesting threads relevant to your research question as they emerge.

While at some level qualitative research findings stem from the researcher's personal judgements, those judgements must be based on clearly identified data and defined analytical processes. To support your qualitative knowledge claims, use quotes from research participants or written content, images and/or detailed descriptions of first-hand observations of the activities you're studying further. Good qualitative research links social scientific concepts to data at every stage.

We have provided instructions to walk you through a commonly used method of analysing qualitative data that we call 'pattern analysis'. It involves breaking your data (often sentences and paragraphs) down into pieces that connect together in some logical way. Once you decide on the patterns to include in your report, you reconnect the pieces with their original context in order to explain how the patterns play out and should be interpreted. You will then need to select particular quotations to include in your report to represent the patterns you have identified. You should select quotations that very clearly show the pattern you are explaining. Resist the temptation to select well-phrased quotations from your participants that don't represent the overall pattern very well. Your goal should be to provide your reader with a general description of the pattern, and then a set of representative quotations (or image elements) that demonstrate the various facets of that pattern.

Ensuring robust analysis is just as essential in qualitative research as it is in quantitative studies. One reason it's so important to follow rigorous procedures in qualitative analysis is to 'counter claims that you have simply cherry-picked your data for instances that support [your original assumptions and] interpretations' (Maxwell, 2010). This means that you as the researcher need to be systematic and disciplined from the outset of your research project. For example, we advocate keeping an audit trail of your key research decisions and the rationale behind them. This is something you need to start at the beginning of your study and continue methodically throughout your work. You can't start part-way through or do it sporadically or you will end up with a patchy record of your decisions. Ultimately, your goal should be to avoid expecting your readers to simply trust that you've interpreted your data accurately. Rather, you should present your readers with the context and evidence you're using as the basis for your interpretations. This empowers your readers to decide for themselves whether they accept your knowledge claims.

▬▬ SUGGESTIONS FOR FURTHER READING ▬▬

Importance of Context for Interpreting Qualitative Data

- **Russel, A., & Mewse, A. J. (2009). Evaluating internet interviews with gay men.** *Qualitative Health Research, 19(4), 566–576.* This article reflects on the ways qualitative data can be affected by who is being interviewed, about what and by whom, using an internet-based interview study with gay men as an example. The article will help you think about the kinds of contextual factors that may have affected your data collection, and therefore need to be considered and acknowledged in your methods section and data analysis.
- **Riley, M. (2010). Emplacing the research encounter: Exploring farm life histories.** *Qualitative Inquiry, 16(8), 651–662.* This article argues for the importance of the physical setting in which a study takes place for interpreting the resulting qualitative data during the analysis process. The article will help sensitize you to the importance of this element of context when you're conducting qualitative data analysis.

Using Software for Qualitative Data Analysis

- **Sandelowski, M. (2009). On quantitizing.** *Journal of Mixed Methods Research, 3,* **208–222.** If you're considering using qualitative software to quantify your data as outlined in this chapter, this article will help you work through epistemological and methodological issues affecting this process.

Quality in Qualitative Research

- **Clary-Lemon, J. (2010). 'We're not ethnic, we're Irish!' Oral histories and the discursive construction of immigrant identity.** *Discourse Society, 21(1), 5–25.* This article shows how you can present your participants' accounts as 'constructions' or framing, rather than implying they are giving you direct access to what happened.
- **Silverman, D. (2007).** *A very short, fairly interesting and reasonably cheap book about qualitative research.* **London: Sage.** This is a very well-written and insightful book that will help you reflect on the quality of the qualitative research you are producing. It raises important questions about common qualitative research practices that have developed, particularly within ethnographic and postmodernist qualitative traditions.

Other Types of Qualitative Analysis

- **Atkinson, P. (2015).** *For ethnography.* **Thousand Oaks, CA: Sage.** Paul Atkinson is an authority on ethnography, and this comprehensive book reflects his extensive experience. The chapter on accounts and narratives is particularly useful for students doing ethnographic research for the first time.

- **Fetterman, D. M. (2010).** *Ethnography: Step-by-step* **(3rd ed.). Thousand Oaks, CA: Sage.** Fetterman's text is appropriate for beginner and experienced researchers. His writing is approachable and capably breaks down complex ethnographic concepts into easy-to-understand explanations. Students may find his chapter on analysis especially useful.
- **Heath, C., Hindmarsh, J., & Luff, P. (2010).** *Video in qualitative research.* **London: Sage.** For all qualitative researchers using video, this book is an essential read. The authors provide useful advice, especially on how to navigate practical problems when analysing video data.
- **Phillips, N., & Hardy, C. (2002).** *Discourse analysis: Investigating processes of social construction.* **Thousand Oaks, CA: Sage.** If you decide to use discourse analysis for your qualitative data, this book offers a good introduction to get you started. In particular, it shows you how to analyse discourse to identify the social construction that lies beneath the surface.

Visit the companion website at **https://study.sagepub.com/jensenandlaurie** to gain access to a wide range of online resources to support your learning, including editable research documents, weblinks, free access SAGE journal articles and book chapters, and flashcards.

GLOSSARY

Audit trail – An audit trail documents the steps you took during the process of conducting your qualitative data collection and analysis, as well as the reasons for the decisions you made.

Background information – Facts, figures, records, visual images, brochures, website information, etc. that are not the specific focus of your analysis but still help you understand the issue you're researching. You cite this information just like other literature, with full references provided in your bibliography/references section.

Computer-assisted qualitative data analysis software (CAQDAS) – Software specifically designed to help you analyse qualitative data, such as NVivo and ATLAS.ti.

Data – In this chapter *data* is what you systematically analyse. You can either gather data yourself (primary data collection) or use what other people have gathered for different reasons (secondary analysis).

Data extract – This term is used to describe a quotation or equivalent piece of qualitative data that is presented directly in a qualitative research report to represent a pattern identified by the researcher.

Deviant-case analysis – A method of quality control where you specifically seek out deviant cases in your data, the cases that do not conform to the predominant body of findings, and explore why they do not conform. Through this process you are able to test the strength of your findings. You may ultimately redefine your views, recode data in light of the deviant cases, or cite the cases in your research as deviant with an explanation of why.

Discourse analysis – This is a qualitative research method associated with the perspective that our reality is socially constructed through discourse, that is, through the link between words, thoughts and social structures. Many different types of analysis are called 'discourse analysis' so you may need a more specific term to indicate what *type* of discourse analysis you're using (e.g., critical discourse analysis).

Grounded theory – This approach to qualitative research is based on the idea of the researcher starting the process with a blank slate. The goal is to begin with data, rather than with reading about the existing research and theory on a topic. The goal with this kind of approach is to build up from data to a mid-level theoretical explanation about your topic.

Memo writing – The process of recording emerging thoughts, ideas, connections, areas of future research and links to theoretical concepts and other literature that arise when coding qualitative data. Memos are an integral feature in most qualitative data analysis software.

NVivo – A brand of computer-aided qualitative analysis software.

Reflexivity – A method of quality assurance where you as the researcher acknowledge your central role in the knowledge generation process and identify areas where you may have biases, preconceived notions or other ideas that may influence your interpretation of the data.

Pattern analysis – The term we are using to refer to the method of qualitative analysis presented in detail in this chapter. The method we articulate here is not taken from a single approach in the methodological literature, but it does correspond to often-used practices in published qualitative research across different social science disciplines. We have presented this approach because we feel it is straightforward and usable across social scientific disciplines.

Thick description – A quality assurance technique where you provide the reader with extended verbatim extracts from your data. This way the reader can have a broader perspective on the context of the quotations and so can decide to what extent you have made an accurate interpretation of the participant's account.

Transparency and procedural clarity – A quality assurance method in which researchers keep records, clear descriptions and evidence of their key decision-making to enable themselves (and potentially others) to assess their procedural pathway through their research.

━ REFERENCES ━

Angen, M. J. (2000). Evaluating interpretive inquiry: Reviewing the validity debate and opening the dialogue. *Qualitative Health Research*, *10*, 373–395.

Atkinson, P. (2015). *For ethnography*. Thousand Oaks, CA: Sage.

Biggerstaff, D., & Thompson, A. R. (2008). Interpretative Phenomenological Analysis (IPA): A qualitative methodology of choice in healthcare research. *Qualitative Research in Psychology*, *5*(3), 214–224.

Carmel, E. (1999). Concepts, context and discourse in a comparative case study. *International Journal of Social Research Methodology*, *2*(2), 141–150.

Charmaz, K. (2001). Grounded theory. In N K. Denzin and Y. S. Lincoln (Eds.), *The American tradition in qualitative research* (Vol. 6, pp. 244–270). Thousand Oaks, CA: Sage.

Eatough, V., & Smith, J. (2008). Interpretative phenomenological analysis. In C. Willig & W. Stainton-Rogers (Eds.), *The SAGE handbook of qualitative research in psychology* (pp. 179–195). London: Sage.

Elliott, R., Fischer, C. T., & Rennie, D. L. (1999). Evolving guidelines for publication of qualitative research studies in psychology and related fields. *British Journal of Clinical Psychology*, *38*, 215–229.

Fairclough, N. (2003). *Analysing discourse. Textual analysis for social research*. London: Routledge.

Fetterman, D. M. (2010). *Ethnography: Step-by-step* (3rd ed.). Thousand Oaks, CA: Sage.

Finlay, L. (2002). Negotiating the swamp: The opportunity and challenge of reflexivity in research practice. *Qualitative Research*, *2*(2), 209–230.

Flick, U. (2002). *An introduction to qualitative research* (2nd ed.). Thousand Oaks, CA: Sage.

Gaskell, G., & Bauer, M. W. (2000). Towards public accountability: Beyond sampling, reliability and validity. In M. W. Bauer & G. Gaskell (Eds.), *Qualitative researching with text, image and sound: A practical handbook* (pp. 336–350). London: Sage.

Gill, R. (2000). Discourse analysis. In M. W. Bauer & G. Gaskell (Eds.), *Qualitative researching with text, image and sound: A practical handbook* (pp. 172-190). London: Sage.

Glaser, B. G., & Strauss, A. (1967). *The discovery of grounded theory: Strategies for qualitative research.* New York: Aldine de Gruyter.

Glaser, B. G., & Strauss, A. L. (2001). The discovery of grounded theory and applying grounded theory. In N. K. Denzin & Y. S. Lincoln (Eds.), *The American tradition in qualitative research* (Vol. 2, pp. 229-243). London: Sage.

Glăveanu, V. P. (2010). Creativity in context: The ecology of creativity evaluations and practices in an artistic craft. *Psychological Studies, 55*(4), 339-350.

Goffman, E. (1990). *The presentation of self in everyday life.* London: Penguin.

Green, J. (1998). Grounded theory and the constant comparative method. *British Medical Journal, 316,* 1064-1065.

Hammersley, M. (2003). Conversation analysis and discourse analysis: Methods or paradigms? *Discourse & Society, 14,* 751-781.

Heath, C., Hindmarsh, J., & Luff, P. (2010). *Video in qualitative research.* London: Sage.

Johnson, R., & Waterfield, J. (2004). Making words count: The value of qualitative research. *Physiotherapy Research International, 9,* 121-131.

Jupp, V., & Norris, C. (1993). Traditions in documentary analysis. In M. Hammersley (Ed.), *Social research: Philosophy, politics and practice* (pp. 37-51). London: Sage.

Kelle, U. (2000). Computer-assisted analysis: Coding and indexing. In M. W. Bauer & G. Gaskell (Eds.), *Qualitative researching with text, image and sound: A practical handbook* (pp. 282-298). London: Sage.

Lincoln, Y. S., & Guba, E. G. (1985). *Naturalistic inquiry.* Newbury Park, CA: Sage.

Maxwell, A. J. (2010). Using numbers in qualitative research. *Qualitative Inquiry, 16*(6), 475-482.

Omari, O., & Wynaden, D. (2014). *Interpretative Phenomenological Analysis: The Lived Experience of Adolescents with Cancer.* SAGE Research Methods Cases. London: Sage.

Potter, J., & Wetherell, M. (1994). Analyzing discourse. In A. Bryman & R. G. Burgess (Eds.), *Analyzing qualitative data* (pp. 47-66). London: Routledge.

Russel, A., & Mewse, A. J. (2009). Evaluating internet interviews with gay men. *Qualitative Health Research, 19*(4), 566-576.

Silverman, D. (2007). *A very short, fairly interesting and reasonably cheap book about qualitative research.* London: Sage.

Stoler, A. L. (2002). *Carnal knowledge and imperial power* (2nd ed.). Berkeley: University of California Press.

Strauss, A., & Corbin, J. (1998). *Basics of qualitative research: Techniques and procedures for developing grounded theory.* Thousand Oaks, CA: Sage.

Thorne, S. (1997). The art (and science) of critiquing qualitative research. In J. M. Morse (Ed.), *Completing a qualitative project: Details and dialogue* (pp. 117-132). Thousand Oaks, CA: Sage.

Tindall, C. (1994). Issues of evaluation. In P. Banister, E. Burman, I. Parker, M. Taylor & C. Tindall (Eds.), *Qualitative methods in psychology: A research guide* (pp. 142-154). Buckingham: Open University Press.

Valsiner, J. (2000). *Culture and human development.* London: Sage.

Wagoner, B. (2009). The experimental methodology of constructive microgenesis. In J. Valsiner, P. Molenaar, N. Chaudhary & M. Lyra (Eds.), *Handbook of dynamic process methodology in the social and developmental sciences.* New York: Springer.

Willis, P. (1977). *Learning to labour: How working class kids get working class jobs.* Farnborough: Saxon House.

Yardley, L. (2007). Demonstrating validity in qualitative psychology. In J. A. Smith (Ed.), *Qualitative psychology: A practical guide to research methods* (pp. 235-251). London: Sage.

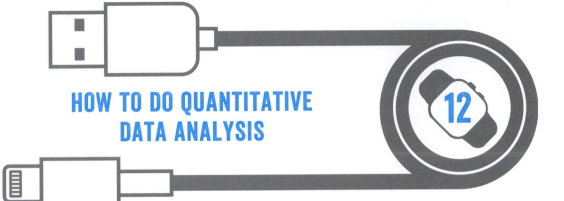

HOW TO DO QUANTITATIVE DATA ANALYSIS

12

12 ● 1 INTRODUCTION

It is not surprising that quantitative methods in social research have gained a strong position in many countries, given that generalization and prediction are highly prized by governments, businesses and other outcome-oriented institutions. Counting and comparing are the primary activities in quantitative analysis. Quantitative analysis tends to prioritize objectivity and impartiality, generally taking the view that truths exist independently of human opinions about them and can be discovered through empirical observation and/or measurement. Quantitative analysis follows standardized, transparent approaches that can be replicated by others. This chapter guides you through the process of developing your quantitative analysis step by step, from selecting an appropriate type of analysis to implementing it with **statistical software**.

While primarily focused on detecting overall patterns rather than individual variation, statistics can be used to uncover patterns within and across different groups. That is, after finding the overall patterns for the population, the next question is what kind of patterns there might be below that population level. You can achieve this by running analyses comparing people with different demographic characteristics (e.g., did men and women respond differently? Did people's responses vary with age?). You can also separate the sample based on the outcome data collected: for example, you can separate your data into deciles (dividing into 10 groups) to see what patterns apply to each 10 per cent step within your sample (e.g., bottom 10 per cent, next 10 per cent, etc.).

You can answer some research questions by adding up the number of individuals with a certain characteristic or by calculating how often something is said or done. Answering this kind of research question requires what is known as **univariate** (one **variable**) statistics. Using such one-variable statistics, you can:

- Find the frequency, that is, a simple count.
- Identify the proportion of times something occurs, for example, using a percentage or ratio.
- Calculate a measure of **central tendency**, such as a **mean** or **median**.
- Calculate the level of variability in scores, for example by using **standard deviation**.

Other research questions require a comparison between two or more categories of participant or points in time. For example, you might want to know whether there are any differences in your data on the basis of age, gender, ethnicity, income, psychological orientations, etc. You can answer this kind of research question by using:

- Content analysis to quantify qualitative data.
- Crosstabular analysis to evaluate whether two variables are related.
- **Correlation** analysis to evaluate the strength of relationships between variables.
- Comparing means to assess whether two groups are significantly different in some way (*t-test*).

This chapter builds on guidance we have provided in previous chapters about quantitative sampling and knowledge claims (Chapter 5) and survey design (Chapter 7). Here, we begin by describing the main principles of quantitative analysis, then offer guidance on when and how to use the different types of analysis listed above. While this chapter addresses some key statistical concepts, there are no formulae or other mathematics. This is a brief introduction to the most essential practical information you need to know about the statistical tests you're most likely to need. For more detail and advice on a greater number of statistical tests, see the suggestions for further reading at the end of this chapter.

12●2 RELY ON THE PRINCIPLES AND CONCEPTS OF QUANTITATIVE ANALYSIS

Quantitative data analysis involves both finding an appropriate explanation and testing that explanation. There are some essential concepts for you to understand in order to make good decisions as you develop your quantitative data analysis.

First, you should know the distinction between cases and variables. Social scientists seek to identify cases – people, organizations, events – about which they will assemble evidence. Any phenomenon for which change can be observed from case to case (e.g., employees' awareness of institutional aims or political attitudes) can be a *variable*. Variables may be observed, surveyed and otherwise measured. Once captured, they can be subjected to statistical analysis.

It is a well-established principle in statistical theory that the normal distribution of values in a population follows a set pattern. This distribution of data is most commonly recognized from its bell shape. This bell-shaped distribution has the following characteristics:

- The mean is located in the centre of the distribution.
- The greater the distance from the mean, the lower the frequency of occurrence.

As will be discussed later, this normal distribution can be evaluated statistically.

12●2●1 DEVELOP AND TEST YOUR MODELS AND HYPOTHESES

Quantitative analysis is based on the idea that you can establish generalizable knowledge about a social phenomenon through deductive reasoning. That is, you first develop a **hypothesis** (a statement about how a particular phenomenon works or how variables are related) based on theory or prior research, etc. (or initial inductive observations). Once you have a hypothesis, you can then identify what you would expect to find from particular **dependent variables**, if the hypothesis is correct. You then collect 'observed data' to test its 'fit' with expected outcomes defined by the hypothesis. Evidence supporting the model increases faith in its accuracy, while evidence that contradicts the model detracts from belief in its accuracy. For example, if we had a hypothesis that 'money is the root of all evil', we could test this hypothesis by analysing in a survey whether people who have more money are more likely to report committing evil acts. If we found a statistical relationship between self-reported earnings and propensity to commit evil acts (however we choose to define those), this would support a broader model linking money and evil.

Statistical analysis uses a rather peculiar and long-winded logical structure. Instead of directly evaluating the accuracy of a hypothesis (e.g., men will earn larger salaries than women due to advantages gained from gender inequality), statistical analyses operate by testing the opposite proposition (e.g., there will be no difference between men and women's salaries). If this opposite view (or **null hypothesis**) is shown to be unlikely to be true by the statistical analysis, then it is rejected and the **alternative hypothesis** is considered to be the likely truth.

In addition, there is a crucial distinction in quantitative analysis between the variables that you think might be causing or predicting an outcome (**independent variable**) and the variables that you think of as outcomes or effects (dependent variable). For example, if you were researching whether the saying 'money is the root of all evil' is accurate, money would be the independent variable and evil would be the dependent variable.

12•2•2 UNDERSTAND THE TYPES OF VARIABLES

Your data can take the form of different types of variables. You must be able to identify these different types of variable in order to use the statistical analysis that corresponds with the variable type(s) of your data. There are three different types of quantitative data, although they are sometimes referred to with different names.

- **Categorical (nominal) variables**. A categorical or nominal variable is one that has two or more categories, but there is no intrinsic ordering to the categories. For example, you can't calculate an average sexual orientation, gender, ethnicity or hair colour for people: people with blond, red or black hair are simply in different categories. Other examples of categorical variables include gender (male/female), place of birth (native-born/immigrant) and marital status (married/single).
- **Ordinal variables.** The difference between an ordinal and a categorical variable is that there is a clear, natural ordering within ordinal variables. For example, the categories of social class and education level are clearly ordered, such as from higher to lower. However, even though the categories within each variable can be ordered, the spacing between each category may not be the same. For example, the size of the step from 'working class' to 'middle class' is not the same (in terms of income) as the step from 'middle class' to 'upper class'. Likewise, the step from bachelor's degree to master's is not the same as the step from master's to doctorate. This makes education level an ordinal variable.

- *Interval (continuous or scale) variables*. An interval variable is similar to an ordinal variable, except that the intervals between the values of the interval variable are equally spaced. For example, annual income measured in British pounds or US dollars would be interval data because the step from $1 to $2 is the same as the step from $125 to $126, and so on: it is always the same interval (i.e., space) between each value within the variable. The same goes for age as measured in years.

Variable type matters greatly because particular statistical analyses are intended for use with only certain types of variables. You can't compute an average level of hair colour in a room because the statistical calculation of the arithmetic average requires an interval variable.

12●3   USE CONTENT ANALYSIS TO CONVERT QUALITATIVE INTO QUANTITATIVE DATA

Content analysis is a systematic method of converting qualitative content (such as words or images), for example from a survey or existing data, into quantitative data. The method provides you with the tools to ensure this quantification process is done in a reliable way. It uses a process of categorization called content analysis **coding** (see also Chapter 11 for discussion on coding). This involves categorizing raw data using a limited number of options (cf. Hayes & Krippendorff, 2007). Your coding must lead to numerical data in order for you to analyse it statistically (even if you start with categories, you must assign numbers to those categories).

A key fork in the road for your content analysis is whether you need to analyse your content for manifest or latent meaning.

- **Manifest content**. This is the objective, surface-level or concrete content. Examples of this kind of research include counting the number of times the word 'homosexual' appears on a news website, the number of pictures of men versus women in a science textbook or the number of times a set of wildlife conservation-related words are used in open-ended survey responses.
- **Latent content**. This is defined by a focus on underlying or implicit meanings. For example, you might consider how approvingly or disapprovingly homosexual behaviour is mentioned in a newspaper, or whether women are performing traditionally masculine or feminine tasks when they are pictured in a textbook, or whether there is evidence that learning has occurred when comparing a survey response from an individual at the beginning of the year and the end.

While identifying manifest content is relatively straightforward, latent meaning is much more difficult to reliably code. It is possible to use automated text analysis tools to identify manifest content. However, using human coders can be particularly valuable when analysing latent content as (with training) they will be able to identify implicit meaning that may evade an automated analysis tool.

12•3•1 DEVELOP CATEGORIES THROUGH OPEN CODING

While you can get pre-made categories for your analysis from theory or prior research, one of the ways to develop your categories for the content analysis is an initial inductive analysis (from data) known as open coding (see Glaser & Strauss, 1967). Often this will involve identifying more specific categories that can be collapsed into an overarching one. For example, in Figure 12.1 four similar codes on eugenics were collapsed into a final all-encompassing code called 'Unnatural', while two outlier (infrequently mentioned) codes were not included, as they would have belonged to different overarching themes and did not appear in a cluster with other similar codes.

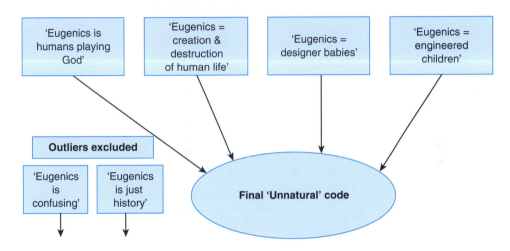

Figure 12.1   Example of final code development from open coding for 'Unnatural'

There are different ways of showing the content analysis categories you've developed. However, you should usually prepare a table that includes category names, definitions and examples (see Table 12.1). This kind of table can help maintain clarity for all involved in the study, including the reader, by showing the key steps involved in going from specific quotations to the coding category.

12•3•2 EVALUATE INTER-CODER RELIABILITY

Inter-coder reliability (also called inter-rater agreement) refers to the extent to which independent analysts (or 'coders') evaluating the same content characteristics will reach the same conclusion. A high level of agreement is taken as evidence that the content analysis has identified characteristics that are objectively evident in the texts being analysed. As Neuendorf (2002, p. 141) argues, 'given that a goal of content analysis is to identify and record relatively objective (or at least intersubjective) characteristics of messages, reliability is paramount. Without the establishment of reliability, content analysis measures are useless.' The practice of testing for inter-coder reliability serves two major purposes. Firstly, it is a quality assurance mechanism that can signal when there are problems with your content analysis design: 'High levels of disagreement among judges suggest weaknesses in research methods, including the possibility of poor operational definitions, categories, and judge

Table 12.1 Example of codes for open-ended survey responses to pre-festival question: 'What comes to mind when you think of the Silicon Valley Technology Festival?'

Code	Code Description	Code Examples
Lack of awareness	Comments by people who have never heard of or never before visited the Silicon Valley Technology Festival expressing uncertainty about the event	• 'I don't know, first time attending' [Master's, Male, age 33, White] • 'Wasn't aware of it before this week' [PhD, Male, age 35, White] • 'My first time hearing about the festival so opinions will be formed from here henceforth' [No formal qualifications (still in education), Male, age 23, White]
Silicon Valley	References to the city which plays host to the Silicon Valley Science Festival	• 'A big event in an industrial city' [Foundation Diploma or equivalent, Female, age 20, White]
Educational	Reference is made to having the chance to learn new things and being educational both for children and adults. Providing youth with opportunities for the future	• 'That we will as adults be learning too! :)' [Degree, Female, age 36, Asian/Asian American] • 'Learning for kids, broadening horizons, the "wow" factor that science has. I want my daughter to be marvelled by science' [Master's, Male, age 44, White] • 'Public education' [Degree, Male, age 62, White]
Interactive Engagement	Focus is on the interactive nature of the Technology Festival and 'learning through doing'. Participants comment on taking part in activities and experiments	• 'Experiment interaction (no reading)' [Degree, Female, age 37, White] • 'Hands on approach, fun and interactive, inspires our children to ask questions and find out more' [Master's, Male, age 45, White] • 'Innovative science, interesting presentations, a University of Stanford academic pouring liquid nitrogen onto my kids shoes (it was safe and I knew the academic, the kids loved it)' [High school, Male, age 38, White]
Technological Advancement	Participants comment on the future of technology, science and new inventions	• 'Technology for the future' [Foundation Diploma or equivalent, Female, age 34, White] • 'Scientific progress and spirit of future innovation' [Master's, Female, age 41, White]

training' (Kolbe & Burnett, 1991, p. 248). Secondly, inter-coder reliability establishes the value of your analysis for the reader: high inter-coder agreement means that you've produced results that are worthy of being believed by readers.

The first step in testing for inter-coder reliability is to have the members of your coding team independently code the same (randomly selected) subset of your sample texts. The rule of thumb is that you want to randomly select at least 10 per cent of your articles for overlapping coding. Once you have a set of items that have been coded by at least two analysts, you can statistically test for inter-coder reliability. There are many different statistics options available to you for evaluating the level of consistency between coders' scores, each with different strengths and limitations. We recommend using Krippendorf's alpha (or Kalpha), because it can handle almost any relevant research situation, and because it is the most valid measure of inter-coder reliability (Krippendorff, 2004). Another reason for choosing Kalpha is that there is a simple SPSS macro you can use for calculating this statistic, with easy-to-understand instructions for downloading, installing and running the macro. To access this information, visit http://www.afhayes.com. See also Hayes and Krippendorff (2007).

REAL WORLD EXAMPLE

Content analysing news coverage of eugenics

Dimitri conducted a study of representations of eugenics in different kinds of news magazines and newspapers. News coverage of eugenics across three distinct genres of US-based news publications was subjected to content analysis. This content analysis addressed the research question: what concepts and rhetorical themes dominate mainstream, pro-science, and Christian fundamentalist news coverage of the human cloning debate? He conducted a preliminary qualitative analysis of the data, which pointed to the importance of 'unnatural' rhetoric, resulting in a reorientation towards coding for unnatural-related content during the quantitative content analysis. His study identified four thematic coding categories (see Figure 12.1), which all connected to the issue of the perceived unnaturalness of eugenics. Here is how the inter-coder reliability procedure and results for this study could be explained:

> Inter-coder reliability was calculated based on a random sample of 900 cases in three distinct genres of US-based news publications. The second coded random sample showed an excellent level of inter-coder reliability with Kalpha = .87.

This example shows how a content analysis study can establish its reliability.

It is generally advisable to test for reliability near the beginning of the coding process, during the coding process and again at the end of the coding process (MacQueen, McLellan, Kay, & Milstein, 1998). Begin by having the full coding team analyse about 15–30 randomly selected articles (no more than 5 per cent of your total sample), and then run your reliability statistics. Then have your team meet together (if practicable) and examine where there were disagreements. If there was a particular code with poor reliability, it may indicate that you need to rephrase, or rewrite, the coding procedures. Once you feel comfortable that your coding team members are all on the same page, have everyone continue analysing the rest of the articles. As the overlapping coding procedure continues, and as you begin to get results, make sure that you are regularly rerunning your inter-coder reliability statistics to ensure everyone is still maintain consistency.

The question of what constitutes a 'good' level of inter-coder reliability often depends on the nature of your research. Generally, it is more acceptable for a complicated or new coding procedure to have somewhat lower inter-coder reliability than a simple or well-established procedure. Regardless of the circumstances, a Kalpha coefficient above 0.9 should be seen as very good. Unless there is previous research establishing that the coding mechanism employed should be higher, anything above a 0.8 is considered good. For more exploratory research or complex coding procedures a score of 0.7 may be acceptable. Anything below a 0.6 should be considered unreliable. A score of 0 indicates that the level of inter-coder agreement was not better than a completely random distribution. A negative score indicates that there was systematic disagreement on how to apply particular codes (Krippendorff, 2008).

REAL WORLD EXAMPLE ━━━━━━━━━━━━━━━

Content-analysing children's zoo visit drawings

Eric conducted a study at London Zoo to evaluate the educational effects of visiting the zoo on schoolchildren (Jensen, 2014). The main measure of educational impact was an open-ended survey question that asked children to draw their favourite wildlife habitat and all the plants and animals that live there (putting labels on everything). Children did this the day before the zoo visit and the day after the zoo visit. The pre- and post-visit drawings for the same children were matched up and then analysed using the following simple content analysis system:

1 = negative change in accuracy of representation (animals/habitat)
2 = no change in accuracy
3 = positive change

Learning was defined for the purposes of this measurement as including:

- Level of elaboration in terms of accurately showing the physical characteristics of the animal
- Level of conceptual sophistication in terms of use of scientific concepts relating to animals or habitats
- Accuracy of depiction and labelling of animal's habitat

For example, the two drawings in Figure 12.2 are from the same child, and were coded as 'positive change'. This was because of the specific criteria set out for the content analysis: the nose had become more accurately represented, there was evidence of increased conceptual sophistication as the child shifted from the term 'sand' to the more abstract scientific concept of 'desert' (a habitat category). Also, the child showed an understanding of the purposes served by the camel's humps.

Figure 12.2 Pre- and post-visit drawings by the same child around a visit to London Zoo

It is worth highlighting that the criteria for this particular study are not concerned with other forms of inaccuracy in the drawings, such as representations of animals in human-like terms (known as 'anthropomorphism'). So the drawings in Figure 12.3 were coded as showing 'positive change', despite the fact that the meerkat in the example is given shoes in the post-visit drawing and the desert is represented using pyramids.

This is how content analysis works. You set criteria that are made clear to both analysts and to readers, and then these are applied strictly and consistently across the entire sample. At the end

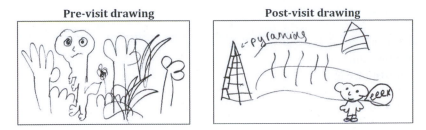

Figure 12.3   Pre- and post-visit drawings around a visit to London Zoo showing positive change

of this process, Eric had systematically converted the open-ended visual data into statistical data that he was able to analyse using some of the techniques discussed in this chapter.

12•3•3 ACCOUNT FOR THE STRENGTHS AND WEAKNESSES OF CONTENT ANALYSIS

The strengths of content analysis include that you can create quantitative data that can be used in statistical analyses, easily repeat portions of the analysis if necessary and apply the same analysis to data collected over different points in time. It is a way of reliably measuring the meaning communicated in content in a way that is in principle inter-subjective (i.e., its meaning is shared across individuals). Moreover, the level of inter-subjectivity achieved is known (through inter-coder reliability). Finally, it offers a clear, well-established method, enabling transparency and procedural clarity for both the researcher and readers/users of the research.

Meanwhile, the main weakness of content analysis is that you can develop inaccurate understandings of the meaning communicated in content because you are working with static information (i.e., you can't normally ask follow-up questions to clarify). This can lead to attributing meanings to a text that are not actually there. This issue is particularly challenging when it comes to analysing latent content, which inevitably involves subjective interpretation (although this can be mitigated through clear documentation of categories and inter-coder reliability measures). Overall, however, some form of content analysis is likely to be required to convert qualitative data into quantitative data that can be analysed statistically.

12•4 USE SPSS TO CONDUCT YOUR QUANTITATIVE DATA ANALYSIS

IBM® SPSS® statistics software (SPSS)* is a software package that performs a wide variety of statistical tests. Both data management and analysis can be conducted with it. You can use it to produce graphs and perform statistical analyses ranging from calculating simple percentages to very sophisticated analyses well beyond the scope of this chapter. There are other statistics software providers, including the free open-source software R (http://www.r-project.org), which is widely accepted as a good (if less user-friendly) alternative to SPSS. However, we focus our guidance in this chapter on SPSS because it is the most widely used across the social sciences. This section provides you with a basic introduction to SPSS to help you get comfortable with its main features.

---

*SPSS Inc. was acquired by IBM in October, 2009.

File types associated with SPSS include:

- **Data:** filename.sav
- **Output:** filename.spo
- **Commands:** filename.sps

SPSS can open these files as well as Excel, CSV and other file formats.

The first SPSS program window is the Data Editor, which has two views: Data View and Variable View. The Data View (Figure 12.4) is where you enter your data, or where your data will appear if you are importing them into SPSS from another programme such as Excel. In this view, the columns are where the variables are indicated (not editable in this view) and the rows are where the individual cases are recorded (editable in this view).

The SPSS Variable View (Figure 12.5) is where you enter your list of variables and define their characteristics. You enter details into the Variable View by clicking on the cells in each row. You normally only need to adjust the following categories:

1   **Name**. Enter a variable name. This name has to be all one word, such as GenderCategory or HairColour.
2   **Decimals**. If your data only appear as whole numbers (e.g., age in years), then change this to '0'. This will apply to most of your variables. If it is important to have the data show decimal places (e.g., 1.22), then enter the number of decimal places you would like to appear here.
3   **Label**. This is where you can enter a variable name with spaces in it. Enter the label for the variable that you would like to have appear in any reports, as this label is carried through onto any results tables or charts produced through SPSS.

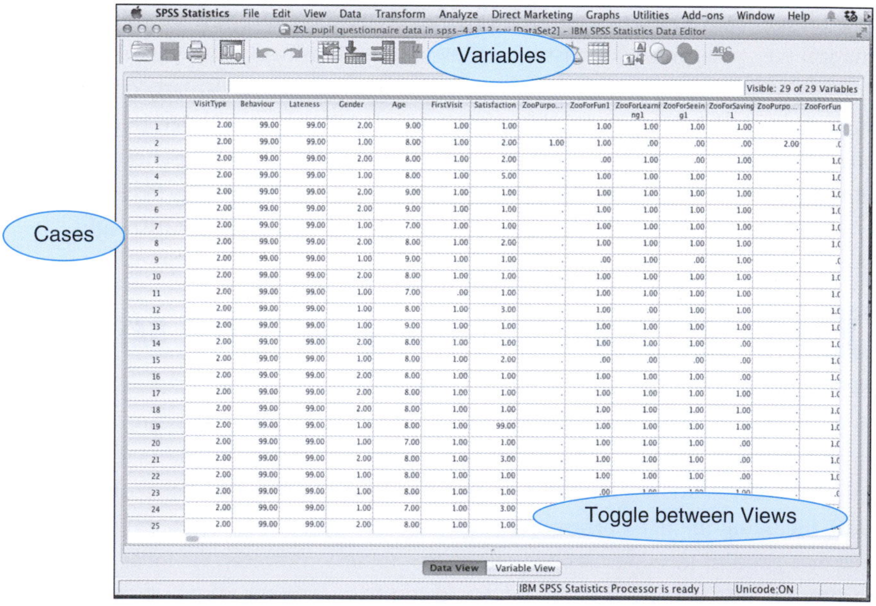

Figure 12.4   Data View in SPSS

(Reprint Courtesy of International Business Machines Corporation, © International Business Machines Corporation)

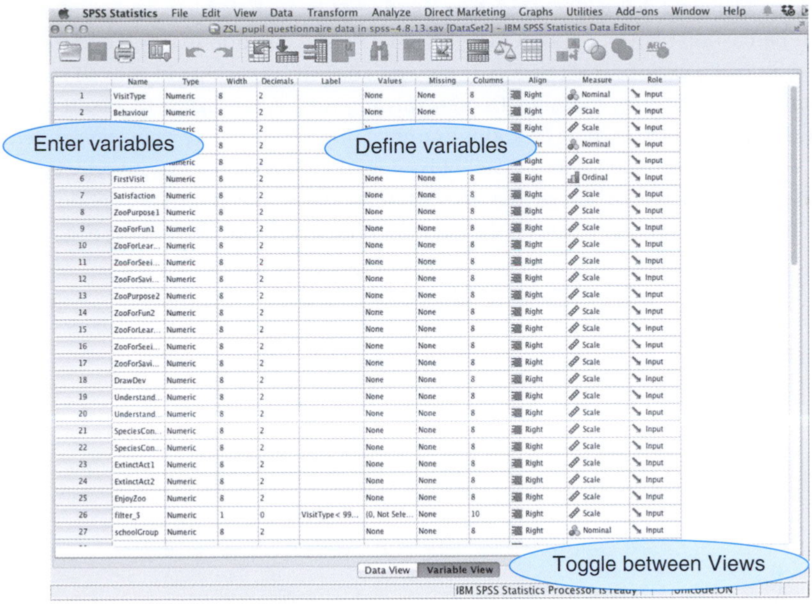

Figure 12.5   Variable View in SPSS

(Reprint Courtesy of International Business Machines Corporation, © International Business Machines Corporation)

4   **Values**. For many variables, you need to assign an arbitrary number to its different categories to be able to use them in statistical analysis (see Figure 12.6). For example, you might enter the variable gender as follows: 1 = Female, 2 = Male, 3 = Other. You make these entries here in the Values cell. When you click in the Values cell, you will see an ellipsis (…). Click on this and a small window will come up that says 'Value Labels'. Here you put the value ('1' for Female in the example above), then the category name associated with that value goes below that in the Label field ('Female' in the example above). Then click on the Add button to save this label. Repeat this process until all of the categories for the variable have been entered. Finally, you can leave the Values cell in its default position of 'None' for variables that are created in a numerical form such as age in years or weekly income in American dollars or British pounds.

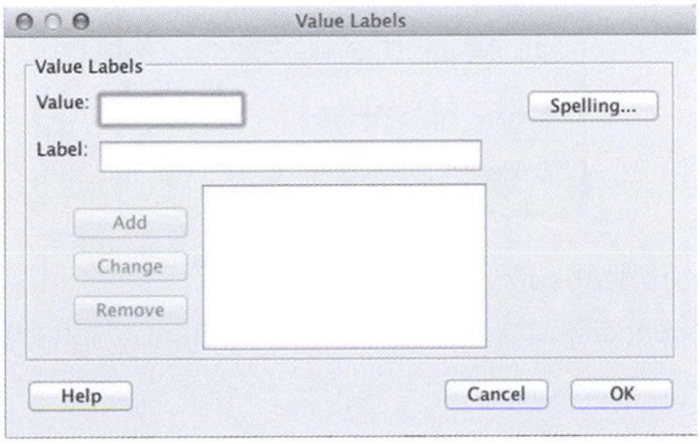

Figure 12.6   Value Labels window in SPSS

(Reprint Courtesy of International Business Machines Corporation, © International Business Machines Corporation)

5   **Missing**. Here you define the values that should not be included in calculations. For example, if you had a 'don't know' response category on a survey question that was entered as '9' in SPSS, you could exclude this category from your analysis by clicking in the cell of the Missing column for the variable, choosing 'Discrete missing values' (see Figure 12.7) and then entering the value you wish to exclude (9 in this example). If you have more than three different codes that signify missing data (as in the case of having more than three reasons why the data is missing) you can use the 'Range plus one optional discrete missing value' option. Here, you enter a range of numbers where all the values should be considered missing (e.g., –99 to –10).

Figure 12.7   Missing Values window in SPSS

(Reprint Courtesy of International Business Machines Corporation, © International Business Machines Corporation)

6   **Measure**. This is not essential to complete, but you can use it to note down the variable type as a reminder for yourself. SPSS uses the following terms for variable type: Nominal (categorical), Ordinal and Scale (interval) (see Figure 12.8).

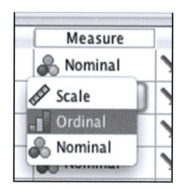

Figure 12.8   Entering the Measure column

(Reprint Courtesy of International Business Machines Corporation, © International Business Machines Corporation)

The second SPSS Program Window is the Output Viewer (Figure 12.9). This is where the results of your statistical tests appear once you run them in the Data Editor. This division between conducting analyses and viewing their results means that you have to know to go looking in the Output Viewer once you hit OK to run a statistical analysis.

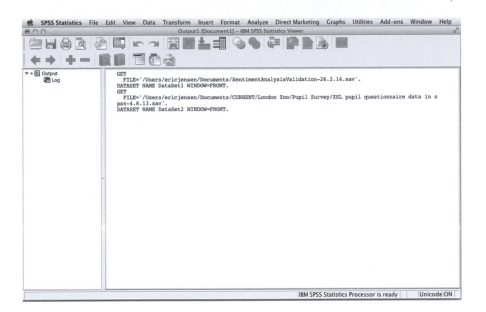

Figure 12.9 Output Viewer in SPSS

(Reprint Courtesy of International Business Machines Corporation, © International Business Machines Corporation)

12 ● 5 CONDUCT DESCRIPTIVE STATISTICAL ANALYSIS

Descriptive statistics tend to be based on analysis of one variable at a time. Many of the statistics we hear about in the news and from government are descriptive statistics, such as the percentage of people holding a particular attitude, the fractions of the population in different ethnic categories and the median income in a population. Most descriptive statistical analyses you'll need to do will fit into three categories:

- Measuring the **prevalence of a characteristic** in the population based on data from a sample.
- Identifying the **general pattern** in a sample and population.
- Evaluating the **extent to which a characteristic varies** across a sample and population.

These three categories of descriptive statistical analysis will each be addressed in this section. Throughout this section, the focus will be on generalizing from sample to population. Therefore, it is important to keep in mind the distinction between the results for the sample (also known as the 'observed values') and the results for the population, which we estimate based on the sample data.

One important concept that relates to this distinction between sample and population results is the *confidence interval*. Imagine you want to know how many people hold a particular political viewpoint in a large city. As we discussed in an earlier chapter, if you systematically gather a sample from that population, you can generalize within a specified range and level of certainty. The results of such an analysis will include a confidence interval, that is, a range of values (based on your *sample*) within which the true value for the *population* is very likely to be (Cohen, Cohen, West, & Aiken, 2003, p. 15). For example, imagine you randomly selected a sample of people in the city of London to ask about whom they supported in the last mayoral election. If you found that 51 per cent supported the Conservative Party candidate, that would not mean that the real percentage of Conservative support in the larger population of millions of Londoners was 51 per cent. Your statistical analysis would give you a range, for example, plus or minus 5 per cent within which the real value is likely to be (95 per cent or better level of probability for statistical significance). This would mean that the confidence interval was from 46 per cent to 56 per cent. The real value could be anywhere in this range (with 95 per cent probability or better); it could also be outside this range, but that would be much less likely (5 per cent probability or less).

A related concept is *statistical power*, that is, the ability of a statistical test to detect a real pattern that exists in the broader population based on your sample data. This is traditionally defined as $1 - \beta$, that is, one minus 'the probability of failing to reject the null hypothesis when it is false' (Cohen et al., 2003, p. 51). This statistical power is affected by sample size (a larger sample size increases statistical power) the size of the real pattern in the population (a larger population effect is easier to detect through a sample), and where you set your α probability, meaning the probability of failing to accept the null hypothesis when it is true (Cohen et al., 2003, p. 52). For example, if you change your confidence interval from 95 per cent to 99 per cent, you decrease the statistical power.

12•5•1 DESCRIBE THE POPULATION

The simplest form of statistical analysis in social research is describing the distribution of characteristics or behaviours in a population using data you've gathered (i.e., your sample). Examples of this kind of analysis include the following:

- **Gender** – The number of women, number of men, proportion of women compared to men.
- **Religiosity** – How many people go to church once per year, per month, per week or never?
- **Age** – What's the oldest/youngest person you gathered data from? What's the average age of people in your sample?
- **Ethnicity** – How many people in your sample belong to each ethnic group?

These are important pieces of information, and they can be used to learn about the characteristics of the population.

CLARIFYING YOUR RESULTS

You may want to simplify and thus clarify the story your data are telling by merging response categories together at the analysis stage. For example, imagine you and 100 other people are asked the following question: 'On a scale of 1 (strongly disagree) to 5 (strongly agree), please indicate your response to the following statement: "I am enjoying learning about statistical analysis."' The responses would likely range from strongly disagreeing to strongly agreeing, but we might only need to have the overall picture of whether the learning experience is positive or negative. With that in mind, the categories of 'agree' and 'strongly agree' could be merged into one positive category, 'neutral' could be entered as a 'missing value', and 'strongly disagree' and 'disagree' could be merged into one negative category. The results remaining would then present a simplified view of the rate of positive versus negative responses to learning about statistical analysis.

The way you do this in SPSS is to go to the Transform menu and select Recode into Different Variables. This option creates a new transformed variable rather than making the changes in the original variable (see Figure 12.10). Then highlight the variable you want to adjust and move it over to the right to the Numeric Variable -> Output Variable box.

1   Fill in a Name and Label for the new variable.
2   Click on Old and New Values.
3   Specify the Old Value (e.g., 1 to 10, 11 to 20, etc.).
4   Specify a New Value (e.g., 1 [for 1–10], 2 [for 11–20], etc.).
5   Click on the Add button.
6   Repeat until all old and new values are specified (you will get errors if you leave any of the old values unaccounted for, so specify the translation even if it is going, for example, from 6 (old value) to 6 (new value).
7   Old values can be defined as single values, ranges or missing values.

Finally, if you do this recoding procedure, be sure to make a note describing how data categories were merged so that you can interpret your data without having to refer back to the Variable View in SPSS.

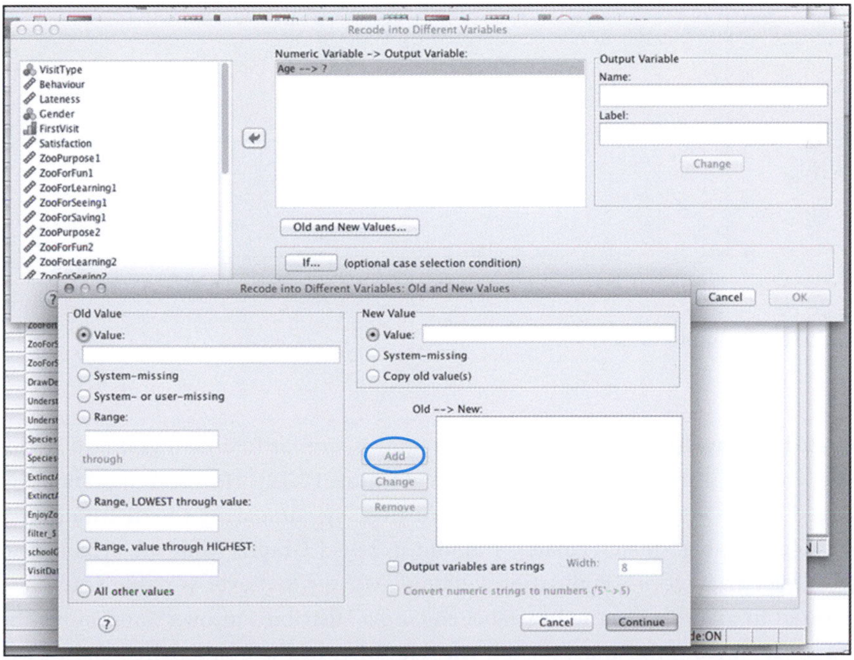

Figure 12.10   Merging categories in SPSS using Recode into Different Variables

(Reprint Courtesy of International Business Machines Corporation, © International Business Machines Corporation)

REPRESENTING UNIVARIATE DATA: USING SPSS TO VISUALIZE YOUR DATA

When presenting your data in charts, your goal should be to provide the reader with an accurate understanding of the data, while presenting it in a manageable form. There are three specific types of charts that are especially useful: the histogram, population pyramid and scatterplot.

- **Histogram**. A histogram is a simple chart for showing the distribution of your data (see Figure 12.11). To build it, select Graphs from the SPSS menu, then Legacy Dialogs > Histogram. Select the variable on the left you wish to graph, and drag it over to Variable. Check the box labelled 'Display normal curve', and then click OK.

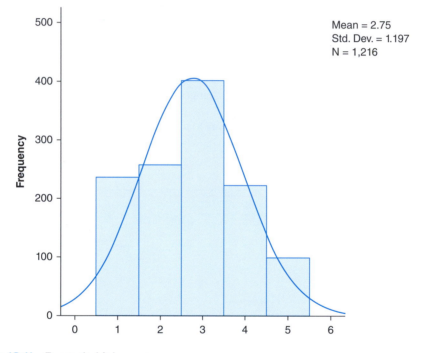

Figure 12.11   Example histogram

- **Population pyramid**. A population pyramid is similar to a histogram, in that it shows you the distribution of your data (see Figure 12.12). However, a population pyramid allows you to take this one step further, by comparing the distribution across two categories (e.g., Male/Female). To build it, select Graphs from the SPSS menu, then Legacy Dialogues > Population Pyramid. Move whichever variable you're interested in graphing to the box labelled 'Show Distribution over', and move the categorical variable you want to split the data by into the box labelled 'Split by'. If you would like to display a normal curve over your distributions, select 'Scale options', and select the box labelled 'Display normal curve'. Click OK, and then OK again.

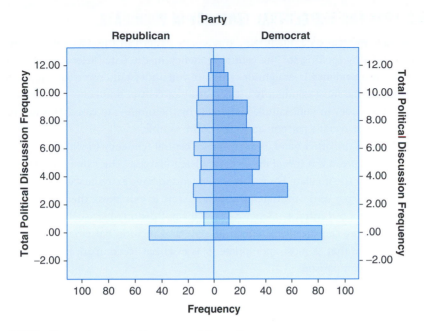

Figure 12.12 Example population pyramid graph

- **Scatterplot**. Scatterplots help you to visualize the relationship between two variables, and are useful for testing important statistical assumptions (as will be discussed later). To build it, select Graphs from the SPSS menu, then Legacy Dialogs > Scatter Dot. Select Simple Scatter and then click Define. Move your outcome variable to the Y-Axis box, and your predictor variable to the X-Axis box. Click OK. You will then get a scatterplot (see Figure 12.13).

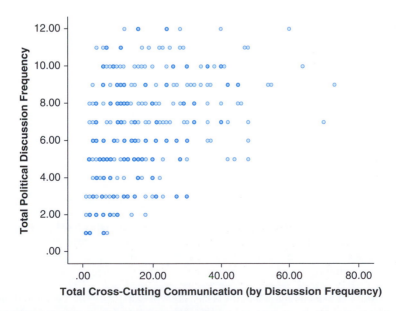

Figure 12.13 Example scatterplot from SPSS

12•5•2 LOOK FOR THE CENTRAL TENDENCY IN YOUR DATA

When you have interval data, identifying the typical pattern in the data can be very useful. This can be done by looking for the central tendency in the data. Selecting an appropriate measure of central tendency is straightforward once you understand some basic principles. The mean is probably the most commonly used measure of central tendency. To calculate it, you add up all of the values in your sample and divide by the number of cases. This can provide a general sense of the average pattern across the entire sample.

The median, on the other hand, is a measure of central tendency in which all of the values in the sample are spread out into a list from smallest to largest. The value that is in the exact middle of this list is the median. For variables that tend to have extreme values such as income (where the richest 1 per cent can stretch the income scale to extremes), the median is the more appropriate measure of central tendency because it's not distorted by such extremes. Indeed, the outcome measure can drastically affect the statistical picture that emerges, so it is important to use the one that is most appropriate. It is essential to compare like with like when making statistical comparisons.

 **REAL WORLD EXAMPLE**

Gender inequality and statistical analysis

Gender inequality is a long-standing problem in Western societies, with women systematically paid less than men for doing the same or similar work. However, this gender pay gap has narrowed in recent years. In an effort to maintain pressure on the issue, however, campaigners have (mis)used the statistical evidence to make the problem seem more pervasive than it really is.

For example, the UK equal pay campaign group the Fawcett Society published a report describing the pay gap as follows:

> More than 40 years after the Equal Pay Act was enacted in 1970, women's hourly earnings continue to be significantly lower than men's with the gender pay gap (mean) for full-time employees in 2013 sitting at 15.7 per cent. This means that women effectively stop earning relative to men on the 4th November 2014 – this day is referred to as Equal Pay Day. ... A woman working full-time now earns, on average, £5,000 less a year than a man. For all workers – both part-time and full-time – the gender pay gap stands at 19.1 per cent ... . This means for every £1 earned by a man in the UK, a woman earns only 81 pence. (Fawcett Society, 2014, p. 2)

The use of the mean creates an inaccurate picture of central tendency for income because it is heavily affected by the richest people's income. In a footnote in the report, this fact is acknowledged and highlighted as the reason for using the mean rather than the median:

> A note on why we use *the mean measure*: Using median estimates mostly leads to lower estimates. This is because it neutralises the effect of having a small group of very highly paid male employees. ... Using the mean measure is helpful precisely because it highlights that the economic elite in the UK is still predominantly male. (Fawcett Society, 2014, p. 4)

The problem with this explanation is that the claims presented in their report are about the central tendency, with references to an 'average' pay gap between men and women of £5,000 per year.

This presents a misleading picture of the problem, as the real source of the mean level of inequality is a relatively small number of men at the highest levels of the income spectrum. Men and women lower down the pay scale have much more similar earnings (although there is still a small gender pay gap even at the lower income levels). Moreover, once gender differences in job type, job role, length of employment and number of hours worked per week are taken into account, the gender pay gap is very small in Western developed nations. This example highlights the importance of selecting appropriate statistical measures to gain an accurate understanding of the real sources of social problems.

12•5•3 LOOK AT HOW YOUR DATA SPREAD TO IDENTIFY INTERESTING PATTERNS

While the central tendency is a key of the picture, it is also important to understand how your data are spread out. That is, you need to know how widely scattered your data are. Do they cluster tightly around your mean? If they don't, then that indicates your mean is a poor summary of your overall results. 'Standard deviation' is a measure used to summarize how spread out your data is: it is a measure of the average level of variability away from the mean in your data. If the standard deviation is larger than the mean, that suggests your data are highly spread out. If it is much smaller than your mean, then the data are likely to be clustering together around the mean.

If you have data that are spread out, then you need to be able to identify the implications of that spread. One way of doing this is to split your data into what are called 'deciles', that is, break your data up into 10 parts (each part being one decile). Once you do this, you will sometimes see some interesting patterns, particularly at the extremes. (For more on this subject, see Williams & Monge, 2001, pp. 31–46.)

━━━━━━━ **REAL WORLD EXAMPLE** ━━━━━━━

Variability in drinking behaviour

In Phillip Cook's book *Paying the Tab* (2007) about alcohol policy and consumption, he points out that while the central tendency for those who drink alcohol in the United States is a median of three drinks per week, this statistic masks a surprising level of variability. If you split all the adults in the United States into deciles, you find that the first three deciles (30 per cent) don't drink any alcohol at all. The next three deciles have average consumption levels of 0.02 drinks per week, 0.14 drinks per week and 0.63 drinks per week, respectively. So 60 per cent of the US population is consuming less than 1 drink per week. The seventh and eighth deciles are closer to the median, with 2.17 and 6.25 drinks per week, respectively. But it is the top two deciles that account for the vast majority of all alcohol consumption in the USA, with averages of 15.28 and 73.85 drinks per week, respectively! 'That works out to a little more than four-and-a-half 750 ml bottles of Jack Daniels, 18 bottles of wine, or three 24-can cases of beer. In one week' (Ingraham, 2014). This means that 10 per cent of the population is consuming the majority of all the alcohol that people are drinking in the USA. This paints a very different picture of the situation than the measure of central tendency.

12•5•4 HOW TO USE THE DESCRIPTIVES FUNCTION TO CALCULATE A MEAN, STANDARD DEVIATION AND RANGE IN SPSS

To calculate the mean in SPSS, you can use the Descriptives function to create tables with summaries of values for variables (see Figure 12.14). To do this, take the following steps:

1   Go to the Analyze menu, select Descriptive Statistics, then Descriptives.
2   Highlight variables to create tables, click on the arrow (or drag and drop) to add to the Variable(s) list, then click OK.

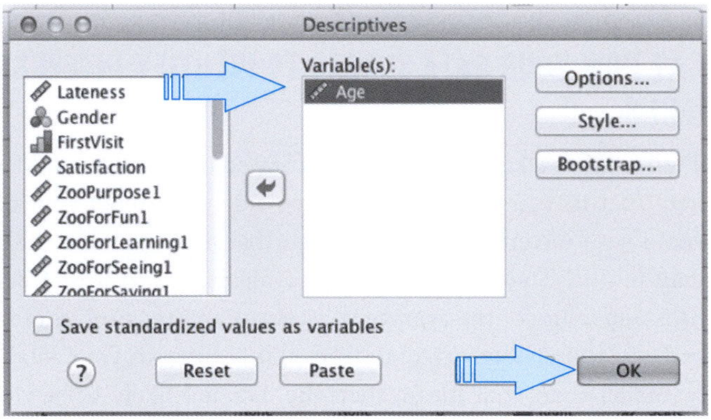

Figure 12.14   Using the Descriptives function in SPSS to calculate the mean

(Reprint Courtesy of International Business Machines Corporation, © International Business Machines Corporation)

This will give you an SPSS output like the one pictured in Figure 12.15, which shows you the mean and number of cases included in your analysis (N).

→ Descriptives

[DataSet2] /Users/ericjensen/Documents/CURRENT/London Zoo/Pupil Survey/ZSL pupil questionnaire data in spss-v

Descriptive Statistics

	N	Minimum	Maximum	Mean	Std. Deviation
Age	3018	7.00	99.00	9.9235	4.94274
Valid N (listwise)	3018				

Figure 12.15   Using the Descriptives function to calculate the mean – Interpreting the SPSS output

(Reprint Courtesy of International Business Machines Corporation, © International Business Machines Corporation)

This output also provides the minimum and maximum (lowest and highest) values in the sample for the variable, as well as the standard deviation. Of course, these are only the default outputs. If you select Options prior to clicking OK, you will be given the ability to specify additional (although often unnecessary) statistics, including: variance, range, standard error of the mean, kurtosis, skewness and sum (i.e., the sum of all response values within the sample). You can also alter the order in which the variables are displayed in the output, by changing the option under Display Order'

12•5•5 HOW TO USE THE FREQUENCIES FUNCTION TO CALCULATE THE MEAN, MEDIAN, STANDARD DEVIATION AND QUARTILES IN SPSS

To calculate the median in SPSS, you can use the Frequencies function to create tables with counts of cases for each value of the variable (see Figure 12.16). To do this, take the following steps:

1   Go to the Analyze menu, select Descriptive Statistics, then Frequencies.
2   Highlight variables to create tables, click on the arrow to add to the Variable(s) list, then click OK.
3   Click on the Statistics button.
4   Tick the Mean and Median boxes. You can select 'Std. deviation' and Quartiles if you would also like that information.
5   Click Continue twice.

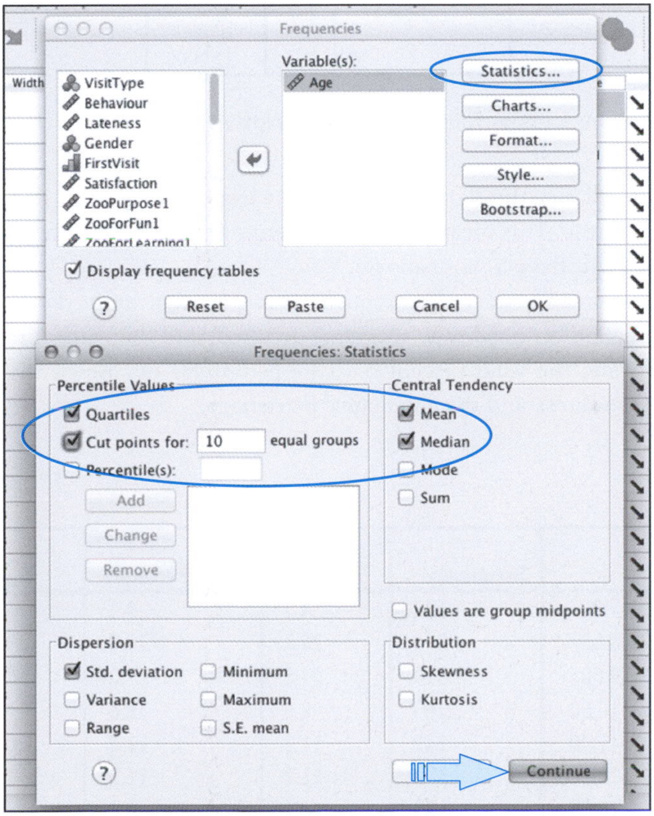

Figure 12.16   Using the Frequencies function in SPSS to calculate the mean, median, standard deviation and quartiles

(Reprint Courtesy of International Business Machines Corporation, © International Business Machines Corporation)

The output for the Frequencies function provides two tables. The first (labelled 'Statistics') provides the mean, median, standard deviation, and percentile values (see Figure 12.17). Percentiles (including the cut points for 10 equal points) are evaluated by

Statistics

Age

N	Valid	3010
	Missing	8
Mean		9.6867
Median		9.0000
Std. Deviation		1.82861
Percentiles	10	8.0000
	20	8.0000
	25	8.0000
	30	8.0000
	40	9.0000
	50	9.0000
	60	10.0000
	70	11.0000
	75	11.0000
	80	12.0000
	90	12.0000

Figure 12.17 Frequencies output in SPSS: descriptive statistics for the Age data set

looking at the number on the right column. In the example in Figure 12.17, a value of 10 is at the 60th percentile. This means that 60 per cent of the sample have a score below that value (and 40 per cent have a score above).

The other table contains data on the frequencies of each value in the data set (Figure 12.18). It provides information on how often the value occurred, and the percent of cases with that value. It also provides the valid percent (i.e., the percentage of cases with that value, after removing 'missing' values), and the cumulative percentage.

Age

		Frequency	Percent	Valid Percent	Cumulative Percent
Valid	7.00	123	4.1	4.1	4.1
	8.00	855	28.3	28.4	32.5
	9.00	818	27.1	27.2	59.7
	10.00	260	8.6	8.6	68.3
	11.00	342	11.3	11.4	79.7
	12.00	338	11.2	11.2	90.9
	13.00	185	6.1	6.1	97.0
	14.00	66	2.2	2.2	99.2
	15.00	21	.7	.7	99.9
	16.00	2	.1	.1	100.0
	Total	3010	99.7	100.0	
Missing	99.00	8	.3		
Total		3018	100.0		

Figure 12.18 Frequencies output in SPSS: frequency of each value in the Age data set

12●6 CONDUCT INFERENTIAL STATISTICAL ANALYSIS

The role of *inferential statistics* is to generalize to a larger population (e.g., a community or nation) from your sample (i.e., the smaller group selected from that population) with a quantifiable risk of error (Cohen et al., 2003, p. 41). That is, through inferential statistics you can find out whether a research result is likely to indicate a real effect in the population (i.e., it is statistically significant) or whether it is due only to chance variation in the selection of a sample from that larger population.

One of the key turning points in your statistical analysis will be a decision about whether to use parametric or non-parametric methods. Parametric statistics are generally used with probability (or near-probability) samples, while non-parametric statistics are used with non-probability samples (see Chapter 5). If you're using parametric statistics, then you'll need to know the key assumptions underpinning this type of statistical test. One of the most common assumptions for parametric statistics is 'normality'. While the precise nature of this assumption differs depending on the statistical test you are using, the important point is that you can run tests to confirm it. These tests will be discussed where they are needed under specific statistical analysis options later in this chapter.

Another common assumption required when using certain parametric statistics is that the levels of variability across all parts of the sample data are equivalent. This is called 'equality of variance' ('homogeneity of variance' or 'homoscedasticity'). When comparing groups, this assumption can be confirmed using an inferential test called 'Levene's test'. This test is built into the SPSS functions for the independent samples *t*-tests, and will be discussed in more detail in those sections later in the chapter.

As with the descriptive statistics, the correct statistical analysis will depend on the type of data that you have and the kind of analysis you want to conduct. To find the relevant statistical analyses covered in this chapter, consult Table 12.2.

Table 12.2   Matching data type, analysis purpose and statistical test

Research Question	Number and Type of Dependent Variable(s)	Number and Type of Independent Variable(s)	Test
Group differences	1 categorical or ordinal	1 categorical or ordinal	Chi-square
	1 interval (continuous or scale)	1 categorical (with only two categories, e.g., male/female)	*t*-test
Degree of relationship	1 interval (continuous or scale)	1 interval (continuous or scale)	Pearson correlation

Once you've identified the correct statistical test to use, you can begin to understand how it works. Let's start with the chi-square test.

12●7 USE CHI-SQUARE AND CRAMÉR'S *V* TO DETERMINE SYSTEMATIC RELATIONSHIPS

You may want to evaluate the statistical relationship between categorical variables such as gender, ethnicity and religious affiliation. When both variables are categorical, you can't produce a mean. Therefore, to conduct this analysis, you use what is called a contingency table, which shows the frequency with which cases fall into each combination of categories such as 'man' and 'Christian'.

When you conduct statistical analysis of categorical data like this, what you are trying to work out is whether there is any systematic relationship between the different variables being analysed or whether cases are randomly distributed across the cells in the contingency table. You do this by comparing what you find in your sample data with what would be expected if there were no relationship between the two variables (this 'no relationship' scenario is the null hypothesis in this case).

For each cell in the table there is an expected frequency, which SPSS will calculate for you and then compare with the observed frequencies from your sample data to see how much difference there is. The expected frequency is what you would get in each cell if there was an exactly equal spread of the data across the different categories in the table. The statistical test that tells you whether the difference is large enough to reject the null hypothesis and conclude that the variables are related is called a **chi-square test**.

If the result of this test, the chi-square statistic, is large enough to be statistically significant, this means that the difference in our sample is large enough that we would see it less than 5 per cent of the time *if there were no real difference between them in the population* (which is the null hypothesis). This would mean you could reject the null hypothesis, and say that there is in fact a relationship between the variables you are analysing.

As is always the case, there are some assumptions to keep in mind for the chi-square statistic.

- You can only use chi-square tests where at least 80 per cent of the cells in the table have an expected value of at least 5 (and all should be 1 or greater). If this assumption is violated the test loses power and may not detect a genuine effect (Yates, Moore, & Starnes, 1999, p. 734).
- The categories must be discrete. That is, no case should fall into more than one category (e.g., a respondent cannot be both male *and* female at the same time).

Once you have verified these chi-square test assumptions, you can run your chi-square test. To do so, take the following steps:

1 From the Analyze menu, select Descriptive Statistics (see Figure 12.19).
2 Select Crosstabs.
3 Highlight the variables you want, clicking the arrow to add to the Row(s) and Column(s) variable lists, then click OK.
4 Select Statistics (see Figure 12.20). Tick Chi-square. Tick Phi and Cramer's V. Click Continue, then click OK.
5 Select Cells, look in Percentages and tick Column. Click Continue, then click OK.

Your first SPSS test result output will be a crosstabular table (see Figure 12.21), which presents the percentages and raw numbers in each category of your analysis, as well as the row and column totals.

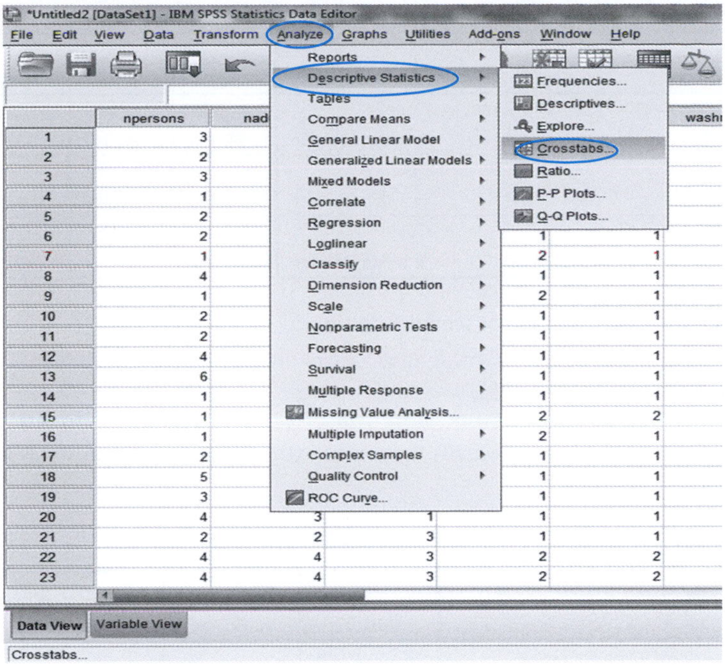

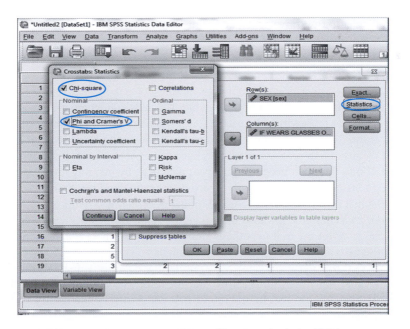

Figure 12.19   Running the chi-square analysis

(Reprint Courtesy of International Business Machines Corporation, © International Business Machines Corporation)

Figure 12.20   Selecting chi-square and Cramér's *V* analysis in SPSS

(Reprint Courtesy of International Business Machines Corporation, © International Business Machines Corporation)

HaveyouvisitedChesterZoobefore * Gender Crosstabulation

			Gender		Total
			Boy	Girl	
HaveyouvisitedChesterZo obefore	Yes	Count	133	117	250
		% within Gender	89.9%	98.3%	93.6%
	No	Count	15	2	17
		% within Gender	10.1%	1.7%	6.4%
Total		Count	148	119	267
		% within Gender	100.0%	100.0%	100.0%

Figure 12.21 SPSS output – crosstabular table

The second part of the test result output in SPSS will be your chi-square results table (see Figure 12.22). The important details for you to extract from this table are as follows:

Chi-Square Tests

	Value	df	Asymp. Sig. (2-sided)
Pearson Chi-Square	165.785[a]	5	.000
Likelihood Ratio	164.320	5	.000
Linear-by-Linear Association	76.914	1	.000
N of Valid Cases	6303		

a. 0 cells (0.0%) have expected count less than 5. The minimum expected count is 165.69.

Figure 12.22 SPSS output – chi-square test result

1 Look at the footnote at the bottom of the table. This tells you whether there are any cells in the crosstabular table with an expected count less than 5. If this number is 0, you are fine to continue. If not, then check to ensure you have at least 80 per cent of cells with expected counts of 5 or greater and all cells have values of at least 1. If so, then you can continue. If not, then you need to adjust your data (e.g., by merging low-frequency categories) to reduce the number with expected counts that are less than 5.

2 Look at the first row ('Pearson Chi-Square') under the column 'Asymp. Sig. (2-sided)'. This is your p-value. If it is less than 0.05, then the result is statistically significant. This means you can reject the null hypothesis and conclude that there is a relationship between the two categorical variables in this analysis.

3 Look at the first row ('Pearson Chi-Square') under the column 'Value'. This is your chi-square value, which is your evidence that the result is (or is not) statistically significant. You will need this information when your write up the results of your chi-square analysis.

At this stage, if you've determined that your chi-square result is statistically significant, you'll next need to determine the strength of the relationship between the two variables.

12•7•1 FIND THE EFFECT SIZE FOR YOUR STATISTICALLY SIGNIFICANT CHI-SQUARE RESULT

If you find a statistically significant relationship with your chi-square analysis, this means there is likely to be a real pattern in the population from which you sampled. However, to determine the size of the effect, you must run a second test called **Cramér's V**. This is a proportional reduction in error statistic, which indicates the strength of associations in contingency tables. It also enables us to compare different associations and decide which is stronger. Another way of describing proportional reduction in error is how much better your prediction of the outcome variable will be if you know something about the predictor variable. Proportional reduction in error statistics such as Cramér's V range from 0 to ±1. Roughly speaking, the following guidelines indicate the strength of the relationship between the variables (Cohen, 1988):

- 0.10 – Small effect size
- 0.30 – Medium effect size
- 0.50 – Large effect size

The example in Figure 12.23 shows a very weak effect (0.046 is very close to 0). This very weak relationship means that other variables are needed to provide a more complete explanation for the outcome variable being measured in this analysis.

Symmetric Measures

		Value	Approx. Sig.
Nominal by Nominal	Phi	.065	.013
	Cramer's V	.046	.013
N of Valid Cases		3018	

Figure 12.23 Cramér's V results table from SPSS output

12•7•2 WRITE UP YOUR CHI-SQUARE AND CRAMÉR'S V RESULTS

The chi-square result tells you if there is a relationship between two variables (yes or no). When there is a relationship, Cramér's V is used to determine the strength of that relationship. When writing up your results, it is important to include information on both.

Begin your write up by restating the problem. For example: 'A chi-square test of independence was conducted comparing the previous attendance at Chester Zoo across boys and girls.' Follow this by telling the reader whether the result was significant, and by providing the relevant statistics: 'A significant interaction was found (χ^2(#) = #.##, $p = 0.\#\#\#$, Cramér's $V = 0.\#\#\#$).' The values provided are the degrees of freedom (df), followed by the chi-square test value, the p-value, and finally the value for Cramér's V. Conclude the write-up by restating the findings, and by providing the proportions: 'boys ($n = \#$) were more likely than girls ($n = \#$) to be attending the Zoo for the first time'.

As a final piece of advice, avoid using contingency tables with interval variables such as age in years, as most people would fall into different categories and so the tables would be enormous and unmanageable.

12●8 CONDUCT CORRELATION ANALYSIS TO MEASURE RELATIONSHIPS BETWEEN VARIABLES

Correlation analysis measures the relationship between two interval variables. This form of analysis tracks whether deviations from the mean 'covary' (i.e., vary together) in a systematic way.

Based on this covariance, Pearson's sample correlation coefficient (r) represents both the direction and the strength of the association between two numerical variables. A correlation can be either positive or negative. A positive correlation occurs when two variables change in the same direction together (going up together or down together). A negative correlation occurs when two variables change together but in opposite directions (as one goes down, the other goes up). You can tell how strong the correlation is just by looking at the r-value. The closer the r-value is to 1 (which represents a perfect positive correlation) or to –1 (which represents a perfect negative correlation), the stronger the correlation. When the r-value is closer to 0 (which represents no linear correlation at all), you know the correlation is weaker.

KEY TIPS

Avoid inflating the risk of Type I error with lots of correlation analyses

It may be tempting to just run your correlation analyses on as many different variable combinations as possible until you get one that is statistically significant. However, you should only run this test when you have a good reason to do so. The statistical significance threshold is that there is only a one out of 20 chance of getting a significant result that is due to random sampling error. So, if you run 20 correlation tests, the odds are that one of them will come up as a false positive, that is, it will show as statistically significant when there is no real correlation in the population (Leek & Storey, 2011).

12●8●1 TEST THE ASSUMPTIONS OF PEARSON'S CORRELATION TEST

As you prepare to use a Pearson's correlation test, you must take a moment to check that the test's assumptions are met by the data you're using. We've already covered the fact that the Pearson correlation test assumes you will be using interval data. However, there are other assumptions it shares in common with other parametric statistical tests:

- **Normality**. The easiest way to determine if a variable is normally distributed is simply by looking at the histogram (as discussed earlier in this chapter). If the distribution of the variable appears to follow the shape of a bell curve, then it is usually safe to assume that the variable is normally distributed.
- **Linear relationship**. As with normality, the easiest way to determine whether two variables share a linear relationship (as opposed to a curvilinear relationship) is visually. Create a scatter plot (as discussed earlier in this chapter) placing the outcome variable on the y-axis and the predictor variable on the x-axis. You may assume a linear relationship as long as there is not a U-shaped curve.
- **No significant outliers**. The scatter plot is also a good way to look for significant outliers. If, when you look at the plot, there is one value that appears far away from the rest of the

data, it is most likely an outlier. While there are mathematical ways to determine whether a case is an outlier, a simple scatter plot is sufficient for the purposes of this book.

12•8•2 RUNNING YOUR CORRELATION ANALYSIS AND INTERPRETING THE SPSS OUTPUT

If the correlation assumptions have been upheld, you can now conduct your correlation analysis by selecting Analyze → Correlate → Bivariate (see Figure 12.24).

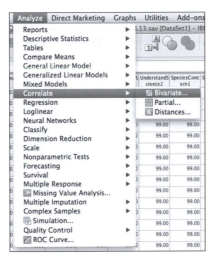

Figure 12.24 Selecting bivariate Pearson correlation in SPSS

(Reprint Courtesy of International Business Machines Corporation, © International Business Machines Corporation)

In the Bivariate Correlations dialog box, you will need to move the variables you wish to analyse over into the Variables field (see Figure 12.25). Be sure to only use interval variables!

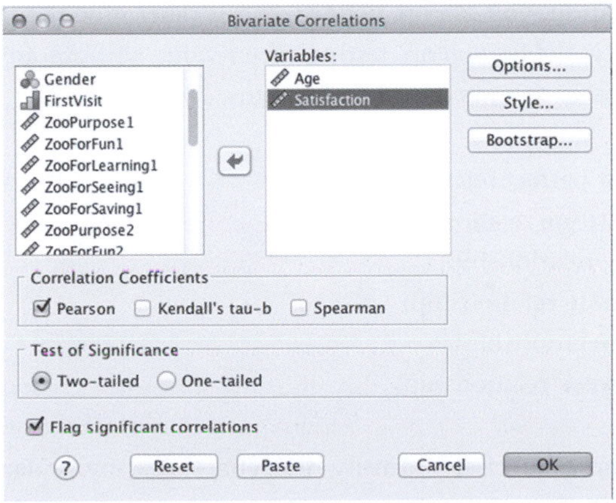

Figure 12.25 Bivariate Correlations dialog box in SPSS

(Reprint Courtesy of International Business Machines Corporation, © International Business Machines Corporation)

When you click OK, what you get from SPSS is a correlation matrix (see Figure 12.26). This is a table that shows how each variable correlates against each of the other variables, including itself. In the table, Sig. is the *p*-value and *N* is the number of cases. So in this case, the *p*-value is 0.127 (not statistically significant, because this number is larger than 0.05), and we have $r = -0.028$ and $N = 3018$. As the result is not statistically significant, we would conclude that there is no relationship between age and satisfaction.

Correlations

		Age	Satisfaction
Age	Pearson Correlation	1	-.028
	Sig. (2-tailed)		.127
	N	3018	3018
Satisfaction	Pearson Correlation	–.028	1
	Sig. (2-tailed)	.127	
	N	3018	3018

Figure 12.26   Correlation matrix (non-significant result)

12•8•3 EVALUATE THE EFFECT SIZE FOR YOUR PEARSON CORRELATION RESULTS

For the Pearson correlation, you can use your *r*-value to determine the strength of the association between the two variables you are testing. The *r*-value without any adjustment gives an indication of effect size, as follows (based on Hopkins, 2013):

- 0.90 to 1.00 (almost perfect relationship)
- 0.70 to 0.90 (very strong relationship)
- 0.50 to 0.70 (strong relationship)
- 0.30 to 0.50 (moderate relationship)
- 0.10 to 0.30 (weak relationship)
- 0.00 to 0.10 (very weak relationship)

However, you can more precisely identify the effect size by squaring the *r*-value (i.e., multiplying it by itself). This is how you get r^2 (also called the coefficient of determination). The coefficient of determination tells you the percentage of the variation in one variable that is explained by variations in the other variable. Here's an example. If you have an *r* value of

0.3, then r^2 would be $0.3 \times 0.3 = 0.09$. If $r^2 = 0.09$, this means that 9 per cent of the variation in one variable can be explained based on variation in the other variable.

WRITE UP YOUR PEARSON'S CORRELATION RESULTS

Using the key details from the SPSS results output, you can present your findings. If your result is significant, you could explain it as follows:

> A Pearson's correlation analysis showed that there is a statistically significant relationship between variable A and variable B ($r = 0.6$, $n = 98$, $p = 0.004$). The r^2-value is 0.36, which indicates that the correlation between variable A and variable B accounts for 36 per cent of variance.

On the other hand, if your result is non-significant, you could simply explain it as follows:

> A Pearson's correlation analysis showed that there was no relationship between variable A and variable B ($r = 0.02$, $n = 98$, $p = 0.07$).

12•8•4 NON-PARAMETRIC ALTERNATIVE TO THE PEARSON CORRELATION

If you find that one or more of the key assumptions for parametric statistical tests has been violated, you will need to turn to the non-parametric alternative test known as *Spearman's rank-order* correlation. This test does not give you *r*-values and it is less sensitive to patterns in your data set than the Pearson correlation, which is why it is considered a second-best option only to be used when violated assumptions make it unavoidable.

The test statistic for the Spearman rank-order correlation is known as 'Spearman's rho' (or ρ). The process for calculating Spearman's rho in SPSS is almost identical to that for calculating Pearson's *r*. Set up the test just as you would set up the *Pearson correlation* test, by selecting Analyze > Correlate > Bivariate. Move the two variables you want to compare into the Variables box. Under Correlation Coefficients, uncheck the Pearson box, and instead check Spearman. When this is done, click OK.

The output for this test is almost identical to the output for Pearson's *r*, and can be interpreted in a similar way. As with the other form of correlation, the important information includes the significance level (*p*-value), the correlation coefficient (rho) and *N* (the number of cases).

WRITE UP YOUR SPEARMAN'S RHO RESULTS

Using the key details from the SPSS results output, you can present your findings. If your result is significant, you could write it as:

> A Spearman's rank-order correlation shows that Group A tended to rank higher in OUTCOME than Group B, $r_s = 0.\#\#$, $p = 0.\#\#\#$.

On the other hand, if your result is non-significant, you could simply write it as follows:

> A Spearman's rank-order correlation showed no difference in OUTCOME between Group A and Group B, $r_s = 0.\#\#$, $p = 0.\#\#\#$.

12•8•5 INTERPRETING CORRELATION

Correlation does not necessarily indicate causality, because the statistics don't tell you the direction of causation and there may be some other variable affecting the relation between the two variables. For example, a study finding a correlation between annual income levels and brain size might conclude that larger brains lead to higher incomes. However, both brain size and income could be affected by many other factors such as physical size of person, which may in fact be the real causal factor involved. In sum, the correlation coefficient says nothing about which variable is *causing* the other to change.

 **REAL WORLD EXAMPLE**

Facebook and life satisfaction

Kross, Verduyn, Demiralp, Park, and Lee (2013) conducted a study of the relationship between Facebook use and moment-by-moment happiness and life satisfaction. They did this by text-messaging 82 people over a two-week period, sending them questions five times per day about how they felt at the time of receiving the text message. They then ran statistical analysis on the data they got back and found that Facebook use at one time point was correlated with negative shifts in mood and 'life satisfaction' the next time they contacted the participants. They also found that there was a general correlation between the amount of Facebook use over the two-week period and their life satisfaction levels (as Facebook use went up, life satisfaction levels went down). They concluded: 'Facebook use predicts declines in the two components of subjective wellbeing: how people feel moment to moment and how satisfied they are with their lives' (Kross et al., 2013, p. 4). Thus, the authors of this study are implying that Facebook use causes declines in people's perceived well-being.

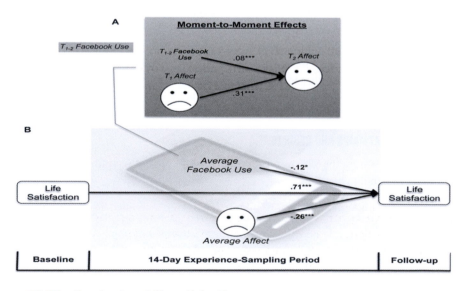

Figure 12.27   Facebook and life satisfaction

Source: Kross et al. (2013)

However, this claim of 'prediction' is actually only referring to correlation. This study only asked about a few things during the 'experience sampling' five times per day: measures of feelings, stated Facebook use and self-reported level of social contact through face-to-face or phone interactions. This means that anything else outside of these factors could have affected people's feelings. For example, perhaps a factor not accounted for in the analysis such as the time of day might have affected people's decision to use Facebook. Or a text message (not measured in the study) from a friend or loved one could have triggered negative feelings. With such a limited frame around the analysis, the causes of the outcomes measured in the study are mostly unknown. It is important to be very careful about drawing causal inferences in such cases.

12.9 USE *T*-TESTS TO COMPARE MEANS

If you have one interval outcome variable (e.g., income) and you want to compare means across two categories (e.g., men and women), then the *t*-test is where you should start. There are two different types of *t*-tests that will be discussed in this chapter:

- *t*-tests with two independent samples ('independent samples *t*-test'). You might use this statistical analysis to compare boys' and girls' results on a math test. The defining feature of this kind of statistical analysis is that the data you're comparing come from different groups of people.
- *t*-test with two paired samples (also called the 'dependent samples *t*-test'). This statistical test compares two means using data gathered from the same people measured at different times. For example, if you compared responses before and after a visit to the zoo for the same sample of children. That is, these data are from 'matched' samples.

When two samples of data are collected and the sample means are calculated, these means might differ by either a little or a lot. If the samples come from the same population, then we must start with the expectation that their means will be roughly equal (this is the null hypothesis). Although it is possible for their means to differ by chance alone, we would expect large differences between sample means to occur very infrequently. We compare the difference between the sample means that we collected to the difference between the sample means that we would expect to obtain if there were no effect (i.e., if the null hypothesis were true). If the difference between the samples we have collected is larger than what we would expect if the null hypothesis is true, then we can conclude one of two things:

1　**There is no effect.** Sample means in our population fluctuate and we have, purely by chance, gathered two samples that are not representative of the population from which they came.
2　**There is a statistically significant difference**. The two samples come from different populations but are typical of their respective parent population. In this scenario, the difference between samples represents a genuine difference between the samples (and so the null hypothesis is false).

As the observed difference between the sample means gets larger, there can be more confidence that the second conclusion is correct (i.e., that the null hypothesis should be rejected). In sum, the *t*-value is effectively the difference between what you would expect if the null hypothesis (identical means in population) is true and the actual sample data you've collected. If the data you've collected indicates a large enough difference, you can reject the null hypothesis and say you have discovered a statistically significant difference between the two means. For the independent samples *t*-test, the main assumptions are *normality* and *equality of variances*. For the paired samples *t*-test, the main assumption is normality. Once you've decided the *t*-test is appropriate for your analysis, you need to test its assumptions. However, in this case, you can test the assumptions in SPSS as part of your *t*-test analysis.

To check whether your data have equality of variances, Levene's test is used; it tests the hypothesis that the variances in the groups are equal. If Levene's test is statistically non-significant ($p > 0.05$), then equality of variances is confirmed (i.e., all is well and you can carry on with your analysis as planned). If Levene's test is statistically significant ($p < 0.05$), this means that the variances are not equal (the assumption is violated). This indicates that you shouldn't be using the standard *t*-test. If you find that the *t*-test assumptions are not supported, then you should skip to the non-parametric alternatives (see Section 12.9.3).

12•9•1 RUN YOUR *T*-TEST

If the *t*-test assumptions have been supported, you can now run your *t*-test (see Figure 12.28). Select Analyze → Compare Means → *t*-test (choose between Independent-Samples T Test and Paired-Samples T Test). Each type of *t*-test will bring up a different dialog box.

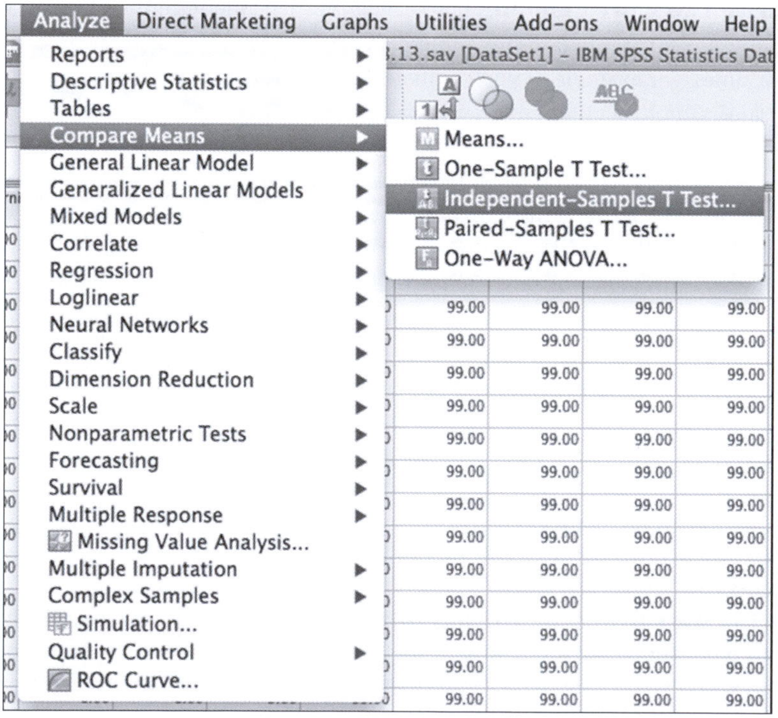

Figure 12.28 Running a *t*-test in SPSS

(Reprint Courtesy of International Business Machines Corporation, © International Business Machines Corporation)

INDEPENDENT SAMPLES *T*-TEST

For the independent samples *t*-test, you need to take the following steps (see Figure 12.29):

- Choose an interval variable as your Test Variable.
- Choose a categorical variable as your Grouping Variable.
- Click on Define Groups and identify the numbers that have been assigned to each group for this variable (e.g., 1 and 2). Then click Continue, then OK to run the analysis.

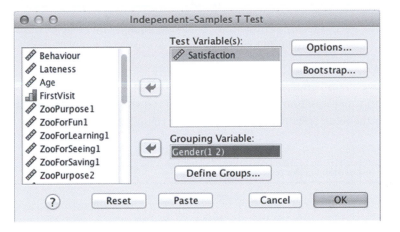

Figure 12.29   Selecting variables for independent samples *t*-test in SPSS

(Reprint Courtesy of International Business Machines Corporation, © International Business Machines Corporation)

You will receive a multi-part output from SPSS. The top part of the output (see Figure 12.30) provides information on the mean, standard deviation and standard error of the mean for the two variables you're analysing, as well as the sample sizes for each category you're looking at (N). You will need the sample sizes and standard error of the mean when you write up your results.

The Levene's test shown in Figure 12.31 has a statistically significant result (Sig. is less than 0.05). This means that the equality of variances assumption of this statistical test may have been violated. This in turn indicates that you shouldn't use the *t*-test, but will need to switch to a non-parametric alternative.

Group Statistics

	Gender	N	Mean	Std. Deviation	Std. Error Mean
Satisfaction	1.00	1452	17.3485	35.81107	.93980
	2.00	1526	14.2192	32.56893	.83373

Figure 12.30   Top part of *t*-test SPSS output: summarizing your data

		Levene's Test for Equality of Variances	
		F	Sig.
Satisfaction	Equal variances assumed	26.082	.000
	Equal variances not assumed		

Figure 12.31 Part of *t*-test SPSS output: checking equality of variance assumptions – equality of variances assumption violated

If you have a non-significant Levene's test result (i.e., Sig. greater than 0.05), then you can continue with your *t*-test. Your independent samples *t*-test will have an SPSS output, which tells you whether the result is statistically significant (see Figure 12.32).

Independent Samples Test

		t-test for Equality of Means			95% Confidence Interval of the Difference	
t	df	Sig. (2–tailed)	Mean Difference	Std. Error Difference	Lower	Upper
2.497	2976	.013	3.12928	1.25336	.67174	5.58683
2.491	2915.467	.013	3.12928	1.25631	.66593	5.59264

Figure 12.32 Example *t*-test results output in SPSS

You can immediately see if a result is statistically significant by checking the column labelled 'Sig. (2-tailed)'. If this number is lower than 0.05, then your result is statistically significant. This means you would be able to reject the null hypothesis and conclude that there is a real difference between the two groups in the population from which your sample was drawn.

In order to write up your results, the important details you need to gather from this table are the sample sizes (N), standard errors of the means (SE), *t*-value and degrees of freedom (df), the Sig. value ($p = .013$ in the example above), as well as your measures of effect size. Here is an example of a write-up using this information:

> An independent two-samples *t*-test was conducted to compare the mean levels of satisfaction when zoo visits were self-guided or education officer-led. The results show that self-guided visits yielded significantly greater satisfaction levels ($M = 1.821$, SD = 0.988): $t(1592) = 3.944$, $p = 0.000$,* when compared with education officer-led visits ($M = 1.659$, SD = 0.913). These results indicate that education officer led visits lead to *lower* levels of satisfaction with the zoo.

---

*Levene statistic = 5.549, $p < 0.05$ (outcome suggests non-equal variances, therefore variance ratio calculated to confirm *t*-test assumption of equality of variances; this assumption was confirmed by Hartley's $F_{max} = 1.170$ ($n = 2415$).

While you can use different words when you write up your *t*-test, you should be sure to include the key statistical information provided here.

PAIRED SAMPLES *T*-TEST

For the paired samples *t*-test, you'll get a dialog box that has spaces for you to place your two paired variables (see Figure 12.33). Select the variables and then click 'OK'.

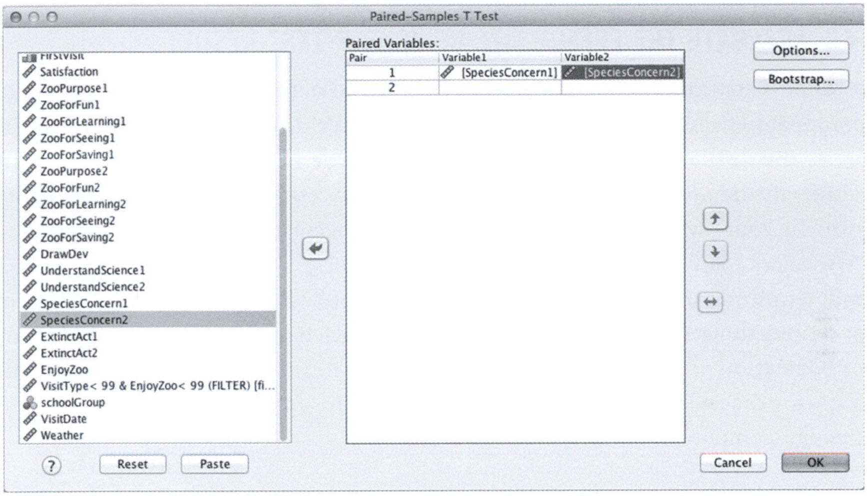

Figure 12.33 Selecting variables for paired samples *t*-test

(Reprint Courtesy of International Business Machines Corporation, © International Business Machines Corporation)

Your paired-samples *t*-test results output includes a set of three tables. The important details for you to extract from the top table (Figure 12.34) are the mean, the sample size and the standard deviation, and from the bottom table, the *t*-value, degrees of freedom (df), and *p*-value (Sig.).

T-Test

Paired Samples Statistics

		Mean	N	Std. Deviation	Std. Error Mean
Pair 1	SpeciesConcern1	88.4344	3018	30.36727	.55277
	SpeciesConcern2	88.0457	3018	30.85138	.56158

Paired Samples Correlations

		N	Correlation	Sig.
Pair 1	SpeciesConcern1 & SpeciesConcern2	3018	.868	.000

Paired Samples Test

		Paired Differences					t	df	Sig. (2-tailed)
		Mean	Std. Deviation	Std. Error Mean	95% Confidence Interval of the Difference Lower	Upper			
Pair 1	SpeciesConcern1 - SpeciesConcern2	.38867	15.71088	.28598	-.17207	.94941	1.359	3017	.174

Figure 12.34 Paired samples *t*-test output in SPSS

Here is how you could write up a paired samples *t*-test result:

A paired samples *t*-test compared pre- and post-visit data on children's concern for the conservation of animal species before and after a visit to London Zoo. There was no significant difference on this measure assessing pre-visit scores ($M = 88.43$, SD = 30.37) and post-visit ($M = 88.05$, SD = 30.85): $t(3017) = 1.359$, $p = 0.174$. These results indicate that the zoo visit had no effect on this outcome for children.

12•9•2 EVALUATE THE EFFECT SIZE OF YOUR *T*-TEST RESULT

If your result is statistically significant, you next need to determine the effect size. For *t*-tests, the appropriate effect size measure is known as Cohen's *d*, which is simply a standardized measure of the difference between two means. This value is not automatically calculated in SPSS, although the *t*-test output does provide all the necessary elements for calculating this effect size on your own. To avoid having to do these calculations yourself, we suggest using http://www.uccs.edu/~lbecker/ for calculating Cohen's *d*.

For determining the effect size for a comparison of two groups (whether between subjects or within subjects), all you need is the mean of each group (i.e., M_1 and M_2), and the standard deviation of each group (i.e., SD_1 and SD_2). These values are found in the first set of outputs for each *t*-test. Enter the information into the appropriate boxes on the website, and click on Compute.

12•9•3 HOW TO USE NON-PARAMETRIC ALTERNATIVES TO THE *T*-TEST

If the *t*-test assumptions are broken, your results may not be valid. Specifically, if the *t*-test assumptions are violated, it can result in a lack of statistical power, meaning that you may fail to reject the null-hypothesis when in fact you should have (that is, a false negative). It may also result in seemingly nonsensical results. This is especially true if you have small sample sizes and/or drastically unequal groups you're comparing. In these cases, you should use a non-parametric test instead.

NON-PARAMETRIC ALTERNATIVE TO INDEPENDENT SAMPLES *T*-TEST (MANN–WHITNEY)

An alternative to the independent samples *t*-test is the Mann–Whitney *U* test. The basic function of the Mann–Whitney *U*-test is similar to the *t*-test, except that you compare differences from within the *mean rank* rather than differences in the *mean*. The 'mean rank' refers to where each individual in the sample sits in reference to the other individuals. For example, the 10th highest score would be given a rank of 10, and the 11th highest a rank of 11. Then, for each group, the test is run on the mean of these ranks, instead of on the mean of the scores themselves. Of course, you don't need to rank each case by hand: This is done automatically by SPSS. To run a Mann–Whitney *U*-test, take the following steps:

3   Go to Analyze > Nonparametric Tests > Legacy Dialogs > 2 Independent Samples.
4   You'll now see a dialog box that is very similar to the one for the independent samples *t*-test. Move your outcome variable to the Test Variable List box, and the predictor variable to the Grouping Variable box.

5   Under the grouping variable box, click Define Groups.
6   Input the grouping values, just as you would for the *t*-test.
7   Click Continue.
8   Make sure the Mann-Whitney U box is checked, and no others. Click OK.

To determine whether the test is statistically significant, look at the value labelled 'Asymp. Sig. (2-tailed)' (i.e., asymptotic significance). If this value is less than 0.05, then your test is statistically significant. You can report the results of the Mann–Whitney *U*-test exactly the same as you would with a *t*-test, just substituting *U* for *t* (i.e., *U* = ###, *p* = 0.###), and noting that there are no degrees of freedom" to report.

NON-PARAMETRIC ALTERNATIVE TO PAIRED-SAMPLES *T*-TEST (WILCOXON SIGNED RANK)

An alternative to the paired-samples *t*-test is called the Wilcoxon signed rank test. Similar to the Mann–Whitney *U*-test, the Wilcoxon signed rank test shares the same basic function as a *t*-test, although instead of comparing means, it compares rank means. To run the Wilcoxon signed rank test, take the following steps:

1   Go to Analyze > Nonparametric Tests > Legacy Dialogs > 2 Related Samples.
2   Transfer the variables you are interesting in analysing into the Test Pairs box, making sure that the time 1 scores go into Variable1 and the time 2 scores go into Variable 2.
3   Under Test Type, make sure that Wilcoxon is selected, and no others.
4   Click OK.

Next you will need to interpret the results. There should be two output tables, one labelled 'Ranks' and one labelled 'Test Statistics'. The first gives you an indication of how many individuals improved their rank from time 1 to time 2, while the second tells you whether the score is significant. In the Ranks table, 'Negative Ranks' are the number of individuals who scored lower at time 2, 'Positive Ranks' are the number of individuals who scored higher at time 2, and 'Ties' are individuals who scored the same at time 2. This information is interesting, although you generally don't need to report it.

The Test Statistics table gives you everything you need in order to report the significance of the test. The *p*-value is labelled 'Asymp. Sig. (2-tailed)'. If this value is less than 0.05, then your test is statistically significant.

You can report the results of the Wilcoxon signed rank test in exactly the same way as you would a *t*-test, substituting Z for *t* (i.e. Z = #.###, *p* = 0.###). As with the Mann–Whitney test, there are also no degrees of freedom to report.

12 ● 10 LOOK TO THE STATISTICAL HORIZON BEYOND THIS CHAPTER

As can be seen in Figure 12.35, there are several other statistical tests you may need to use that are not covered in this chapter. In Table 12.3, we signpost some of the statistical analyses beyond the scope of this chapter so that you know where to go next if your statistics needs are not addressed here. If your situation calls for statistical tests not covered in this chapter, we recommend you consult Field (2014) for detailed guidance.

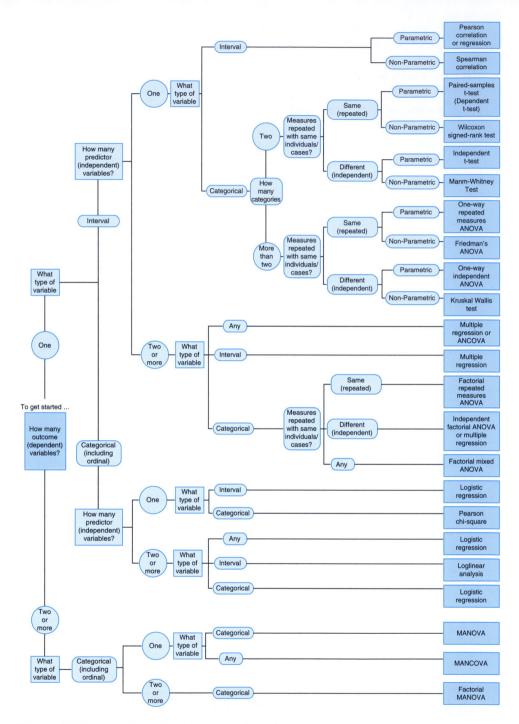

Figure 12.35 Map of statistical test options by number and type of variables

Table 12.3   Steps to the statistical horizon

Type of Research Question	Number and Type of Outcome Variable(s)	Number and Type of Predictor Variable(s)	Covariates	Test to Use
Group differences	1 Interval	1 Categorical	–	One-way ANOVA
		1 Categorical	1+	One-way ANCOVA
		2+ Categorical	–	Factorial ANOVA
			1+	Factorial ANCOVA
	2+ Interval	1 Categorical	–	One-way MANOVA
			1+	One-way MANCOVA
		2+ Categorical	–	Factorial MANOVA
			1+	Factorial MANCOVA
Degree of relationship	1 Interval	2+ Interval	–	Multiple Regression
	1+ Interval	2+ Interval	–	Path Analysis
Prediction of group membership	Nominal with 2 levels (e.g., Male/Female)	2+ Categorical, Ordinal or Interval	–	Logistic Regression

12 ● 11 CONCLUSION

Quantitative analysis aims to create efficient descriptions and summaries of patterns using standardized data sets and statistics. This chapter began with an introduction to content analysis as a method of converting qualitative data into a systematic numerical form that can be used in statistical analysis. The linchpin in the content analysis process is inter-coder reliability, which is a necessary (although not a sufficient) criterion for validity in the study. Without it, all results and conclusions in the research project may justifiably be doubted. We emphasized that all content analysis projects should be designed to include the assessment and reporting of this crucial quality assurance measure.

Whether created through content analysis or other methods, your quantitative data can be used to describe patterns in your data and make comparisons. They can also be used to test hypotheses using statistics to calculate whether a result is 'statistically significant', that is, whether it points to a real pattern in the population. For example, the chi-square statistic can tell you whether there is a 'significant' association between two categorical variables (or whether there exists an association that would be unlikely to be found by chance). Once a significant pattern is detected, you'll need to determine the strength of association using a different test (Cramér's V in the case of a significant chi-square result).

Statistical tests often have assumptions that must be met in order to use them. Parametric statistical tests tend to assume both normality and equality of variances. Correlation analysis also assumes linearity. If these assumptions are satisfied, you can use the Pearson correlation to investigate whether there is a relationship between two interval variables. However, it is important to limit the risk of a false positive result by only running correlation analyses when there is a good reason.

We then discussed options for comparing means between different categories of a predictor variable. If two samples come from populations with identical population means, then you would expect the difference between the sample means to be (close to) zero. Thus, the larger the difference between the two sample means, the more likely it is that the two population means are different. This is what the *t*-test evaluates.

Finally, we highlighted a range of other statistical options you can learn more about in other books or articles. This chapter only provides the bare essentials for you to be able to run statistical analyses in SPSS. It's likely you'll need to do some further reading if you have any unusual situations or analysis needs that are not covered here.

■ SUGGESTIONS FOR FURTHER READING ■

- Field, A. (2014). *Discovering statistics with IBM SPSS Statistics.* London: Sage. This book discusses the theoretical and practical aspects of a number of key statistical concepts and analyses. It strikes a very informal tone, but provides a good level of detail about how to conduct statistical tests using SPSS and related contextual information about these statistics.
- D'Agostino, R. B., Belanger, A., & D'Agostino, R. B. (1990). A suggestion for using powerful and informative tests of normality. *American Statistician, 44,* 316-321. This article provides guidance about different options for assessing whether normality assumptions have been met in your statistical analyses.
- Kotrlik, J. W., Williams, H. A., & Jabor, M. K. (2011). Reporting and interpreting effect size in quantitative agricultural education research. *Journal of Agricultural Education, 52*(1), 132-142. This article identifies different options for measuring effect size for a range of statistical tests.
- Cohen, J. (1992). Power primer. *Psychological Bulletin, 112*(1): 155-159. This article is a brief, accessible and prescriptive look at the concept of statistical power. Perhaps the most notable thing about this article (and the reason it has been cited over 8500 times!) is the simple rules of thumb Cohen provides for interpreting effect size measures. This article is a quick read, and an incredibly useful citation.
- Williams, F., & Monge, P. (2001). *Reasoning with statistics: How to read quantitative research* (5th ed.). Boston: Wadsworth Cengage Learning. The world of quantitative statistical testing expands far beyond what we cover in this chapter. This book offers an excellent cursory look at many additional statistical methods which you may run into as you read social science research. Importantly, the book is not (primarily) designed to teach you *how to do* statistics, but instead on *how to read and understand* a large verity of advanced statistical analyses.
- Krippendorf, K. H. (2013). *Content analysis: An introduction to its methodology.* Thousand Oaks, CA: Sage. Krippendorf is by many accounts the father of modern-day content analysis. This textbook covers everything you need to know in order to be an expert on doing and critiquing content analysis.

Visit the companion website at **https://study.sagepub.com/jensenandlaurie** to gain access to a wide range of online resources to support your learning, including editable research documents, weblinks, free access SAGE journal articles and book chapters, and flashcards.

■ GLOSSARY ■

Central tendency – This is the typical pattern in your data, which can be assessed by calculating the mean or median.

Chi-square test – This test is used when you want to evaluate whether two categorical variables are related.

Coding – The process of systematically converting qualitative content into quantitative data by categorizing raw data using a limited number of standardized categories that are suitable for analysis.

Correlation – The extent to which two variables have a relationship dependent on each other. For example, there is a correlation between eating high quantities of fatty foods and gaining weight.

Cramér's V – This test is used as a follow-up after a statistically significant chi-square result to determine the size of the effect.

Dependent variable – The variable that is changed or altered in a study. For example, the amount of exercise, the voting preference or the amount eaten can all be changed in a study. The easiest way to remember the difference between dependent and independent variables is to insert the variables into the following sentence: (your independent variable) brings about a change in (your dependent variable) and it is not possible for (your dependent variable) to bring about a change in (your independent variable).

Descriptive statistics – Mathematical methods used to summarize and interpret data properties. They are distinct from inferential statistics in that they do not infer the properties of the population. For example, the percentage of goals scored during a football season is a descriptive statistic of individual player or team performance.

Hypothesis – The null hypothesis, usually denoted H_0, states that there is no association/relationship between the variables, while the alternative hypothesis, denoted H_1, states that there is an association/relationship between the variables.

Independent variable – The variable that stands alone and is not changed by any process in your analysis. For example, someone's age could be an independent variable and is not going to change no matter how much exercise they do, how they vote or what they eat.

Inferential statistics – Mathematical methods that are based on probability theory to deduce or infer the properties of a population larger than that of the sample tested. This is done, for example, by testing hypotheses and deriving estimates.

Mean – Result of dividing the sum of the values by the total number of cases to give an average of all values.

Median – The exact mid-point in your data.

Mode – The most frequently occurring attribute in your data.

Standard deviation – A standardized measure of the variability in the sample. It tells you how good a 'fit' there is between the full data set and the mean as a measure of central tendency.

Statistical software – Computer programs, such as SPSS and STATA, that specialize in analysing statistical data. These purpose-built programs make it far easier for you to carry out a host of basic analyses from descriptive statistics to more complex regressions.

t-test – Analysis of two population means used to understand whether or not the difference between the means of two populations is significant. For example, a *t*-test could help you determine if there is a significant difference in alcohol consumption between men and women.

Univariate analysis – Simplest form of statistical analysis, used to describe a single variable.

Variable type – There are three main types of variable: categorical/nominal, ordinal and interval. *Categorical variables* have no intrinsic ordering to them. Gender, ethnicity and hair colour categories (e.g., blonde, brunette, ginger) are examples of categorical variables: male and female are just categories, not an attribute you can have more or less of. *Ordinal variables* do have an intrinsic order. However, the steps between each value are not equal. For example, educational qualifications are ordered (some are higher or lower than others) but the steps between qualifications are not equal. The step from bachelor's degree to master's is not the same as from master's to doctorate. *Interval variables* have intrinsic ordering and the steps between each value are equal. For example, money (e.g., US dollars) is this kind of data. An interval variable is similar to an ordinal variable, except that the intervals between the values of the interval variable are equally spaced.

Glossary of Quantitative Analysis Symbols

Symbol	Symbol Name	Meaning / definition
μ	population mean	average/arithmetic mean of population values
σ^2	variance	variance of numbers in population from mean
σ_x	*standard deviation*	standardised measure of population variance
$\bar{x}$	sample mean	average/arithmetic mean for sample
s^2	sample variance	variance of numbers in sample from mean
s	sample standard deviation	standardised measure of sample variance

▬ REFERENCES ▬

Cohen, J. (1988). *Statistical power analysis for the behavioral sciences* (2nd ed.). Hillsdale, NJ: Lawrence Erlbaum.

Cohen, J., Cohen, P., West, S. G., & Aiken, L. S. (2003). *Applied multiple regression/correlation analysis for the behavioral sciences* (3rd ed.). New York: Routledge.

Cook, P. J. (2007). *Paying the tab: The costs and benefits of alcohol control.* Princeton, NJ: Princeton University Press.

Fawcett Society (2014). The time to act is now: Fawcett's gender pay gap briefing. Retrieved 22 February 2015, from http://www.fawcettsociety.org.uk/wp-content/uploads/2014/11/Fawcett-Equal-Pay-Day-report-November-2014.pdf

Field, A. (2014). *Discovering statistics with IBM SPSS Statistics.* London: Sage.

Glaser, B. G., & Strauss, A. (1967). *The discovery of grounded theory: Strategies for qualitative research.* New York: Aldine de Gruyter.

Hayes, A. F., & Krippendorff, K. (2007). Answering the call for a standard reliability measure for coding data. *Communication Methods and Measures, 1,* 77–89.

Hopkins, W. G. (2013). A scale of magnitudes for effect statistics. Retrieved 24 February 2015, from http://www.sportsci.org/resource/stats/effectmag.html

Ingraham, C. (2014, 25 September). Think you drink a lot? This chart will tell you. http://www.washingtonpost.com/blogs/wonkblog/wp/2014/09/25/think-you-drink-a-lot-this-chart-will-tell-you/

Jensen, E. (2014). Evaluating children's conservation biology learning at the zoo. *Conservation Biology, 28*(4), 1004–1011.

Kolbe, R. H., & Burnett, M. S. (1991). Content analysis research: An examination of applications with directives for improving research reliability and objectivity. *Journal of Consumer Research, 18*, 243–250.

Krippendorff, K. (2004). Reliability in content analysis. *Human Communication Research, 30*, 411–433.

Krippendorff, K. (2008). Systematic and random disagreement and the reliability of nominal data. *Communication Methods and Measures, 2*(4), 323–338.

Kross, E., Verduyn, P., Demiralp, E., Park, J., & Lee, D. S. (2013). Facebook use predicts declines in subjective well-being in young adults. *PLoS ONE, 8*(8), 1–6.

Leek, J. T., & Storey, J. D. (2011). The joint criterion for multiple hypothesis tests. *Statistical Applications in Genetics and Molecular Biology, 10*(1), article 28.

MacQueen, K. M., McLellan, E., Kay, K., & Milstein, B. (1998). Codebook development for team-based qualitative analysis. *Cultural Anthropology Methods, 10*(2), 31–36.

Neuendorff, K. (2002). *The content analysis guidebook*. Thousand Oaks, CA: Sage.

Williams, F., & Monge, P. (2001). *Reasoning with statistics: How to read quantiative research* (5th ed.). Boston: Wadsworth Cengage Learning.

Yates, D., Moore, D., & Starnes, D. (1999). *The practice of statistics*. New York: W. H. Freeman.

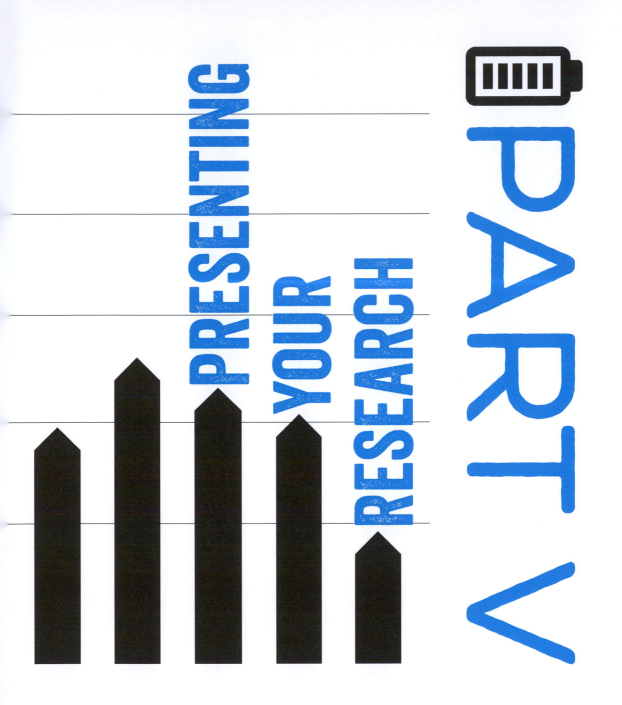

PART V

PRESENTING YOUR RESEARCH

HOW TO WRITE UP YOUR RESEARCH

13●1 INTRODUCTION

Writing your report involves gathering all the content you've compiled so far in your research (your research design, **literature review**, **methods**, data analysis, notes, etc.) to create a complete account of your research and its findings. Whether your write-up is a report, dissertation, conference paper or article, you'll need this account to be well organized, clearly written and analytical. As we have done throughout the book, we will use the term 'research report' to refer to the document you're creating based on your research.

This chapter begins with guidance on developing a report template for laying out your content in an organized manner. You can then place the content you've developed in this report document. We then explain how you define your audience (i.e., who reads your completed written work) and then prepare your report in a format your audience will find most useful and persuasive. Next, we take you on a step-by-step tour through each section you need in your report. The chapter guides you through each step, highlighting what content you need and how to frame it. Finally, we identify common challenges that affect the writing-up phase, along with strategies for resolving them. This chapter focuses on how to write up research reports using a structure recognized across the social sciences. However, you will need to make adjustments for your specific circumstances and requirements.

13●2 START WITH A REPORT TEMPLATE AND MAKE A PLAN

Before you begin writing up your research, start by evaluating what content you've already completed during your research project. A good plan showing what you already have and what you are missing can prevent you wasting weeks or even months of writing you might not ultimately need.

13●2●1 DEVELOP YOUR WORD-PROCESSOR TEMPLATE

To get started, create a template for your research report. Create this template in your word-processing software (e.g., Microsoft Word or Apple's Pages) to centralize and unify all the work you've done for your research project. You don't need content or even a title to do this because you can add information as you go.

We explain in more detail later in the chapter, but the standard sections in a research report are: **Title page**, **Abstract**, **Table of contents**, **Introduction**, **Methods**, **Results**, **Discussion**, Conclusion and **References**. Separate each section with a 'section break', a way for your word-processing software to recognize that one section has ended and another one has begun. You should also set up the following:

- Insert **page numbers**, usually in the header in the top right of the document (Figure 13.1).
- **Table of contents** (including figures and tables) that will automatically reflect the major headings created in your report (Figure 13.2).

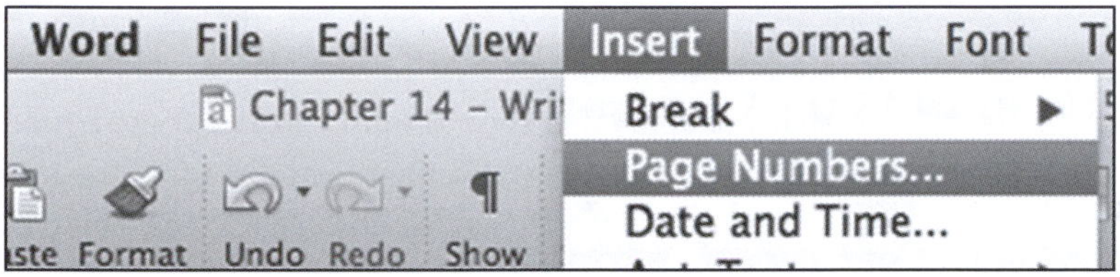

Figure 13.1   Insert Page Numbers function in Microsoft Word

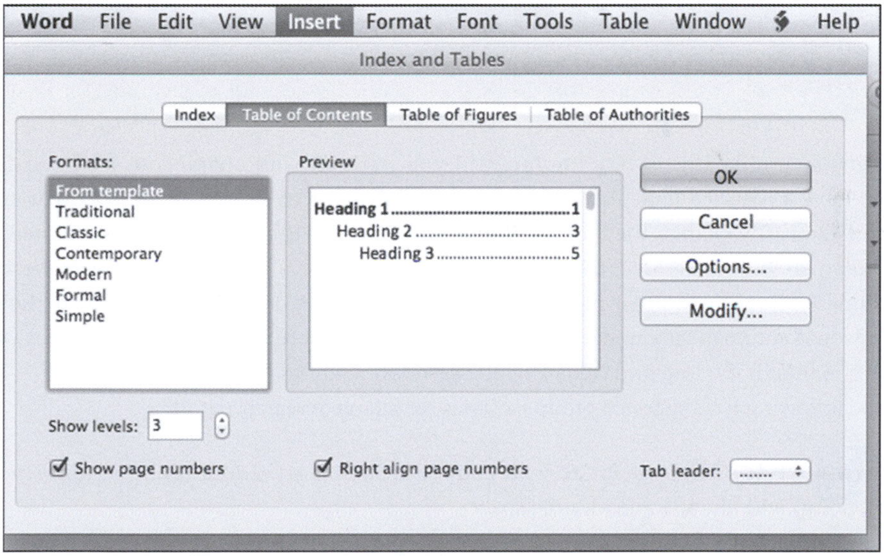

Figure 13.2   Insert Table of Contents function in Microsoft Word

In your report template you need to define what 'styles' you'll be using throughout your document. Styles create the 'look and feel' of the report and the way that you visually organize your sections and subsections. You first decide how many heading levels you want (in most cases, you'll need at least three levels). Then you define how your styles will look, such as the size of the font, whether the text will be centred on the page, etc. (Figure 13.3).

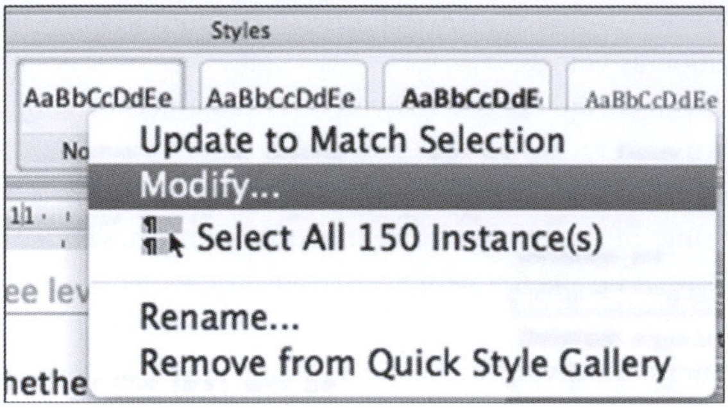

Figure 13.3   Modifying styles in Microsoft Word

Once you've set up each style, you can start applying it to the relevant parts of your document. For example, if you set your Heading 1 style to be boldface, Times New Roman in 12-point font, then any text that you apply that style to would take on those attributes. Every word in your report needs to be defined by one style or another, including the main body of the text in each paragraph, which is usually assigned the style called 'Normal' (Figure 13.4).

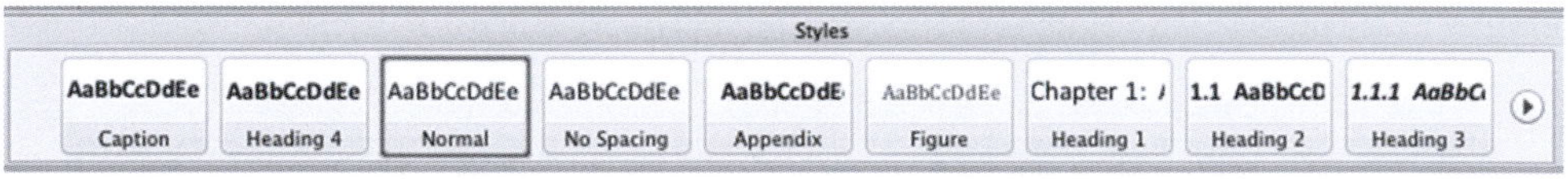

Figure 13.4   Styles in Microsoft Word

Using styles like this is very important if you want all your chapters to look consistent and to have a polished look and feel. Also, by establishing styles and assigning them as you go, you can easily change the look of your entire report with just a few clicks (Figure 13.5). For example, if you decided that you wanted to change all your second-level headings ('Heading 2') from Calibri to Times New Roman font, all you'd need to do is modify the style and it would automatically update the entire document. The alternative without styles would involve manually finding and updating all these subheadings one at a time.

The following is a suggested group of styles for a large research report:

- **Normal style** – The style for all your body text. Sample style: font (Calibri), font size (12 point) and line spacing (double space).
- **Heading 1 style** – Defines the title of each chapter, which means you will rarely use them. You will want this style to stand out so that the reader knows a new chapter is beginning. Sample style: font (Calibri, bold), font size (12 point), line spacing (single space, 0 points before and 12 points after), alignment (centred) and includes auto-numbering.
- **Heading 2 style** – Your first major subsection in each chapter. You will normally use several instances of these styles per chapter. Sample style: font (Calibri, bold), font size (12 point), line spacing (single space, 0 points before and 12 points after), alignment (left), indent (none) and includes auto-numbering (x.1). For example, the first section in Chapter 3 would be 3.1, the second section would be 3.2, and so on).

- **Heading 3 style** – A more fine-tuned subsection of Heading 2, so you may have multiple Heading 3s under each Heading 2. Sample style: font (Calibri, bold italic), font size (12 point), line spacing (single space, 0 points before and 12 points after), alignment (left), indent (left, 0.5 cm) and includes auto-numbering (x.1.1). For example, the Heading 2 in Chapter 3 would be 3.1, so the first Heading 3 would then be 3.1.1, the second section would be 3.1.2 and so on.
- **Heading 4 style** – This is your most detailed subheading because it is a subheading of Heading 3. Therefore, you may not use it very often. Sample style: font (Calibri, bold), font size (12 point), line spacing (single space, 0 points before and 12 points after), alignment (left), indent (none) and no auto-numbering.
- **Bullet point style** – You need a style to consistently define your bullet points. In almost all cases you can just use one style, but then assign either bullet points of numbers. We therefore recommend not automatically adding bullet points to the style since it can also be used for numbered lists as well. Sample style: font (Calibri), font size (12 point), line spacing (single space, 0 points before and 6 points after), alignment (left), indent (left: 1.3 cm) and no auto-numbering.
- **List style** – Useful for ensuring a uniform look to your tables. Sample style: font (Calibri), font size (10 point), line spacing (single space).

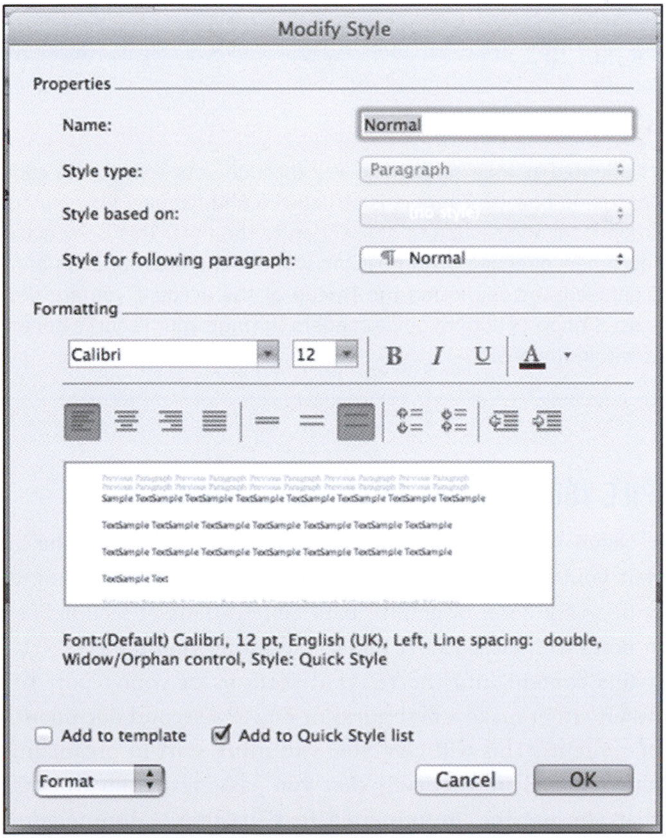

Figure 13.5 Modify Style window for adjusting a style

Here is one example of what these styles can look like:

Normal style
[Chapter] 1: Heading 1 style

1.1 Heading 2 style
1.1.1 Heading 3 style
Heading 4 style

- **List style with bullet point (or)**
- **List style with numbers**

Example table style
Lorem ipsum

When you set up these styles, you can have the headings be auto-numbered. Doing this numbering manually is needlessly time-consuming and likely to lead to mistakes. Your word-processing software offers you useful functionality to handle it automatically.

KEY TIPS

Use 'signposts' to guide your readers

Keep your readers oriented as they make their way through your report. You can do this by sign-posting; that is, describing how your report is structured and flagging up what content is coming next as you transition from one section or subsection to the next. This is especially useful if your discussion is taking a new direction or digression: without the appropriate signpost your reader may feel lost or confused, thereby losing the thread of the account you are developing in your report. Therefore, use signposts both to guide readers through your report's general structure and any shifts in focus within the report.

13•2•2 COMPILE YOUR EXISTING RESEARCH INFORMATION

If you've already begun key elements of your research project such as the literature review, you'll need to start your write-up by compiling everything you've already completed. This information may be in the form of graphs, data tables, drafts of sections or subsections, or perhaps even just notes with ideas you've had so far during your project.

Start placing this content into the relevant sections of your report (if you're unsure where to put it, then either make a best guess or create a second document to temporarily park this kind of content). This will give you a running start in organizing your research report. We strongly recommend that *every time* you paste text from an outside source into your template that you use the 'unformatted text' pasting feature (Figure 13.6). Pasting without selecting 'unformatted text' can introduce changes to your styles, disrupt your automatic numbering, etc.

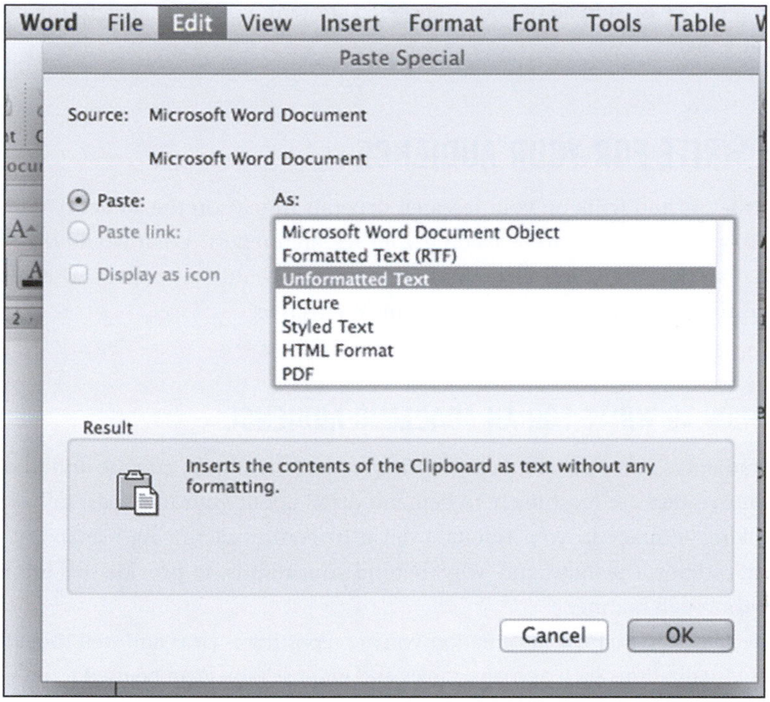

Figure 13.6   Paste Special as Unformatted Text

This one, easy step is a virtually foolproof way of preventing unwanted style changes to your template that can be difficult to fix later on. We also recommend that when you add figures you format use the 'Insert caption' feature in your word processor to create the caption, because this will also then enable you to easily create an automated list of figures. Likewise, follow the same procedure when you create tables. First, create the table framework using your word processor's tables feature, add the text by using the 'unformatted text' pasting feature and then add a caption using the 'Insert caption' feature (Figure 13.7).

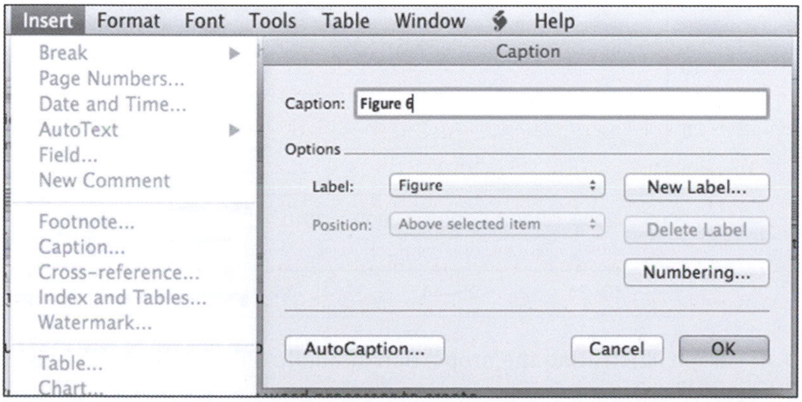

Figure 13.7   Inserting captions for automatic numbering

Once you have pasted in all of your completed content, you can start refining it and filling in the missing pieces.

13 • 3   WRITE FOR YOUR AUDIENCE

How you structure and write up your research depends in part on the audience you're writing for. Think about who is likely to be reading your research report. What would they find interesting? What level of detail and theoretical engagement would they expect? Use your answers to these questions to craft your writing to be most effective.

13•3•1   HOW TO WRITE FOR AN ACADEMIC AUDIENCE

Academic audiences for social research generally expect organized, concise and in-depth writing. Academic readers are most likely to demand detail about your methods, full explanations and painstaking accuracy in your results, even if it requires sacrificing readability. Academic readers want to know the 'how' and 'why' behind your results, so provide this information in a clear and thorough manner.

One way to ensure that the information you are reporting is clear and well thought out is to make use of visualizations such as maps, tables and graphs. Tables can be used to provide important details from your results in a brief and concise manner, while maps can be used alongside additional information from your research to show spatial patterns and visual arrangements much more clearly than words. For example, as part of a research project investigating the relationship

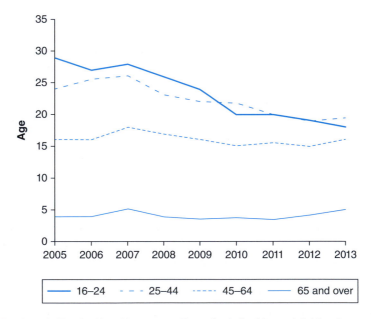

Figure 13.8   Graph illustrating the proportion of adults binge drinking by age in Great Britain, 2005-2013

Source: Office for National Statistics (2015)

between material deprivation and specific types of crime, the use of a district-level crime map could be used to show the frequency of a selected crime within a geographic region overlaid with earnings data and other socio-economic indicators. The use of graphs as an additional visualization tool can also be helpful in reporting key findings in a detailed and comprehensive way. The example in Figure 13.8 is taken from a statistics bulletin from the Office for National Statistics illustrating adult drinking habits in Great Britain.

As can be seen in the example, the use of a visualization clearly illustrates the proportion of adults binge drinking according to age between 2005 and 2013. The inclusion of a graph to visualize statistical change over time can be used to complement your writing and allow your reader to clearly establish the main finding(s) from your research.

Your methods section should be detailed and rigorous, accounting for possible lines of criticism. Your audience will include critics and sceptics who will scrutinize your methods for weaknesses and implications, so be thorough and provide reasons for your research decisions. At the same time, don't try to conceal your project's weaknesses. All research involves compromises, so rather than try to hide them (which is likely to fail with savvy academic readers), show that you have thought about them, explain your decision-making around them and acknowledge limitations. Don't make claims that exceed your methods and evidence.

Drawing on your literature review and theory at multiple points during your report is another hallmark of academic writing. The relevant research and theory you identified during your literature review needs to be applied to establish where you are making a contribution to your field. Moreover, your readers will often be familiar with relevant literature, thus by referencing it you create a bridge of understanding between their base of knowledge and your work.

13•3•2 HOW TO WRITE FOR A NON-ACADEMIC AUDIENCE

Some readers of this book will be writing for audiences outside academia. Any number of professions can involve social research, including corporate research on customers and employees, NGOs that need to understand those they are engaging with, and teachers. When it comes to writing for non-academic audiences, less is more. This type of audience is usually not interested in methodological detail, so there is no need to provide a full methods section. You need to summarize what methods you used and why, perhaps providing example questions, but not much more than that.

Your writing needs to be highly accessible for non-academic readers. You can't assume familiarity with academic jargon, so keep it to a minimum. Make sure that your writing is clear, approachable, easy to read and to the point. Clarity and brevity are usually most important, even if that means sacrificing detail. Indeed, your content needs to be shorter and very direct in explaining key points throughout your report. At the same time, non-academic, practice-oriented audiences especially value detail about the implications of your research. They are much more likely to want detailed recommendations that suggest how the research findings can be put into action to help the organization achieve its goals.*

---

*Non-academic research reports commissioned by the government may differ on this point, with government representatives sometimes preferring to avoid clear recommendations to minimize the risk of appearing partisan. There are also more likely to be particular requirements imposed on such government research reports, which may include greater methodological detail but most likely avoiding theory.

13●4 START WRITING UP

Once you've set up your template, populated it with your existing content and decided what audience you're writing for, you're ready to begin the writing up phase of your research. We have three key pieces of advice as you begin this stage of your research:

1   Write the sections when you are ready.
2   Keep returning to sections to refine them.
3   Write outlines for each section.

Don't try to start at page 1 and work through your write-up from start to finish. Writing doesn't tend to flow in such a convenient manner. Instead, try to make breakthroughs wherever you can by beginning with sections (or even subsections) that you can complete relatively easily or that you are the most interested in writing. This will mean that you can more rapidly (and enjoyably) get into the writing mode by getting words on the page. For some people this will mean starting with the methods section because it is relatively straightforward: it describes your research actions and decision-making (a section we generally advocate beginning with unless you have a strong preference for another section), or it may mean starting with a results section where participants' quotations and your notes provide a jumping off point for the report. We have advocated taking detailed notes about your ideas during the research process precisely to help you at this stage. It's much harder to start with a blank page than to have notes that you can use to flesh out a section. Having figures, tables and pages of detailed notes can kick-start your writing.

We also strongly recommend that you write in waves, achieving gradual improvement through multiple attempts at the same (sub)section, rather than expecting to get it right on your first draft. A first draft of a section is simply not going to achieve everything you need, including the following:

• Capturing all your important research ideas relevant to the section.
• Ensuring the section is coherently structured.
• Keeping the writing clear yet detailed.
• Making sure that the current section ties in with your other sections.

Create a first draft that gets as many of your ideas as possible written down. Then, in successive passes, you refine the section over and over again. This is a vastly better way of writing because it gives you time to gain perspective, see what can be improved and where the gaps are. Between drafts, you can work on other sections, benefiting from seeing how the report as a whole is coming together.

In order to have a coherent, well-rounded and focused section, think in advance about how it will be structured. Prepare an outline that indicates the content of each section and its subsections, with some notes about the kind of content and some of the sources you'd like to use there. This way when you start writing you're following a kind of roadmap to help you stay focused. It is important to stress at this juncture that although you don't have to write your report in precisely the right order, you must make sure that each section flows intuitively from one topic to another. Your report must make sense and flow as a whole piece of writing.

It is therefore useful to keep your prepared outline at hand to help guide the shape and structure of the whole document, and keep you mindful of how each section or subsection fits into your final report.

13•4•1 TITLE PAGE

The title page usually contains only the full title, your name, institution, department and date of report submission. Some researchers will also include contact details here.

13•4•2 ABSTRACT

The abstract enables readers to understand the most important information about your research project in summary form. It should answer the following:

1   What topic did you research? (1–3 sentences)
2   Why is this topic important? (1–2 sentences)
3   Who did you collect data from, and how? (1–2 sentences)
4   What were your high level findings? (2–3 sentences)
5   What are the implications of this research? (1–2 sentences)

Your abstract should state clearly why your research is significant (i.e., why should anyone want to read it?). It should then briefly summarize your results. The abstract is normally one long paragraph of about 200–300 words. It doesn't usually include citations.

━━━━━━━━━ **REAL WORLD EXAMPLE** ━━━━━━━━━

Abstract

The following abstract comes from a journal article Eric co-authored (Moss, Jensen, & Gusset, 2015):

The United Nations Strategic Plan for Biodiversity 2011-2020 is a key initiative within global efforts to halt and eventually reverse the loss of biodiversity. The very first target of this plan states that 'by 2020, at the latest, people are aware of the values of biodiversity and the steps they can take to conserve and use it sustainably'. Zoos and aquariums worldwide, attracting more than 700 million visits every year, could potentially make a positive contribution to this target. However, a global evaluation of the educational impacts of visits to zoos and aquariums is entirely lacking in the existing literature. To address this gap, we conducted a large-scale impact evaluation study, using a pre- and post-visit repeated-measures survey design, to evaluate biodiversity literacy – biodiversity understanding and knowledge of actions to help protect biodiversity – in zoo and aquarium visitors. Our findings are based on the largest and most international study of zoo and aquarium visitors ever conducted worldwide; in total, 5661 visitors to 26 zoos and aquariums around the globe participated in the study. The study's main finding is that aggregate biodiversity understanding and knowledge of actions to help protect biodiversity both significantly increased over the course of zoo and aquarium visits. There was an increase from pre-visit (69.8 per cent) to post-visit (75.1 per cent) in respondents demonstrating at least some positive

(Continued)

(Continued)

evidence of biodiversity understanding. Similarly, there was an increase from pre-visit (50.5 per cent) to post-visit (58.8 per cent) in respondents who could identify a pro-biodiversity action that could be achieved at an individual level. This study provides the most compelling evidence to date that zoo and aquarium visits can contribute to increasing the number of people who understand biodiversity and know actions they can take to help protect biodiversity.

13•4•3 TABLE OF CONTENTS

Your table of contents needs to be a somewhat detailed, yet short and clear, outline of the major headings in your report. We recommended including three heading levels in your table of contents (see Section 13.2.1) to provide your reader with a reasonable level of detail. In addition to the table of contents, you can also include a list of figures and a list of tables (which will show their captions).

13•4•4 INTRODUCTION

The introduction is one of the most difficult sections to write. On the one hand, it seems intuitive that you would write it first. Yet the wording you use in the introduction needs to match what appears in all the other sections. We suggest writing the introduction in three stages:

1   Write some content for your introduction early (but not necessarily first) in your writing-up process. This way you can begin committing thoughts to paper and aligning the direction of your report.
2   Return periodically to add content to the introduction as your other sections evolve. For example, if you finish a subsection in your results, you could go back to your introduction to make sure it accounts for this content. Doing this for each new (sub)section you complete means that you flesh out more and more of your introduction as you go.
3   When you have finished writing all your other sections, including a first pass of your conclusion, go back to heavily revise your introduction to bring it close to a final stage.

A well-written introduction should be immediately engaging for the reader. You want to hook the reader in right away with an interesting problem, controversy or opportunity that shows a key motivation for your research. An attention-grabbing introduction can help establish your reader's interest in the rest of your report. For academic audiences, this hook can connect to, for example, a theory or challenging social or political problem. For non-academic audiences, you'll need a broad framing, connecting your specific study to issues of general public or professional concern.

It's worth over-investing in getting your introduction just right, as this will establish your reader's initial impression of your report. Focus especially on ensuring the first several paragraphs are extremely clear. Keep your sentences short, minimize jargon and easy to understand. You are also making a case for why the reader should want to continue beyond the introduction.

Just because you think that a specific issue is interesting it doesn't meant that other people will feel the same way, so you need to persuade them of the value of your research.

Without repeating the abstract, your introduction should:

- **Clearly identify the problem** you're investigating.
- **Contextualize your problem** within the broader research context. For example, if you're researching gender bias in a workplace, you need to link this problem to broader societal concerns (e.g., women's place in society, participation of women in the labour market).
- **Acknowledge existing work** on which you are building, including theoretical issues and major research, but hold the in-depth discussion for the literature review.
- **Define the scope** of your forthcoming report. What will you be covering and why?

The introduction usually finishes with you outlining a roadmap for the rest of the report, so the reader knows what sections are coming up and how they are linked together.

13•4•5 LITERATURE REVIEW

Your literature review serves three main purposes (see Chapter 2 for an in-depth discussion):

1 Show your readers that you've **read and understood the key relevant literature** in your field.
2 Demonstrate **where your research fits in a broader field of study,** why it is important and how you're making an original contribution.
3 **Explain, evaluate and contextualize research and theory** that you engage with throughout your write-up to give your research broader relevance and importance.

13•4•6 METHODS

This section provides a detailed description of your sampling, data collection and data analysis methods. In this section you should detail (where relevant) the following:

1 The theoretical assumptions that are directly affecting your methodological choices.
2 How you did your research.
3 Which data collection strategies you adopted and why.
4 What research design you used and why.
5 How and why you chose your research location.
6 Important information about your research location(s) in terms of potential biases.
7 Any other factors that may have affected your data in a way that is relevant to your research question.
8 Why your research strategy and methods were appropriate for this research context.
9 Which data analysis approach(es) you selected and why.

You can usually start writing this section early on in the research process, even before you've started collecting any data.

13•4•7 RESULTS

The number of results sections you write depends on your particular study. Smaller pieces of research may only have one or two results sections, and larger studies may have five or six sections. Keep in mind that each results section should focus on one major issue. This is where your section outline is especially important for maintaining the overall focus and identifying the subsections that make sense under a particular section. Your sections should also relate to each other in a coherent sequence. Think about what order makes the most sense for your particular research. You might start with the more general theme and then address the more specific ones, for example. If there is no obviously appropriate sequence, just select an order and ensure you have good transitions to make the set of results sections seem coherent.

REAL WORLD EXAMPLE

Ageing and the economy in Japan

Fumiko studied the economic impacts of an ageing population in Japan. She wanted to know how Japan's ageing and shrinking population would affect the national economy over the next 20 years. To explore this issue she laid out her sections as follows:

1   Introduction
2   Literature review
3   [Results section] Demographic profile of Japan's ageing population: past, present and future
4   [Results section] Ageing workers and the pensions dilemma
5   [Results section] Impact of ageing workers on youth employment
6   [Results section] Immigration as a solution to ageing populations
7   Discussion
8   References
9   Appendices

With this layout her results sections were individually and collectively coherent. She began with a broader descriptive section laying out the key demographic information on Japan's ageing population. Then came a section on a key challenge caused by ageing workers. She then moved to consider how these problems affect the future, first by analysing how young workers are affected. Finally, she evaluated the potential of immigration as a solution to plug employment gaps. This follows a rough pattern of going from broad to narrow and from past to present to future.

13•4•8 DISCUSSION

As with all sections, we recommend adding notes to the discussion section when ideas occur to you while writing other sections so that you have content to build from. Start preparing your first full draft of your discussion section when you've completed all your results sections, but just before you write your first full draft of your introduction. Once your draft discussion is complete, you can begin refining both the discussion and introduction.

Your discussion section should begin by briefly restating the research problem and research question(s) you are investigating. That is, re-establish the overall focus for this piece of research. You will then want to summarize the headline findings from your results sections. Strictly avoid introducing new evidence at this stage, but instead focus on developing clear statements about the significance and implications of your results. Think about whether there are any 'take-away' points for readers from each individual finding as well as the project as a whole.

A good discussion of your research findings also requires explicit reference back to the theory and empirical research discussed as part of your literature review (see Chapter 2). Locating your findings within the context of previous social research and theory enables you to contextualize your findings within the wider academic literature (perhaps offering supporting or contrary evidence to existing knowledge or claims). The extent to which you should refer back to your literature review depends on the extent to which a particular theory or empirical study is informing your own research. If you are looking to disprove a well-established theory, for example, then it would be appropriate to engage with such work in relation to your own findings regularly during the discussion section. It is important, however, to use the discussion of your findings (to whatever extent) to show your readers how your investigation relates to the wider global picture, and whether or not you have adequately addressed your research question(s).

The last part of the discussion section is a subsection called 'Conclusion', which provides the closing argument you would like to make based on your research.

13•4•9 REFERENCES

Your references section should follow the citation style specified by your department. For example, many social science departments require the American Psychological Association (APA) citation style. As we've said previously, we strongly advocate using citation management software such as Endnote to save you an enormous amount of time and reduce citation entry errors.

13•4•10 APPENDICES

If you have non-essential details that you think some readers might wish to consult, you can provide them after the main body of the research report in an **appendix**. Some reports have no appendices, while others have several. For example, if you needed to keep the main report short in a qualitative project, you might provide a table outlining demographic information about your interview participants and the duration of each interview. Occasionally, full anonymized transcripts are provided in appendices; however, this is unusual because interview transcripts tend to be so long they could quickly dwarf your actual report! Quantitative researchers sometimes use appendices to provide the original survey forms used in a project or extra statistical detail. When deciding whether to add content to an appendix, ensure that it is directly relevant to your research and important for the reader to have available.

13●5 WORK THROUGH COMMON WRITING-UP CHALLENGES

Writing up is hard work. You have a lot of pages to write, many thoughts to present and a desire to produce an original, high-quality piece of research. While you will undoubtedly feel proud of your achievement in the end, you will also likely face bumps in the road during the writing-up process. Below, we present a number of common challenges that can affect the writing-up process, and our recommended solutions.

Challenge: You feel overwhelmed by the size of the writing-up task.

Solution: Reduce the size of each task by breaking it into smaller units that you can tackle one at a time. For example, think of the write-up as a series of sections that you can focus on one at a time. If one section is daunting, think of each section as being made up of a series of subsections that you can address one at a time. It is now a cliché, but nevertheless true: a journey of a thousand miles begins with a single step!

Challenge: It's hard to get started writing each day.

Solution: Set yourself a goal for writing each day. At the end of each day when you have met that goal, *do just a little bit more to give yourself a head start on the next day*. For example, if your goal is to finish a subsection by the end of a day, make sure you write some notes for the next day's subsection, draft a couple paragraphs for it or lay out some general ideas. This approach helps you feel that you've got ahead at the end of the day. Then, the next morning you feel like you've got a running start with some ideas to build on.

Challenge: You find that days are going by and you aren't writing very much. You feel the need to do a bit more reading, analysis, etc. before you can write. Then you find yourself searching the internet for hours, reading literature without writing about it or toying with ideas you ultimately decide not to use. These are signs you're procrastinating!

Solution: Writing is hard work and it is easy to get busy with other tasks that seem important but in truth are only there so you can avoid the writing work. Make sure that you produce written content on every possible day. Even if the content is just notes, a draft section or a rough overview of ideas for a paragraph: write, write, write! Keep moving forward by putting words on the page at every opportunity, however rough or undeveloped they may feel.

Challenge: You find yourself confused by an idea or uncertain how to frame it in your writing.

Solution: One of the best solutions is to work on a different part of your research report for a while to clear your head. Talking to your supervisor and colleagues can also help you gain clarity. We also recommend isolating a particularly difficult piece of writing by working on it in a blank document, not within your report. Here you can take an experimental approach, trying out different ways of expressing your ideas.

Often you find that one version comes out how you want it, and you can then copy it back into your report.

Challenge: You're facing a tight schedule and aren't sure how to structure your day to get everything in on time.

Solution: Take on a full-time working approach by setting up a set schedule that you stick to each day.

- Have a set start time each morning; try to avoid giving yourself the excuse to start 'when you feel like it' because it's human nature to find delays.
- Set up a reasonable writing schedule for yourself. Most people can't concentrate heavily for long periods, so it will be unrealistic – and unpleasant – to try to make yourself type for eight straight hours each day. You will probably not be able to sustain this and will then feel that you are always behind. Find tasks that require less concentration, which you can switch over to when your mind is feeling over-taxed.
- We recommend committing to four–six hours of focused writing per day. We then recommend spending two–four hours each day undertaking other tasks that will keep you moving forward but require less intense concentration. These can be gathering or typing up notes and outlines for your next sections, preparing visualizations such as graphs, or 'housekeeping' tasks such as entering citations into your citation software (e.g., Endnote).

13 ● 6 FOLLOW PRINCIPLES OF GOOD WRITING AND EDITING

One of the worst myths in social research circles is that good writing is a 'gift', that is, a natural talent you are either born with or sadly lacking. Good writing is a skill like any other. You can develop your writing skills by following well-established principles, putting in the hard work of editing and polishing your writing long after your first draft is complete. In this section, we draw heavily on the classic text *Writing for Social Scientists* by Howard Becker, which engages with the problem of bad social scientific writing.

Bad writing is a rampant problem in published social research. Given that the goal of social scientific writing is to communicate ideas to readers, 'bad' in this context means unclear, long-winded and poorly structured writing that is difficult for the reader to follow. C. Wright Mills (1959, pp. 218–219) argued that unclear social scientific writing often stems from a desire to make a topic seem more complicated in order to gain academic status:

> Lack of ready intelligibility [in scholarly writing], I believe, usually has little or nothing to do with the complexity of the subject matter, and nothing at all with profundity of thought. … Desire for status is one reason why academic men [*sic*] slip so easily into unintelligibility.

Becker and others point to the dangers of picking up bad writing habits from the scholarly literature in your field. They argue that students '"learn" to write by reading what is written. They generally find dull, verbose, pretentious writing, perpetuating the problem and suggesting that most referees expect such a stilted style' (Becker, 2007, p. 42). As you become familiar with social scientific writing, be sure to learn from the style of those who write clearly.

   **REAL WORLD EXAMPLE**

Edit for clarity and quality

Becker tells the story of an exchange with one of his students about her work. This illustrates the process that you will likely need to go through to make your writing as clear as possible. He starts by describing the student's writing, then explains how it could be improved:

> It was a very good piece of work – rich data, imaginatively analysed, well-organized – but it was very wordy and academic. I had removed as much of the redundancy and academic flourish as I thought she would stand for. We went over it, a page at a time, and she quizzed me on each point. ... Where she wrote 'unified stance' I substituted 'agreement,' because it was shorter. I replaced 'confronted the issue' with 'talked about,' because it was less pretentious. A longer example: where she wrote 'This section will examine the impact of money or, more specifically, independent incomes on relations between husbands and wives with particular regard to the realm of financial affairs,' I substituted 'This section will show that independent incomes change the way husbands and wives handle financial affairs,' for similar reasons. I removed meaningless qualifications ('tends to'), combined sentences that repeated long phrases, and when she said the same thing in two ways in successive sentences, took out the less effective version. (Becker, 2007, p. 27)

This kind of careful line-by-line editing is essential to producing a high-quality research report.

Good social scientific writing is active, concise and coherent. These features are described in detail below.

USE AN ACTIVE WRITING STYLE

Maintain an **active writing voice**. This means that you clearly specify who is taking the action(s) in your sentence. For example 'I visited the store to buy groceries' is preferable to 'There was a visit to the store that involved the purchase of groceries'. Our advice is to use the first person, 'I', when it would make your point most clearly and concisely. Tortured writing that bends over backwards to use a third person voice makes for an unpleasant reading experience.

Billig (2013, p. 7) argues that social scientists should describe their research findings, while avoiding overly long and vague words that make writing difficult for your reader to follow:

> Here, then, is the centre of my argument: the big concepts which many social scientists are using – the ifications and the izations – are poorly equipped for describing what people do. By rolling out the big nouns, social scientists can avoid describing people and their actions. They can then write in highly unpopulated ways, creating fictional worlds in which their theoretical things, rather than actual people, appear as the major actors. The problem is that, as linguists have shown, using nouns and passive sentences is a way to convey less, not more, information about human actions. ... At root, there is a problem in preferring the big technical noun to the shorter, humbler verb.

Follow Billig's advice and your writing will come alive. State your argument directly without unnecessarily long words or sentences.

BE CONCISE AND COHERENT

When you write your first draft, it is likely to contain far more words than necessary to deliver your intended message. For example, the italicized words in the following sentence are unnecessary:

> *It is essential to consider the fact that* gender norms *today* directly affect *many* people's *subjective experience of their* lives.

These extra words waste space on the page and the reader's attention, undermining the clarity and effectiveness of your writing. Reread the sentence above, looking at only the non-italicized words (this reduces the sentence from 20 to 6 words): Has any meaning really been lost?

Becker (2007, p. 81) offers the following advice that can help you streamline your writing:

> I find unnecessary words by a simple test. As I read through my draft, I check each word and phrase to see what happens if I remove it. If the meaning does not change, I take it out. The deletion often makes me see what I really wanted there, and I put it in.

The other major way to reduce excessive words is to eliminate repetition, so that your readers don't lose patience.

To ensure that your readers don't get lost, ensure that each sentence, paragraph, subsection and section clearly and logically flows into the next. You can make your report coherent by using connecting phrases to link different points within your research report. 'On the other hand', 'however', 'similarly', 'furthermore', 'moreover', 'in addition', 'by contrast' and 'as such' let you move from one idea to another. You also need to create a logical sequence for the development of your ideas within and across sections.

Finally, you should regularly self-evaluate your writing. Here is a checklist of questions you can ask yourself along the way, adapted and expanded from Taylor & Beasley (2005, p. 101):

- Have I signposted my main points at the beginning of this section or report?
- Could I make my arguments/analyses clearer?
- Is each sentence as focused and clear as it could be?
- Have a developed smooth transitions from point to point in my report?
- Have I provided evidence for the points that I've made?
- Are my conclusions clearly stated?
- Have I made links between this section and other parts of the report?

Self-assessing your writing helps to keep you on track as your research report develops.

13.7 LOOK BEYOND WRITING

While the written report is undoubtedly the dominant format, the social sciences are increasingly opening up to alternative ways of presenting research results. Qualitative researchers in particular are using a variety of media, including video documentaries, artistic exhibitions and even performances such as theatre and dance to present research insights. More broadly, blogs, podcasts, interactive websites, games and many other tools are used to communicate social research. Web-based publishing allows researchers to have a dialogue with others interested in their topic, which can affect how findings are interpreted and prompt future research. You can even publish your data in hopes that other researchers will analyse them further. As you think about the potential audiences for your research, don't forget about the people around the world that you can reach through online platforms such as Twitter, academia.edu and ResearchGate.

13●8 CONCLUSION

'Scholarly writers have to organize their material [and] express an argument clearly enough that readers can follow the reasoning and accept the conclusions' (Becker, 2007, p. 43). Writing up your research can be gratifying as see your research ideas, data and analysis come together in a single document that you craft and polish until it's ready for submission. To help you efficiently prepare this document, we showed you how to create a template in your word-processing software. You can think of your template as like a filing cabinet with drawers and folders: Place your content into these folders for both neatness and clarity. Once you've filled each drawer/section with relevant content, you can take stock to see what information you have and need to complete your research report.

Your audience affects how you write up your research. Academic readers expect detail and analytic rigour. Academic readers will expect to see a comprehensive methods section that explains in detail the 'who?', 'what?' and 'how?' of your research project. In contrast, practitioner audiences typically expect to be told the headline findings with brief explanations and a minimal methods section. You need to devote much greater focus to the research implications and recommendations.

Regardless of audience, we strongly advise writing your report in layers (i.e., multiple drafts) and not attempting one full and final write-up, going from start to finish. This strategy of building up a full draft with multiple passes at a section allows your thinking to evolve and mature.

Your report will likely need the following sections: Title page, Abstract, Table of Contents, Introduction, Literature review, Methods and Conclusion chapters. It also needs results sections, each of which presents a coherent set of findings. For each of your sections we strongly recommend that you draft a rough outline before you start writing.

Get words on the page early and often, and when you gather some momentum in your writing, keep going until you run out of steam. It's easy to get side-tracked on various tasks that feel like research but are actually distracting you. If you are reading something at this stage, you should either decide early on that it's not useful or write about it (typing up good quotes, summarizing relevant arguments and findings, etc.). In sum, we urge you to write, write, write! Even if the words aren't perfect, you're in a much stronger position when you have some content to build on and refine. Don't waste a single day surfing the internet, reading material that you can't use or toying with ideas without writing about their application to your topic.

If you feel overwhelmed at the thought of writing up your research, reconceptualize it as a series of much smaller tasks that you can tackle one at a time. Go beyond your writing target each day to give yourself a head-start each day, making your ideas connect more coherently together and easing the process of starting the next day's writing. Editing, rephrasing and polishing your writing will come later once you have content to work with. As Becker (2007, p. 89) argues, 'writers need to pay close attention to what they have written as they revise, looking at every word as if they meant it to be taken seriously. You can write first drafts quickly and carelessly exactly because you know you will be critical later.' Remember Billig's (2013, p. 8) advice about the 'importance of using ordinary terms where possible and using verbs in the active voice'. Make the most of your hard work on the literature review, data collection and analysis by creating a clear and concise research report that tells your research story.

▬ SUGGESTIONS FOR FURTHER READING ▬

- **Becker, H. S. (2007). *Writing for social scientists: How to start and finish your thesis, book, or article* (2nd ed.). Chicago: Chicago University Press.** Renowned sociologist Howard Becker astutely identifies the reasons why bad (convoluted, overly complicated) writing is so common. The book provides some excellent detail and examples of how you can improve your writing.
- **Billig, M. (2013). *Learn to write badly: How to succeed in the social sciences.* Cambridge: Cambridge University Press.** Like the classic book from Howard Becker, Billig explores why social scientists tend to write in such unclear ways. At base, he argues, social scientists' unnecessarily long and jargon-filled sentences represent a vain attempt at self-promotion.
- **Bui, Y. N. (2014). *How to write a master's thesis* (2nd ed.). Thousand Oaks, CA: Sage.** Bui's book is geared for master's students who may face a theory-practice gap, that is, students who have taken research methods courses but lack experience putting this knowledge into practice. The book will be especially useful for students who need help conceptualizing and writing a typical master's thesis.
- **Joyner, R. L., Rouse, W. A., & Glatthorn, A. A. (2013). *Writing the winning thesis or dissertation: A step-by-step guide* (3rd ed.). Thousand Oaks, CA: Corwin.** The authors address the challenges of writing head-on. Their guidance is thorough, taking you from the first steps of writing your report all the way to thinking about how to publish your research. Their practical guidance is especially useful, covering topics such as addressing institutional requirements.
- **Krause, S. D. (2007). *Alternative ways to present your research.*** Retrieved 29 March, 2015, from http://www.stevendkrause.com/tprw/Chapter%2011.pdf This web-based resource will advise you on how to use web publishing. This freely accessible chapter provides a clear summary of the challenges and opportunities available to you if you decide to publish your research online.
- **Oliver, P. (2014). *Writing your thesis* (3rd ed.). London: Sage.** This book offers practical and highly accessible advice and strategies for tackling your write-up. The depth of the guidance may be more suitable for doctoral students, although the first part of the book, which discusses academic writing, would benefit a broad range of students writing research reports.
- **Wolcott, H. F. (2009). *Writing up qualitative research* (3rd ed.). Thousand Oaks, CA: Sage.** This book gives excellent suggestions on each phase of writing up a qualitative research project. The guidance on incorporating theory is particularly useful, as well as the advice on how to move from thinking about your research to actually writing it.

Visit the companion website at **https://study.sagepub.com/jensenandlaurie** to gain access to a wide range of online resources to support your learning, including editable research documents, weblinks, free access SAGE journal articles and book chapters, and flashcards.

▬ GLOSSARY ▬

Abstract – A short summary at the beginning of a report that concisely presents the arguments and findings in the research.

Active writing style ('active voice') – A style that clearly specifies who is taking the action in a sentence and avoids the third person. For example, 'I played tennis' rather than 'Tennis was played'.

Appendix – An appendix is a section of additional material placed at the end of your research report containing information that may not be critical to your main discussion but could be important for your readers to consult if needed. Information that would 'clutter' your main discussion, but is still necessary to include, can be placed in an appendix. For example, an appendix could include anonymized transcripts or a copy of your survey form.

Discussion – The discussion section should re-establish the focus of your research, summarize the key findings from your results section, and take those results further by discussing their significance and implications, especially about how they relate to existing literature and theory. This section should not introduce any new evidence.

Introduction – The first main section of a report, usually made up of a background discussion that identifies the broader research context, the clear identification of the research problem and why it matters, and your proposed solution to this problem.

Literature review – A literature review goes beyond merely describing other people's research. It's an opportunity to analyse and critically evaluate existing literature so that you can apply it to your topic clearly and coherently. It also allows you to identify gaps in the broader research context that your research can address.

Methods – A detailed report of your sampling, data collection and data analysis decisions and processes. This should have sufficient information that someone else would be able to replicate your approach.

References – A way of acknowledging the books, papers, audio-visual and other sources you use in your research. The use of references helps to credit other researchers' work, explains to your readers from where you have drawn ideas and information, and helps to critique, substantiate and inform your own research. Follow the referencing style preferred by your department or institution. Referencing software will make this process much easier to manage.

Report template – A document set up in your preferred word processor that includes the selected fonts, formatting and styles for your report. It may also include sections such as Title page, Abstract, Table of Contents, Introduction, Methods, Results, Discussion, Conclusion and References where you can start to place relevant content.

Results – The results of your research and analysis, that is, what you found out after gathering and analysing your data. The number of results sections you have will be dependent on the size of your study, but each results section should focus on one key issue and be laid out in a logical sequence.

Table of contents – A detailed, but short and clear, overview of the major headings in your report.

Title page – The first page of your report that includes the report title, your name, institution, department and date of report submission. It may also include contact details, as well as other relevant information specifically requested by your institution.

■ REFERENCES ■

Becker, H. S. (2007). *Writing for social sciences: How to start and finish your thesis, book, or article* (2nd ed.). Chicago: Chicago University Press.

Billig, M. (2013). *Learn to write badly: How to succeed in the social sciences.* Cambridge: Cambridge University Press.

Moss, A., Jensen, E., & Gusset, M. (2015). Evaluating the contribution of zoos and aquariums to Aichi Biodiversity Target 1. *Conservation Biology, 29*(2), 537–544.

Office for National Statistics (2015). *Adult drinking habits in Great Britain, 2013* Retrieved from http://www.ons.gov.uk/ons/dcp171778_395191.pdf

Taylor, S., & Beasley, N. (2005). *A handbook for doctoral supervisors.* Abingdon: Routledge.

Wright Mills, C. (1959). *The sociological imagination.* New York: Oxford University Press.

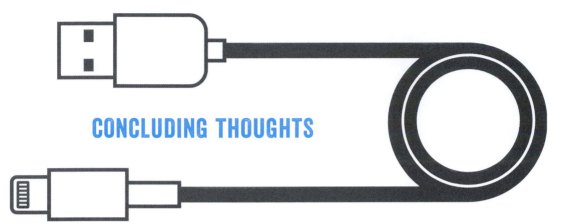

CONCLUDING THOUGHTS

Social research offers you the opportunity and privilege to develop knowledge about the rich and varied societies and cultures in which we live. As social researchers, we know how difficult the process can be, especially for students new to research. Indeed, it can be daunting to stand at the beginning of your research project and look at the path ahead with all the steps that you'll need to take before submitting your completed work. This path may take you days, weeks, months or years (in the case of doctoral projects).

If you are feeling uneasy about this journey, you're in good company! The best researchers in the world have all felt this way at some point. You too will soon discover, however, that your curiosity, careful and continuous (re)planning, creative problem-solving and relentless focus on your topic are the keys to completing good research.

In this book, we have defined a pathway that enables you to take your quantitative or qualitative research from the very earliest stages of development and planning to a final report that you can present with confidence. Our focus on the practical aspects of social research means that at each stage we've identified and explained the issues you are most likely to face. We have highlighted challenges other researchers have faced and highlighted practical solutions at each stage. These solutions will help you navigate often unexpected and challenging real world conditions, whether you are investigating social problems in your local neighbourhood, or facing unfamiliar research contexts far from home.

We hope that this book helps you along your research journey. We aimed to show you how to get the most from each stage of your project and navigate the numerous hurdles every researcher is bound to face. For our part, we think back fondly to the early days of our research training when we were at university together learning the tools and processes to becoming effective social researchers. We hope we have conveyed our enthusiasm for the process of developing reliable knowledge. It's a process inflected with surprises, unexpected findings and sudden insights. What you encounter may be heart-warming, uncomfortable or tragic, but coming to understand and share the knowledge you develop is always rewarding.

INDEX

surveys, xxiii, 133, 138–169
   combined with other methods of
      research, 146
   open-ended and *closed-ended*, 142
   strengths and weaknesses of, 138, 141
systematic error in surveys, 143

t-tests, 315, 325–30, 334–5
target population, 162
Taylor, S., 259
telephone interviews, 179
templates used in research reports, 342–8,
   360, 362
Tesfaye, C.L., 166
theoretical framework for a piece of research,
   45–6, 255
'thick description', 92, 279, 288
third-party servers for storing data, 198
Thorne, S., 211–12, 279
Thrift, N., xix
time-limited events, research on, 7
time management, 21–5
time required
   for any participation in research, 129
   for data analysis, 142, 149
   for interviews, 180
   for qualitative research, 103, 109, 173
   for transcription, 238, 244, 278
time-series analysis, 147
time-wasting practices, 22–3
timeline software, 24, 26
timelines for research, 20–6, 231–2, 246
Tolich, M.B., 64
tracking of data, 229–30
Tracy, K., 92
Tracy, S., 92
transcription, 23, 25, 201, 233–9, 244, 246,
   249, 278
   amount needed, 234, 237
   of qualitative data, 233–9
   training others in, 239
   verbatim or *standardized*, 234, 246
transcription services, professional, 238–9
transparency, 288
travel costs, reimbursement of, 119
triangulation, 13, 212, 215, 219
trust of participants in researchers, 121–2,
   126, 130
trusted institutions, 125
Tuskegee syphilis experiment, 131
Twitter, 57, 115, 212, 214, 216, 360
Type I error and Type II error, 106–7,
   109–10, 320

U test, 330–1
United States
   Bureau of Consular Affairs, 79
   Centers for Disease Control and Prevention,
      77–8
   Department of State, 85
univariate statistics, 293, 335
utilization-focused evaluation, 18

V analysis, 317–19, 333–5
validity of survey methods and measures, 143,
   167, 219
Varese, F., 105
variables, types of, 295–6, 335
   categorical, 295
   continuous, 296
   dependent, 295, 335
   independent, 295, 335
   interval, 296, 336
   nominal, 295
   scale, 296
variance-equality assumption, 315, 327, 333
Venkatesh, S., 133
verbally-administered surveys, 147–8, 167
video data, analysis of, 248
video recording, use of, 196
visualizations used in research reports, 348–9
Vogel, R.J., 218
vulnerable groups, research with, 60, 63,
   65, 122

web-based surveys, 162–4, 213
Wegner, D.M., 6–7
Wilcoxon signed rank test, 331
Williams, F., 334
Williams, H.A., 334
withdrawal from participation in research, 58
Wolcott, H.F., 361
Wood, F., 226
word frequencies, 271–3
word-processing software, 240, 342–4
writing skills, 357–9, 361
   active writing, 358, 362
   conciseness and *coherence*, 359
writing up research, xxv, 277, 342–62
   overarching narrative in, 283
   standard sections in reports, 343,
      349–55, 360
   use of templates, 342–8, 360, 362
written consent, 57–8

Yardley, L., 283
YouTube, 56